THE DRAMATIC

ART OF

ATHOL FUGARD

THE DRAMATIC ART OF ATHOL FUGARD

From South Africa to the World

ALBERT WERTHEIM

Indiana
University
Press

BLOOMINGTON AND INDIANAPOLIS

This book is a publication of

Indiana University Press
601 North Morton Street
Bloomington, IN 47404-3797 USA

http://www.indiana.edu/~iupress

Telephone orders   800-842-6796
Fax orders   812-855-7931
Orders by e-mail   iuporder@indiana.edu

The paper used in this publication meets the minimum
requirements of American National Standard for Information
Sciences—Permanence of Paper for Printed Library Materials,
ANSI Z39.48-1984.

Manufactured in the United States of America

Library of Congress Cataloging-in-Publication Data

Wertheim, Albert.
    The dramatic art of Athol Fugard : from South Africa to the world / Albert Wertheim.
       p.   cm.
    Includes bibliographical references (p.   ) and index.
    ISBN 0-253-33823-9 (cl : alk. paper)
    1. Fugard, Athol—Criticism and interpretation. 2. South Africa—In literature. 3. Fugard,
Athol—Technique. 4. Drama—Technique. I. Title.
    PR9369.3.F8 Z95 2000
    822´.914—dc21
                                                                              00-039627

1 2 3 4 5   05   04   03   02   01   00

CONTENTS

Introduction   vii

ONE
Early Work and Early Themes   1

TWO
The Port Elizabeth Plays:
The Voice with Which We Speak from the Heart   17

THREE
"Acting" against Apartheid   69

FOUR
Dimetos: Fugard's First Problem Play   100

FIVE
The Drama as Teaching and Learning:
Trauerspiel, Tragedy, Hope, and Race   117

SIX
The Other Problem Plays   153

SEVEN
Writing to Right: Scripting Apartheid's Demise   177

EIGHT
Where Do We, Where Do I, Go from Here?
Performing a New South Africa   203

Notes   239

Works Cited   259

Index   267

INTRODUCTION

If one were to list the six or seven most significant English-language playwrights alive in the last decade of the twentieth century, that list would undoubtedly include the names of Arthur Miller, Tom Stoppard, Harold Pinter, Edward Albee, and perhaps August Wilson and David Hare. It would also surely include South African playwright, director, and actor Athol Fugard. Beginning with his first extant play, *No-Good Friday,* initially performed on 30 August 1958 at the Bantu Men's Social Centre in Johannesburg, Fugard has made a name for himself as a serious playwright who has often dared to challenge the social system of his country and the ways whites, blacks, and coloureds think of race; and who has expanded our horizons about the nature of human psychodynamics. To this one should add that his plays provide illuminating, important insights into the nature of art, creativity and the ways in which acting in the theatrical sense and acting in the political one are identities.

No-Good Friday was staged ten years after the 1948 initiation of apartheid in South Africa, and from that time to the present Fugard's plays have been milestones and signposts of apartheid's devastating progress, its demise, and the future that is unfolding in its wake. A thorough discussion of his plays, which this book proposes, will reveal the development and growth of a major playwright of our time as well as his reaction to the vexed questions of art, politics, and race both in his country and more universally.

Happily, Fugard, like Nathaniel Hawthorne and Henry James, is a keeper of notebooks, in which he records his ideas, his thoughts for possible plays, and some record of how his work germinates. It is our good fortune that the very fine scholar and personal friend of Fugard, Mary Benson, has edited and published Fugard's 1960–1977 notebooks, and that she has also published her own memoir of Fugard.[1] Fugard himself has likewise been generous to interviewers, and thus newspaper, magazine, television, and playbill interviews abound. In preparing this book, I have had the benefit of consulting the original typescripts for many of Fugard's plays (often amended in the author's hand) held by the National English Literary Museum

1. Athol Fugard, 1983. Photo by Ruphin Coudyzer.

(NELM) in Grahamstown. These and other Fugard materials have recently been sold to the Lilly Library at Indiana University. Thus when the text that follows indicates material held at NELM, the originals are now at Indiana University and copies at NELM.

Fugard's plays and the ideas expressed in his work are the main concern of this study. But Fugard is no reclusive, ivory-tower playwright. He is an engaged, consummate genius of the theater who has struggled with the staging of each production; fought the authorities to produce his plays; striven to end the racial segregation in South Africa on the stage and in the seating areas of the theatre; initiated the careers of at least three brilliant black actors, John Kani, Zakes Mokae, and Winston Ntshona; and found it necessary to premiere some of his plays in America, especially at the Yale Repertory Theatre under the aegis of Lloyd Richards, in order to have them produced without banning in South Africa.

There is little need for this study to rechart the history of Athol Fugard as director and actor or recount the vicissitudes of his actors and productions since that has already been done extremely well in two fine books, both published in 1985, one by Russell Vandenbroucke and the other by Dennis Walder.[2] At the same time, however, in considering Fugard's dramatic works, it is important to remember that they are written by someone whose connection with theatre practice is immediate. He has been the manager of theatre groups, such as the Serpent Players and the Space Theatre, and has directed numerous plays, including most of his own. He has trained actors, and his own experience as an actor is wide-ranging. And he has frequently appeared in his own plays, acting major roles in *The Blood Knot, Boesman and Lena, A Lesson from Aloes, The Road to Mecca, A Place with the Pigs, Valley Song* and *The Captain's Tiger.* And some of the plays, most notably *Sizwe Bansi Is Dead* and *The Island,* are directly derived from acting exercises. Unlike dramatists who are not themselves theatre practitioners, Fugard is never far from a theatre or stage and, consequently, his plays contain an awareness of the possibilities of acting and of actors. His works reflect a sophisticated understanding of the connections between stage action and political action, between roles assumed in the theatre and those assumed in life. In this regard, Fugard's intimacy with theatre, his awareness of the analogies between one's life in theatre and one's life as a citizen in the world, puts him in a class with Harold Pinter, Edward Albee, Chekhov, Brecht, Shakespeare, and Molière.

The study of Fugard's dramatic works that follows is meant as a discussion of all his plays to date, focusing on what Eric Bentley called "the playwright as thinker" and examining Fugard's ideas as well as his ability to use the dramatic form in order to give shape to his ideas, to present them live and make them alive, on stage for modern theatre audiences. Like all writers, Fugard has sometimes won praise and other times taken his lumps from the reviewers and critics. Likewise, not all Fugard's plays have been box office successes or universally admired.

In some instances Fugard has suffered at the hands of those who wish to ghettoize authors who write in English but are not from Great Britain or the United States, castigating them if they dare write about something other than their native country. We want Indian, African, and Australian writers to tell us respectively only about India, Africa, and Australia. To them we implicitly sometimes deny the rights, unquestioningly given to British and American authors like Defoe, Kipling, Dryden, Henry James, or Melville, to set their work off their native soil. In the case of Fugard, he is applauded when he writes—as he generally does—about South Africa and its politics. But when he writes about other matters—as he does in *Dimetos* or *A Place with the Pigs*—reviewers, critics, and audiences seem either at sea or disconcerted that he has presumed to dramatize anything other than South African matters.

In other instances, Fugard has been criticized for being a white playwright whose skin and Eurocentric education prevent him from knowing the South African black majority and their problems in a truly intimate and, therefore, meaningful way. The issues of attack are that, given the racially separate development structure of apartheid South Africa, Fugard has not resided in a black township and therefore cannot know in any firsthand way the realities of oppression; his languages are English and Afrikaans, but he is not a speaker of an indigenous African language; and his plays tend to focus on racialism rather than on the underlying exploitative economic structure that fosters apartheid. The most pugnacious of Fugard's detractors, Robert Kavanagh Mshengu, influenced by the political philosophy of Antonio Gramsci, wrote in 1982:

> Fugard's opposition to apartheid confines itself to an indictment of racialism, but not of the exploitative and destructive nature of capitalism as it operates in South Africa. The effect of emphasizing the former is to obscure the latter, especially when a playwright's work can command an audience in the capitalist countries whose ruling classes reap the superprofit the creation of such labour reservoirs, to name but one example, produces. . . . But South African history testifies to the daily struggles of the oppressed majority. There have been and still are strikes, boycotts, uprisings, sabotage, urban guerilla actions, passive resistance, stonings, killings, creativity, music, dance, protest literature and journalism, political theatre, poems and recitations, political parties and associations—all manner of struggle. Yet where in Fugard's work is any of this?[3]

Mshengu's accusations deserve some attention because they do make us aware of what is *not* there in Fugard's work. At the heart of such attack is the presumption that a white writer is incapable of writing cogently about the lives of blacks. Of course the work of any white writer presenting black lives will necessarily be compromised by the fact that the writer does not live inside a black skin. To follow the implications of Mshengu's argument to its natural conclusion, along with Fugard's, the works of Nadine Gordimer, André Brink, or Alan Paton must be deemed nugatory. For those with strong political agendas, like Mshengu, a writer's work must necessarily be diminished when he or she fails to consider the "exploitative and destructive nature of capitalism." Jane Austen's *Mansfield Park,* for example, is, then, a compromised work, for it fails to point its readers to capitalist exploitation by not indicating that the luxury of Mansfield Park is derived from Mr. Bertram's sugar plantations in Antigua, which are likely run with slave labor and based on colonialist land appropriation. Mshengu's touchstones should not lightly be passed over for they enable us in useful ways to see the limitations of works, including Fugard's, that we read or see.

An astute and objective treatment of Fugard's playwriting and politics is given by Dennis Walder, who discusses ways of understanding how Fugard as a playwright has borne witness to the political and social history of apartheid South Africa.[4] Fugard's works about race are often more symbolic than realistic, and his audiences are generally aware that the characters in *The Blood Knot, Boesman and Lena, Statements after an Arrest under the Immorality Act, My Children! My Africa!,* or *Playland* are representations of issues far more than they are Africans whose living conditions Fugard has personally experienced. Fugard does not share Mshengu's Gramscian bent and thus does not write his plays, as Mshengu would have him, in such a way that they "lead to the artistic enrichment of his work and the adoption of the democratic ideology of socialism."[5] Fugard uses the art of drama to reach the minds and hearts of his audiences, to make them aware of political issues. And it is with Fugard the dramatist rather than with the incorrectness or correctness of his politics that this study concerns itself.

The reality is that Fugard is a world-class playwright, who often uses the South Africa he knows so intimately as a setting for more universal examinations of human life, human interactions, and the powers of art. His several plays about South African apartheid may be set in a specific place and time, but they deftly use the space/time coordinates to graph far more imposing and larger, generally applicable patterns of race and racism. Plays such as *The Island, A Lesson from Aloes,* or *Playland* clearly have as much or more to say about the human toll racism, wherever it is practiced, leaves in its wake than they do about the specific destructiveness of localized South African apartheid.

The goal of this study is to examine Fugard's dramatic works in chronological order and in a straightforward way, discussing the issues they examine and analyzing the ways in which Fugard uses drama and dramaturgy to present his insights. I am interested, moreover, in charting his growth as a playwright and in marking the ways his South African experience gives him a way of talking about issues that extend well beyond the borders of his homeland. I feel little need to chart the theatre history of his work, since that has already been done so well by both Vandenbroucke and Walder. There are those who write scintillatingly and with great fervor about Fugard, but who are mostly concerned with criticizing, disputing, or rejecting what they see as the politics of his plays. Let me say at the start that this study is not a politically theorized one, not one that is meant to support my own political ideas or revile Fugard's, but rather one that wishes to understand how Fugard puts his ideas on stage and makes them live for an audience. There is more interest here in how one writes plays with a political and social edge than in caviling over the particularities of a play's political and social issues and over Fugard's implicit political stance. It is, after all, possible to admire the playwright's art in Shakespeare's *Julius Caesar* without rejecting that play for its antidemocratic and elitist thrust.

Because Athol Fugard, like Harold Pinter, Edward Albee, David Mamet, and Tom Stoppard, is a "son of Sam," a disciple of Beckett, more than four actors on his stage seems a crowd. Although not quite the minimalist Beckett was, Fugard creates spare plays with little change of location and requiring a small space in which a paucity of actors create meaning from the motion of their bodies and the words of the text. By contrast, this study has benefited from an extensive cast and a range of locations. It has taken me to a large number of libraries, archives, and theatre collections primarily in the United States, South Africa, and Germany, where I have not only read material relevant to this study but been able to see performances of the entire Fugard canon with the exception of *No-Good Friday, Nongogo,* and *Dimetos.*

The first Fugard play I ever saw was *Statements,* which a touring group performed in 1975 at the Malersaal of the Staatschauspielhaus in Hamburg, Germany. I was struck by the power of the play and moved to read more by this new (to me) South African author. Years later, it was an especial pleasure to see Fugard himself on stage in the revival of *The Blood Knot* and *A Place with the Pigs* at the Yale Repertory Theatre; in the New York productions of *Valley Song* and *The Captain's Tiger;* and in the McCarter Theatre (Princeton) and Kennedy Center (Washington) stagings of *Valley Song* and *The Captain's Tiger.* When I witnessed the New York production of *The Road to Mecca,* feeling the play come to life and take on meaning through the chemistry among Fugard, Yvonne Bryceland, and Kathy Bates, I knew I had to write this book. I was likewise inspired by seeing Zakes Mokae in the Yale Rep revival of *The Blood Knot* and in the New York production of *"Master Harold" . . . and the Boys,* and by John Kani and Winston Ntshona when they revived *The Island* at the 1995 Grahamstown Festival and then, a few days later, in Cape Town. Especially important for me was the 1983 production of *A Lesson from Aloes* at the Berkeley Repertory Theatre in California, where, under the auspices of an Eli Lilly Faculty Fellowship, I served as the dramaturg, witnessed the rehearsal process, and authored the playbill's program notes. Writing cogently about drama is not just about reading texts in a library but about attending performances and knowing what happens when a play goes from page to stage. This is unusually important for understanding Fugard, who is, after all, both playwright and playmaker: writer, director, and actor.

In the course of researching and writing this study, I have been helped immeasurably by the input, friendship, and generosity of others, and I owe thanks to many. Some of this study was written with funds from the National Endowment for the Humanities; the Eli Lilly Foundation; the offices of the Research and the University Graduate School, International Programs, and the College of Arts and Sciences at Indiana University; and the Universität Bayreuth. I am indebted as well to Indiana University's Institute for Advanced Study and the Institute for the Study of English in Africa at Rhodes University.

Much of my research was conducted at the National English Literary Museum (NELM) in Grahamstown, South Africa. My debt to the staff there can never be repaid. Most especially, though, I want to acknowledge the unusual kindness of my good friend Malcolm Hacksley, the director of NELM, who not only placed the resources of NELM at my disposal but made me feel a family member at NELM and in his home. There are no words to thank adequately the very extraordinary and indefatigible senior archivist at NELM, Ann Torlesse, who more than once found material I did not know existed, made my stays at NELM unusually productive occasions, and continued to send materials and to answer questions long after I had left Grahamstown. A word of thanks, too, must go to Jeremy Fogg, NELM's genial associate director. I was honored to be made a fellow of the Institute for the Study of English in Africa at Rhodes University, and I am grateful to the director of the institute, Professor Laurence Wright, and to his staff. While I was in South Africa, my work was much enhanced by productive talks with Guy Butler, who combines with elegance the talents of writer, critic, and sage. I am unusually blessed at Indiana University by having at hand a first-class library run by premier librarians. And there I am especially indebted to Tony Shipps, Perry Willett, and Ann Bristow as well as to Lisa Browar at Indiana University's Lilly Library.

One of the joys of writing about Fugard's plays is that I came to know Athol Fugard himself. Even after strenuous performances, he was never too busy to spend time with me, to talk to me about his plays and his projects. In this book I acknowledge my respect for him as a playwright. I respect him as well for his warmth, humility, and patience. He is not merely a gifted man of theatre, he is also a fine human being and a friend.

In the course of doing the research and writing for this study, I also got to know three truly remarkable scholars who aided my work in significant ways and whom I admire for the breadth of their knowledge and depth of their friendship. Stephen Gray, himself a renowned scholar and writer, put all his Fugard materials and astonishing personal knowledge of South African literature at my disposal. His great interest in my properly understanding Athol Fugard's plays and personal background was heartwarming; he went so far as to drive me through Fugard's South Africa giving me informed tours of Middleburg, Colesburg, Noupoort, Cradock, Nieu-Bethesda, Graaff-Reinet, Beaufort-West, and Somerset-East. The vegetation, wildlife, topography, and sense of place in the Karoo and environs became known to me through Stephen, who has also managed over the years to supply me with clippings from the Johannesburg papers about Fugard productions. He is generosity itself and gives new meaning to collegiality and friendship.

It is hardly surprising that in 1982 André Brink dedicated his novel *A Chain of Voices* to Tim Huisamen, his then-colleague in the Afrikaans department at Rhodes University. Tim's knowledge of both English and Afrikaans South African literature is nothing short of encyclopedic, his insights into that literature often astonishing, and his friendship without bounds. More than once he was able to help me see works with new eyes, and my sections on *Boesman and Lena* and on *The*

Blood Knot are significantly better than they might otherwise have been for our lively discussions of the plays and for Tim's astute guidance. I shall never forget his friendship, collegiality, and remarkable knowledge.

Likewise in Marcia Blumberg, who has herself written so well on some of Fugard's plays, I found a colleague and friend of like mind and one eager to share her own insights on Fugard's plays and productions in order to make mine better. Our readings and understandings of Fugard's are not always congruent, but I never fail to gain important new insights from her interpretations. She generously took time, moreover, from her many commitments to read my manuscript with great care and to make many important suggestions for its amelioration. In more instances than I care to admit, she saved me from tactlessness.

In the course of my education, I had the good fortune to sit in the classrooms of some particularly fine teachers, who taught me much of what I know about the drama and who gave me a lifelong love for theatre. I very much hope this study will reflect the best of their teaching. My greatest debt is surely to my teacher at Yale, friend, and role model, Eugene M. Waith. In a sense, my serious study of drama (and consequently this study of Athol Fugard's plays) began years ago in Gene Waith's graduate seminar on English playwrights from Beaumont and Fletcher to Addison and Steele. I was fortunate, too, as a graduate student to study with Cleanth Brooks, E. Talbot Donaldson, and Charles T. Prouty. As an undergraduate at Columbia, my understanding of drama was vastly enriched by studying nineteenth- and twentieth-century German drama with Walter H. Sokel, modern drama with Eric Bentley, and Shakespeare with Andrew Chiappe. At Columbia, too, I encountered great teachers of literature who influenced my critical sensibilities in strong but ineffable ways: Steven Marcus, Richard Chase, Susan Taubes, Mark Van Doren, and George Nobbe. As a young faculty member at Princeton, I was privileged to work with Alan S. Downer, from whom I learned much about the structure of drama and the connections between drama and theatre.

For this project, I have enjoyed the warm support of two especially kind and close friends, John Barlow of Indiana University and Joseph Kissane of Columbia University. With great care, they read and proofread the entire manuscript of this study, giving me their incisive comments on how the text could be improved, and saving me from many infelicities. I appreciate as well the generous and useful comments I received from my valued colleague at Indiana, Tim Wiles. Indeed, the support and friendship I have known at Indiana University have meant a great deal to me; and I am especially indebted to Brian Winchester, Patrick O'Meara, Keith and Marion Michael, Morton Lowengrub, Trevor and Charlene Brown, Budd Stalnaker, Henry Cooper, Kenneth Johnston, Alvin Rosenfeld, George Walker, David Hoegberg, Judith H. Anderson, Murray McGibbon, and Paul Strohm. At Indiana University Press, I want especially and warmly to thank my editors Joan Catapano, Michael Lundell, and Susanna J. Sturgis.

Friends and scholars around the United States and the world have given me the advice and warm support that made this study possible. I wish, therefore, to offer my warmest thanks to: Paul Walters and the late Barbara Bosch (Rhodes University), Temple Hauptfleisch (Stellenbosch University), Oscar Brockett (University of Texas), Nancy Bazin (Old Dominion University), Robert King (Elms College), Tony Heilbut, Eckhard Breitinger (Universität Bayreuth), Jean-Pierre Durix (Université Dijon), Kyung-won Lee and Suk-koo Rhee (both of Yonsei University), Peter and Marie-Anne Brasch, Bill McGaw (University of Wollongong), Yasmine Gooneratne (Macquarie University), Jack Turner (Humboldt State University), Michael Harper (Scripps College), Shirley Kenny (SUNY–Stony Brook), Arthur C. Kirsch (University of Virginia), C. J. Gianakaris (Western Michigan University), Chris Hudgins (University of Nevada, Las Vegas), Ann Fox (Davidson College), Jerry Dickey (University of Arizona), Joseph W. Donohue (University of Massachusetts), Robert Vorlicky (New York University), Kimball King (University of North Carolina), Jackson Bryer (University of Maryland), Errol Hill (Dartmouth College), Henry Schvey (Washington University), James Bulman (Allegheny College), Norma Jenckes (University of Cincinnati), and C. Roger Davis.

My Cape Town cousins, Harry, Pam, and Alfie Wertheim, were always there for me in South Africa and made sure I got to see the South African landscape as well as mountings of Fugard plays in Cape Town. My California cousins, Allan and Diane Wertheim and Claire and Carl Reisman, kept me abreast of Fugard productions in Los Angeles, and made it possible for me to attend a rare performance in Los Angeles of *My Life*.

I leave for last my greatest debts. Neither this study nor my career would have been possible without the considerable sacrifices, financial and otherwise, of my mother and late father, Gerta and Gustav Wertheim. As refugees from World War II Germany, they arrived on American shores with very little, but managed to give me, their child born in free America, so very much. What they did can never be repaid. My wife, Judy lived this book with me. Taking time from her own demanding career, she attended and discussed performances of Fugard's plays with me, and later read and proofread the words of my text. Her critical eye and her critical insights have been invaluable. Indeed she is and has always been there to encourage my projects and discourage my excesses. To Judy and to my children, Lewis and Ellie, and Gerald and Raluca, this book is dedicated with love.

THE DRAMATIC

ART OF

ATHOL FUGARD

ONE

Early Work and Early Themes

One of the high points of New York's Museum of Modern Art's 1992 retrospective exhibition of the works of Henri Matisse was the attention devoted to his earliest works. There one could immediately see his origins in works of seventeenth-century Dutch still life painters and the subsequent French painters Courbet and Chardin.[1] One could see as well the starting points for the directions his later work would take. With Athol Fugard, as with Matisse, the earliest works—*No-Good Friday* (1958) and *Nongogo* (1959)—have innate merit, suggest early literary influences on Fugard (e.g. O'Neill and Beckett), and indicate directions either taken or eschewed in his later work. Approaching *No-Good Friday* and *Nongogo* with a knowledge of the plays Fugard is to write in the decades that follow, one can recognize the markings of Fugard's style and some situations and themes he will develop in later plays. At the same time, however, it is important to recognize and discuss the power and values of these plays in and for themselves.

Born in Middleburg on 11 June 1932 the son of Harold Fugard and Elizabeth Magdalena Potgieter, Athol Fugard combines the two major European strains in South Africa. His father, a sometime jazz pianist and a cripple, was of English-speaking, Anglo-Irish ancestry; his mother, an Afrikaner, was a descendant of a Voortrekker family. In 1935, the Fugards moved to Port Elizabeth, where Athol Fugard grew up and where his mother ran a boardinghouse and later the St. George's Park Tea Room, the setting for *"Master Harold". . . and the Boys.* After attending a Port Elizabeth technical college, he enrolled at the University of Cape Town, which he left in 1953 shortly before he would have earned a degree.[2] After hitchhiking from South Africa to Sudan, Fugard signed on for ten months as a hand on the SS *Graigaur.* That journey and his attempt to write a novel while at sea are recorded in *The Captain's Tiger* (1998). Upon returning home in May 1954, he took up a position as a freelance writer for the *Port Elizabeth Evening Post;* and in 1956, he married actress Sheila Meiring, also of mixed English and Afrikaner ancestry. Two years later, the couple moved to Johannesburg. Fugard was employed there as a clerk in the Fordsburg Native Commissioner's Court, where pass law violations were tried. Very likely that experience and his time on the SS *Graigaur*, where he had met men of many races and nationalities, played a role in making him poignantly aware of South Africa's racialism and its troubling effect on the lives of South Africans of all races.

After Fugard arrived in Johannesburg in 1958, he was introduced by his Cape Town classmate Benjamin Pogrund, who had also come to Johannesburg, to Sophia Town, the black township (later razed) one could enter without a pass. There he became associated with a group of black artists that included Lewis Nkosi, Bloke Modisane, and saxophonist-actor Zakes Mokae. Together on 30 August 1958, they performed what was essentially Fugard's first full-length play, *No-Good Friday*, at the Bantu Men's Social Centre with Fugard directing and Sheila Fugard serving as manager of their African Theatre Workshop company.[3] To produce a play with a racially mixed cast was a daring move in 1958; and when *No-Good Friday* had a one-night performance in Johannesburg's Brooke Theatre, a white audience venue, Lewis Nkosi acted the role of Father Higgins, which Fugard had been playing.

The members of the African Theatre Workshop seem to have been as much engrossed in the theory of drama as in production itself. As Vandenbroucke, quoting from an interview with Mokae, points out, the group members "were more theoretical than practical and would discuss what Beckett, for instance, was trying to say."[4] Eventually Fugard would profit from Beckett's minimalist dramaturgy as well as from Beckett's ideas; but in *No-Good Friday* with its eleven characters, Fugard crowds his stage, allowing the force of his drama to become diffuse. Nevertheless, much of that force does remain.

No-Good Friday is a play bedeviled by a problem that has haunted the reception of Fugard's work throughout his career. The play is set in Sophia Town, the black township, which would later be destroyed, at the edge of Johannesburg. As a white writer, Fugard necessarily sees black and coloured life at a remove, a remove that can provide some objectivity but that also always keeps him from truly understanding what it is to be "non-white"[5] in South Africa, what it is to live in a non-white township and suffer the human indignities, the physical and mental blows, that blacks and coloureds know with terrible immediacy. The dilemma is that Fugard has often been, will continue no doubt to be, taken to task for writing about the degradation of blacks and coloureds while himself being afforded the privileges enjoyed by South African whites.[6] At the same time, however, it would for Fugard be impossible not to write about these things, for silence is acquiescence.

When recent literary theorists complain that Fugard's plays, like *No-Good Friday*, have not been radical enough, they fail to acknowledge that an artist may be forced to sacrifice political correctness for larger political ends. Had Fugard's plays been as acerbic as these theorists would have them, they would likely not have been produced or made an effective appeal to their audiences. White writers like Fugard and novelist Alan Paton are nowadays rejected for their moderation by post-apartheid critics, but one must remember that it was their moderation that drew world attention to the outrages of apartheid. *Cry, the Beloved Country* and the plays of Fugard may not have rendered all the aspects of apartheid to suit the agendas of contemporary theorists, but Fugard and Paton achieved something far more significant: they used their art to bring South Africa to world attention as few anti-apartheid activists were able to do.[7]

For Fugard, imagination and acting are identities. And the word "acting" has at once a theatrical and a political meaning. Theatre is a place to enact both realities and dreams, and it is thus a microcosm and a possible model for the world beyond the playhouse doors. If all the world's a stage, then the stage and the *acting* and *performance* it witnesses can also be played out in the world.

Aware of both the advantages and the limitations his skin affords, Fugard, especially (but not only) in his Sophia Town and so-called Port Elizabeth plays, touches his works with realistic detail he has come to know through his contacts with townships and township dwellers, but then wisely and usefully tempers that realism with symbolic, nonrealistic moments. And thus *No-Good Friday* and *Nongogo,* Fugard's first plays, both of which are set among Sophia Town blacks, are much more than the "thin slice of township life" that Vandenbroucke, for example, claims *Nongogo* to be (23). They are, rather, plays that often effectively weave together the realism or naturalistic setting of a township clothesline or shebeen with the unrealistic or symbolic killing of a naive black man newly arrived in Sophia Town or the sudden magnetism between a shebeen queen and a tablecloth salesman. That mixture, that interweaving of real and symbolic, is what distinguishes *No-Good Friday* and *Nongogo,* and what, when perfected and burnished by Fugard, will be the source of dramatic power in his later works.

No-Good Friday achieves its vision through a curious combination: it pictures some of the realities of township life but then connects its pictures by tying them all to the force that rules the lives of the characters and existence in the township. Bringing his knowledge of white life to bear, Fugard effectively dramatizes how the economic structures of black townships disastrously replicate and intensify those of white South Africa, which has created those townships and set their way of economics. All the characters of the play are, finally, victims of an economic system that demeans and alienates them.

In *No-Good Friday* the characters in one way or another all face the same issue: the poverty imposed on blacks in South Africa. Fugard recognizes that to be black in South Africa is to be poor, and that black existence is imbued with the struggle to find release from the cycle of poverty and the mean quality of life indigence creates. That black problems are no different from white ones is suggested by Father Higgins, the well-meaning white cleric acted by Fugard himself in *No-Good Friday*'s initial production. But the priest's well-meaning innocence is treated ironically and satirized by an embittered Willie, the play's main character (played by

Lewis Nkosi in the original production), whose education has allowed him to see with more clarity than others the realities of township life:

> WILLIE. Sophia Town is a fertile acre for troubles, Father.
>
> HIGGINS. Every garden has its weeds, even the white ones.
>
> WILLIE. Yes, I've seen them. I was walking down a street the other day with neat white houses on each side and a well-trained dog snarling at me behind every gate. Those gardens were neat all right, the grass so green I couldn't believe my eyes. And in one of them is a dear old lady with a fork looking for a weed which she finds dying among the flowers, so she digs it out and everything is just fine and blooming nice again. (126)[8]

When Father Higgins then asks Willie to aid Tobias, a man who has come from the economic despair in rural areas to find economic relief in the jobs Johannesburg offers, Willie describes Sophia Town as Hamlet describes the Danish court—"'Tis an unweeded garden / That grows to seed. Things rank and gross in nature / Possess it merely":

> HIGGINS. This is Tobias, Tobias Masala. He has just arrived here from the Eastern Transvaal. A simple man, Willie, like so many of our people. I was wondering if you could help. He'll do anything provided there is enough in it for him to live and maybe save a little each month. . . . he only wants to live, Willie. You know better than I do the stories they bring with them of sick women and hungry children.
>
> WILLIE. When it rains over here we have to walk up to our ankles through muck to get into our shacks. There is another patch of muck we have to slosh through every day, the tears and sympathy for our innocent brothers.
>
> HIGGINS. His life is a supreme gift. He must cherish it. He asks for nothing but a chance to do that.
>
> WILLIE. It's muck, I tell you. This is Goli, not a quiet reserve. He wasn't made for this. They flounder, go wrong, and I don't like seeing it. (126–127)

Underlying this interchange are the economic realities at work in black South African life, and underlying it as well is the literal picture of the mired landscape of Sophia Town connected to the metaphorical human bog Sophia Town represents. Such a fusion of literal and metaphorical image is the underlying strength that will characterize the best of Fugard's plays and that gives meaning here to *No-Good Friday* as a drama that is more than a series of tragic snapshots chronicling the meanness of township life.

A plot outline of *No-Good Friday* might suggest that Willie is the play's tragic protagonist, for he is pitted against his township antagonists, Shark and his *tsotsi* thugs, who appear every Friday to collect weekly protection money from Sophia Town inhabitants bringing home their meager pay packets. Such a view of the play makes it a good deal less than it is, for Shark is a "heavy" whose brief appearances on stage are merely functional and do not pose a meaningfully articulated opposition to Willie. The real antagonist of *No-Good Friday* is economics and the economic system, a white system that blacks have unwittingly replicated.

Tobias, the East Transvaal innocent, comes to Johannesburg (or Goli, the city of gold) to earn enough money to survive and "maybe save a little each month" to send home to his wife and hungry children. His situation is no different from that of the other characters. It is just simpler and more naive. Guy, the saxophonist, is in the township looking without success for a job playing his instrument, but is disheartened by the realities of the vocational marketplace: "I knocked on the door of every recording shop in town. If I'd known how many chaps were playing the sax I would have stuck to penny whistle. When my break comes, I won't have enough wind left to blow a false note" (121–122).

The travails of Pinkie, the "tea boy" in a white firm, are more complicatedly tied to the system of race and economics as it is played out in South Africa. Van Rendsburg, a white employee, has not paid Pinkie with a required tea coupon, and when Pinkie does not pour his tea, Van Rendsburg complains to the management. Pinkie, the black "boy," has no rights and is told his job is in jeopardy unless he apologizes. Pinkie's dilemma, to take the moral high road and be fired or suffer the humiliation of apologizing to the white man who has cheated, is raised by Fugard because it is important in terms of the larger moral dilemma of the play. Guy and Peter, Pinkie's friends, teach Pinkie the lessons of economic survival he clearly knows but has momentarily lost sight of in the heat of his moral anger:

PINKIE. What would you do, Peter?

PETER. It's like Guy said. Find out what hurts you most: apologizing or losing your job. Then you got your answer.

. . .

GUY. Well, you're sober, you're calm, you got control of yourself. Now think. It's a good job. It's good pay. It's Friday night. You're going to have yourself a good time. Right?

PINKIE. Right.

GUY. So what! This van Rendsburg's not in Sophia Town. You only see him for five minutes every morning and five minutes every afternoon. Why worry about him! Apologize and keep your job.

PINKIE. That makes sense. Guy, you've helped me. That pay packet was welcome, you know, what with Shark coming round. I wouldn't like to be here without five bob when he comes. Of course. It's a job like you said, it's regular pay! That old van Rendsburg, we know he was wrong, don't we? So I say:

"I'm sorry, Mr. van Rendsburg" and I laugh at him in the kitchen. You're right, Guy! (130–131)

The discussion here does not merely present the easy sacrifice of moral principles to economic pragmatics; it also sets the stage for the entrance of Shark.

The white oppressive world of van Rendsburg, Pinkie's boss, and the affluent executives who ride in the elevators run by poorly paid black men is not shown, but it is nonetheless dramatized with feeling by the characterization and appearance of Shark and his gang, who simply replicate the way of the South African world, only that they are a step lower than the white *baas* on the food chain of oppression. Shark's humiliation and exploitation of Sophia Town residents are a coarse copy of van Rendsburg's. Men like Pinkie and Guy and Willie cannot speak out against the wrongs of Shark's extortion racket any more than they can against van Rendsburg's indignities. They must, rather, suppress their moral feelings and, as it were, "laugh at him in the kitchen." And the comments on the black system in the township could just as easily be applied to the white system in the town:

> WILLIE. He's sure got us trained, hasn't he?
>
> GUY. As Shark would put it: I've put a lot of money and time into training you boys. God help the chap that forgets.
>
> WILLIE. I reckon he's about the only one God would want to help.
>
> GUY. If he'd forgotten about Shark the only help God could give would be a free pass into heaven. You'd be finished with the good old earth if you ever forgot eight o'clock on Friday night. . . . Pay up and you'll at least have the seven days to next Friday. (132–133)

The earlier interchange among Pinkie and his friends and these comments about Shark are Fugard's way of indicating that the dynamics in the township are a version of the dynamics enacted daily between whites and blacks. It is a dynamic based on oppressive power, obedience training, money, and the pass, whether that be the passbook or the ability to pass in safety.

In a moment that foreshadows a more extended satirical scene in *Sizwe Bansi Is Dead*, Guy instructs Tobias in the ways of the city:

> GUY. We're meant to be dumb. What's more important is a little lesson in grammar. Now, what did you call the white induna on the farm where you worked?
>
> TOBIAS. Mr. Higgerty.
>
> GUY. No, Toby. Over here it is "*Baas.*" Do you understand? Just: yes *baas*, no *baas*, please *baas*, thank you *baas* . . . even when he kicks you on the backside. (128)

In the scene that follows, this theme is picked up by Willie in a new key as he exclaims, "What a future! Everybody wants a backside to kick in this country" (131). And when he is told to forget his studies and his discontent for the night, Willie's response touches the nub of his problem and that of the play:

> GUY. Forget the books tonight if they make you feel so bad.
>
> WILLIE. Forgetting is the problem.
>
> GUY. I always just thought of it as a bad habit.
>
> WILLIE. It is, the way most people do it. What I was getting at was being able to forget just what you wanted to. Learn to do that, Guy, and you'll be the most contented man in the world. You got accounts? . . . Forget them! They summons you? . . . Forget it. They jail you? . . . Forget there's any better place to be. (131–132)

In line with Willie's cynical, pragmatic advice, Tobias must forget his manhood and Pinkie must practice moral amnesia. Likewise, the citizenry of Sophia Town must forget to condemn and resist the likes of Shark. Like Guy's explanation of *baas*, these are simply the ground rules, the rules for survival in an exploitative, dehumanizing system practiced upon blacks by whites and by other blacks like Shark, who merely re-enact the larger paradigm.

If he bucks the system, Pinkie knows he will be heartlessly sacked. For bucking the system, the innocent Tobias is heartlessly murdered. And in both cases, the others stand by, see it happen, and avert their glances. *Forgetting* equals survival. They all know too well on which side their stale and meager crust of bread is buttered, but they understandably hold on to that crust rather than face the peril of starvation. Here, one might argue, is Fugard's cue to shout, "Black workers of the world, unite." But neither in his first play nor in his later ones is Fugard a playwright who calls for arms, for physical action. Some would hold this against him. Indeed, Fugard in *No-Good Friday* mocks the would-be revolutionaries, their rhetoric, and their calls to arms in one of his most baldly lampooning caricatures, that of Watson, the township politician, who says:

> Round about lunchtime, I had an idea. A stirring call for action! "The time for sitting still and submitting to every latest injustice is past. We gotta do something about it." But then I remembered that this was a meeting of the Organizing Committees and they might not like that. Just now, I had another idea. "We must weld ourselves into a sharp spearhead for the liberatory movement." That'll have to do. (124)

The kind of resistance Fugard seems to demand is one not of storming the barricades but of existential courage. A deep reader of Camus, Fugard seems to suggest that real revolution, real distress, real dismantling of racial and economic injustice will come from individual existential self-realization.

At the heart of *No-Good Friday* lies Willie's coming of age and tragic struggle. The most intelligent of the group of Sophia Town residents Fugard presents, Willie is earning a B.A. degree through a correspondence course because this will result in "a better job . . . more pay" (122). It has given him as well a facility with words and, as Rebecca, the woman with whom he lives, unhappily recognizes, a sense of independence. Throughout the initial scenes of the play, Willie is shown to be the one whose education makes him verbally facile, enables him to spell difficult words and to draw artful distinctions between the words like "pride" and "admiration." But the hand of Fugard the accomplished man of theatre is already evident in this first play, for Willie's verbal accomplishment is presented dramatically within a context that satirizes the use of words, which are used as the building blocks for empty rhetoric like Watson's and more sinisterly as the basis for a vocabulary of racial oppression. What is the use of Willie's mastery of polysyllabic language when the necessary language in South Africa is based on monosyllables like "*baas*" and "boy"? And when the black replication of white oppression takes place, when Tobias is dubbed *Stupid* and peremptorily murdered by Shark and his thugs for not knowing his role of subservience to them, Willie's words fail him and he stands on stage bearing tacit witness to Tobias's murder, acquiescing to it by his silence.

No-Good Friday's central and powerful dramatic moment stems from the onstage juxtaposition of swift action, the murder of a naive and innocent Tobias, who has just ironically exclaimed, "I'm not a baby" (140), with the stage picture of inaction, whereby the cast of township dwellers mutely, without protest, stands by permitting the murder to take place and not reacting to it after it has happened. The moment marks Willie's awakening. He has beforehand already achieved, we are told, a nebulous sense of independence, but to no clear purpose. His loss of innocence is marked as he says of his prior "cosy" life, "But something has shaken it and I've fallen out of the nest. It's not so cosy and warm down here and I don't see how I can kid myself that it is" (142).

Willie's tragedy and the point of view of the play are neatly designed by Fugard. Willie cannot summon the requisite words as he tries and fails to compose a letter that will inform Maxulu, Tobias's widow, of her husband's death while covering over its circumstances. Such words would be words that once more looked the other way, forgot the violence of Tobias's murder, and thereby accepted the life of oppression that defines existence for the resident of Sophia Town and of the townships throughout South Africa. The death of Tobias serves to crystallize for Willie the plague that besets the society in which he lives, and he says sarcastically, "The only way we can soften life is by softening ourselves. . . . Like forgetting a silly bastard was killed out there and we stood around because that way life was easy." To this, his friend Guy asks, "Do you want to end up dead?" And Willie replies, "How else does a man hope to end up?" (147–148)

Willie's rhetorical question significantly moves *No-Good Friday* toward its impressive and unique end. The dramatic lines of the play suggest a buildup toward an agitprop, activist ending. The underpinning of life in the township is economics. All the relationships in the play—even Willie's with Rebecca—are tainted by monetary matters. This Fugard clearly shows, as he also shows the lines of inter- and intraracial oppression. Willie's loss of innocence and consequent realization of how things are will, a seasoned theatergoer might guess, lead to an ending like that of Clifford Odets's *Waiting for Lefty*, a call for the oppressed, under Willie's intelligent leadership, to rise up as one and take arms against the oppressors, to destroy the underlying capitalism that fosters their oppression. But Fugard impressively veers the play in quite another direction.

Willie's awakening is an existential one, and his answer to Shark and the realities of life is to acknowledge that by acquiescence, by forgetting, by looking the other way, he is not a passive victim of a bad world but has played a part in its creation and survival:

> You know one of the ideas I've come out with? The world I live in is the way it is not in spite of me but because of me. You think we're just poor suffering come-to-Jesus-at-the-end-of-it-all black men and that the world's all wrong and against us so what the hell. Well I'm not so sure of that any more. I'm not so sure because I think we helped to make it, the way it is. . . . There's nothing that says we must surrender to what we don't like. There's no excuse like saying the world's a big place and I'm just a small man. My world is as big as I am. (160–161)

Willie then acts with existential enlightenment, facing and facing down the plague by severing his ties with Rebecca and the others who would have him capitulate to the situation and thereby save his life. But to the inspired existentialist Willie has become, such a life would not be worth the having.

Stoically and alone, except for the company of a blind man, Willie waits at the close of the play for his inevitable death at the hands of Shark. The stage picture at the conclusion of *No-Good Friday* is one of remarkable power. Although there is no sense that Willie's existential Friday night martyrdom will bring about a revolution and a new week on Sunday, the curtain nevertheless comes down on an audience chilled by what they have witnessed. From that time forward they will not be able to "forget" or not to know. Eschewing either oratory or combat, Willie's dramatic power is that of an immured Antigone awaiting tragic death for opposing a tainted system. That notion of existential heroism, of acting in accord with higher enlightened principles rather than with the fervor of a pugnacious revolutionary, is not to every viewer's or reader's liking, but it is a notion that will mark nearly all of Fugard's work to follow.

Beginning with his very first plays, it is clear that Fugard finds in the South Africa he knows the elements of tragedy. Although Fugard sets many of his plays in South Africa and more specifically in Port Elizabeth, he is not writing specifically South African tragedy, for he uses his South African setting and his presentation of South African life under apartheid rule to define a tragic situation imbued with meaning far beyond the geographical boundaries of South Africa. In his growth as a tragic playwright, Fugard, probably influenced by the ancient Greek tragedians and by Samuel Beckett, comes to recognize that to convey his ideas effectively, he must focus his plays on a few characters and be guided by, though not follow slavishly, the unities of time, place, and action.

Fugard's first play, *No-Good Friday*, though in many ways a work of considerable strength, is weakened by its many characters and several locations, which diffuse its focus and power. The dozen actors on stage and the play's two sets create a panorama where more concentrated dramaturgy would have served Fugard better. When Fugard comes to write *Nongogo*, his second play, he wisely pares his cast down to four actors and keeps to a single time, place, and action. And after *Nongogo*, Fugard trims and shapes his scripts further so that every one of his plays, with the exception of *Dimetos* and *People Are Living There* (which each have four roles), is either a two- or a three-hander. The panoramic quality of Shakespeare's and Marlowe's tragedies or Goethe's *Faust* notwithstanding, there is surely, Fugard seems to learn, a dramatic economy and a tragic power to be gained by reducing a play, its characters and its situation, to its essentials. Of course, from a purely pragmatic point of view also, it is easier for a playwright or director—and Fugard is usually both—to work intensely with two or three actors than to manage crowds or to reposition characters in several different settings. The elemental and tragic questions of human existence seem for Fugard to be most effectively presented when the play contains two or three actors and one setting.[9]

Nongogo, which opened on 8 June 1959 and which featured Zakes Mokae in the role of Blackie, is a tighter, stronger play than *No-Good Friday* in large part because Fugard confines himself to one significant set, Queeny's shebeen, and because he has trimmed his dramatis personae to four. Indeed, it is arguable that the play might have benefited further had it been constructed just around the triangle of Queeny, Johnny, and Sam. Nevertheless, even at this early stage in his career, Fugard already displays his particular and considerable playwriting strengths, which emanate from his ability to use set and stage objects in remarkably powerful ways and to conceive the language and semiotics of characters in such a way that the audience can achieve great depths of understanding in a relatively short dramatic time frame.

At the heart of *Nongogo* is Queeny's shebeen, a black township pub where the battered souls created by South African racialism congregate and drink. The denizens of Queeny's place are not the derelicts of Harry Hope's saloon in *The Iceman Cometh*, but like Eugene O'Neill's characters they find at Queeny's the alcohol that will serve as a temporary anodyne to their painful lives. And into the shebeen comes Fugard's own version of O'Neill's Hickey, a salesman selling tablecloths and, at least for Queeny, a special brand of salvation.

As Fugard tells the reader in his opening stage direction and as the audience eventually comes to understand, the shebeen is the physical embodiment of its proprietress. The furniture is expensive and first-class, but the general decor has been neglected and the room has an aura of slovenliness. Odd bits of female apparel have been left about, curtain rings are missing, and what could be elegant has a slatternly look. When Queeny enters, Fugard's stage directions assert, "*She is a personification of the room: the very best but neglected*" (59).[10]

When Johnny comes into Queeny's shebeen with his salesman's sample case of colored tablecloths, there is an almost instant, ineffable attraction between the two characters. Johnny, hoping to sell to Queeny, explains how the disorderly main room of the shebeen can be straightened up and made attractive, how his table-cloths can be used to cover the stains on Queeny's expensive, high-quality furniture:

> JOHNNY. All I do is sell table cloths. Which reminds me . . . It's not a very big range, only red and blue, but the colours don't run.
>
> QUEENY. What do I want with a table cloth?
>
> JOHNNY. For your table. Look, that's good wood. [*He examines the table closely.*] . . . And here, see! Stains! I say, it's essential for a respectable shebeen with a good table like this to have one of my table cloths.
>
> [*Queeny has been watching him carefully. She starts smiling and at the end of his little sales talk bursts into laughter. Her personality changes . . . the moody aggressive person is gone.*] (61)

Queeny's handsome table is marked with the stains of glasses from all the men who frequent her establishment; and though Johnny's cloths will not remove the stains, they will cover them up and give a new, well-kept, coordinated look to the room. And at some unspoken level, Queeny seems to recognize that what Johnny can do for the room bespeaks what he can also do for Queeny herself: restore her worth and looks, coordinate and lend new color to the meaning of her life by helping her cover up the stains and damage that men have inscribed on her life and body. The way in which Fugard here uses the stains on the table from numerous moist barroom glasses to symbolize the many men whom Queeny has known sexually is indicative of the astonishing dramaturgical savvy that characterizes Fugard's entire playwriting career.

Queeny, who stands at the center of *Nongogo* and is its protagonist, finds herself in the course of the play at the crossroads of her life. Her friend and protector, Sam, who seems to be the organizer of house break-ins and a fencer of stolen goods, in the past was her pimp and is now her fellow entrepreneur. Implicitly Sam accepts that exploitation and poverty are the lot of non-white Africans in South Africa, and his pragmatic philosophy is based on making the best of the way of the world, of making the most money he can from the given situation. And he has encouraged Queeny to do likewise in her shebeen, which, as an institution of township life, takes money from those who can ill afford to spend it, offering them in drink a mo-

2. Dambisa Kente as Queeny in *Nongogo*, Civic Theatre, Johannesburg, revival 1994. Photo by Ruphin Coudyzer.

mentary escape from their bitter lives. Queeny is relatively affluent because her shebeen essentially makes its considerable profit from the misery and lowest needs of those caught in economic hopelessness.

As becomes clear in the play and as its title essentially tells us, Queeny has previously been a *nongogo*, "a woman for two-and-six, a term especially used of prostitutes soliciting amongst the lines of gold-mine workers queuing for their pay." Though she does not yet understand it as such, her new vocation as shebeen queen is simply a replication in a new key of the past life and profession she wishes so desperately to bury.

Residing at the heart of the tragedy Fugard formulates in *Nongogo* are Fugard's insights into the notions of freedom and enslavement, and the role money and economics play in those matters.[11] The play of course depends on the particularities of black township life and the struggle for existence within that life, but the power of *Nongogo* resides in its larger truths and the general applicability of the lessons taught within the Johannesburg township setting. Uncovered and displayed in *Nongogo* are the unfortunate truths of economic reality when the inequities of capitalism are exacerbated by the constraints of racialism.

Under a system that keeps blacks as an indigent underclass, black economic survival depends on enslavement to the system or discovering ways to beat or circumvent the system. All the characters in the play are in their special ways victims of the system. Patrick and his wife are caught in a hopeless life cycle, leading lives of desperation because they are simply cogs in the economic mechanism and are reduced to being merely the means of providing human fodder for a mighty economic machine they will never control or own. Patrick's passionate, poignant lament is that of a man experiencing a moment of insight into the life he and thousands like him lead:

> It's hell. In every way it's hell. You know they should make it that we blacks can't have babies . . . 'cause hell they make it so we can't give them no chances when they come. They just about made it so we can't live. But with babies it's hell! They cry, you don't get no sleep, they need things . . . and they suck the old woman dry. (76)

The "they," the generalized other of the speech, stands for the inexorable economic system and perhaps more particularly that system as South African whites have fashioned it. Is it any wonder, then, that Patrick spends the evening in Queeny's shebeen obliterating the thought of another child, another exploited being, about to be born instead of spending that time at his wife's bedside?

Standing at the edges of the hell Patrick invokes seem to be Sam and his incubus, Blackie. They cope with the system through illegal activities and through force. For Sam especially, money, regardless of how it is earned, is tantamount to beating the system, to economic freedom. He genuinely believes that he and Queeny, erstwhile pimp and prostitute, have found salvation by becoming fence and shebeen queen:

> SAM. In the old days when we were . . . you know what I mean . . . I used to talk about the shop and you used to talk about having your own shebeen. It was just the same. And we both got what we wanted. I bet if you kept books you'd find you was making more than me. . . . If you mean I still believe in this . . . [*rubbing his thumb and forefinger together to indicate money*] you're right. That's the only difference between the full belly I got now and an empty one, between these clothes and rags. . . . This is what we worked for and this is what we got. So let's be happy. . . . Show me another woman around here with half of what you got.
>
> QUEENY. What about the things they got that I haven't?
>
> SAM. Such as?
>
> QUEENY. A man.
>
> SAM [*bursts into rude laughter*]. Didn't you have enough . . . ? Well you know what I mean. What's the matter with you? A man. You'll be saying a home next, with kids . . . and then you've had it. We got no complaints, Queeny. We live comfortable . . . no attachments . . . We're free . . .

QUEENY. Free!

SAM. Yes, free. Who is telling you what to do or where to go? Nobody. (67)

With the instincts of a Marxian in a Brecht play mastering what he believes to be capitalism, Sam believes money and a "full belly" equal happiness, and that freedom is achieved by remaining free from the bourgeois fetters of home, marriage, and children. Observing the plight of Patrick, one can well understand the wellsprings of Sam's reasoning.

But for Queeny and Johnny, freedom means something more than affluence. And both of these characters have been, far more than Sam or Patrick, the victims of economics. Johnny's story is a common one among black men who go as adolescents to the Johannesburg mines, lured there by the tales of money to be made and as the would-be saviors of their impoverished families:

> I was a kid. Seventeen years old. It was the big story about the mines. The good food, the clean rooms, the money. My parents bought that one all right. Money! So I came here, ten years ago. (92)

Of course he found none of these things, and especially the dreams of money did not come true. What did instead come true was a nightmare that bespoke the whole system: he was sodomized by the sex-starved older inhabitants of the all-male compounds. Johnny's repeated rape by people of his own gender and race is a dazzling image of the way the need for money and the enslavement of blacks within the economic system turns blacks to violate each other in the most violent, most brutal of ways. Even more than Tobias and Willie, who are killed by black gang members in *No-Good Friday*, Johnny, who is sexually penetrated by the mine workers, falls victim to a way of life that forces men to batten on each other's flesh for survival.

Likewise, Queeny has also been brutalized by the exigencies of economics. Her life as a child was precisely that of Patrick's children. She explains to Johnny, ". . . my father used to drink his pay packet down on a Friday night while we waited hungry at home" (92). Impressively, she says that since then she dreamed to herself, "'One day you'll have a shebeen and get fat.'" (92)—that is, essentially, she dreamed of becoming a captain of industry instead of one of industry's abused. Indeed, as she tells Johnny at the play's climactic moment, she was a *nongogo*, a woman for two-and-six, who made money through the most denigrating form of prostitution. And again, money, economic survival, compelled her to let her body be penetrated in the most intimate ways. And in so doing, she reduced herself to a receptacle; and the men were reduced to animals waiting for their turn to feed their lust:

> I did it because I was hungry, because I had sworn to myself I was going to make enough to tell the rest of the world to go to hell. And nothing makes money like Sam organizing the business. We started with queues around the mine dumps at night. I can also tell you a few things about compounds,

Johnny. But we ended big . . . one man at a time. That's how I got here and Sam got his shop across the street. (113)

As Queeny suggests in this speech, her history and Johnny's are curiously parallel.

What draws these two bruised characters to each other is that both seek to overcome their history, and see in the other a means for doing so. Both characters, moreover, seek a special kind of freedom from the ravages of money. Sam organizes businesses and, with reasoning like that of George Bernard Shaw's Mrs. Warren, argues that the path to salvation is to own the business and exploit others rather than to be one of the exploited workers. For Johnny, however, the idea of freedom is vastly and significantly different. Having been exploited and, both figuratively and literally, raped by business, his idea is to protect his freedom by eschewing the capitalist trap of human exploitation and by using money instead to ensure personal freedom, freedom from the exploitation and power paradigm capitalism entails. And in explaining his stance, Johnny utters the first of many parables in Fugard's drama. One sees the beginnings of what is to become a hallmark of Fugard's style, the parabolic story like that of the drought and the aloes in *A Lesson from Aloes*, the kite and the ballroom dancing in *Master Harold*, or the dominee's potatoes in *The Road to Mecca*. Johnny tells the parable of Joe and his horse:

I knew a fellow once . . . had a horse and an old cart . . . people used to laugh at him 'cause he didn't make much and what he had he always spent on the horse and cart. Sometimes he went without supper just so the horse could eat! Everyone thought he was mad but he carried on like they wasn't there. One day I asked him: Joe, why don't you sell that horse and buy yourself some good clothes and eat well for a month. He looked at me: What do I do after the month? Get a job, I said, like everybody else. He shook his head: Johnny, you're asking me to sell my freedom for a good meal and clothes. (74)

Understanding the parable, Johnny sees that Queeny's savings can be her salvation. He says to her, "Money. It could mean security, three meals a day, a roof over your head and independence . . . like Joe" (74). For himself, he hopes to have the money some day so that no one "can kick you around and feel like a white man" (75). For Johnny, then, freedom means independence from a system in which one man is enslaver and the other enslaved, in which one man is white and the other black.

Johnny's attitude is, furthermore, that of a visionary and of an artist. He sees himself first as an interior decorator on a small scale, literally brightening people's lives, covering up their stains and unsightly rooms with tablecloths and curtains and bedspreads and cushion covers. And this, in turn, opens up into a large vision of social reform:

You see, it's important, Queeny . . . trying to make life better. I'm not saying my idea is going to change the world, but maybe it will give us a bit more guts, and make waking up tomorrow a little bit easier. (80)

Clearly Johnny here captures what Fugard is beginning to realize is the function of the artist in society and the function of the play he has written and the plays he will write. To be sure, Johnny's vision is central to Fugard's career-long concept of his role in society as an artist.

For Queeny, the idea of freedom is less clearly spelled out than it is for Johnny. He is the artist, and she is the spectator for whom vistas of freedom begin to become perceptible through the power of Johnny's magic. For Queeny, freedom is summarized as "We'd be respectable" (82), having a "clean start" (93), and "It's good to need someone" (105). In short, she believes in Johnny's vision that interior decoration can make life better, that stains can be covered up and forgotten, that it is possible to find a life where one is not owned or used. She believes that through Johnny and the new start in life he can give her, she can reach a state where, in Johnny's words, "you're really safe when you can tell the rest of the world to go to hell" (105).

In *Nongogo*, Queeny invests in Johnny. She invests her capital but, more importantly, she invests her hopes in his vision and in him as her redeemer. The tragedy in the play evolves when Sam and Blackie, fearful of losing Queeny as their peer, suggest to Johnny that Queeny is not respectable. Johnny, for all his rhetoric about change, is mired in that oldest of male prejudices about women: that they are either angels or whores. And when it is suggested that Queeny is less than an angel, his idealism escapes like air from a balloon and he reverses his prior optimism, saying, ". . . sometimes I get the crazy idea that a man can change the world he lives in. Hell! You can't even change yourself" (109). And when Queeny reveals that she has been a *nongogo*, he abandons her. The tragedy for Johnny is that of the artist who does not finally believe in his own vision. The tragedy for Queeny is that she has glimpsed independence and freedom but has been betrayed by her liberator. And not knowing how to achieve freedom without him, she slips back with vehemence into the world of Sam and Blackie, reopens her shebeen, and, as the stage directions dramatically reveal, "*She goes to the mirror, puts on lipstick . . . rouge . . . earrings . . . bracelets, and dolls herself up into a real tart*" (114). Tragically, she embraces business, the business of making money by lining her purse through the sexual and alcoholic weaknesses of men. If she cannot achieve her own liberation, she will enslave others.

The concluding moments of *Nongogo*, the confrontation of Johnny and Queeny, and of Queeny's dazzling transformation as she reverts to the *nongogo* she once was, are both gripping and moving. As Queeny falls back into the capitalist, exploitative world and philosophy of Sam, the audience feels something akin to the tragedy of Faust unable to escape his hellish fate. At the same time, the play offers the audience a sense that Johnny's tragedy lies in his failure to believe in his own vision of social and personal amelioration. The audience, however, can see that Johnny's philosophy can work, that the tragedy of the protagonists need not have been, and that that tragedy can be averted by the audience members if they have heeded the lessons inherent in Fugard's dramatic art.

TWO

The Port Elizabeth Plays:
The Voice with Which We Speak from the Heart

In 1959 and 1960, the Fugards spent a not very successful or happy time in Europe. Fugard's attempts to find work in the London theatre were largely abortive. In 1961, Athol and Sheila returned to South Africa, where their daughter Lisa and Fugard's new play *The Blood Knot* were born. Fugard did not return to the African Theatre Workshop but selected one of those actors, Zakes Mokae, for one of the two roles in *The Blood Knot*. Fugard himself played the other. It opened on 3 September 1961 at Dorkay House, a former clothing factory turned into a playing space, which Fugard had previously used to rehearse *No-Good Friday*.

In his 1994 memoir, *Cousins*, Athol Fugard speaks of *The Blood Knot* (1961) as a "watershed play." Robert King recognizes it as the gateway to a range of later Fugard plays, and Russell Vandenbroucke asserts, "The play was to the stunted South African theatre what O'Neill's *Beyond the Horizon* was to the American theatre in 1920."[1] These comments all bear witness to the importance of *The Blood Knot* not only for launching the playwright's career as a highly regarded playwright but, beyond that, for acting as a significant marker both in the development of Fugard's thinking and in the development of a theatrical style not divisible from that thinking.

When Dennis Walder speaks of *The Blood Knot* as containing "a more transgressive urge than has generally been admitted,"[2] he refers to the play's daring presentation of a black and a white actor on the same stage in an apartheid-bound, Verwoerdian South Africa, where before *The Blood Knot* such a gesture would have been considered nearly unthinkable and daringly radical.[3] Indeed, as Vandenbroucke reminds us, four years after the play opened, mixed casts were deemed illegal (fig. 3).[4] As important and transgressive an act as having black and white actors—in this case Zakes Mokae and Athol Fugard—on stage may have been in

TOGETHER ON THE STAGE

Special Correspondent

JOHANNESBURG.—Theatre history was made in Johannesburg this week when a White man and a Black man acted together publicly in the same play.

Play makes S.A. theatre history

They were Athol Fugard and Zakes Mokae, the only players in Fugard's exciting three-hour "The Blood Knot", a play about race in South Africa. It is set in a Korsten, Port Elizabeth, shack.

Municipal by-laws purport to prohibit racially mixed performances but some lawyers think the by-laws are ultra vires.

Anyway, producer Leon Gluckman has taken a chance and "The Blood Knot" opened in the Y.M.C.A.'s intimate theatre on Wednesday night before a fashionable and wildly applauding (White) audience.

Nadine Gordimer, the South African author who has just returned from receiving a literary award in London, was there and also Mrs Helen Suzman, the only Progressive M.P.

UNCOMPROMISING

The authorities have taken no action (yet) to stop the performance, possibly because the legal aspect has been delicately avoided so far.

In a rave notice, the Rand Daily Mail put it this way: "Two brothers, one light-skinned and with European features (Athol Fugard) and the other dark-skinned and with uncompromisingly African features (Zakes Mokae) . . ."

This is the way Leon Gluckman wants the play appraised — purely as a play. He thinks "The Blood Knot" is making a different kind of theatre history as the first genuinely top-rate South African play.

"This is the birth of South African playwriting", he said enthusiastically on the morning after the first night.

"I hope 'The Blood Knot' will do for South African playwriting what 'The Summer of the Seventeenth Doll' did for Australian playwriting."

ILLITERATE

Gluckman wants to put the play on "everywhere". He has promised Fugard that it will go on in London.

Fugard and Mokae will be the players. "The Blood Knot" is remarkable as a feat of memory alone. It will be trimmed a little and some people who have seen it think it needs a few minor adjustments in construction.

They declare, however, that it has moments that are inspired.

The two brothers share a room. Against the background of this simple set some of South Africa's racial madness is acted out.

The illiterate African, with the help of his literate brother, gets a pen friend and then discovers that she is a White Afrikaner girl.

Fugard, 32, a White South African born in a Cape village, managed to scrape enough

ATHOL FUGARD

money together to get a university education and then went on the road for more than three years.

He claims there is not a highway or byway he has not waited on hitching lifts.

He has written seven plays, of which "The Blood Knot" is the third to be performed. It is the only one that looks like hitting the jackpot.

Zakes Mokae has been acting for four years including a part in the South African film "Tremor".

He appeared in the productions of Fugard's two previous plays. Fugard and Mokae have a great affection for each other.

A CHANCE

While it has been possible to take a chance with "The Blood Knot"—the financial loss would be small if the performance was stopped suddenly by the authorities — it is not possible to take a chance with another multi-racial play "The Red Silk Umbrella" by Johannesburg author James Ambrose Brown.

Brown's play is a musical, a happy show, but with eight players and expensive sets and costumes the producers could not take the risk of having it shut down summarily.

It will open in Johannesburg shortly with an all-White cast.

Die Transvaler, of Johannesburg, devotes about five inches beneath a two-column heading to the play.

"This piece lasts for three hours, with only two players and no change of scene. Normally this would be an invitation to boredom, but this tragedy is an exception.

"The play deals with the mixing of the races and is set in a Coloured slum in Port

Elizabeth, where two brothers live together. One brother is White, the other Black.

"The frustration resulting from racial mixing is the theme of the story."

The reviewer observes that Athol Fugard, playing the part of the White brother, is also the author — "but he is more successful as an actor."

There were also times when the play deteriorated because it was a sequence of situations more than a definite intrigue which was developed.

THINKING

The reviewer concludes: "'The Blood Knot' is a successful presentation. It makes the audience think about the solution for this tremendous problem."

Footnote: Mr Fugard is the son of Mrs Harold Fugard, of Bird Street, Port Elizabeth. He matriculated at the Port Elizabeth Technical College and went to Cape Town University, leaving on a world hitch-hiking tour a few months before his finals in social science and philosophy.

After his return to Port Elizabeth in 1954, he joined the S.A.B.C. and later became a freelance journalist. He has also worked for the Johannesburg Native Affairs Department.

Since then he has written several plays, one of them winning an award at the 1960 Brussels Festival.

He went to Europe in 1959 to learn more about the theatre. Mr Fugard is married to Sheila, daughter of Dr Ernest Meiring, of Kirkwood.

MARMITE DECINE OF

3. Review from unknown South African newspaper. Courtesy the Lilly Library, Indiana University, Bloomington, Indiana.

1961, *The Blood Knot* is transgressive in other and equally important ways as well. And one must remember, as the original audience knew only too well, that the play's transgressions came just a few months after the atrocities of the infamous Sharpeville massacre.[5]

A two-hander, *The Blood Knot* concerns two brothers living in Korsten, a coloured area of Port Elizabeth. The brothers share the same brown-skinned mother, but it is not clear from the playtext whether they have a common father.[6] One of the brothers, Morris (played in the original production by Fugard), however, is light-skinned and Zachariah (played by Zakes Mokae), the other, is black.[7] In the course of the play, we learn that Morris has tried in the past to pass, or in South African parlance "try," for white, but that now he is trying on Zachariah's clothes and Zachariah's life to learn what it is to have a black skin in South Africa. Likewise, Zachariah comes to project himself into a white role through his correspondence with Ethel Lange, a white girl from Oudtshoorn whose address he has obtained through the personals section of a newspaper. As Zach and Morrie try on each other's roles, as they try on and try out being white and being black, they transgress every which way across color lines. For the audience of the first production, there was the added transgression of a white and a black actor appearing on stage together playing the parts of light- and dark-skinned coloureds. And most subsequent productions have also cast a white and a black actor in the roles of the two coloured brothers. The play's two characters and its two actors while on stage are, consequently, racialized bodies.

Of course *The Blood Knot* is also transgressive in that the two coloured men are writing to a young white woman who has placed an ad in a newspaper personals column so that she can meet an eligible young man. Clearly dark-skinned Zach Pietersen of coloured Korsten is *not eligible* to court the fair-skinned Ethel Lange of Oudtshoorn. And in still another dimension, that of style, *The Blood Knot* is transgressive, for it deftly combines and juxtaposes scenes and moments of realism with ones of Beckettian symbolic minimalism, and with ones that exemplify what is perhaps Fugard's greatest gift to the modern theatre, the voice of inner truth. Describing that voice in *Cousins*, Fugard writes:

> . . . as a director in rehearsal rooms . . . I have tried to help actors embrace their own personal moment of truth. It is the voice with which we speak from the heart, the voice with which we lower all our defences and try to tell our deepest and most painful truths.[8]

With its several diverse transgressions, *The Blood Knot* is the first of Fugard's plays to achieve the unique dramatic voice that is to mark much of his subsequent work. It is a voice that is able at once to articulate realities of South African life, speak eloquently of life's larger verities, and find an appropriate channel for evoking "the voice with which we speak from the heart."

The opening moments of *The Blood Knot*, during which Morris winds his alarm clock and fussily checks the contents of his room followed by Zach's wordless entrance and Morrie's subsequent Chaplinesque attention to Zach's aching feet and footbath, echo dramatic moments in *Endgame* and *Waiting for Godot*, and serve to create a Beckettian atmosphere.[9] And the opening moments of the play, filled as they are with extended discussion of the smells, relative efficacies, and prices of the foot-salts Morrie has purchased, continue to suggest a Beckettian environment.[10]

Working counter to a Beckettian indeterminacy of space and time, however, *The Blood Knot* offers the specifically South African accents of its two characters. Zach and Morrie's English is peppered with Afrikaans words and phrases; moreover, the mention of Korsten as their place of residence gives a recognizable local habitation and name to their existence. Situated as it is next to a noisome body of stagnant water rank with industrial waste, Korsten is a poor coloured area of Port Elizabeth. Although Morrie and Zach appear to the audience as white and black respectively, the fact that in 1961 South Africa was divided into group areas cues the audience that the two brothers who live in their small space in Korsten must, by virtue of their location, be classified as coloured. Thus Fugard paradoxically creates a space that is at once the everywhere of Beckett yet has the specificity of a particular Port Elizabeth coloured area. In Martin Orkin's judgment, Fugard's world in *The Blood Knot* is not that of Beckett's "'muckheap'" but rather, he writes in *Drama and the South African State*, "the dead lake at Korsten suggests, more particularly industrial waste" (98). Orkin is not altogether wrong, but what he misses here is that it is not a matter of one or the other, for what Fugard manages to do is blend what are in *The Blood Knot* sometimes coexistent and sometimes hybridized Beckettian and realistic environments. It is this sometimes mixture, other times compound that allows Fugard to forge dramatic truths that uncannily and sometimes dazzlingly transcend both the minimalistically symbolical and the doggedly realistic.

The Blood Knot is not a simple play to understand or discuss. Speaking of the St. George's Tea Room which his mother ran and which serves as the setting for *Master Harold*, Fugard describes it in a phrase that has obvious meaning for *The Blood Knot:* "a place where we all came together to tie and untie the rosary of knots that is every family's unique story" (*Cousins*, 80). *The Blood Knot* is surely a play about such knots, about the making and undoing of family ties. And the role of the audience as well as of the two characters is to unravel or at least to understand the knot that binds Morrie and Zach.

Dreams and the imagination are close to the heart of Fugard's play. In the first scene of the play, Morris says, "There's always two sides to a sad story" (6),[11] and the two sides to the brothers' sad story is evoked by the competition between Morrie's dream of the future and Zach's of the past. For the former, the future consists of his dream of "a small two-man farm, just big enough for you and me" (9). For the latter, the past consists of sexual remembrances:

> Hey! I remember now! By hell! . . . How did I forget? Where has it gone? It was . . . *ja* . . . *ja* . . . It was woman! That's what we had when we went out at night. Woman!! (11)

In a sense, the two visions bespeak the tragic present-tense limbo in which the brothers exist.

In Zach's case, his thoughts are very much about immediate pleasures of physicality and coitus. They have nothing to do with procreation, family, or improvement of his rude situation. In the years of his adulthood, Zach has apparently never ceased living in Korsten or in the one-room shack where the play takes place. A man of limited imaginative capabilities (at least as he is shown in scene 1), Zach lives from day to day with no visions of a future. Morris, by contrast, has traveled and has, perhaps thereby, grasped the pointlessness of their lives in the city. For him, the bright future lies in escape to a farm in the countryside:

> City streets lead nowhere . . . just corners and lamp-posts. And roads are no different, let me tell you . . . only longer, and no corners and no lamp-posts which, in a way, is even worse. I mean . . . I've seen them, haven't I? Leading away into the world—the big empty world.
>
> But when we go, Zach, together, and we got a place to go, our farm in the future . . . that will be different. (10–11)

But it is clear to the audience that this is a vision that will likely never be realized in a South Africa where coloureds like Morrie and Zach can easily become farm laborers but are almost certainly not going to become farm owners.

Fixed on the future, Morris feels life passing away as time passes away. "That's life for you. The passing of time and worthless friends" (13), he asserts. Controlling time and controlling friendships is thus of great importance for him. Appropriately, then, he measures his life with the play's important inanimate actor, an alarm clock that is set to go off at regular intervals. In part, Morrie's need for control is manifested in the way he seeks to restrain Zach's urges by replacing Zach's need for interpersonal and sexual encounters with the control gained by social intercourse through letter writing:

> Morris. In fact I think we got it.
>
> Zachariah. What?
>
> Morris. The answer to your problem, man.
>
> Zachariah. Woman?
>
> Morris. That's it! You said talking to one would help you, didn't you? So what about writing? Just as good, isn't it, if she writes back?
>
> Zachariah. Who . . . who you talking about?
>
> Morris. A pen-pal, Zach! A corresponding pen-pal of the opposite sex! (16–17)

Although the disparate mentalities of Morris and Zach emerge in the first scene of the play, the nature of their brotherhood does not, nor does the reason for Morris's having a year ago evidently returned to their *pondok* (shack).

Morris's role in *The Blood Knot* begins to make good sense if we see him as an artist, a Prospero, a playwright who seeks to control story and narrative, time and tempo, character and psychic development. Writing about music and theatre more than thirty years after *Blood Knot*, Fugard provides useful insights that can be projected back upon the play and upon Morris as would-be playwright. Fugard writes:

> The parallels between music and theatre as a whole, and not just my particular dramas, are very striking. Both have time, actual experienced time, as one of the major dimensions built into them. . . . Beginning, middle, and end. I call them "time machines" because that is what they are designed to do, take you on an emotional and intellectual journey lasting a very specific time. Both have metronomes and clocks ticking away as pacemakers at the heart of their engines. (*Cousins*, 37)

And he goes on to say how his timing usually leads, as in *The Road to Mecca*, to an aria. He says, "I don't think I have written a play without it having at least one aria in this fashion. It is no coincidence that rehearsal room talk is about rhythm, tempo, pause, beat and crescendo as much as about the words and sentences" (38). But unlike Fugard, Morris is not a practiced playwright nor is he controlling a work of art outside himself, for he is unwittingly one of the major players in his own play.

Appropriately, it is Morris himself who comes to sing a Fugardian aria at the close of the first scene. Instead of working as an effective playwright and stage manager who moves Zach to a new interest in the future, Morrie's verbalizing literally puts Zach to sleep. And instead of Zach, it is Morrie himself who is caught up in the rhythm and timing of the scene. He is brought around, as it were, through his own playwriting or orchestration, to voice an aria of guilt that concludes the scene and brings the audience of *The Blood Knot* to a new level of awareness and meaning.

As though about to deliver a sermon on a biblical text, Morris prefaces his aria or soliloquy with the lines from Genesis 4:10: "And he said: What hast thou done? The voice of thy brother's blood crieth unto me!" (19). As the play's title suggests, the relationship between the two brothers in *The Blood Knot* is considerably more complex than the relatively archetypal fraternal rivalry between Cain and Abel in the biblical narrative. Indeed, it is Morrie, the Abel figure, favored by both his mother and his white blood, who has abandoned the black-blooded Zach. And the blood that crieth is not the blood of physical murder but the blood of race and brotherhood denied. Having abandoned Zach and the racial stigma that Zach represents, having abandoned Zach in order to "pass," to "try for white," Morris has returned to Zach's Korsten tin-roof shack to do penance, be forgiven, and acknowledge his oneness with his black-skinned brother.

In this play about passing or transgressing, Morrie's soliloquy ends with a significant visual act of racial and brotherly transvestism: he puts on Zach's coat, rife with the black man's strong sudoriferous bodily odors; evocative, in its stains and in its feel, with the definitions of Zach's life:

> You get right inside the man when you can wrap up in the smell of him, and imagine the sins of idle hands in empty pockets and see the sadness of snot smears on the sleeve, while having no lining and one button had a lot to say about what it's like to be him . . . when it rains . . . and cold winds. It has helped a lot. It prepared me for your flesh, Zach. Because your flesh, you see, has an effect on me. The sight of it, the feel of it . . . it . . . it feels, you see. Pain, and all those dumb dreams throbbing under the raw skin, I feel, you see. (21)

Fugard here puts into Morrie's mouth what all playwrights, directors, actors, and cross-dressers know: that to don someone else's clothes is to assume and begin to understand that other person's life. One is able, too, by assuming another's clothes and shape to see oneself with new objectivity.

Transgression in another form takes place as the two brothers peruse the personals of three young women in the newspaper Zach has brought home. As they read the self-descriptions of the women, Zach, prompted by Morris, projects himself into a vicarious romantic or sexual relationship with each. And at one point, he does so by conceptualizing the young woman in the newspaper ad as Connie, a woman whom he has actually known as a sexual partner:

> ZACHARIAH. I can't get hot about a name on a piece of paper. It's not real to me.
>
> MORRIS [*outraged*]. Not real! [*Reads*] "I am eighteen years old and well-developed." . . . eighteen years old and well-developed! If I called that Connie it would be real enough, wouldn't it?
>
> ZACHARIAH [*his face lighting up*]. *Ja!*
>
> MORRIS. So the only difference is a name. This is Ethel and not Connie . . . which makes no difference to being eighteen years old and well-developed. Think, man! (23)

The dramatic irony here is that the audience realizes from the names and addresses of the women what the men at this point do not: that the woman about whom they are fantasizing is white, and that the interchangeability of Ethel Lange of Oudtshoorn and Connie Ferreira of Korsten is, in South Africa, an unthinkable racial interchangeability of white and coloured.

Continuing in his role of playwright and stage manager, Morrie verbally annihilates Zach's friend Minnie, so that Zach becomes wholly dependent on Morrie; then Morrie reshapes his brother through epistolary formalities and the rules of answering a personals column ad.[12] Clearly what Morrie wishes to do is rewrite the script of their lives, for in South Africa it is scripted that these two brothers, white and black, should be driven apart. It is scripted as well that coloureds like Zach live crude, indigent lives in a Korsten *pondok* contiguous to stagnant water redolent with the odors of pollution and industrial waste. And it is scripted that their lives be as static and moribund, as physically and spiritually foul-odored as the body of water that defines their neighborhood (and indeed much is made of Zach's offensive bodily smells). What Morris thus attempts to do is write a new script that will allow the brothers to leave their shanty for a farm. This will allegedly re-form Zach into a gentleman, allow Zach to substitute epistolary courtship for a sexuality that has been little better than rape, and rinse away the foul smells of urban life from Zach's body.

When Ethel Lange writes back to Zach, the brothers must come face to face with both the imaginative possibilities and the folly of Morrie's scripting, as well as with the realities of South African racialism. The photo Ethel Lange sends of herself reveals her as incontrovertibly white. Just as the brothers have not surmised from her name and address that she is white, so she, living in Oudtshoorn and unfamiliar with Port Elizabeth geography, has not recognized Korsten as a coloured area or Pietersen as a relatively common coloured name. These misunderstandings enable Fugard rather brilliantly and incisively to present and explore both the comedy and tragedy of errors possible in the given situation. Zach sees from the photo that Ethel is white, enjoys the error, and sees the comic possibilities that the racial transgression affords:

> ZACHARIAH. You mean that this Ethel . . . here . . .
>
> MORRIS. Is a white woman!
>
> ZACHARIAH. How do you know?
>
> MORRIS. Use your eyes . . .
>
> ZACHARIAH [*studying the photo*]. You're right, Morrie. [*Delighted.*] You're damn well right. And she's written to me, to a *hotnot*, a *swartgat*. This white woman thinks I'm a white man. That I like! [*Zachariah bursts into laughter*]. (40)

The situation, filled with classic dramatic irony of comedy, becomes increasingly funny for Zach and for the audience as Ethel's letter is read aloud to its concluding salutation, "'To Zach, with love, from Ethel'" (42). And for Zach, his ability to imagine himself crossing the lines of racial taboo is a better, more delightful script than those Morrie has conceived for him:

> It's because she's white! I like this little white girl! I like the thought of this little white girl. I'm thinking it, now. Look at me. *Ja*. Can't you see? I'm serious, but I'm also smiling. I'm telling you I like the thought of this little

white Ethel better than our future, or the plans, or getting away, or foot-salts, or any other damned thing in here. It's a warm thought for a man in winter. It's the best thought I ever had and I'm keeping it. (44)

The comedy of errors and the safety of a letter allows Zach, black as he is, imaginatively to try for white as Morris has done. In a sense, it enables him to be Morris, to know what it means to be housed in a white skin. And at the same time, of course, it enables him vicariously to flout South Africa's Immorality Act barring interracial sex and marriage.

Morris, who has known the dangers of trying to pass for white and thus risking the consequences of crossing South African color bars, immediately sees the possibly tragic consequences of the situation, and wishes to burn Ethel's letter. From his own travels through Oudtshoorn, he knows that the whites of the town are not the sort to be welcoming to people of color. With some significance, he remarks of Oudtshoorn, "Both times I went straight through. I didn't make no friends there" (25). Understanding to whom they have written and the racial dangers thereby invoked, Morrie is brought to the larger realization that for non-whites even their dreaming is forbidden and potentially perilous:

> Do you think a man can't hurt himself? Let me tell you, he can. More than anybody else can hurt him, he can hurt himself. I know. What's to stop him dreaming forbidden dreams at night and waking up too late? Hey? Or playing dangerous games with himself and forgetting where to stop? I know them, I tell you, these dreams and games a man has with himself. . . . You think that's a letter? I'm telling you it's a dream, and the most dangerous one. (46)

Of course, what is true for the sexual dream is equally true for the dream of owning a farm.

In this scene, Fugard does not first posit Zach's comic view of racial dreaming and then follow it with Morris's. Rather he has Zach and Morris, tenor and bass, sing their insights in duet. The combination or knot of their separate visions creates for the audience and perhaps for them as well a transcendent state of tragicomic enlightenment. There is much to be said for each brother's perspective, but for Fugard, there is still more to be said for the perspective that combines these two racially and temperamentally opposite brothers into an enlightened whole greater than the sum of the parts.

The racial dilemma of the play intensifies when a second letter from Ethel arrives announcing her plans soon to visit Port Elizabeth in the company of her brother the policeman. This causes a series of important moments in the play. On one level, the turn of events, as Fugard surely recognizes, is reminiscent of comic farce like *Charley's Aunt* or *The Importance of Being Earnest.* On quite another level, those events replace the alarm clock that literally goes off in the first scene of the play with a more menacing metaphoric clock set to touch off a tragic explosion if Ethel should meet Zach. That combination, an event at once potentially comic and tragic, initiates one of the trans-real moments that mark *The Blood Knot,* one of those moments when larger truths are reached through "the voice with which we speak from the heart." The characters suddenly speak in a Fugardian dramatic *Sprechstimme.* First, under Morrie's guidance, Zach is forced to exorcise and expiate his transgression; and in so doing, he confronts the central taboo, the nuclear transgression that defines the permissible limits of the South African imagination:

> MORRIS. You see, we're digging up the roots of what's the matter with you now. I know they're deep; that's why it hurts. But we must get them out. Once the roots are out, this thing will die and never grow again. . . .
>
> ZACHARIAH. Ethel is white and I am black. . . . Ethel is so . . . so . . . snow white. . . . And I am too . . . truly . . . too black. . . . I can never have her. . . . She wouldn't want me anyway. . . . *The whole, rotten, stinking lot is all because I'm black!* (60–62, italics mine)

Then Zachariah realizes that for his light-skinned sibling the dreams are possible and even permissible if he can pass and avoid getting caught.

And with that realization, Zach assumes new power, for, as those who have discussed passing have explained, the game of passing is a tripartite power relationship consisting of the person who passes (the passer), the person who is fooled by the passer (the dupe), and the person who sees what is going on and knows that the passer is passing and the dupe is being fooled.[13] In this relationship, the greatest power is in the hands of the one who knows the game being played. The power of the dupe resides only in the event that he or she becomes aware of the scam and brings down punishment on the passer. Thus, in *The Blood Knot,* the passer (Morris) exerts a power over his dupe (Ethel), but the greatest power is placed in the hands of the one (Zach) who knows the true identity of the passer, knows the dupe is being duped, and has the power to reveal the passer's identity. It is Zach, consequently, who in the middle of scene 4, in the middle of Fugard's seven-scene play, begins to assume power and to script a transgression for Morrie:

> Look. I can't use her. We seen that. She'll see it too. But why throw away a good pen-pal if somebody else can do it? You can. You're bright enough, Morrie. I don't know why I never seen it before, but you're pretty . . . a pretty white. I'm telling you now, as your brother, that when Ethel sees you all she will say is: How do you do, Mr. Pietersen? She'll never know otherwise. (66)

And from that point, the two brothers vicariously create Morrie as someone who can pass in the white world not merely in terms of skin color but in terms of clothing (a hanky in the breast pocket) and etiquette ("chew it small, and swallow before you speak").

The imaginative cross-dressing proceeds into literal cross-dressing when the brothers spend the money they have saved for a farm and their future in order to buy clothes for Morrie to wear when he will presumably take Zach's place and meet Ethel. At this point, with Zach's help, Morris dons white man's dress and thereby recognizes that a coloured man in white racial drag is about more than clothing, for it has to do with demeanor, style, bearing, attitude, and the ineffable sense of security that bespeaks whiteness:

> The clothes will help, but only help. They don't maketh the white man. It's that white something inside you, that special meaning and manner of whiteness that I got to find. . . . the first-fruit of my thought is that this whiteness of theirs is not just in the skin, otherwise . . . well, I mean. I'd be one of them, wouldn't I? Because, let me tell you, I seen them that's darker than me. Yes. Really dark, man. Only they had that something I'm telling you about. . . .They look at things differently. Haven't you seen their eyes when they look at you? . . . They're born with that sort of courage. (73–74)

As Morrie's cross-dressing takes hold, he, like Zach before him, must realize and confront the racist wellspring of white hegemony. Role-playing, Morrie pretends to escort Ethel on a stroll, and Zach assumes the role of a peanut vendor who offends Morrie's assumed white manhood by ignoring him. Zachariah, like an astute director, pushes Morrie from a coloured, subaltern mind-set to the racist rhetoric that comes with full acceptance of the white privileged role. "You must learn your lesson, Morrie. You want to pass, don't you?" Zach says. Finally falling into his white role, Morris snarls: "[*with brutality and coarseness*]. Hey, *Swartgat!*" (78). With this expletive, which means black arse, Morrie touches the wellsprings of racial *difference* in South Africa, *difference* that will be echoed decades later in *Master Harold,* when that racial epithet "*swartgat*" is made manifest as Sam literally bares his black Basuto arse to Hally and to the theatre audience.

What is so remarkable and singular about *The Blood Knot* is that even as Fugard contrasts in relatively realistic ways the lives, styles, attitudes, and skin pigmentations of the two brothers, he also constantly moves the dialogue to psychologically interior and Beckettian planes. In most scenes, the interchange between Zach and Morrie suddenly leads to interior monologues, arias, which are not disjunctive but rather enhance and open out the action from within the playing space of a very realistic *pondok* on stage into a different and larger, but related, allegorical space. Thus, for example, trying on white man's clothes and white man's demeanor and body language leads, in brilliantly seamless ways, to Morris's allegorical tale of following a man walking ahead of him in the bleak, empty, "grey and cold" South African veld (75). Like some shadow of himself, Morrie sees the man always on the path ahead of him; and he keeps increasing his pace to catch up with the man, whose fire and its warm glow he can see in the distance. But as Morrie approaches, there is a moment of epiphanous racial truth:

> When I was even nearer he saw me coming and stood up, but when he saw me clearer he picked up a stick and held it like a hitting stick, stepping back

for safety and a good aim . . . so what could I do but pass peacefully. [*Pause.*] Because he was white, Zach. I had been right all along . . . the road . . . since midday. That's what I mean, you see. It's in the way they walk as well. (76)

The action and dialogue of the play here move deftly from a literal cross-dressing or vestment level of racial passing to the allegorical level of a coloured man pursuing a whiteness that is always several steps ahead of him. When Morrie does finally reach the figure of whiteness and his warm fire, he reaches an idea of protective turf ownership that marks racial separation. Protecting his space and who he is, the white man pugnaciously raises his stick ready for combat. And Morrie, instead of "passing" as white, must pass him by, recognize the truth of his colouredness, and silently walk his own path, a path that brings him back to the coloured Korsten township and to his dark-skinned brother. Fugard's remarkable and remarkably effective blending of meanings through an amalgam of realistic and allegorical modes—in this case with reference to racial passing—is one of the great strengths of *The Blood Knot,* for it allows Fugard to reach areas of his audience's feelings and understanding unaccessible by allegory or realism alone.

The story of Morrie and the white man immediately precedes and is juxtaposed with Morrie's donning white man's clothes, falling into white body language and mind-set, and calling his brother *swartgat.* Morrie's light-skin, his ability to pass, gives him the ability to act two racial roles and through his acting to cross apartheid's racial divisions. Acting allows him to become two racially separate people. He is, moreover, so convincing an actor or passer that his own brother Zach doesn't recognize him:

ZACHARIAH. It's you.

MORRIS. Yes!

ZACHARIAH. That's funny, I thought . . .

MORRIS. I know. I saw it again.

ZACHARIAH. What?

MORRIS. The pain, man. The pity of it all and the pain in your eyes.

ZACHARIAH. I was looking, I thought, at a different sort of man.

MORRIS. But don't you see, Zach? It was me! That different sort of man you saw was me. It's happened, man. And I'll swear, I'll take God's name in vain that I no longer wanted it any more. I turned around on the road and came back here because I couldn't stand that look in your eyes any more. . . . I'll tell you the whole truth now. . . . Because I did try it! It didn't seem a sin. If a man was born with a chance at a change, why not take it, I thought. . . . why not stand up the next morning, Different . . . Beautiful! . . . We all know that some are not caught, so . . . so . . . so what was worrying me? You. Yes, in my dreams at night, there was you, as well. What about you? My own brother. What sort of a thing was that to do to a *ou's* own flesh-and-blood brother? (79)

All of this is spoken and understood on that Fugardian plane where realism and the allegory of inner truth combine and thereby transcend each of the component parts. Morrie, we come here to understand, has found his way literally and psychologically back to Korsten and to his "flesh-and-blood brother," and he has done so through coming to understand two roles and knowing what it means to act them.

Here we see Fugard's special ability not merely to make theatre but to use the elements of theatre to create political awareness. The on-stage presentation of *acting* two racial roles provides insight not merely to Morrie but to the audience, which is made aware, through the deconstruction of racial roles, that those roles are very much a form of acting, that apartheid is a form of theatre and theatrical performance. Moreover, Fugard the playwright and Fugard the white actor playing the ambivalently coloured Morrie also make us aware that theatre, role-playing, *The Blood Knot*'s inner truth forged through an amalgam of realistic and nonrealistic, and apartheid are all analogous creations based on the ineffable hybridity of the real and the fictive. Just as the audience knows that the Morrie they see on stage is a coloured man who is Fugard's fictional creation and at the same time the person standing before them is a real white actor (Fugard himself in the first production), their binocular perception extends as well to the language of the play, to the nature of theatre, and to the nature of apartheid.

In a theatre, as Fugard makes plain, the audience does not entirely, contrary to Coleridge's phrase, willingly suspend its disbelief. At the same time, neither are they entirely disengaged, *verfremdet*, as Bertolt Brecht might wish them to be. Rather there is a coexistence of accepted engagement with the stage fiction and a disengaged recognition that it is a fiction played by actors. Fugard makes us aware in *The Blood Knot* that that same tacit understanding, of a fiction based on assigned roles played out by real people, is what constitutes the performance of the South African apartheid system. Revealing the scaffolding of theatre art and acting, then, Fugard allows us to realize how theatre craft, dramaturgy, can be and is employed to create the theatre of apartheid; but he demonstrates as well how that same dramaturgy, in his hands, can also be employed as a forceful weapon directed against apartheid.

The all-important character who never appears on stage in *The Blood Knot* is Ethel, whose power is extraordinarily effective despite her physical absence. As Morrie and Zach come painfully to realize, the power of a white skin can easily penetrate the walls of a *pondok* and their non-white lives. It is she, moreover, who forces Morrie and Zach to confront who they are in apartheid South Africa. To confront Ethel's power, they plan to have Morrie "pass" into the enemy camp, cross-dressing as a white and thereby creating a diversion so that Ethel and her policeman brother will not discover Morrie and Zach's colouredness. In scene 5, as

Morrie practices passing, he puts on the white man's clothes, becomes momentarily a privileged white, and then pulls back in horror exclaiming, "I'm no Judas!" (80) as he "tears off the jacket and hat in a frenzy" (78), accepting his colouredness and his fraternity with both Zach and his race. This is followed by scene 6, comprising exclusively Zach's bizarre monologue, and barely more than a page of text, wherein Zach also cross-dresses his way toward truth.

In that scene, Zach gets up in the middle of the night and ludicrously replicates his brother's racial transvestitism. The stage directions read:

> *Without looking at Morris he gets up, goes to the corner where the new suit of clothes is hanging, and puts on the suit and hat. The final effect is an absurdity bordering on the grotesque. The hat is too small and so is the jacket, which he has buttoned, while the trousers are too short. Zachariah stands barefooted, holding the umbrella, the hat pulled down low over his eyes so that his face is almost hidden.* (81)

Part of the absurdity of course stems from the fact that, quite apart from the clothes not fitting, these are the clothes of passing, and given Zach's black face, that is, clothes or no, an impossibility. In the interior monologue that follows, Zach addresses his mother, whom he hears asking him whether he is Morrie: "What's the matter with you, Ma? Don't you recognize your own son? No, no! Not him! It's me, Zach." Then he asks her the primal question about which son she loved: "Whose mother were you really? At the bottom of your heart, where your blood is red with pain, tell me, whom did you really love? No evil feelings, Ma, but, I mean, a man's got to know" (81). Is white innately to be preferred and loved over black? Does even a blood mother make this distinction? Running through the play are remembrances of moths and butterflies. The moths seek the light and are singed, the butterflies live in light and are beautiful. The racial analogy is forceful. Offering his mother a butterfly he has nursed—even as he has taken care of white Morris—black Zachariah asks, "This, old Ma of mine, is gratitude for you, and it proves it, doesn't it? I got it, here in my hand, I got beauty . . . too . . . haven't I?" (82). The question goes unanswered, but its formulation is a significant prologue to Zach's sense of self and to the audience's touching the underpinning of racialism, which essentially assumes that one race is butterflies and the other moths.

The recognitions of scenes 5 and 6 prepare for *The Blood Knot*'s final scene, in which Zachariah and Morris undergo and undertake a series of exorcisms. In part, the brothers have reversed roles, so that Zach becomes the more verbal and active, encouraging an at first taciturn and morose Morris sitting with his few belongings packed in a bundle and preparing to make a departure. In Morris's eyes, Ethel has stolen their future—stolen it because they have spent their savings to buy clothes for meeting Ethel, and more largely stolen it because their discovery and possible arrest seems inevitable. She has also stolen their dreams of themselves by making them come face-to-face with the fact that unless you are white in South Africa, you have no meaningful future.

Knowing the conventions of the well-made play, Fugard suddenly, tongue-in-cheek, allows a letter from Ethel to remove her as an impediment and to remove her as well from the play. Everyone can breathe a sigh of relief that disaster will not strike in the form of white Ethel and her policeman brother. But rather than signal a happy dénouement, Fugard uses the conventional resolution as the initiation of new understanding. Zach's pen-pal romance and the danger of the situation are over:

> [*Morris looks vacantly at Zachariah, whose attitude has hardened with bitter disappointment*]

> ZACHARIAH. So?

> MORRIS. So I think we can begin again.

> ZACHARIAH. What?

> MORRIS. That's a good question. [*Pause.*] Well, let's work it out. Where are we? Here. That's a good beginning. What is this? Our room. Me and you, Morrie and Zach . . . live here . . . in peace. Yes. It's coming now, Zach. I feel it. I'm filling up again with thoughts and things. We're living here in peace because the problem's gone . . . and got engaged to be married . . . and I'm, Morrie . . . and I was going to go, but now I'm going to stay! [*With something of his old self Morrie goes to work. Opens his bundle and packs out his belongings.*] Hey, Zach! [*Holding up the clock.*] It's stopped. Like me What time shall we make it? (86)

The alarm clock apportioning the time of their lives has stopped, and the events that have transpired will not allow them to go back to where and what they were. Instead they must continue on the path of enlightenment that Ethel initiated. She has not been the element of danger she seemed but a catalyst to new understanding that they have not yet reached.

To get there, they return to cross-dressing in the white clothes. This time Morris puts them on not to practice a script for meeting Ethel but, as Zach says, "Just for size," just to feel whiteness. At first he struts exaggeratedly but then, as the clothes confer his role, he wheels around on Zach and exclaims, "Hey, *Swartgat!*" After an initial stunned moment, Zach plays his own part in response, "*Ja, Baas*" (87). With these words, they reach apartheid's lowest common denominator, "*Baas* Morrie and his boy, Zach!" (88). Then, using the art of theatre, they play-act Zachariah's employment as a non-white guarding the gates of a whites-only park from incursions by black children. Together Morris and Zach vicariously experience the meanness and demeaning nature of Zach's job, his invisibility to whites, his depersonalization.

On the path to discovering their lives, Zach and Morrie continue to act out their black and white roles with increasing tension and pugnacity. But they must also exorcise the figure of their mother, who has represented their fraternal bond. If they are to be brothers in more than a literal family-ties way, their mother must cease being their common reference point; and thus in their acting they chase her off, pelting her with stones and shouting racial expletives at her. With their mother gone, the two men can face their anger with each other. Morris attacks Zach savagely with the umbrella and tells him:

> You know something? I hate you! What did you mean crawling around like that? Spoiling the view, spoiling my chances! What's your game, hey? Trying to be an embarrassment? Is that it? A two-legged embarrassment? Well, I hate you, do you hear! Hate! . . . Hate! . . . Hate! . . . [*He attacks Zachariah savagely with the umbrella. When his fury is spent he turns away and sits down.*] (93)

And then Zach takes over the acting out by locking Morris into the whites-only park, which suddenly becomes a place of terror and danger. Indeed, it is a vision of angry black wish fulfillment, of locking whites up in their own area and attacking them for their sins. It is Zach's turn to be savage as he "*stands above Morris on the point of violence*" (95). And then, as the alarm clock suddenly rings, Morris is literally saved by its bell and the curtain comes down on their racial and psychological theatre.

In the last moments of the play, after all the possibilities have been acted out, the two men find themselves in a Beckettian static relationship within a Beckettian landscape. This is their endgame. The stagnant, noisome, ecologically dead body of water outside their quarters in Korsten is the landscape of their existence. "It's the mystery of my life, that lake. I mean . . . It smells dead, doesn't it?" (96), says Morris. And then he outlines the nature of their endgame:

> We were carried away, as they would say, by the game . . . quite far in fact. . . .One thing I'm certain is sure, it's a good thing we got the game. It will pass the time. Because we got a lot left, you know! [*Little laugh.*] Almost a whole life . . . stretching ahead . . . in here. . . . I mean, other men get by without a future. In fact, I think there's quite a lot of people getting by without futures these days. (96)

Like Hamm and Clov, Morrie and Zach have a pastime to pass time, a relationship to occupy them while they live out their lives without a future. They are destined to continue on hopelessly, like so many other blacks and coloureds, their lives devoid of meaning because they can look to no future. All they have is each other, their blood knot.

When *The Blood Knot* was doing well in performance, Fugard moved on to write his next play, *People Are Living There*. Fugard's *Notebooks* indicate that his first image of the play came to him in May 1962 (51–52). The first draft, bearing the provisional title *Silkworms,* was completed in March of the following year (77). It was not until six years later, 13 March 1968, that *People Are Living There* found its way into a theatre. It was performed in Glasgow and given another one-night charity performance a few weeks later in London on 28 April. But it was not formally produced until its Cape Town opening more than a year later, on 14 June 1969. Although *People Are Living There* was written well before both *Hello and Goodbye* and *Boesman and Lena,* the former was produced four years earlier and the latter only a month later. Thus, despite the fact that *Hello and Goodbye* appeared on stage earlier, *People Are Living There* should be regarded as the work that follows *The Blood Knot.*

Neither *People Are Living There* nor *Hello and Goodbye* is directly about race.[14] Both plays remind us that although Fugard frequently writes about race and South African apartheid, his primary concerns are the human condition and characters' moments of self-discovery. Racial issues (as in *The Island*) are given force by those moments of self-discovery, and sometimes those moments of self-recognition are brought about through racial conflict (as in *Master Harold*). In their rush to pigeonhole Fugard as a regional writer who produces dramas about the intensity of South African political and racial issues, reviewers and critics tend to lose or push to the periphery the essential matters of self-discovery that are the heart and power of a Fugard drama.

Above all, Fugard is concerned about human relationships, about those often epiphanous moments when characters reveal their secrets to themselves and others. At those times—often sudden and fleeting but nonetheless pellucid—characters gain insight into themselves, their lives, and their situations. The drama comes from sharing the secrets and the insights with themselves and the audience. Fugard hints that he realized the power of such moments as a young boy, when his cousin Garth momentarily confessed his homosexuality to Fugard and then quickly closed the door on it. Fugard writes of that moment:

> In opening his heart to me Garth had given me my first empowerment as a writer. Because that is my real territory as a dramatist: the world of secrets, with their powerful effect on human behaviour and the trauma of revelation. Whether it is the radiant secret in Miss Helen's heart or the withering one in Boesman's or the dark and destructive one in Gladys, they are the dynamos that generate all the significant action in my plays. (*Cousins,* 74)

Race and apartheid have imbued and continue to imbue so much both of life as it is lived in South Africa and of Fugard's dramatic output. Certainly they are the important concerns of modern South African writing. But to see Fugard merely as a playwright concerned with race is to miss the revealed secrets and human insights that are, finally, the basis of his dramatic works. *People Are Living There* and *Hello and Goodbye,* neither of which concern the strictures of apartheid and both of which contain only white characters, are unusually powerful plays and provide unusually fine means for understanding what Fugard is about as a playwright.

A nearly perfect and dramatically powerful work, *People Are Living There* is a milestone in Fugard's career as a major playwright. Like so many of his stage works, it maintains a unity of time and place. Learning from playwrights he admires, particularly Samuel Beckett and Arthur Miller, he makes the most not merely of his dialogue but also of his costumes, set, and stage properties. Indeed, in the seedy Jo'burg boarding house of *People Are Living There* Fugard launches a happy marriage of playtext and dramaturgy.

The opening moments embody the very essence, the meaning of the whole. The play begins in near darkness, the set first illuminated only with the lights of the Saturday evening traffic passing outside the window of the shabby, old-fashioned kitchen. A figure of undetermined gender appears in a dressing gown. "*The figure stands motionless, obviously listening, then calls out in a husky voice:* Hullo! Anybody home? [*Pause*] Help!" (101). It is not until we hear the voice register that we know the figure is female. Four chimes of a grandfather clock are heard; the woman goes to a back passage, hits the clock; and three more chimes emerge, telling us it is seven in the evening. She then turns on a single dim bulb, and we see Milly, a fifty-year-old woman "in an old candlewick dressing gown" who has just risen from sleep. Calling aloud for Shorty and Don, two other residents of the house, she looks up at the ceiling to hear if there are sounds from someone above.

These short opening moments, as in *Waiting for Godot*, epitomize the play as a whole. As the stage manager and playwright she attempts to be throughout *People Are Living There*, Milly lights the stage, calls for the principal actors, and sets the action in motion. Like Milly herself, the stage set is shabby and out-of-date. The lights from the passing cars that periodically illumine the set evoke the contrast between the life of people with places to go on a Saturday night and the static lives of the people washed up in Milly's boardinghouse. Milly has awakened from her sleep and appears in her dressing gown, but it is seven in the evening, not seven in the morning. The dressing gown alerts us that something is surely out of joint with the rhythm and schedule of Milly's life. And this is unmistakably italicized as well by the clock that does not toll all the hours without a needed jolt from Milly. Indeed, like the lives of the characters, the clock has gotten stuck and needs a push before it can finish its allotted time.

The static quality of the characters' lives, their hopelessness, and Milly's fear of what lies ahead for her are encapsulated in the play's first speech: "Hullo! Anybody home! [*Pause*] Help!" That we are momentarily unsure of the gender of the robed figure, moreover, helps prefigure Milly's menopause and the slow death of her fertility. And her look to the ceiling listening for a response introduces Mr. Ahlers, who has cast Milly off, who no longer cares for her, whom she desperately wishes to impress, and who, in the course of the play, does not respond to her by making an appearance in either Fugard's play or the one Milly will try to script.

After this opening, the first major actions of the play are Don's flushing the lavatory and Milly's lighting her cigarette. The pulled chain of the toilet announces the play's leitmotif of bodily wastes (defecation, urination, masturbation, pimples) and of rubbish imagery. Milly's cigarette smoking throughout the play is Fugard's inspired visual analogue of life going up in smoke, leaving behind only a residue of ashes. Smoking punctuates the action and dialogue; and its meaning is not merely visual but olfactory as the aroma of burning tobacco flows from stage to audience. Milly's cigarettes become the clock time of the play, ticking off the waste of Milly's life. Like T. S. Eliot's Prufrock, who measures his life in coffee spoons, Milly measures hers in cigarette butts.

In *People Are Living There,* Fugard presents a sad trio—Milly, Shorty, and Don—the days of whose lives are grains of sand that will never have shape or meaning. Don, recording his insights and observations on ephemeral cigarette packs, cannot find an occupation or face the future. Despite his intelligence and, ironically, his belief in Camus' proactive existentialism, he is most often recumbent on his bed, an eternal bystander unwilling to act or move his life forward. His present is his future, his life a waste. Shorty, a postman and aspiring boxer of less than ordinary intelligence, has a young wife, Sissy, who belittles and emasculates him, and who withholds herself from him sexually while she seeks sexual pleasures elsewhere. A failure as postman, boxer, and husband, Shorty pathetically and comically tries to deny the deficiencies of his life and make the best of an unfulfilling present. And the fifty-year-old Milly, the central figure of the triumvirate and the fulcrum of Fugard's drama, comes in the course of her traffic on stage to realize that she has wasted her past and now has no meaningful future. Spurned by Ahlers, to whom she has given herself during ten years of "beer and sausages at the Phoenix" and what she thought was premarital sex at home, Milly spends Fugard's play drawing up battle plans to avenge herself on Ahlers and for the life she has lost.

With a good deal of bitter comedy, Milly organizes her two cohorts, Don and Shorty, into the forced gaiety of a party meant to convince Ahlers that she is neither downcast nor defeated; and the party these three arrange is at once pathetic, tragic, and comic. Although they do not best the enemy, they do create a tragicomic camaraderie of the defeated and the helpless. Shortly before conceiving *People Are Living There,* Fugard wrote, "Talking to Sheila about Beckett's humour, I said, 'Smile, and then wipe the blood off your mouth'" (*Notebooks,* 67). And this is precisely the effect Fugard achieves in this play. One could almost say that *People Are Living There* is the sad, realistic analogue of *Endgame.*

More than that, *People Are Living There* lucidly demonstrates how Fugard adapts Beckettian dramatic style to a realistic setting. It shows as well Fugard's debt to the careful dramaturgy of Ibsen and Arthur Miller in the play's use of physical details, stage properties, and the stage picture. Milly's cigarettes and the clock are obvious examples. But it is important to recognize Fugard's skill—a skill he seems to hone with each successive play—in forging dramatic complexity through simple detail. A striking example is the way he nicely creates an analogy between Milly and Shorty through something as simple as Ahlers's shoes and Sissy's stockings.

Milly has had a ten-year affair with Ahlers, who has not married her or enabled her to have a family. Having used up Milly's youth and childbearing years, Ahlers has ended his amorous connection with her and is, on the evening of the play, preparing to dine with a new female friend. In preparation for the occasion, he has given his shoes to Shorty to be polished. The large black shoes, the inanimate actors representing him on stage, are all we ever see of Ahlers. They signify, moreover, his walking out on Milly, his stepping on her, and Milly's downtrodden state.

Like Milly, Shorty is abused by his partner. Although Shorty is married to Sissy, it is not clear that she has ever allowed him to consummate their marriage. Like Ahlers, Sissy is a user. Taking Shorty's pay packet, she goes off dressed for a date with a man named Billy, abandoning Shorty in the boardinghouse, a knowing cuckold. Her verbal abuse and abandonment is carried on as she takes a pair of stockings from the clothesline, complaining that they are her only pair and making much of putting them on her legs. Don comments afterward, "the way she put on her stockings? Did you catch that? I saw the suspenders, you know. I think that was deliberate" (114). Like Ahlers's shoes, Sissy's stockings emphasize walking out on a downtrodden victim. The shoes and stockings donned for a night out and potential lovemaking, moreover, underscore the fact that Ahlers and Sissy leave the others behind bereft of love. Carefully dressed, Ahlers and Sissy disappear into the Braamfontein world represented by the lights of passing cars headed for Saturday night pleasures. A slatternly Milly, Shorty in his postman's clothes, and an unkempt Don remain in the dimly lit room for the forced gaiety of the sad, stay-at-home party Milly scripts for them.

Following through on her stage-managerly entrance when the play begins, Milly spends her time in *People Are Living There* writing a revenge play, one ostensibly directed against Ahlers, who has taken advantage of her and done her psychological injury, who has failed to pay her his monetary debts as well as his personal ones. Like a twentieth-century Hieronymo or Vindice, Milly lets her imagination run riot as she conjures up an elaborate revenge against her foe:

> The plan is as follows. Shorty tells us where he is going. Our first move is to get dressed. We tog up to kill the cats. My white costume with matching gloves! You'll see something tonight, my boy. That done we then descend on the enemy. Ha! That will be triumph. He's sitting there, you see, with his so-called friend from Germany, and in we march, sit down and have a good time of our own! And right under his nose where he can see us. Then when he comes crawling to ask if he can join in, I'll have him arrested for molesting. (119)

The elaborateness of her revenge scheme seems at first out of proportion to the injuries done her.

As Milly lashes out, we begin to realize what has given rise to her anger and her spirited revenge plot. When the unseen Ahlers makes his exit from the house, Milly shouts out her sarcastic invective:

> Enjoy yourself . . . with your old friend from Germany. And please don't worry about me. I'll just sit here in the kitchen and twiddle my thumbs. After all, it was only ten years. Why worry about them! [*Her anger and resent-*

ment beginning to break through] Well, you'd better, because they were mine. Those were ten years of my life and you had them cheap . . . I'm also going to have a good time tonight. You bet. I'm going to have the best good time of my life . . . Yes, go on! Go on, get the hell out of here, you rotten stinking thief. *Thief!* (121)

The speech is punctuated by the clock's chiming getting stuck after one stroke, being hit by Milly so it rings seven more times, and then Milly's lighting up another cigarette. Ahlers may be the human focus of Milly's anger, but her rage is really about time, a word that reverberates through her speeches. She wants the "good *time*" that is somehow owed her. Ten years of her life have disappeared, been stolen. And clearly it is Time, not Ahlers, that is the real thief. The stage business with the clock and the cigarette italicize the play's concern with time. And indeed, that stage business in the original typescript provided a dramatic conclusion to what Fugard indicated as the first scene of the play.[15]

But time is not a tangible commodity. Clocks and calendars measure it, yet it has no shape. So how can it be stolen? And if time is neither tangible nor visible, how does it take on positive and negative qualities? Milly poses important existential questions about time when she points to the people in the cars outside her window and asks:

Where are they going? They're going to have a good time. Every Saturday night they drive past on their way to have a good time. And don't try to tell me they're going to the movies! So what I want to know is, where is it? . . . Go out there and stop one of those cars and say "Milly wants to know where is it? Where do you get this good time every Saturday night?" (122)

Furthermore, the slippage of time, the loss of the time of one's life, is a concept that cannot be documented, and yet it can cause pain.

In *People Are Living There,* Fugard leads his audience into a tragic much ado about nothing world akin to that of Shakespeare's *King Lear,* a play in which the word "nothing" resounds again and again. Lear's tragedy stems from his desire to objectify love, which, like time, is an intangible concept. To Lear's demand that she say what her filial love is, his daughter Cordelia replies, "Nothing, my lord," and Lear answers, "Nothing will come of nothing." In the course of Shakespeare's tragedy, Lear learns to his great pain that love cannot be delineated and that *nothing* is, paradoxically, very much *something.* Like Lear but without his tragic grandeur, Milly must come to know that time, which cannot be delineated, is also a *nothing* that is a *something,* and that it is capable of rendering very real pain:

MILLY. "It took its time." My time . . . bit by bit . . . yes! That sounds better. Slow and sly. What I mean is I try to remember when. The Moment When—the way they say: "And from then on so and so" . . . and so on. But I can't. There doesn't seem to be a day or a date. Once upon a time it wasn't, now it is, but when or where . . . ? It's not easy to pin down. Believe me, I've tried.

Don. Milly, do *you* know what it is? [*She smokes.*] You mean you *don't* know? . . .

Milly. Sometimes I could brain you! What do you know about it?

Don. Apparently as much as you. Nothing. Which most likely means there is nothing.

Milly. Nothing! I said it hurts, didn't I? Can nothing hurt? I'll say it again, as God is my witness, it hurts. And it took time. Mine. And once upon that time there was a little girl in a white dress, full of hope, and she was happy. But now she's not any more. Is that my imagination? Those are facts. (128)

Much as she may wish to, Milly cannot stop time. The boardinghouse's run-down clock does not stop time. Nor can that other run-down timepiece: Milly's body clock.

Contrary to Milly's original revenge vision, she, Shorty, and Don do not leave the house to confront Ahlers with their merriment at the place where he is entertaining his new lady friend. Instead and significantly they never leave the boardinghouse; they put on party hats and stay home to celebrate Milly's fiftieth birthday. Milly's intention is to confront Ahlers and, for Shorty's sake, the equally traitorous Sissy with the "good time" they have been having at home. In the course of the party, Milly has a long monologue in which some of the play's secrets are revealed by Milly to the other characters, to the audience, and to Milly herself.

The party begins with Milly's situating herself in her middle years and saying, "Someone once said you start to die the moment you are born" (146). She is likely referring to some variant of an aphorism in The Wisdom of Solomon (5:13) in the Apocrypha, but Fugard is likely also reminding us of Pozzo's speech in *Waiting for Godot:*

> Have you done tormenting me with your accursed time? . . . one day we were born, one day we shall die, the same day, the same second, is that not enough for you? They give birth astride of a grave, the light gleams an instant, then it's night once more. On![16]

In short order, the party celebrants wolf down and finish their half bottle of muscatel, cool drinks, potato chips, and the shabby, rectangular slab cake that Shorty has purchased in lieu of a properly frosted, round birthday cake. The less than festive quality of the party food does little to relieve or brighten the dingy room and Milly's slatternly appearance. The rapidity with which the birthday food and drink are used up, moreover, underlines the central ruminations of the scene about the speed with which one's life and time are exhausted. As food and drink running out

signifies time running out in Beckett's *Endgame,* so the end of the edibles and pota-
bles more literally marks a *fin de parti* in *People Are Living There.*

When food, drink, jokes, songs, and gaiety have expired; when, according to
Milly, the party has hit "rock bottom"; when Milly has soured the atmosphere by
giving her candid and stingingly true appraisals of Shorty and Don (one wonders
whether Fugard was influenced by O'Neill and Harry Hope's birthday party in *The
Iceman Cometh*), she launches into a monologue that reveals both her secrets and
those of the play. Milly begins her monologue by commenting, with quintessen-
tial Beckettian insight, on the nature of her life and of life more generally: "I've
been cheated. The whole thing was just a trick to get me to go on. Otherwise who
would? Who wants to get up tomorrow if this is it?" (156). With near tragic irony,
on this day celebrating her birth, Milly comes face-to-face with the fact that she is
moving relentlessly toward death.

The secret that Milly reveals in her monologue is that she has begun menopause.
Her body clock is tolling the time of her life. Ahlers has had her fertile years, and
when he discovers her life as a childbearing woman is drawing to a close, he casts
her aside as obsolete, regarding her as no longer gendered:

> Then he said, matter-of-fact I'll admit, not meaning to hurt, that therefore
> strictly speaking I'm not a woman any more. It sounded logical the way he
> put it. To do with function. The function of a thing, and being a woman, that
> meant babies. And you see, suddenly he sat up and said he wanted a family!
> (157)

But Ahlers, whom Milly has posited all along as the villain, the enemy, is merely
the object upon whom she has transferred her anger toward the true but unseen enemy: Time.

In one of those moments of epiphanous insight that Fugard affords his characters, Milly recognizes that the thief is not Ahlers but Time:

> So you see it's gone. Or just about. A little left but mostly in the way of time.
> The rest just gone. Not broken, or stolen, or violated—which might make it
> sound like there's been no crime, I know. But I did have it and now it's gone
> and nobody ever gets it back so don't tell me that doesn't make us victims.
> Don't ask me how! Somehow! Victims of something. Look at us. All flesh
> and bone, with one face hanging onto your neck until you're dead!
>
> [*Inside the house the clock begins to chime. They listen in silence for a few seconds,
> then . . .*]
>
> Ignore that! Where were we? Today! What was I saying? Today . . . to-
> day. . . . Hold on! This one I won't let go! Today, today. . . . All right! You
> win, damn you. Yesterday! [*The clock mechanism is again at fault. It chimes on
> and on and on.*] (157–158)

Don: ~~Darwin's theory of Descent~~. Evolution.

Milly: Good lord. Are they still carrying on about ~~that~~? That one's as old as the hills my boy. Monkey glands and why do Adam and Eve have navels if they were made out of dust, spit and spare ribs. I heard that lot when I will still in bloomers. Anyway are you coming. ~~tomorrow~~?

Don: I'll think about it.

Milly: That's all you seem to do about anything. Cant you decide?

Don: Its never been easy. (15a)
(pause while Milly puts the kettle on the stove.)

Milly: (sitting down) Ready in a jiffy. (lights a cigarette) watches don slyly) ~~So what do you think?~~

~~Don:~~ ~~About what.~~

~~Milly:~~ ~~Tonight. The goings on.~~

~~Don:~~ ~~I've made a few notes. I'll work it out.~~

Milly: ~~So~~ You reckon its psychological.

Don: Was that your secret. You and Ahlers. ~~What happened to you~~. *his promise*.

Milly: In a way, I suppose its more of a tragedy really, than a secret. (Don writes on his cigarette box)
So?

Don: Nothing?

Milly: Good. (pause) What else did I say?
Lets say
Don: / I cant remember.

Milly: Thank you. There's a streak of decency in you Don, somewhere.

~~Don:~~ ~~On a point of interest,~~ What would you say happened to night.

~~Milly:~~ Lets see. I'd ~~say~~..Letting of steam? Hows that? ~~And I think thats a~~ ~~good thing as if the lids on and the kettle's boiling.~~
~~(Shorty returns.)~~

~~Shorty:~~ ~~Got them. (to the shelf and his box of silkworms)~~

~~Milly:~~ ~~So then thats that. Iniedently when he (calling) comes home we had a good time. Okay?~~

~~Don:~~ ~~Okay.~~

Shorty: Hey. Gues what? They're all in silk. (To Milly) I dont need the leaves Milly. Look. ~~One is still~~ spinning. *Theyre*

Milly: So that's how they do it. ~~Well I'll be~~....Congratulations Shorty! ~~And Good luck to you~~. What happens now?
Well done.

Shorty: Now?

Milly: With them man. ~~(~~Shorty looks to Don for guidance) ~~What do~~ ~~you do with them~~. The next step?

Shorty: I dont know. (pause) Nothing.

4. A page from the original typescript of *People Are Living There* showing Fugard's textual changes. Courtesy the Lilly Library, Indiana University, Bloomington, Indiana.

Important here is not merely the quality and nature of Milly's momentary insight but the way in which Fugard orchestrates it. It is a dramatic aria composed of short sentences and heavily punctuated phrases whose choppiness contrasts with the long and unpunctuated sentence beginning "But I did have it . . ." to form a speech delivered or chanted by the voice of the soul. The mad chiming of the usually stalled clock provides an appropriate cacophony for Milly's final discordant exclamations.

This is one of those stunning characteristic Fugard moments when the drama and the dramatic construction allow a stage character to abandon body and normal speech, and to realize the soul and its voice. Fugard is quite clear about consciously constructing such moments. About Miss Helen's long speech in *The Road to Mecca*, Fugard explains:

> . . . I can remember very clearly how conscious I was when writing it of the need to organise the flow of thought and feeling in the same way for example that Mahler had done with that last magnificent "Farewell" in his "Song of the Earth" cycle. I don't think I have written a play without it having at least one extended aria in this fashion. It is also no coincidence that rehearsal room talk is about rhythm, tempo, pause, beat and crescendo as much as about the meaning of words and sentences. (*Cousins*, 38)

Milly's poignant aria, it is important to see, is a momentary epiphany sung by the soul. Almost immediately, however, she resumes her more usual character and attitude:

> To begin with don't take what I said too seriously. I got excited—flushed— if you really want to know. Hot and bothered. It's a symptom. We'll survive. (158)

The hot flash of insight Milly has had, she amusingly attributes to a hot flash of the menopausal kind. And her comment, "We'll survive," is at once one of grim Beckettian resignation and a flip, comic rejoinder to her own insights. Indeed, as Fugard himself asserts (*Cousins*, 66–67), *People Are Living There* is a richly comic, funny play, but the humor and laughter always have a tragic edge. Once more one is reminded of the playwright's characterization of Beckett's humor: "Smile, and then wipe the blood off your mouth" (*Notebooks*, 67).

Enriching the pathos that centers on Milly are the lives of her tragicomic lieutenants, Shorty and Don. In addition to using Shorty's relationship with Sissy as analogous to Milly's situation, Fugard introduces through Shorty the silkworms that gave the play its first provisional title. Shorty, like some higher Being, feeds and nurtures the silkworms, protecting them from random destruction at the hands of Sissy, who would poke them to death. Like God tending his creatures, dispensing manna, Shorty provides beetroot leaves for his silkies. Immediately following Milly's aria, Shorty peers into his shoe box of silkworms and excitedly exclaims, "They're all in silk. I don't need the leaves now, Milly. Look! One is still spinning"

(159). Yet when the silkworms stop spinning, they will become moths; and Shorty has no interest in having moths. For Milly and for the audience, Shorty's silkworms are suddenly translated into an emblem of her life:

> MILLY. Why Have You Kept Them Alive?
>
> SORTY. To see them spin. To see the silk. . . .
>
> MILLY. You're going to chuck them away. . . . To starve! To die! . . . Must it always be the muck-heap? Isn't there another solution? (160–161)

Like the silkworms, Milly and mankind are the playthings of some higher Being who provides sustenance to see them spin their silk but who will consign them to the muckheap when their period of fruition has passed.

Throughout the play Don functions as the most insightful of the triumvirate, the one who brings Freudian perspicacity and Camus' existentialism to bear. Indeed, Don seems in part Fugard's comic rendering of himself as a young man, an idea made probable by Fugard's playing the role of Don when the play opened. But Don's position as the play's *raisonneur* is undermined by his unkempt physical appearance and the references to his acne and his dirtiness. An actor equal to the part, like Fugard himself, will make the odors of an unbathed Don seem real to the audience. Throughout the play, Don positions himself as commentator or satirist outside the action, outside Milly's and Shorty's plights, disinterestedly examining them. As the play draws to a conclusion, Don gets to sing his own aria, through which we discover that he is in a state of existential paralysis; he sees but cannot act:

> I'm dumb. When things happen, I watch. Even when it's to my self . . . all I do is watch. I used to think the right word for me was Numb . . . that there wasn't even Feeling. But I think that's wrong . . . I'm sure I would feel. My trouble is I wouldn't protest. . . . The worst that can happen to me is that I'll be forgotten a bit before my time. . . . If I were to sit down somewhere, unseen, and was quiet for a very long time, and the instinct to return to the herd petered out. All you need is four walls, and a lid. (167)

The last two sentences above speak volumes. The first, an "if" clause with no conclusion, is, like Don himself, observation without subsequent action. The second evokes the apt image of Beckett's *Endgame* and of Nagg and Nell in their ash cans.

The final moments of *People Are Living There* contain the image from which Fugard claims the whole play sprang: "'Milly is unnerved at finding herself still in her nightclothes from the previous night'" (*Notebooks*, 77). Milly's plight rushes upon her as she suddenly realizes she has never left the confines of her house and has never put on daytime clothes:

> MILLY. But there's a street outside there, Don! All the people! Rush-hour traffic. Right outside that front door!

DON. Yes. But you've got to open it, Milly. Did you today?

MILLY [*suddenly conscious of herself and her predicament*]. I'm still in my nightie. I haven't gotten dressed . . . yet. . . . You mean . . . it can happen like this? In a dressing gown? (167)

The narrowing of space and time as well as her failure adequately to address her situation come rushing upon Milly in her moment of recognition, a recognition that she has not entered the world of movement and headlights outside the confines of her kitchen, a recognition that she has not changed the clothes of sleep for those of life.

Influenced though he is by Beckett, Fugard does not share Beckett's darkly pessimistic world view. Fugard's innate optimism is a source of warmth and hope within even his most dire plays even as it is also a soft spot upon which critics sometimes pounce. In bleak plays such as *The Island, A Lesson from Aloes,* and *My Children! My Africa!,* Fugard's hope shines through the darkness. His post-apartheid works—*Playland, My Life, Valley Song*—are sometimes lyrical with optimism. *People Are Living There* also ends on an upbeat if not thoroughly positive note. Fugard writes in his *Notebooks,* "Ultimately—Pessimism. But heroic. Heroic Pessimism. 'Courage in the face of it all'—Milly in *People are Living There:* 'Surrender? Never!'" (96). In the face of the passage of time and the meaningless of existence, Milly demands recognition and an heroic, courageous defiance of time and the muckheap:

> There must be something we can do! Make a noise! . . . Lest they forget, as the monument says. I can still do that. I'll make it loud, make them stop in the street, make them say: People are living there! (167–168)

When Milly asks Don what the score sheet for their evening's combat reads, he says it's a draw.

The curtain comes down not on tragic defeat but on Milly's raucous laughter and with Don, characteristically, watching her laugh. The laughter is a laughter at the absurdity of life, but it is also the laughter that embraces life. The play darkly questions the meaning of life, but it abounds in comedy, the genre that affirms life. The play contains tears and laughter, but they cancel each other out. Don is right: "On paper it looks like a draw" (168). Paradoxically, the tragedy is that Milly's life—or, for that matter, the play itself—is neither tragic nor comic. The tragedy is that Milly's life and life itself are not tragic but merely sad, tragicomic, absurd.

Fugard launched his career as a major playwright with his three "Port Elizabeth" or "Family" plays. The first, *The Blood Knot,* centers on race questions in a comparison of coloured and white. The second, *Hello and Goodbye,* presents the world of poor Afrikaners. And the third, *Boesman and Lena,* treats displaced coloureds. On October 26, 1965, his two-hander, *Hello and Goodbye,* opened at the Library

Theatre in Johannesburg. The production was directed by Barney Simon, who eventually became the co-founder of Johannesburg's now famous Market Theatre. It featured Fugard himself playing Johnnie and Molly Seftel in the role of his sister, Hester. As Fugard says in *Cousins, Hello and Goodbye* is his "personal celebration" of the "world of the alienated working-class Afrikaner."[17] Fugard can sing more than one note. And throughout his career this has been his great strength as a writer. Although many of his plays are about apartheid and race, others treat abstract or symbolical matters (e.g., *Dimetos* or *A Place with the Pigs*), and still others, such as *Hello and Goodbye* and *People Are Living There*, are plays for a white cast and have little or nothing directly to do with racial confrontations.

Hello and Goodbye continues to be one of Fugard's most powerful plays, for it movingly presents two characters, a brother and a sister, finding their meaning and the direction of their separate existences. Fugard seems to take the struggle for self-definition and survival spread among the poor white characters of *People Are Living There* and marry it to *The Blood Knot*'s exploration of siblings who share a familial starting point but who choose separate paths toward self-definition.[18] Fugard's spare single-set stage (based on his own parents' front room)[19] first contains just the figure of Johnnie but grows to become crowded with Johnnie and Hester Smit, their unseen but very present parents, the physical artifacts of their life that become strewn on the stage, and the vividly described figures of the outside world whom Hester despises. From one set and two actors, Fugard builds a drama teeming with anger, the past, and the dramatis personae that shape one's life. Learning as he does from Beckett, Fugard builds a world from very little and touches on the meaning of existence.[20] In this play and for Fugard more generally, less is more.

Late in 1962, at the Rehearsal Room in Johannesburg, Fugard directed a startling and successful production of Beckett's *Waiting for Godot* with an all-black cast using actors from the arts and drama workshop AMDA (African Music and Dance Association). As he wrote *Hello and Goodbye*, he surely had Beckett's play and its minimalism in mind. Even more, he was patently aware of Beckett's *Krapp's Last Tape*, which he was to direct two years later at the Rhodes Theatre in Grahamstown. As *Hello and Goodbye* begins, the atmosphere reeks of *Krapp's Last Tape* with "a solitary electric light hanging above" a table and four chairs, and Johnnie's monologue, which runs for five pages of text.[21] Instead of Krapp's bananas and alcohol, Johnnie has a bottle of fruit squash and some water in a glass, against which he taps a spoon as he counts off seconds, minutes, and hours, the "petty pace" of his life. The echoes of Krapp are unmistakable:

> [*counting as he taps*] . . . fifty-five, fifty-six, fifty-seven, fifty-eight, fifty-nine, sixty!
>
> [*Stops tapping.*]
>
> Three hundred and . . .
>
> [*Pause.*]

Five minutes—become hours, become days . . . today! . . . Friday some-thingth, nineteen . . . what? . . . sixty-three. One thousand nine hundred and sixty-three! Multiplied by twelve, by thirty, by twenty-four, by sixty . . .

[*Pause.*]

by sixty again! . . . gives you every second. Gee-sis! Millions.

[*Pause.*]

Yes, since Geesis.

[*He starts tapping again but stops after a few.*]

No! I'm wrong. It's six. Sixty goes six times into three hundred and sixty. It's six minutes!

[*Looks around.*]

Walls. The table. Chairs—three empty, one . . . occupied. Here and Now. Mine. No change. Yes there is! Me. I'm a fraction older. More memories. All the others! Same heres mostly. Here. Other nows. Then, and then when this happened and that happened. My milestones, in here mostly. "And then one day, after a long illness, his . . ."

[*Pause. Softly.*]

Which art now in heaven.

[*Pause.*]

Nearly. On the tip of my tongue that time. Just don't rush it. The shock to the nervous system has got to wear off! (173)

To the audience, the references are unclear, but they will become so as the play progresses; even as the three empty chairs will become filled with the seen or felt presences of the other members of the Smit family: Mother, Father, and Hester.

Whereas Beckett tends to leave his time and space general or vague, Fugard provides a date, 1963, and a very detailed "local habitation and a name," as Johnnie recalls in great detail the sights and bus routes of Port Elizabeth. But clearly the world of Port Elizabeth is a remembered space for a Johnnie who has reduced his peregrinations to the limits of this room and the adjoining ones in the small, shabby house. The circularity of Johnnie's monologue and movements is sharply punctuated at its conclusion by an interruption from the outside world in the shape of a blowzy woman who enters from the outside world clutching a cheap and battered suitcase. She seems to know who Johnnie is, but he does not seem to know her. Initial feelings of Pinteresque uncertainty are resolved by the revelation that the woman is Johnnie's sister, Hester Smit, who has been away for fifteen years and who has returned for some as yet mysterious purpose.

One can tell from Hester's looks that she is an aging, weary, rather hardened woman of the streets. Her opening line, "Hello," is the first half of the bracket into which Fugard's play falls. The close of that bracket is her exit line at the play's conclusion: "Goodbye, Johnnie." Fugard shrewdly engineers Hester's arrival to play off against and create meaning through a complexity of dramatic construction. She is, in her own mind, the archetypal returned prodigal of "homecoming" plays,[22] prepared to be embraced and showered with questions and concern. Johnnie shows neither recognition nor emotion, nor does he in the slightest question who the suitcase-bearing stranger might be. The moment for the audience is much like the initial bizarre and disconcerting reception of Ruth in Pinter's *The Homecoming*. Building on the dramatic engagement of Hester and disengagement of Johnnie, Fugard lays down, right to an identifying birthmark, the tracks for a classic Roman comedy "recognition" scene that pointedly runs amok.

The birthmark, the classic signal for the reunification of a happy family, has no effect, giving way to Hester's bitter recognition of the room and of an *un*happy family:

> That was our room; this was a lounge-cum-kitchen but after Mommie died I went on growing which isn't good for little boys to see so you moved in here . . . And when you got big and Daddy got worse it was you used to look after him . . . and that's his room and his lying there with only one leg because of the explosion; and all our life it was groaning and moaning and what the Bible says and what God's going to do and I hated it! Right or wrong? Right! And it was hell. I wanted to scream. I got so sick of it I went away. What more do you want? Must I vomit? (181–182)

And then in another significant reversal of dramatic tradition, it is *she* who does the recognizing: [*Hester moves close to Johnnie—she sees him properly for the first time. When she speaks again it is with the pain of recognition—what is and what was*] "Johnnie! It's been a long time, *boetie*" (182). It is not the prodigal returned after a fifteen-year absence who is recognized; it is she who begins to remember and recognize the grim life that had been shared in those rooms. And it is that recognition, the recognition of what it meant to leave and what it meant to stay in those sad rooms, that this "recognition play" is finally about.

In his marked copy of a typescript of *Hello and Goodbye*, director Barney Simon suggests that as Johnnie begins to know that the visitor is his sister, he "wills her not be Hester. Tries to prove she isn't Hester because Hester is the last creature he wants around."[23] Simon's comment helps to focus the differences between Hester and Johnnie that mark their confrontation with each other and with their lives, and that fuel the dramatic tension of this sibling drama. Johnnie is a master of denial, of repression and regression. Hester, though she does not yet know it, has returned to Port Elizabeth to answer in the affirmative her question, "Must I vomit?" Indeed, the play is punctuated with her references to her nearly vomiting: "I almost vomited" (183), "I'll bring up on the spot like a dog, so help me God" (183), "It's enough to make a dog vomit" (210), "Makes me sick just to look at it" (212). In the face of the past and its meaning, containment and explosion are the dramatic and psychological principles Fugard puts to work in *Hello and Goodbye,* even as the play title itself is one of entrance and exit.

When Johnnie finally recognizes and accepts his sister's return, he remembers her identifying quality, her hate for her family and for the quality of life they led:

> JOHNNIE. . . . your hate! It hasn't changed. The sound of it. Always so sudden, so loud, so late at night. Nobody else could hate it the way you did.
>
> HESTER [*weary scorn*]. This? Four walls that rattled and a roof that leaked! What's there to hate?
>
> JOHNNIE. Us.
>
> HESTER. I've got better things to do with my hate.
>
> JOHNNIE. You hated something. You said so yourself.
>
> HESTER. All right, something. The way it was! All those years, and all of us, in here.
>
> JOHNNIE. Then why have you come back? (182)

Though she does not yet know it, that hatred of family, place, and way of life is the unfinished business Hester has returned to vomit up, confront, and expurgate.

Contextualizing the confrontation of brother and sister is the figure of their father, who is sick, presumably terminally sick, in the adjoining room. As Hester and Johnnie spar and take stock of each other, their discussion is punctuated by Johnnie's periodic visits to his father's bedside to check on the old man's groaning that he alone hears or to administer his father's medication. Johnnie, we learn, has given up a career with the railroad to attend his widowed, lame, deteriorating father. Whereas Johnnie has remained in the house, Hester ran away fifteen years earlier from her father's cruelty, a loveless family, and a down-at-the-heels home. And she ran filled with hate and loathing for her family, her background, and especially for her father. From the outset, the debilitation of the father in the next room serves as a comment on the moribund lives acted out by Johnnie and Hester onstage. The frequently clipped and pause-punctuated dialogue between brother and sister is a linguistic counterpart of the groaning and coughing that transpire, we are told by Johnnie, in the father's adjacent bedroom.

Hester evidently has returned home, to a home she hated, for a purpose that is as yet unclear either to the audience or to herself. The house and the family, their past, are, nevertheless, magnets for both children. Johnnie's mental recitation of the bus routes that lead home (176) is paralleled by Hester's ticking off the stations of her return from "Jo'burg to P.E. second class" (184–185). There is something there in that house over which Johnnie and Hester will struggle antagonistically like siblings over a birthright. Barney Simon astutely pencils in on the title page of his playscript, "A play about accidents. A phrase, a word, a defense leads to new confrontations." When Hester reveals that she believes her father alive, one of the play's major "accidents" transpires: "Accident: Hester's attack has made J. defensive. By thinking Daddy alive she gives Johnny weapon"; and this is followed by Johnnie's stunned silence and "Accident: Johnny's stunned silence makes her think Daddy hates her" (1–13v). And, as Simon recognizes (1–15), from this point on Johnnie begins to behave as though his father is alive.

Although Hester and Johnnie spar, neither of them knows with any clarity over what. Johnnie probingly asserts, "You've come back for something, Hester"; to which she can only reply with a question that is as much directed to herself as to him, "Have I?" Indeed she wants an ineffable something, and she shouts at him, "Well, I'm also ME! Just ME. Hester. And something is going to be mine—just mine—and no sharing with brothers or fathers" (195). And that something has to do with the meaning of her existence, why she has become the human jetsam that hearing and seeing her tell us she is.

Hester and Johnnie's dialogue sends them back into their history—not just the history of specific events in their childhood but the history of their psychological relationship with their father and with one another. Hester feels, has always felt, that she is the hated child. And Johnnie has spent his childhood ingratiating himself with his father, telling him of Hester's misdeeds. It had been Johnnie's weapon against Hester, his way of intimidating his older sister, and it bespoke as well his desperate need to be the favored child. Old family habits do not die easily, and the siblings instinctively revert to their long-established roles:

> JOHNNIE. When you left he said, "We won't speak about her any more." You weren't a real Afrikaner by nature, he said . . . He hated you then. He doesn't dream about you.
>
> . . .
>
> HESTER. Because this is also my home. And him forgetting me doesn't count. She was my mother and he's still my father even if he hates me. So half of everything in here is mine when the time comes. . . . Such as being dead when the time comes.
>
> JOHNNIE [*loudly*]. Wishing for him to die is the wickedest thing in the world!
>
> HESTER. Who's making the noise now?
>
> [*Abrupt silence. Johnnie goes into father's room, returning in a few seconds very nervous and agitated.*]
>
> JOHNNIE. Now you've done it! He's groaning . . . If there's a stroke you know who's to blame! It looks bad.
>
> . . .
>
> HESTER. Fifteen years gone and one hour back but I done it again! Home sweet home where who did it means Hester done it. "I didn't do it. She did

it!" If I laughed loud that did it. Have a little cry and that will do it. Sit still and mind your own business but sure as the lavatory stinks that will also do it. (197–199)

Hester's use of three tenses in this last speech emphasizes the idea that their relationship with their father and each other, their psychological time—as is so often true in families—transcends the borders of past, present, and future. Consequently, Hester's wild search for something in that room and her near-sadistic delight in contemplating her father's decrepitude are countered, as they always have been, by her brother's solicitude for his father and his consistent opposition to the hate-ridden family portrait she paints. As Hester becomes louder and more determined in her antagonism toward her father, Johnnie becomes increasingly attentive to him, busying himself with fetching medication and checking on his father's presumably unstable condition.

As the old family gambits revive for her, Hester gropes toward understanding why she has returned and what she hopes to find in her parents' house. She understands that she wishes to destroy, and that from that destruction she will find relief: "And I'll be happy. It's broken and I'm to blame but I'm happy because this time I'll know I did it. So hello be damned and goodbye for good and go home" (199). But what exactly *it* is, what it is she hopes to destroy or how, remains unknown. With almost the tragic determination of an Oedipus, Hester wishes to find something, to know, to know who she is and to relieve her sense of homelessness and namelessness. She has gone from this house, the house of Smit, and the world of poor Port Elizabeth Afrikaners to the lonely, interchangeable rooms of nameless lower-class Jo'burg flophouses. And Fugard composes for her a moving aria of anomie:

> HESTER. I started waking in the middle of the night wondering which one it was, which room . . . lie there in the dark not knowing. And later still, who it was. Just like that. Who was it lying there wondering where she was? Who was where? Me. And I'm Hester. But what's that mean? What does Hester Smit mean? So you listen. But men dream about other women. The names they call are not yours. That's all. You don't know the room, you're not in his dream. Where do you belong? . . .
>
> JOHNNIE. So what do you do?
>
> HESTER. Wait. Lie there, let it happen, and wait. For a memory. . . . Suddenly there's going to be a memory of you, somewhere, some other time. And then you can work it all out again. In the meantime, just wait, listen to the questions and have no answers . . . no danger or pain or anything like that, just something missing, the meaning of your name. (200)

This is one of Fugard's signature moments in which the harsh language and manner of a stage character gives way to the tragic lyricism of her inner being and inner voice. Seeing Maria Tucci and Zeljko Ivanek in a February 1994 revival of this play at McCarter Theatre in Princeton, I was not surprised by the gripped silence and tears among the audience during this moment, for Hester touches here the common human feelings of disconnectedness, of "something missing," of not knowing your proper home, "the meaning of your name," who you truly are.

Having spoken of doing some ineffable, destructive thing, creating what she calls "ruins" and what Johnnie characterizes as " catastrophe. Calamity. Ruin . . . Smashed to smithereens," Hester conjures up a remembrance of another catastrophe and calamity, another explosion, when her father's leg was smashed to smithereens. Johnnie recalls in some detail how his father's leg was destroyed when, as a railroad worker, he was injured in a dynamite blast. For his injuries, Hester remembers, he received compensation from the railroad. It suddenly dawns on her that *compensation* for the injuries done to her is what she wants, what has brought her back to the scene of her own injuries. And she takes it into her head that the compensation she wants is the monetary compensation she believes her father has hoarded away hidden amid the boxes of possessions in his room. "LISTEN!" she violently exclaims. "He's passing away but I'm still alive. And I'm his daughter. So half of that compensation is mine. . . . I want it now" (204).

When Johnnie counters that her desire for the money now is a sin, she reveals her scorn for her family ties and for all family ties. She reveals as well the secret she has been closeting: her prostitution, which has taught her that pain and degradation can be compensated in cash:

> There's no fathers, no brothers, no sisters, or Sunday, or sin. There's nothing. The fairy stories is finished. They died in a hundred Jo'burg rooms. There's man. And I'm a woman. It's as simple as that. You want a sin, well there's one. I *Hoer*. I've *hoered* all the brothers and fathers and sons and sweethearts in this world into one thing . . . Man. That's how I live and that's why I don't care. And now I'm here and waiting. Because when he wakes up I'm going in there to tell him I want it. My share. (204)

Hester's assertion that "There's nothing" echoes, Fugard tells us, Albert Camus' sense of existential nothingness.[24] Making something within or from that nothing, finding new life is why Hester thinks she has made the long train ride from her seedy prostitute's room in Johannesburg to the shabby family house in Port Elizabeth. She wants her share of compensation money to redeem her life and put it on a new footing. The compensation gotten for her father's physical illness will somehow also now serve as compensation for her spiritual one. She is, after all, as maimed as he.

The first act of *Hello and Goodbye* climaxes with Hester's admitting and speaking to herself as well as to Johnnie the inadmissible and unspeakable—"I *hoer*"—and then demanding the boxes from her father's room that she believes contain the compensation money. In a revealing moment, Johnnie shrewdly bargains with her for his own compensation—"I'll make a bargain. You take the money, all of it. Leave me the home" (205)—which is revealing not so much because Johnnie knows there is no money in the boxes, but because for her the money will allow her to do what she wants, move in new directions, and for him possession of the home will ensure his arrested development and rootedness in those rooms. The compensation money she expects to find is finally only a symbol of the larger compensation she needs. She hopes, in short, to exchange the battered box of a suitcase with which she entered for the life-giving treasure stored somewhere in the battered boxes and suitcases her brother will one by one bring her from her ailing father's room.

The final moments of the act brilliantly develop a complexity of feeling certain to send an audience into an intermission deeply disturbed and moved. As Johnnie brings out the first box, Hester falls upon it ravenously. Barney Simon's notes convey the way that moment feels: "Hester tears open box, greedily pulls at contents. Like ravenously devouring something. Does it in a way that should be private. . . . (Johnny gives her one box, she devours it. He is fascinated) Feeds her as if feeding animal second box" (1–40v). The image and stage picture are that of an animal like a cat pouncing upon its food yet jealously guarding it so that others may not see it or see it being eaten.

Seeing his sister this way brings out for a moment a hitherto hidden side of Johnnie. Father- and home-fixated, seemingly asexual, Johnnie now makes momentary contact with his sexuality as he stares at Hester clawing at the box and its knotted string. Suddenly he asks her, "How much they pay you? . . . the men. The ones you . . . you know. Your boyfriends. What's the tariff or charges?" (205). As Simon pencils in, "Johnny becomes aware of Hester the woman, feels randy. Thinks of getting a woman" (1–40v). What is sadly bracketed here in the dialogue and body language is Johnnie's sexual imagination, which is limited to purchased, loveless sex, and Hester's inability to inspire any more than that from any man.

The tone of the scene changes again as Hester pulls from the now opened box her mother's dress, from which she can, in a Proustian moment,[25] smell her mother's smell that the long-packed-away dress still retains. And then she brings forth her own girlhood Sunday dress. As the curtain falls, Hester has begun to forget the money and to lose herself in the box's contents. Stored in those boxes may after all be her compensation, though not a monetary one.

In the interval between the play's two acts, the contents of the boxes spill out over the floor of the room and cover the once empty space. The fragments of Hester's life spill out as she literally unpacks her childhood, her family, her history, her life. Appropriate to the regurgitative images that beset Hester's dialogue, the boxes and cases here vomit up the Smits and their poor Afrikaner lives. And amid bringing in the boxes, Johnnie has also unearthed his father's no longer used crutches, which remain on stage as a physical representation of the crippled, dying man in the adjacent room and as a reminder to the audience that the boxes and spillage on the floor belong to the father as well as to Hester. Like Grandma's boxes in Edward Albee's *The American Dream*, the boxes in Fugard's *Hello and Goodbye* are the parcels of memory, the pieces of life that are the ingredients of existence.

As Hester rummages through the boxes and suitcases unearthing the memorabilia and memories they contain, she immerses herself in her history, losing sight of the monetary compensation she initially sought. She begins increasingly to see the contents of the boxes as the vomit and rubbish they are; Johnnie, for his part, simultaneously begins to take new life from the crutches he has found:

> HESTER. That's what this is. Second-hand rubbish. What's it good for? [*Johnnie is back on the crutches, examining them, tentatively trying one and then the other. He takes two crutch-rubbers out of his pocket and starts to put them on.*]
>
> JOHNNIE. Our inheritance.
>
> HESTER. All I'm inheriting tonight is bad memories. Makes me sick just to look at it. (212)

While Hester's imagination reverts from the clothes, photos, and odds and ends that are strewn about to the five hundred pounds she hopes to find, Fugard power-fully choreographs the contrasting imaginations and dreams of the Smit siblings.[26] Hester imagines aloud the respectability she will achieve with money in her purse; and while she does so, behind her back Johnnie dances forth his own dreams, "*tries out the crutches—a few steps, different positions, opening an imaginary door, etc., etc.*" (214).

Hester's dreams, based on the assertion "You can do anything with money," however, are conflated with a bitter scorn for respectable family life, a scorn born at once of her own scarred childhood and of her prostitute's experience selling as a commodity the act upon which families are based: "Happy families is fat men crawling on to frightened women. And when you've had enough he doesn't stop, 'lady'. I've washed more of your husbands out of me than ever gave you babies" (214). As she continues to rummage, the search for money is constantly displaced by the search for something else:

> HESTER. Second-hand! Life in here was second-hand . . . used up and old before we even got it. Nothing ever reached us new. Even the days felt like the whole world had lived them out before they reached us. . . . Where's the box? Why the hell did I ever come back? . . . Wasn't there one thing worth saving from all those years?
>
> JOHNNIE. What will you do if you don't find it?
>
> HESTER. I don't know. I don't even know what it is yet. Just one thing that's got a good memory. I think and think, I try to remember. All those years. Just once. Happy.
>
> JOHNNIE. No, I mean the money. The compensation. What will you do if you don't . . . [*pause.*] Have you . . . ? Yes you have, haven't you? [*Hester looks in bewilderment at the chaos around her.*] You've forgotten what you're looking for! (218–219)

Johnnie only partially understands, for what Hester is looking for is finally not money but something that will provide her with self-definition, give her life meaning, and engender her freedom from 57A Valley Road and her poor Afrikaner past.

As she forages through the artifacts of family she has unpacked on the stage, re-living for each, like a patient in therapy, its meaning in her personal history, she finds her way through the underbrush of memory to a central moment of under-standing: her feelings about her mother's death and about her mother's marriage. Of the first, she asserts, "I knew she was dead, and what it meant being dead. It's goodbye for keeps. She was gone for ever"; and of the second:

> I'm saying this was the biggest mistake she ever made. Marriage! One man's slave all your life, slog away until you're in your grave. For what? Happiness in Heaven? I seen them—Ma and others like her, with more kids than they can count and no money; bruises every pay-day because he comes home drunk or another one in the belly because he was so drunk he didn't know it was his old wife and into bed! (222)

She concludes, "All we unpacked here tonight is mistakes" (223). And if there is no meaning to life except perhaps a concatenation of mistakes leading to the ultimate goodbye, then she is free to scream out the ultimate blasphemy against both the family and the religiosity that characterized it: "THERE IS NO GOD! THERE NEVER WAS! We've unpacked our life . . . and there is no God. Nothing but rub-bish. In this house there was nothing but useless . . . second-hand poor-white junk!" (227). The unpacking of the boxes is Hester's poignant and manic threnody for her life.

But as Hester here finds the heart of her disease and her despair, as she touches the body of her hate and anger, she finds the good memory she has sought. Fling-ing the contents of the boxes, the fragments of her life, around the room in her frenzy of despair, she hurls her mother's dress and suddenly realizes that her mother's image is the one thing worth holding on to, the one thing that connects her by a thin thread to life and existence: "I forgot she was here—in here, alive, to touch, to talk to, to love. She was a chance in here to love something, I wanted to. The hating was hard. Hate! Hate! So much to hate I forgot she was here" (228).

Fugard deftly powers *Hello and Goodbye* with three climactic moments in quick succession, of which the first is Hester's discovery of her mother as an object of love. The second is the shocking discovery by both Hester and the audience that there is no father in the next room dying, that the father is already deceased and that his dying during the play was a scenario constructed by Johnnie for our, for Hester's, and most of all for Johnnie's own benefit. But it brings about a kind of catharsis for Hester, revealing at its height Fugard's genius as a forger of dramatic statement. Hester has spent all her bitter words, and with the energy of a soul exploding and purging itself in anger and torment, wordlessly she kicks and pummels her brother until the poison is out of her and she stops from "sheer exhaustion."

In Barney Simon's mounting of the play, Hester chases Johnnie, "hitting at him,

5. Zeljko Ivanek and Maria Tucci as Johnnie and Hester in *Hello and Goodbye*, McCarter Theatre, Princeton, N.J., revival 1994. Photo © T. Charles Erickson.

destroying things, while he rushes round like squealing-half-laughing piglet" (2–31v). In Fugard's stage directions, the beaten Johnnie lies stretched on the floor until Hester's exit. The stage picture with Hester erect and in control and with Johnnie sprawled on the floor is one of Hester's triumph. Her anger and hate spent, she rises to the occasion, can pity her brother, offer to take him away from Port Elizabeth, and finally bequeath him everything: "It's all yours. The house and everything. Tell them I said it's yours" (233).

In a dramatic reversal, Hester leaves *giving* the money and goods she had been so bent on taking. What she does take, however, is a sense of who she is and of her existential responsibility for her life: "That's me—a woman in a room. . . . I want to get back to it, in it, be it, be me again the way I was when I walked in. . . . there she is waiting, here she is going, and somebody's watching all of it. But it isn't God. It's me" (234).[27] With that she closes the bracket of her role, and saying, "Goodbye, Johnnie," she makes her exit.

But Hester is only half the meaning of the play. She shares the stage with her brother, who is present before her hello and after her goodbye. Hester's is the fate of the child who left and leaves again. Johnnie's is that of the one who remained and will continue to remain. When the secret of his father's death is discovered, a secret that audience members may have already guessed, Johnnie's hermetic opening monologue as well as his actions throughout the play take on revised meaning and importance.

For him, his father's presence and debilitation had given his own life meaning.

His room, the room we see on stage, has been for him defined in terms of the other room. And thus his father's demise brought him face to face with his own existential terror:

> I tried to work it out. "This is it," I thought. "The end." Of what? Of him. Of Waiting. Of pain in the other room. "You're on your own, Johnnie Smit," I said to myself. "From now on it's you—just you and wherever you are—you in the middle of a moment. The other room is empty. . . . It's hard to describe. It feels like . . . I'm ashamed. Of me. Of being alone. Just me in my whole life. It was so different with him. He was in there, something else, somewhere else. Even tonight, just pretending it helped. You believed he was in there, didn't you?. . . . If only his ghost would come back and haunt me! Even if I went grey with fright!" (232–233)

He declines her offer to go with her and find a new life in Johannesburg because he is hopelessly rooted to this house and his memories. He cannot say goodbye to them but will wait for the figure of death in the shape of his father: "Suppose—just suppose there are ghosts, and he did come back to haunt and I was gone! I'll stay. Just in case, I'll wait" (233).

The play's third and final climactic moment is Johnnie's. After Hester has made her exit, Johnnie lifts himself from his prone position on the floor, sees his father's crutches, drags himself across the floor like someone disabled, reaches for the crutches, and literally becomes, reincarnates himself as, his dead father, as the maimed and dying parent. It is a breathtaking moment. Johnnie's tragic Resurrection is the final image of the play: "a different me! What's the word? Birth. Death. Both. Jesus did it in the Bible. [*Pause*] Resurrection. [*Pause*] CURTAIN." For Johnnie, his relationship with his dead father is from goodbye to hello.

More than once, Athol Fugard has suggested that Johnnie is his alter ego, that Fugard's own close relationship with his crippled father could have led him to make Johnnie's decision never to leave home.[28] As such, Fugard knows personally the dilemma of the one who leaves and imaginatively that of the one who stays. He masterfully uses that binocular knowledge to create one of his most profound plays. The 1994 McCarter Theatre audience left in tears not because they knew anything of Fugard's life, not because they had any knowledge of poor Afrikaners in Port Elizabeth, but because in *Hello and Goodbye* Fugard reminds us that none of us ever makes peace with our past, our families, and our life choices. We are all part of an often painful dynamic of hello and goodbye, goodbye and hello with our history and our demons. Hester and Johnnie do not resolve their lives, say a final goodbye to 57A Valley Road, or walk off into a new, bright sunrise. Nor is anyone ever able to do that. The nature of our lives is that we visit, take leave, and revisit who we were and who we are: hello and goodbye, goodbye and hello.

Where are Lucky and Pozzo when they are not on stage? Perhaps they are performing as Fugard's Boesman and Lena. The connection of Fugard's *Boesman and*

Lena (1969) to Samuel Beckett and more specifically to Didi and Gogo in *Waiting for Godot* has often been made.[29] But Fugard's couple bear less resemblance to Vladimir and Estragon, the two Chaplinesque, affable comrades who never move from their tree, than they do to the peripatetic, beater/beaten, victimizer/victim, master/slave pair of Pozzo and Lucky. Unmistakably, Athol Fugard is one of Samuel Beckett's progeny, but as he does throughout his work, Fugard gives the generalized Beckettian landscape a very specific geographic place. Indeed, the Swartkops mudflats near Port Elizabeth and the other locations in the Port Elizabeth environs where Boesman and Lena have been are of great significance and made much of in the course of the play. The places that make up the Eastern Cape life-path of Boesman and Lena—Coega, Redhouse, Swartkops, Veeplaas, Korsten, Kleinskool—can be found on any map;[30] and as such, *Boesman and Lena* is able to comment on Beckettian and existentialist questions of human meaning in the universe even as it also comments on South African social and racial situations that provide the poignant underpinnings of those more general questions.[31]

Nowhere is this more evident than in the opening line of the play. Boesman and Lena, carrying their belongings—she carrying some of them, as South African coloured and black women do, on her head—enter on to the stage one at a time. Like Pozzo, Boesman enters the stage first and then is followed by Lena, his Lucky. Though no rope is in evidence, Lena is as tied and subservient to Boesman as Beckett's human beast of burden, Lucky, is to Pozzo. "*She has been*," the stage directions tell us, "*reduced to a dumb, animal-like submission by the weight of her burden and the long walk behind them*" (239). Before setting down the heavy load in her hands and atop her shabby *doek* (cloth turban), Lena opens the play with the question, "Here?" In that one word is contained much that is at the heart of Fugard's play. She is asking somewhat incredulously, "Here? In this totally open, muddy space? Here is where you wish to stop?" She is asking, "Here? Tell me if this spot is where we stop or if we are going on, because I don't want to set down my load and collapse if you plan to go further." Lena's one word question informs us, too, that when and where they stop is Boesman's male decision, that he is ruler and she ruled. And in the play's larger realm, "Here?" is an existential question for a Lena who will spend her time on stage searching for the meaning of her life and for her value as a human being.

The Blood Knot and *Hello and Goodbye,* Fugard's two other so-called Port Elizabeth plays, take place in single rooms. Although clearly related to those plays, *Boesman and Lena* takes the drama out into the open and onto the Swartkops mudflats. As Stanley Kauffmann and Dennis Walder have both noted, *Boesman and Lena* is a play very much about the primal mud which gives rise to human existence;[32] and thus the play's second word, "Mud!," is significant.

As is so often the case in his work, Fugard reaches back to the very fundamentals of theatre, taking two or three figures, a single defined space, and a few stage properties that grow into inanimate actors in order to build a drama imbued with universal meaning well beyond the particular plights of particular characters. In *The Blood Knot,* it is Morrie and Zach, their one-room shack in Korsten, the letters and the new clothes; in *Hello and Goodbye*, it is Hester and Johnnie, the front room of 57A Valley Road, and the boxes and the crutches. In each of those two plays, moreover, the action is carried out in relation to a third character: in the one, the unseen pen-pal, Ethel Lange of Oudtshoorn; in the other, Hester and Johnnie's unseen father allegedly in the next room. In *Boesman and Lena*, the third actor is actually seen on stage in the figure of the black man, Outa, who is given no voice except to mumble incoherently and to utter only one single, but all-important, word: *Lena*. Using as his basic elements the Swartkops mudflats, his title characters' playing off against each other in the face of an essentially silent third person, and the scraps of rubbish that Boesman and Lena transport from one place to another, Fugard constructs what Stanley Kauffmann has astutely called a "beautiful, shocking, unforgettable play."[33]

Who are Boesman and Lena? They are coloureds, miscegenates caught between South Africa's black and white races. Their noticeably inappropriate names—Lena, a European name, and Boesman or "bushman," one of the worst things a South African black man can be called—ironically remind us that they are the mixed breed of coloureds unwanted, unaccepted by either race responsible for their being. And they are itinerant coloureds nomadically roaming the Eastern Cape rural and industrial suburbs of Port Elizabeth looking for work and living in temporary housing, usually a makeshift *pondok* constructed of corrugated iron scraps, cardboard, and whatever other waste materials come to hand. Fugard also manipulates language to characterize his two characters, for as in no other play he had ever written before or has written since is the language so heavily peppered with Afrikaans. It is true their Anglo-Afrikaans patois is a way of reminding us that Boesman and Lena's language would be Afrikaans. But Morrie and Zach, Hester and Johnnie would also certainly have conversed in Afrikaans, as would the characters in *Playland* or *Valley Song*. Except for an occasional word, the language of those plays does not present any difficulties for the non-Afrikaans-speaking audience member or reader. But in *Boesman and Lena*, the probably Xhosa-speaking Outa appears not at all to understand the characters' language, and a white English-speaking audience will not catch all of Boesman and Lena's heavily Afrikaans-laden speech. The racially mixed situation of the characters is thus cleverly and dramatically reinforced by the language they speak.

But Fugard's characters are not rooted in a limiting way to their geographic and racial South African coordinates. Boesman and Lena are also his Everyman and Everywoman trying, again like Beckett characters, to forge meaning and substance from the circular paths and seemingly meaningless routines of their lives. One must see, too, that the most important word in Fugard's title is "and," for the two characters are a bound unit. That "and" connecting Boesman and Lena, defining their interdependence, is as significant as the rope stretched between Pozzo and Lucky. Fugard acknowledges the allegorical importance of his pair when he writes in his *Notebooks*, "Boesman and Lena—their predicament, at the level at which it fascinates me, neither political nor social but metaphysical . . . a metaphor of the human condition which revolution or legislation cannot substantially change" (168).

That "predicament" in *Boesman and Lena* must largely be forged from the actors' bodies and from the stage properties even more than from the words of the text, for the characters are not intellectuals easily able to translate their feelings into the spoken word. They think, act, and feel with their bodies, the primary site at which their history and life have been inscribed. When Lena enters and says, "Mud! Swartkops!" (239), she is indicating that her body, her bare feet which have endlessly traveled the circuit of communities that form the locus of Port Elizabeth's circumference, tell her where she is: if it's mud, it must be Swartkops. Lena's body comprehends rewards and affection at the most basic level, through the bread, water, and cheap wine Boesman metes out. Likewise, she knows punishments and Boesman's anger in the form of his blows to her body that he also, and rather freely, metes out. Her few possessions, all portable, she carries on her head; the bundle of firewood to provide some bodily warmth she clutches under her arm. In Stanley Kauffmann's words, "The rubbish that this pair carry is the detritus of experience."[34] And Lena's shabby, shapeless dress is one of those that, as the stage directions indicate, "*reduce the body to an angular, gaunt cipher of poverty*" (239).

In Fugard's *Notebooks*, it is made clear that *Boesman and Lena* emerges from his seeing men and women like them on the roads and paths of South Africa. In part, Fugard makes a political statement just by placing these two South African nobodies on stage and using them as his protagonists. More importantly, however, his task as a playwright is to endow those faces and bodies of poverty he has seen with being and feelings expressible in dialogue, in words. This problem goes to the heart of the play, since for Fugard, playwriting and theatre are frequently his metaphors for life. Like the playwright's, then, Lena's difficult quest is to find the words and ideas befitting the inchoate register of bodily experiences she has known so that the actions and acts of her life can be given shape, meaning, and value: to enable her to make the leap from plod to plot through the fusion of body and speech.

Although *Boesman and Lena* is written in two acts, it is divided in another way as well by the appearance of its third character, Outa, at almost precisely the play's textual center. In an important way, Outa marks a "before and after" for the eponymous couple. When the play begins, Boesman and Lena have arrived in Swartkops after their Korsten squatters' *pondok* has been razed by the white man's bulldozer, and Lena's remembrance of the day's events and of Boesman's bizarre laughter as his home is destroyed is described with moving comic bitterness:

> "*Vat jou goed en trek!* [take your goods and beat it] Whiteman says *Voetsak!*" [beat it]. . . . *Ja!* You were happy this morning. "Push it over, my *baas!*" "*Dankie, baas!*" "*Weg is ons!*" [Thanks, boss! We're on our way!] It was funny, hey, Boesman! All the *pondoks* flat. The poor people running around trying to save their things. You had a good laugh. And now? Here we sit. Just now it's dark, and Boesman's thinking about another *pondok*. The world feels big when you sit like this. Not even a bush to make it your own size. Now's the time to laugh. This is also funny. Look at us! Boesman and Lena with the sky for a roof again. (240–241)

Lena punctuates her speech with a laughter born of the pathetic meaninglessness of her life. There is more than a touch of *King Lear* here, for without a shelter, she and her man once more stand naked before the world on their own Dover Cliffs: in the dark, in the cold, in the mud, and with no vegetation in sight. Laughable for her is the comic absurdity of their meaningless, earthbound life. It is hardly surprising, then, that her first act is to spot a bird in the sky and curse it as she compares its freedom of flight to her absurd life on earth and flight from Korsten:

> [*She is obviously staring up at a bird. Softly . . .*] *Jou moer!* [You cunt!] [*She watches it for a few seconds longer, then scrambles to her feet and shakes her fist at it.*] *Jou moer!!* [. . . *Her eyes follow it as it glides out of sight.*] So slowly . . . ! Must be a feeling, hey. Even your shadow so heavy you leave it on the ground. . . . Tomorrow they'll hang up there in the wind and laugh. We'll be in the mud. I hate them. (240)

Both she and her shadow are earthbound, in the mud, mocked not merely by whites but even by the birds, a superior animal life she understandably detests.

For Lena as she trails behind Boesman, the graph of her life is one long walk determined by the ordinate and abscissa of the road and Boesman's back (fig. 6), and she laments, "Look ahead, sister. To what? Boesman's back. That's the scenery of my world. You don't know what it's like behind you. . . . It's *me*, that thing you *sleep*

6. Bill Curry and Nomhle Nkonyeni in *Boesman and Lena*, Market Theatre, Johannesburg, revival 1993. Photo by Ruphin Coudyzer.

[drag] along the roads. My life." And she now sees that life as something that "felt old today," a piece of rubbish ready for the scrap heap like a threadbare blanket or a pot with a hole. With an existential cri de coeur, she exclaims, "Time to throw it away. How do you do that when it's yourself?" (244). What she has to show for her life are the bruises from Boesman's beatings and a life that is no more than dry bread and black tea, than bare bones. Boesman and Lena's is a love story that the circumstances of their lives has forced to go awry, replacing the gestures of love with gestures of violence, the language of affection with the language of abuse.

The senselessness of Lena's existence is echoed by their journey through the Eastern Cape towns, a journey that is circular, without memory of start or vision of terminus other than death. And to add to her despair, Boesman denigrates her language, the human quality distinguishing men from beasts, characterizing her speech as glossolalia, as verbal defecation, and as even less than that: "rubbish . . . That *drol* [shit] of nonsense that comes out when you open your mouth! . . . That *gebabbel* [babble] of yours. When you *poep* [fart] it makes more sense. You know why? It stinks. Your words are just noise. Nonsense. *Die geraas von 'n vervloekte lewe* [the noise of a cursed life]" (241, 246).

There is some truth in Boesman's characterization of her life as cursed, for she is doubly a subaltern: as a coloured, victimized by whites and the assault of their bulldozers; as a woman, victimized by a male and the assault of his fists. As Marcia Blumberg shrewdly observes, "her body is a road-map of bruises."[35] She asserts her humanity, nevertheless, by singing, dancing, remembering good times and sweet food, and attempting to orient herself geographically and physically. She harbors a belief that one day "Something's going to happen," and she will then be able to break free from the meaningless circularity of her life: "And then I'm gone. Goodbye, darling. I've had enough. 'Strue's God, that day I'm gone" (252). Boesman acts, however, at every turn to deny her dreams, her worth, her humanity, her selfhood, and any idea that her life could have meaning:

BOESMAN. *Now* is the only time in your life.

LENA. No! Now. What's that? I wasn't born today. I want my life. Where is it?

BOESMAN. In the mud where you are. *Now.* Tomorrow it will be there too, and the next day. And if you're still alive when I've had enough of this, you'll load up and walk, somewhere else. (254)

But just as Lena reaches a moment of despair, exclaiming, "What time is that in my life? Another now. Black now and empty as hell. . . . I'm sick of you too, Boesman!" (254, 255), she suddenly spies a third figure in the darkness.

Boesman can immediately tell even in darkness merely by seeing the outlines of the man that he is black, "When did you see a whiteman sitting like that!" he asks rhetorically. In having Boesman speak this line, Fugard makes us aware that different races have different and identifying postures and body languages. As an astute director, Fugard recognizes that on the stage of life generally and more especially on the stage of life in the South Africa he knows, races enact their disparate roles projecting who they are, what they can and cannot become, through the language of their physical stance and movement. At his visceral level, Boesman knows this too; and his ability to enunciate it creates a whole new context for his relationship with Lena and for the play as a whole. From this central sentence on, the play is fueled with new energy; and both Lena and Boesman have the opportunity to come to terms with their lives, their partnership, and their existence.

The old African, "*an image of age and decrepitude,*" huddled on stage in his shabby overcoat almost immediately alters the dimensions of the dramatic action, for he is a racial "other," against whom Boesman and Lena can play out who they are. Earlier in the day, as so often before, they have been driven off by a racial "other," the white man, superior to them on apartheid's social scale. Now it is their turn to deal with someone who is in their view below them on that scale. The two split apart. Boesman names him "*kaffer*," the lowest, most abusive name for someone of black skin (roughly equivalent to "nigger"); and he wishes to drive the old man off, just as he had been driven off by the white man.[36] Lena, by contrast, names him "*Outa,*" or old man, an appellation of affection; and begs him to "Come over!" and warm himself by their fire. In the face of an unfortunate fellow human, Lena says to Boesman, "Do something. Help him" (256), and Boesman answers by moving back into the makeshift shelter he has constructed. Boesman argues, "He's not brown people, he's black people," and Lena responds, "They got feelings too. Not so *Outa?*" (258). In their response to the old man, Boesman and Lena play out a drama of alterity that reveals who and what they are.

Outa turns Boesman into a racist in whose speech we hear the familiar racist clichés. As Lena goes to call Outa to them, Boesman utters his version of "they lust for non-black women" and let one of *them* in and the neighborhood will be spoiled:

> They like *Hotnot meide* [Hottentot women]. Black bastards! Going to call again? You'll end up with a tribe of old *kaffers* sitting here. That's all you'll get out of that darkness. . . . Turn my place into a *kaffer nes!* [nest]. (359)

And in calling Lena "*Hotnot,*" Boesman uses the most abusive word for coloureds. Boesman, scarred by what whites have done to him and by his own dislocation in a race that is neither white nor black, has learned the lessons of the oppressor and uses them against both blacks and women.

Lena for her part senses her affinity with Outa, and refuses to abuse him as she, a non-white and a woman, has been abused. Clearly, too, Outa is the replacement for her beloved mongrel dog that went astray when the Korsten *pondoks* were demolished. For Lena, that animal was her *hond* [dog] whom she never gave more than a generic name, "*Hond.*" Revealingly, Boesman, who scorns Outa, also scorns Lena's pet, referring to him denigratingly as a *brak* [mongrel dog]. Though the childless Lena has not clearly cognized it, that voiceless mongrel dog was an image of her own racially mixed self that she could love and care for. Now she moves a step forward, replacing her lost *hond* with a human of another race and gender.

In her kindness to another being and in the sacrifices she makes for that other being, Lena begins to find her humanity and her self. She suggests to Boesman that they divide their bread in three, and when Boesman refuses, she divides her own half in two and shares it and her tea with Outa. She trades her share of the rotgut wine and her place in the new shelter for Boesman's sufferance in allowing Outa to share the fire with her. The circumstances enable the indigent Lena to play Lady Bountiful or St. Martin with one still less fortunate than she. The act 1 curtain then comes down on another of those dazzling moments in Fugard's work where he translates a simple physical act into epiphany. Lena says, "Look at this mug, *Outa* . . . old mug, hey. Bitter tea; a piece of bread. Bitter and brown. The bread should have bruises. It's my life" (271).[37] After he had written the moment, Fugard, calling it an "accident in writing," himself saw what he had posited: "Suddenly, and almost irrelevantly, remembered Lisa [his daughter] the other day reading a little book on the Mass—and there it was = Lena's Mass . . . the moment and its ingredients (the fire, the mug of tea, the bread) because sacramental—the whole a celebration of Lena's life"[38]

Outa helps Lena "celebrate" her life in a more important and non-religious way as well. And here Fugard as author, director, and actor uses his heightened understanding of the power of theatre to make his statement both about Lena and about his own commitment to theatre. Lena's dilemma is that Boesman has claimed her as an extension of himself, turning her into a human punching bag, beating her when he is angry with himself or with her disobedience. He has reduced her to a thing he uses to prove to himself his own value. Monica Meinert is very much on target when she comments, "Er prügelt und quält Lena, an den er hängt, weil sie das einzige Lebewesen ist, das zu ihm gehört. Diese negative Kraft ist der einzige Sinn, den sein sinnloses Leben noch hat" [He beats and abuses Lena, to whom he clings, because she is the only being that belongs to him. This negative power is the only meaning his meaningless life still has].[39] Absorbed by his own needs, Boesman, as shown by the actor on stage, physically turns his back on Lena, and that movement bespeaks Lena's more general aloneness: "Boesman's back. That's the scenery of my world."

Adapting Bishop Berkeley's famous question, one asks, "If a person is unnoticed, if an actor has no audience, is he or she alive?" In her loneliness, Lena reaches out to a fellow being, whom she uses as a confessor, to whom she relates her life and dreams, for whom she acts out who she is. The metaphor is theatrical, for Outa becomes the audience to her as player, and like an audience he murmurs garbled syllables, and serves as a human witness to Lena's life. As Fugard says in his *Notebooks*, Lena demands "that her life be witnessed."[40] Clearly, for Fugard the playwright as well, his life and ideas have no meaning unless they are enacted and witnessed by an audience. What gives him being as a dramatist also gives Lena being as a person.

Lena establishes her relationship with Outa by speaking their names, "*Outa* . . . You . . . [*patting herself*] . . . Lena . . . me." And when Outa pronounces her name, she attempts to speak to him in Xhosa and Fugard's stage direction reads, "the whole of the monologue follows this pattern: *the old man mumbles intermittently—the occasional phrase or even sentence quite clear—and Lena surrendering herself more and more to the illusion of conversation*" (261). It is an "illusion of conversation" because it is not two-way. What it is, however, is the special, not altogether one-way conversation between actor and spectator. And Lena proceeds to perform her life to the man who has his face, not his back, to her. With much physical gesture and role-playing, she not merely relates but acts out, performs her life for Outa. And she recognizes Outa's importance to her as a replacement for and a great improvement over her lost dog: "I'll tell you what it is. Eyes. *Outa.* Another pair of eyes. Something to see you. . . . I wanted to look [for the dog], but Boesman was in a hurry. So what! Now I got *Outa*" (262). To Outa, she performs the decline of her marriage ("He walks in front. I walk behind. It used to be side by side, with jokes"), the pain of her meaningless nomadic life ("Those paths on the veld . . . Boesman and Lena helped write them"), the sadness of her failed motherhood ("One, *Outa*, that lived. For six months. The others were born dead"), and the poetic image she gives to the pain she has endured ("Pain is a candle *entjie* [stump] and a donkey's face"). Like an actor, Lena reaches for her inner feelings, brings them out of herself as an actor does, and performs them for Outa. She makes a theatre of the "empty space" of the Swartkops mudflats. Indeed what Fugard and Lena do is precisely what Peter Brook describes in the riveting opening lines of his *The Empty Space*: "I can take any empty space and call it a bare stage. A man walks across the stage while someone else is watching him, and this is all that is needed for an act of theatre to be engaged."[41]

For Lena, the theatre she makes is life-giving and life-affirming. For Boesman, Lena's theatre is threatening. If she finds her own life, her own will, if she leaves him, he is left without definition. Having turned Lena into his female property, follower, slave, victim, and recipient of his blows, and having defined himself in terms of male, leader, master, victimizer, beater, Boesman's life becomes, he begins to realize, meaningless without her. In their power-based relationship, she thus has as much power as he, but has not until now realized it.

Toward the close of act 1, Lena feels her inner strength; and part of that is feeling the power she has in her relationship with Boesman. As she makes her decision to mutiny and remain outside the shelter with the old man, the stage directions tell us of Boesman, "*For the first time he is unsure of himself.*" In Lena's momentary absence, Boesman makes a desperate and unsuccessful attempt to drive Outa off by kicking him, shoving him away, and causing him to fall. Significantly, Boesman says to Outa, "If you tell her, I'll kill you" (270), indicating that Lena is now the authority figure from whom the truth must be kept. And as the act ends, it is she and Outa who have "othered" Boesman: "*They drink and eat. Boesman is watching them from the shelter, his bread and tea untouched before him*" (271). He stands outside their feast, outside their "celebration," his existence threatened.

In a sense, Outa is a catalyst who enables Boesman and Lena's relationship to change. At an immediate level, Boesman finds his assumed superior male intelligence challenged by his simple inability to fathom Lena's attraction to Outa, an aged, indigent racial inferior. When the second act begins and the effect of two bottles of cheap wine have become manifest, what began as Boesman's uncomfortable bewilderment gives way to jealousy and a very real fear of losing his hold over the subaltern Lena. Eager to affirm and maintain his mastery, he creates his own theatre, pantomiming and satirizing Lena and the others who cowered before the white man's slum clearance:

> Give us time, *my baas. Al weer sukke tyd.* [Here we go again.] . . . That's how you said it. That's what you looked like. . . . The lot of you! Crawling out of your holes. Like worms. *Babalas* [in a drunken stupor] as the day you were born. That piece of ground was rotten with *dronkies* [drunkards]. Trying to save their rubbish, falling over each other. (273)

He characterizes the fleeing squatters as dogs with "their tails between their legs" and as baboons evicted from their shelters. With an air of superiority, he separates himself from the rabble by referring to "the lot of you" and by suggesting he has risen above *their* animal level. The destruction of the squatters' camp, he claims, gave him freedom and a new dawn: "The world was open this morning. It was big! All the roads . . . new ways, new places" (275). And he tells her, "we're whiteman's rubbish. That's why he's so *beneukt* [fed up] with us. He can't get rid of his rubbish. He throws it away, we pick it up. Wear it. Sleep in it. Eat it. We're made of it now. His rubbish is people" (277).

Boesman's inebriation helps create a view filled with inconsistency. Clearly his talk of Freedom and new roads is mere bravado, for they have traveled the old roads again. The play finds them in the dark, and they have experienced not freedom but eviction. True enough, as the battered and ragged possessions strewn on stage attest, they carry about what whites have thrown away, their refuse, their rubbish. But to equate coloureds, and himself among them, as the human extension of that rubbish reveals Boesman's terrible underlying self-loathing. As he vacillates inconsistently from patronizing superiority to a sense of himself as coloured trash, Boesman reveals his conflicted self-image, one premised on the assumption that relationships, whether of race or gender, are power-based: one is either master or mastered.

Boesman's assertion of his freedom is patently false, but it is Lena who has found a kind of freedom and who consequently has risen to a new level and speaks a new language that Boesman does not comprehend. Outa's ability to speak her name becomes a signifier of herself as person and not as human pack animal following behind Boesman like an ass carrying his rubbish possessions. She speaks with the voice of a "born-again" believer:

> LENA. That's not a *pondok,* Boesman. It's a coffin. All of them. You bury my life in your *pondoks.* Not tonight. . . . No! I'm on this earth, not in it. Look now. [*She nudges the old man.*] Lena!

OLD MAN. Lena.

LENA. *Ewe* [Yes]. That's me. You're right, Boesman. It's here and now. This is the time and place. To hell with the others. They're finished and mixed up anyway. I don't know why I'm here, how I got here. And you won't tell me. Doesn't matter. They've ended *now*. The walks led *here*. Tonight. And he sees it. (278)

Lena is saying *ewe*, yes, to her life and is endowing the play's opening word, *here*, with its existential meaning. The circuit of their seemingly repetitive and pointless travels have after all led somewhere. They have led *here*. Whereas Boesman has declared, "*Now* is the only time in your life," Lena on this night has realized that Boesman's statement is both unenlightened and false.

Her newfound freedom clearly gives Lena an unwonted edge over Boesman, enabling her to express herself (like Fugard and his actors) through art. She claps and sings her song of "*Ou blikkie kondens milk*" [old can of condensed milk], she dances, and ultimately composes music and lyric poetry celebrating her life.[42] Indeed, in the holograph text, Fugard precedes the song with the later deleted line, "Clap Outa! This is my life":

> Korsten had its empties
> Swartkops got its bait
> Lena's got her bruises
> Cause Lena's *Hotnot meid.*
>
> Kleinskool got prickly pears
> Missionvale's got salt
> Lena's got a Boesman
> So it's always Lena's fault.
>
> Coegakop is far away
> Redhouse up the river
> Lena's in the mud again
> *Outa's* sitting with her. (280)

The actor portraying Lena will necessarily make her body perform Lena's emerging liberation. And Lena's song is impressive not merely for her ability to indite with metrics and rhyme but for her new sense of places. Her geography, now no longer a meaningless treadmill of towns, is connected positively with foods and landscapes. She can also transform into music, dance, and poetry her bruised past and the new fact in her life, "*Outa's* sitting with her."

In Korsten, Boesman had been earning money by collecting and returning empty deposit bottles. He has beaten Lena for breaking some of the bottles in the scurry of eviction. In response to Lena's happy song, her care for Outa, and the new body language she performs, Boesman blurts out, "I dropped the empties." This is a dramatic assertion containing a complexity of disparate meanings. It is an admission of guilt that is as far as Boesman can go in asking for forgiveness and some of the attention Lena now showers on Outa. It is a hurtful statement underscoring his power as her capricious master, and it is one loaded with a powerful psychological punch when she recognizes that she has been the innocent object of his physical abuse. It is a revelation that will enable Boesman to begin asking why he has himself broken the bottles, why he has knowingly laid false blame on Lena, and what inner hurt fuels his domestic violence.

Partially in anger and partially from suddenly recognizing Boesman as a human being more bruised than she, Lena asks the critical questions, "Why must you hurt me so much? What have I really done? Why didn't you hit yourself this morning? . . . Or the whiteman that kicked us out? Why did you hit me?" (281). Fugard choreographs body movement and language as Boesman steps out of the shelter and asks himself the question to which he really has no answer yet, "Why do I hit you?" That step out of the makeshift shelter he has constructed and to which he has withdrawn is a difficult and significant one for Boesman, for through it he reluctantly performs for Lena and for himself the exposure of his vulnerability. Hitting himself, his first action is self-flagellation. With the natural instinct of a psychotherapist and the experienced voice of one who has known pain analogous to what Boesman is beginning to feel, Lena reaches out to him saying, "Maybe you just want to touch me, to know I'm here. Try it the other way. Open your fist, put your hand on me. I'm Lena" (282).

When empathy fails, Lena prompts Boesman to use Outa as she has, as an audience, by having Outa witness either his physical blows to her body or his verbal admission of his wrongdoing: "Say it in *kaffertaal* [nigger language]. 'You hit me for nothing.'" At last Boesman explodes, sings a characteristic Fugard aria revealing his own dark view of existence. And, as with arias in opera, it is one of those moments that appear throughout Fugard's work, when the recitative of realism gives way to the transcendent aria of the inner being:

> All you've got is me and I'm saying "*Sies*" [an expletive of disgust roughly equivalent to "yuk"]. . . . You think I haven't got secrets in my heart too? That's mine. *Sies!* Small word, hey. *Sies.* But it fits. [*parodying himself.*] "*Ja, baas! Dankie* [thanks], *baas!*" *Sies,* Boesman! . . . *Sies,* Lena! Boesman and Lena, *sies!* We're not people any more. Freedom's not for us. We stood there under the sky . . . two crooked *Hotnots.* . . . *Sies wêreld!* [yuk world!] All there is to say. That's our word. After that our life is dumb. . . . One day your turn. One day mine. Two more holes somewhere. The earth will get *naar* [nauseous] when they push us in. And then it's finished. The end of Boesman and Lena. (283–284)

This life-denying aria plumbing the depths of Boesman's despair has its final punctuation with their realization that during Boesman's speech bemoaning their meaningless lives and equally meaningless deaths, Outa has actually passed from life to death on stage. Outa is thus at once a timepiece for *Boesman and Lena,* the living embodiment of Boesman's death in life and his spiritual demise and—when it is clear Boesman could be arrested by the authorities and held responsible for Outa's death—the means for Lena to teach Boesman what it is to be falsely accused.

Boesman's view of their lives and relationship as *sies* indicates his internalization and acceptance of a racial classification system that tells him he is "whiteman's rubbish." He in turn learns and acts out the white man's role toward those he deems beneath him on the social scale, his wife and Africans. As he has beaten his wife, he kicks and pummels Outa's corpse almost as though he is beating his own body in disgust and self-loathing. He and Lena have traded roles and power. It is now she who is in control, she who asserts she is breaking up their relationship and that she will no longer follow him, and she who has found the Freedom he has only boasted of but failed to achieve:

> LENA. Why must I go with you? Because you're Boesman and I'm Lena?
>
> BOESMAN. Are you coming? It's the last time I ask you.
>
> LENA. No. The first time I tell you. No. I've walked with you a long way, *ou ding* [old thing]! It's finished now. Here, in the Swartkops mud. I wanted to finish it this morning, sitting there on the pavement. That was the word in my mouth. NO! Enough! . . . Run! It's trouble. Life's showing you bullets again. So run. But this time you run alone. (290)

As he smashes up the shelter, she exhorts him to take all their belongings: "I want *boggerall.* It's my life but I don't want to feel it any more. . . . What's your big word? Freedom! Tonight it's Freedom for Lena. Whiteman gave you yours this morning, but you lost it. Must I tell you how? When you put all that on your back. There wasn't room for it as well" (291). By breaking from him, by unburdening herself of their rubbish, she is declaring that she and her life are not rubbish, not "whiteman's rubbish," not Boesman's rubbish, not anyone's rubbish. He, standing there "grotesquely overburdened" with all their rubbish piled on his back, standing there like Lucky beleaguered with the baggage he bears, is the tragically comic stage image of man without meaning. He is not free but literally weighed down with things that give neither shape nor meaning to his existence.

It is then, when Boesman is in his most debased and alone state, that Lena turns the play around. She goes to him and makes a crucial one-word demand, "Give!" At the most important level, this is Lena's request for Boesman to be what he has not been: generous. Through her own generosity to someone less fortunate than she, Lena has found her value and her life. Boesman's denial of others, of Outa and of her, as well as his denial of himself have prevented him from seeing himself and his own value as something only negative, as *sies.* If Boesman can now "give," if he can be generous, if he can *surrender* his negative self-concept, he can join with her in a new relationship. That he begins to do so is rendered semiotically as he responds to her "Give" by giving her the bucket in which she has carried their things. Lena comments, "Hasn't got a hole in it yet. Might be whiteman's rubbish, but I can still use it." In the gesture and in the comment resides the idea that their relationship is whole and no longer flawed. That this bucket, though battered, is still intact and serviceable stands in contrast to her initial view of her own life as "Something that's been used too long. The old pot that leaks" (244) as well as to Boesman's pejorative image of her: "You're dumb. When you make a hole in your face the noise that comes out is as good as nothing, because nobody hears it" (183). Their relationship is, in short, finally whole, not holed, and they can exit the play as Boesman *and* Lena, a unit, not master and slave, not male victimizer and female victim. They can leave side by side, not one behind the other, and they can leave with Lena saying optimistically, "I'm alive, Boesman. There's daylights left in me. You still got a chance. Don't lose it" (293).

Boesman and Lena is an extraordinarily moving play that engraves the powerful image of the two main characters, their lives and their pain, upon the mind of viewer. While Fugard developed as a playwright, his wife Sheila launched a career as a poet and fiction writer; and her poem "Lena" captures the essence of her husband's characters remarkably well:

> You walked there
> Along the brown road that struggles on beyond kopjie and grass,
> Into the future, with the stumble of wine bottles and a stale repast
> In the firewalk of your wrinkles, your face a lake of placidity,
> Your mouth a rounded "O" of pain where your cry never escapes
> But remains locked in a dry karoo well
> And in your gaunt body, you too lock up the shape of the woman
> Who falls only from your eyes, a dream in which you drop children
> And they are as tears flowing about your life[43]

The poem, which focuses on the image of Lena and not her speeches, helps one understand that to make an informed judgment about *Boesman and Lena*, one must remember that this play is as much or more a performance script than a playtext of dialogue. It is a play of physical images and body language. It is a play that could easily be mimed, with the exception of a few heavily weighted words or phrases: here, mud, Boesman *and* Lena, Freedom, *sies*, give. With this in mind, it is easy to see how Fugard very naturally moved on to create with John Kani and Winston Ntshona *Sizwe Bansi Is Dead* and *The Island*, performance pieces that grew out of remembered images, mimes, and acting exercises.

THREE

"Acting" against Apartheid

Statements after an Arrest under the Immorality Act (1974) is the first of Athol Fugard's "witness to apartheid" plays. It forces its audience to confront the terrible effects of the South African law that prohibited sexual relations and marriage between members of two different races. *Statements* is one of Athol Fugard's most ambitious and difficult works, and it is also among his least successful with reviewers and audiences. Dennis Walder talks about the typically "clumsy, abstract feel" of the language. Vandenbroucke describes the problems the play had in its genesis, and he suggests that because of its rootedness in a specific apartheid law familiar to South Africans but not to others, it would play better "in Cape Town than in London or New York."[1]

Since the play makes a strong statement about one of the most offensive apartheid legislations, emasculating the play politically while acknowledging its value as theatre was not uncommon among its South African reviewers. Reviewer Elsa Joubert, for example, writing for the Afrikaans newspaper *Rapport,* asserted, "The play has no political message. Honesty and attempt to understand, yes. A superb, neutral rendering by playwright and cast alike. It is just a hypothesis."[2] Her comment is stunning in its remarkable denial of the play's sometimes rather bald politics. But perhaps audience problems with *Statements* are best captured in the acerbic review given the 1984 Durban revival of the play in the *Natal Mercury*: "It is seen to be without any real form and emerges as a curious mixture of theatre *verité* and illustrated lecture.[3]

Statements is a play surely not without its problems, and those that beset it are several. It does seem at first glance to be, as the Durban reviewer asserts, "without any real form." Although this is not finally the case, it can seem that way to theatergoers who do not want their conventional concepts of theatre challenged. But for Fugard, unconventional theatre is certainly an apt weapon against a society that has attempted to impose "real form" on natural selection and sexuality. Nevertheless, it is true that, as Russell Vandenbroucke suggests, *Statements* is not a play that travels well. A non–South African audience is more likely to understand the racial segregation and racism depicted in *Sizwe Bansi* or the incarceration of political dissidents in *The Island* than it is the South African Immorality Act, the legal intervention that makes coital relations across race lines a crime, which is at issue in *Statements*. Racism and repression are known the world over. The Immorality Act is an almost uniquely South African invention.

Furthermore, in *Statements* it helps to comprehend the play's setting. As a non–South African, I must admit that I did not appropriately understand its principal characters until I visited the bleak, rather cheerless Karoo desert town of Noupoort, where the play is set; and until I walked the dusty road from the shabby coloured area to the small, poorly supplied public library. In this desert outpost— like one of those isolated towns in central New Mexico—it is likely that the unmarried white librarian and the principal of the coloured school might be a lone pair of intellectual equals who are separated by the color bar from knowing each other as peers. Apart, their lives are as jejune as arid, dusty Noupoort, which is aptly caught in the throes of drought and in short supply of water.

In creating Frieda Joubert, the forty-two-year-old white Noupoort unmarried librarian and Errol Philander, the thirty-six-year-old married principal of the school in Bontrug, Noupoort's coloured township, Fugard writes himself into a tough corner. Had he set forth a pair of racially different, same age, maritally single lovers, he might have produced a lockstep South Africanized *Romeo and Juliet* or *West Side Story* complete with white Montagues and coloured Capulets or Sharks and Jets. But in eschewing the easy formula, Fugard is faulted on moral grounds for his implicit approval of Errol and Frieda's adulterous relationship. Thus Robert Cushman, reviewer for the play's premiere in London, was offended not by the nature of South Africa's Immorality Act but by the immorality of the characters, commenting, "Mr. Fugard's State-crossed lovers are hardly Romeo and Juliet; the man is an adulterer and the predominant feeling is fear, as much of his family responsibilities as of the law. So their love-scene is given over as much to recrimination as to affection."[4] The objections to *Statements* seem connected to Fugard's having broken the rules by failing to write either *Romeo and Juliet* or *Tristan and Isolde* on the one hand or a marital infidelity play like *Blood Wedding* or *The Fair Penitent* (featuring Philander as an appropriately named Lothario) on the other.[5] What is perhaps not made clear enough or stated forcefully enough in the play is that both the Immorality and the Group Areas Acts, which haunt *Statements*, must bear the blame not merely for the racially transgressive sex but for the adultery as well.[6]

Pointedly, Fugard chooses to begin the play not with the courtship of Frieda and Errol and not with the couple *in flagrante delicto*, but with their tender moments of postcoital affection and repose. As Fugard recognizes, the true intimacy of sex is not so much glandular as it is the intimacy of feelings after orgasm. *Statements* opens with "A man *and* a woman *on a blanket on the floor. Both of them are naked. He*

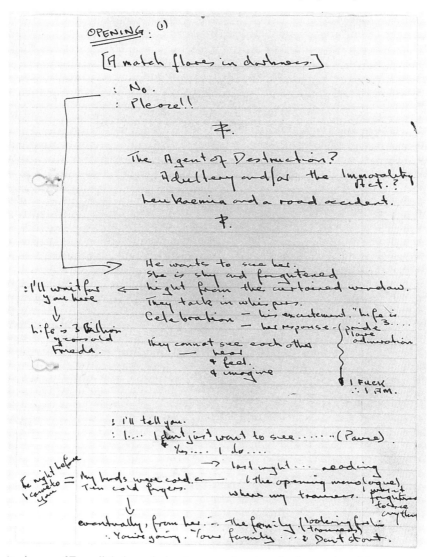

7. A copy of Fugard's holograph showing stage directions for the opening of *Statements*. Courtesy the Lilly Library, Indiana University, Bloomington, Indiana.

is caressing her hair" (81).[7] The sensuality of the hair and the privacy of the moment go more to the heart of their relationship than would a depiction of sexual union. Indeed, the moment is reminiscent of the scene in which the Duchess of Malfi brushes out her hair as she tells of her relationship with Antonio. Furthermore, the moment—with its naked "man" and "woman," and with its references to sun, breezes, trees, birds, locusts, bees—has an Edenic ring, reminding the audience that sex can be an act of creation and as close as men and women come to biblical Creation. The Edenic image subsequently takes on importance when we learn of Philander's interests in creative evolution theory. It takes on importance as well when the state has eaten from what it believes is The Tree of Knowledge and has located what it believes to be Original Sin and Carnal Knowledge in Noupoort; for it is then that the state destroys, dis-creates the relationship between Frieda and Errol. The reason, even after their names are known, the text continues to the end to give the speeches not to Errol and Frieda but to "MAN" and "WOMAN" is that it seems Fugard wants them to be the elemental Adam and Eve of his creation and dis-creation, prelapsarian and postlapsarian drama.

Statements is divided into two nearly equal parts: before and after the arrest of Frieda and Errol by Detective Sergeant J. du Preez. The first is acted in near darkness and outlines the special and necessarily secret island of union Frieda and Errol have created. The second is the exposure and destruction of that relationship in the harsh light of torches (flashlights) and in the bursting light of a flash camera that takes six still photographs of the nude couple. If God creates the universe in six days and thereafter rests, then the State here dis-creates Frieda and Errol's universe with six flashes and thereafter arrests. From the outset, however, the state has been there as the trouble in their paradise. There is pathetic playfulness in Fugard's title, for all along the life and relationship of the principals is haunted by government and law, by "State-ment."

From the outset, *Statements* asks, "Whither has evolution led? To what state has the human species, more particularly, evolved?" These evolutionary questions are emphasized through Philander's comments on his reading of nineteenth- and twentieth-century creative evolutionists, especially Charles Lyell and Julian Huxley. Philander is enrolled in a correspondence course presumably dealing with evolution and genetics, and he has been reading Lyell's *The Principles of Geology* (1830), an early, pre-Darwinian study investigating the development of plant, animal, and geological forms. Philander is particularly struck by and twice quotes the conclusion of Lyell's lengthy, exhaustive study: "'no vestige of a beginning and no prospect of an end'" (84). Actually the conclusion reads:

> To assume that the evidence of the beginning or end of so vast a scheme lies within the reach of our philosophical inquiries, or even of our speculations, appears to be inconsistent with a just estimate of the relations which subsist between the finite powers of man and the attributes of an Infinite and Eternal Being.[8]

As the reviewer of Barney Simon's 1976 Upstairs Market Theatre production of *Statements* astutely comments, "[Philander] expresses the excitement of his initiation to significantly, the secular and theological theories of the origins of man. The relationship as it would be, if unfettered by legalism, breaks through."[9] Indeed, one wonders whether either Fugard or Philander read Lyell's comment, somewhat earlier in his study, concerning mixing of races. This appears in some editions under the heading "*Different races of men are all of one species*," and there Lyell writes, "Yet, notwithstanding this flexibility of bodily frame, we find no signs of indefinite departure from a common standard, and the intermarriages of individuals of the most remote varieties are not less fruitful than between those of the same tribe."[10] What is important for Philander and for the play is that if human beings cannot determine the eschatology, the beginnings or ends, of human life in either theological or evolutionary terms, then the philosophical carpets are pulled out from under the Immorality Act.

Evolutionary matters are emphasized as well by the fact that contemporary paleontologists and paleobotanists feel there is reason to believe the Karoo area around Noupoort may have been the earth's oldest cradle of life and the site of a once great inland sea. As Philander explains, "This little piece of earth, the few miserable square feet of this room . . . this stupid little town, this desert . . . was a sea, millions and millions of years ago. Dinosaurs wallowed here!" (83). That Noupoort and environs are nowadays an arid desert landscape and that the town, and in particular the Bontrug coloured area where Philander resides, is suffering from drought and a water shortage inflects the action of the play and provides a functionally important analogue for the two emotionally parched characters who thirst for (mental even more than physical) contact with one another.

Given South Africa's separation of the races and the assignment of group areas that are an aspect of that division, the contact between Frieda Joubert and Errol Philander, two intellectually and personally compatible people, is problematized. Under law, they may not, even as cordial, like-minded friends, know each other, let alone know each other in the carnal sense. And when they do transgress, they must do so clandestinely and in fear. They are, furthermore, hopelessly and tragically rooted in the "state-ments" or roles the state has scripted for them. This is seen almost immediately in Philander's joking comment that he has that day built a five-room house, and his subsequent anecdote about his talk with Izak Tobias, a preschool child building a structure in the sand. The incident, Philander's first full statement in the play and on the first page of the text, speaks volumes:

> On the way home I passed a little boy. . . . Izak Tobias . . . anyway Izak was playing there in the sand with some old bricks and things. I stopped and watched him. Building himself a house he said. Told me all about it. His mother and father and his baby brother sleep, in one room, and he and his sister and his granny in the other. Two rooms. It's the house he lives in. I know. I've been in it. It's a Bontrug house. [*Pause.*] You know what I made him do? Build a separate room for his granny. Then I explained that when his sister got big she would need a room for herself. So he built another one for her. When I left him he had a five-room house and a garage. . . . That's what it's all about, hey. . . . If you are going to dream, give yourself five rooms, hey. (81–82)

Implicit in the statement is the second-class life of Bontrug coloureds. Unlike privileged white children, Izak has no toy building blocks, only sand, stray building-

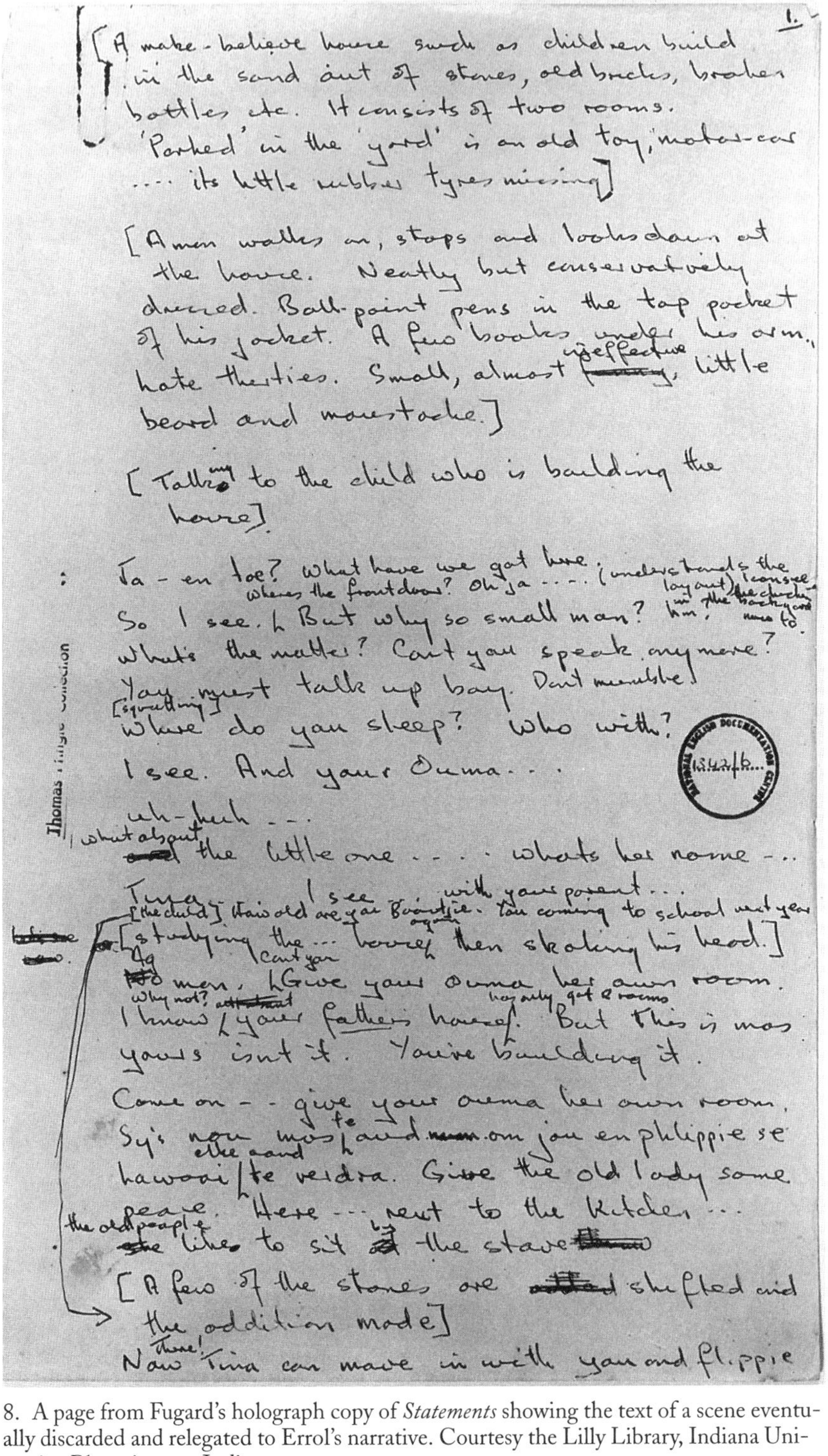
1.

[A make-believe house such as children build in the sand out of stones, old bricks, broken bottles etc. It consists of two rooms. 'Parked' in the 'yard' is an old toy motor-car .... its little rubber tyres missing]

[A man walks on, stops and looks down at the house. Neatly but conservatively dressed. Ball-point pens in the top pocket of his jacket. A few books under his arm. Late thirties. Small, almost ineffective little beard and moustache.]

[Talking to the child who is building the house]

Ja – en toe? What have we got here. (understands the layout) Where's the front door? Oh ja ....
So I see. But why so small man? hm.
What's the matter? Can't you speak anymore?
You must talk up boy. Don't mumble!
[squatting] Where do you sleep? Who with?
I see. And your Ouma...
uh-huh ...
what about the little one ... what's her name ..
Tina ... I see ... with your parent...
[the child] How old are you Boetie. You coming to school next year
[studying the ... house again then shaking his head.]
No man. Can't you give your Ouma her own room.
I know. Why not? your father's house. they only got 2 rooms. But this is mos yours isn't it. You're building it.
Come on -- give your ouma her own room.
Sy's nou mos te oud om jou en Flippie se kawaai te verdra. Give the old lady some peace. Here ... next to the kitchen ...
the old people like to sit by the stove
[A few of the stones are shifted and the addition made]
Now there! Tina can move in with you and Flippie

8. A page from Fugard's holograph copy of *Statements* showing the text of a scene eventually discarded and relegated to Errol's narrative. Courtesy the Lilly Library, Indiana University, Bloomington, Indiana.

site bricks, and whatever scraps he might find. He is building Boesman's *pondok* in miniature. Philander knows the Tobias house only too well, for it is the Bontrug norm, two rooms housing too many bodies and without either amenities or personal space. Earlier in the speech, an older brother, Henry, is mentioned, but there is no clear idea he has a set place to sleep. Because Philander is a school principal, his own home will likely be better, but not markedly better, than Izak's. An educator, Philander teaches young Izak to dream and to create a model for the future, a five-room house with garage that is essentially the modest norm for Noupoort's whites.

The evolution of the next generation must be fueled by this one's dreams. And Philander, who travels in darkness the dusty road from the Bontrug coloured area to the back door of the white library, a repository of knowledge to which he cannot be a subscriber or have legal entry, is also thereby tasting what is at once future possibility and present-tense forbidden fruit. In any case, both Izak constructing a white person's home and Philander entering the white library are indulging in transgressive dreams and pointing to the lines of demarcation separating their world from Frieda's.

Because of the "state-ments" of their world, Frieda and Errol do not meet as equals, and their relationship is necessarily inflected with archetypes of patriarchy. She lends *him* books, she admits him through the back door of *her* library, she offers him *her* water. And even their sexual meeting, their congress, had to be initiated by her, lest he, mistaking her body language, make an inappropriate sexual overture and be arrested for the worst of crimes, attempting to rape a white woman. In a curious way, then, the Immorality Act works to abrogate sexual mutuality, invading even their intimacy and tainting it with a grotesque replication of apartheid's textures of power and the archetypes of racism: assigning Frieda the white, masculine, dominant role and forcing Errol into a subaltern, feminine, passive one.

Philander pulls out all the money in his pocket, a meager forty-three cents. He is possibly the most educated man of any color in Noupoort, but forty-three cents is the extent of the fortune in his pocket. And when he fantasizes about what he would do if he had to manage with just that money, Frieda tells him to buy milk; but he responds, "No. When we're thirsty we drink cooldrink" (87). The "we" here makes clear his awareness of being in an othered group: *they* drink milk, *our* drinks of choice are sweet and carbonated. He calls himself and his identity group "*brak*," mongrel, the same word Boesman used for Lena's mixed-breed dog. And then he links up his own dreams of a day on forty-three cents to the coloured dreams he tries to generate in young Izak Tobias, "But if that one day also had a real chance to start again—you know, to make everything different—and forty-three cents would buy me even just the first brick for a five-roomed house . . . I'd spend it on that and go hungry" (89). What is impressive here is his desire for betterment, the way their sexual relations have enabled his postcoital candor, his ability to share his inmost dreams with a white woman, and his willingness to be vulnerable.

Each one of the pair shares remembrances and dreams, but these underline their different worlds. Dreams of the future are compromised by the water shortage of the present. And when Frieda offers to share with him some of *her* water, he replies sharply, "Thanks, but I'll go along with Bontrug." And here in a different key Fugard introduces the dilemmas of pride and survival, pride and shame he will explore in *Sizwe Bansi* and *The Island*. With shame, Sizwe Bansi will surrender his identity to become Robert Zwelinzima because it is a matter of survival. With shame, Winston will cross-dress as Antigone because playing that role is a matter of survival. In *Statements*, Errol cannot accept Frieda's generosity of the much-needed water because it is a gift bearing the distinct odor of white patriarchy and charity toward inferiors:

> MAN. The reason I don't want your water is just because Bontrug is thirsty.
>
> WOMAN. And that is not pride.
>
> MAN. No. Exactly the opposite. Shame. (91)

And that conflation of pride and shame is the snake in their garden, the irremediable flaw in their relationship. The aftermath of their apprehension just brings into the light the unbridgeable gap that has all along been both consciously and unconsciously suppressed and obscured by them in the darkness of their clandestine affair.

The first half of *Statements* is imbued with a postcoital natural closeness to which the rambling speeches and sharing of reminiscences and dreams provides a verbal background music. More important than the words we hear is the physical closeness we see only in shadow and the honesty between the two that is the affecting subtext of their words. They are, in far more than the mere physical sense, beautifully, pristinely naked to each other. If the actors can achieve it, then the audience will feel the dramatic tension of having on stage, as they are called in the speech lines of the text, MAN and WOMAN untrammeled by anything but their own physical and mental openness to one another; and yet at the same time unable to escape from the mundane definitions that render them forty-two-year-old white Frieda and thirty-six-year-old coloured and married Errol enacting racial and marital immorality. They are simultaneously innocent and united, yet separated by Errol's love for his family and by the strictures of apartheid law.

The closeness of the play's first half is suddenly and unexpectedly violated by the appearance of Detective Sergeant J. du Preez reading to the audience his *statement* concerning the apprehension of Errol and Frieda. With this move, the audience becomes directly implicated in the drama, and the tender, special world the man and the woman have created is rent asunder.[11] From the very first words of the Policeman's report, the man's and woman's place in the apartheid world is made manifest:

> Frieda Joubert. Ten, Conradie Street. European.
> Errol Philander. Bontrug Location. Coloured
> Charge: Immorality Act.

Joubert runs the library in town. Been living here for six years. Unmarried. No previous convictions.
Errol Philander is Principal of the location school. Born here. Wife and one child. No previous convictions. (94)

They devolve into lifeless data, into their addresses—she with a house and number, he with only "Bontrug Location"—racial classification, marital status, and police record. The statement the policeman reads, complete with the deposition of Mrs. Tienie Buys, the spying neighbor, is one about observed laboratory animals and bears only the most superficial relation to the two sentient humans the audience has witnessed on stage.

The report culminates in the six blinding, terrifying, quick-succession flashbulb photos taken of the couple. The suddenly and momentarily illuminated darkness presents Frieda and Errol in grotesque, dehumanized nakedness like frightened animals caught in the glare of headlights:

> *A sequence of camera flashes in the darkness exposes the man and the woman tearing apart from their embrace; the man then scrambling for his trousers, finding them, and trying to put them on; the woman, naked, crawling around on the floor, looking for the man. As she finds him, and tries to hide behind his back, the flashes stop and torches are shone on them.* (96)

The stage directions go on to explain that *"These 'flash-sequences' are nightmare excursions into the split second of exposure and must be approached as 'sub-text' rather than 'reality.'"* As Fugard asserts in his *Notebooks,* "I started to live with what I've always regarded as the central image in their story—those six terrible photographs of Joubert and Philander scrambling around in the dark; twenty seconds of Hell which start with them together and end with them irrevocably apart; the twenty seconds it takes to pass from an experience of life to an intimation of death. These photographs were, and remain for me, the essence of the experience I wanted to explore."[12] Furthermore, the torches that subsequently bear down upon the pair are like annihilating instruments of torture. And when Fugard's stage direction reads, *"This time, however, the torches trap the man against the wall . . ."* (100), it is quite possible that he has in mind the equally horrific moment when in Pinter's *The Birthday Party,* Goldberg and McCann use their torches as a weapon to pin a terrified Stanley against the wall.

The six photos reduce Errol and Frieda ironically to black-and-white stills; but more than that, they destroy all the two lovers have created. It is not too extravagant to say that the camera flashes are the energy of creative evolution and the six days of Creation inverted, for in his rehearsal notes for the original 1974 London production of *Statements,* Fugard pens the note, "One problem to understand and state dramatically the six photographs, what their ten seconds mean—the simplest and most primitive mystery, the reverse of the Act of creation." He also writes in his *Notebooks,* "Those few seconds—the experience between the first photograph and the last. Six seconds in which men destroy something only God could make."[13] What happens, too, is that the lovers' language begins to disintegrate. Frieda's *"first words are an almost incoherent babble"* (96), and her long narrative, and later his, an increasingly inchoate flow of words meant to explain their situation, as though they are two naughty schoolchildren caught out by the teacher.

More important, the audience will have difficulty focusing on the words, so overwhelmed will they be by the stage images of a nude Philander unable to get his trousers on, exposing himself, attempting to cover his genitals with his hat, taking the hat from his genitals to put it on his head and then to doff it for Frieda as a respectful coloured man might to a white madam. It is a terrifying mime that haunts the spectator long after the play is over. The high-minded world of an educator and a librarian gives way to a bizarre and terrible pornography produced not by Errol and Frieda but by the unseen police photographers acting on behalf of the state. Errol is, moreover, essentially emasculated, losing his manhood, sophistication, and virility; and reduced to performing an archetypal racial role: *"The man's 'performance' has now degenerated into a grotesque parody of the servile, cringing 'Coloured'"* (99). In a matter of a few sentences, he goes from "Miss Frieda Joubert," to "Miss Frieda," to "lady," to "Water, Miesies. Please, Miesies . . . water. . . . Just a little. . . . We're thirsty . . . please, Miesies . . ." (99). The coitus, an act of affirmation, that takes place just prior to the opening of the play is here replaced by humiliating negation. The feel of the second half of *Statements* is aptly characterized by Robert Baker-White as a kind of "dystopian, agonized montage."[14]

At the play's conclusion, the erstwhile partners in sexual union are "totally isolated" from one another. Both physically and spiritually, Frieda is externally and internally stripped of Errol: "My hands still have the sweat of your body on them, but I'll have to wash them. . . . In every corner of being myself there is a little of you left and now I must start to lose it" (105). And he is given the long disintegrative monologue that concludes the play. Like the final aria of a dying tenor, Errol's speech is the lyrical poetry of annihilation:

> If they take away your eyes you can't see.
> If they take away your tongue you can't taste.
> If they take away your hands you can't feel.
> If they take away your nose you can't smell.
> If they take away your ears you can't hear.
> I can see.
> I can taste.
> I can feel.
> I can smell.
> I can hear.
> I can't love. (105)

His five physical senses remain intact, but his sense of love has been eviscerated. He can't love: his ability to love has been taken away. He can't love: the state forbids it.

The state has unmade what God has made, and Errol ends the play with a cry of tragic defeat that leaves the audience with a moving realization of the destructive, dis-creative power of the Immorality Act and of the state that enforces it: "They can't interfere with God any more."

Athol Fugard is more than a playwright. He is a total theatre artist. He authors plays, but also directs them, acts in them, directs the work of other dramatists (e.g., Machiavelli, Brecht, Beckett), acts in plays and films by others (e.g., his memorable portrayal of General Smuts in the film *Gandhi*), forms theatre companies, discovers acting talents like Zakes Mokae and John Kani, and generally participates in nearly every avenue of theatre life. His theatre career has taken a number of turns due in part to his own growth as playwright and practitioner, due in part to politics. After his two early township plays, *No-Good Friday* and *Nongogo*, he was essentially banned from entering the black townships. This perhaps led to his writing two plays about whites—*Hello and Goodbye* and *People Are Living There*—and two plays about coloureds: *Blood Knot*, in which he and the black actor Zakes Mokae played two coloured brothers, and *Boesman and Lena*, in which he and Yvonne Bryceland played the coloured protagonists.

In 1963, when he returned to South Africa from the successful London run of *The Blood Knot*, Fugard and his family settled down in his home city, Port Elizabeth, where he soon was drawn to reconnect with the community in New Brighton, Port Elizabeth's black township. Norman Ntshinga, an actor and artist from New Brighton, visited the newly returned Fugard and made him "realize that he had lost touch with the realities of his country."[15] Together with Ntshinga, Fugard created a New Brighton acting company that called itself the Serpent Players and that soon performed a highly successful township version of Machiavelli's *La Mandragola*. One might speculate that the relationship Lena forges with the black Outa in *Boesman and Lena*, a play written while Fugard was co-founding and active with the Serpent Players, represents at one level Fugard's need to re-engage himself with the black township community. The Serpent Players gave him the chance to make that reconnection.

As a theatre practitioner and as an admirer of Grotowski's methods, Fugard began to develop ideas for plays through acting exercises with the Serpent Players and through the personal experiences his actors used as a basis for their performance of those exercises.[16] That the personal life of the actor should be important for Fugard is hardly strange for he is an artist whose own personal experiences and memories, as evidenced in *Notebooks* and *Cousins*, are almost always the seeds that burgeon into his dramas. Working with bright, able actors like John Kani and Winston Ntshona, Fugard was able, through their life-experience-based acting, to return to the world of the black townships from which he had been banned. The result was a dynamic combination that gave rise to two memorable plays: *Sizwe Bansi Is Dead* and *The Island*. Together with *Statements*, these plays form Fugard's most serious interpellation and condemnation of South Africa's apartheid laws. Fugard, Kani, and Ntshona workshopped the plays, produced them, and eventually set them down on paper. The combination was symbiotic and near perfect.[17] When asked by Michael Coveney in a 1973 interview whether it were possible to distinguish the separate contributions of the three creators of *Sizwe Bansi,* Fugard replied:

> Because I am the eldest and most professionally experienced I bring possibly an excess contribution to our work at the moment. I know something about what dramatic structure involves, and obviously I did a hell of a lot of actual writing. But I've not been allowed inside a black township in South Africa for many years, so I am very dependent on the two actors for a basic image, a vitality, an assertion of life.[18]

Each performance, moreover, left room for spontaneous innovations and changes.[19] The opening scene in which Styles reads newspaper headlines was one such spot at which improvisation helped keep the play au courant.[20]

But *Sizwe Bansi Is Dead* is not merely *based* on acting, it *is* about acting and about theatre. Influenced as he is by Brecht, Fugard never lets the audience forget that they are in the theatre, and the Brechtian *Verfremdungseffekt* is always at work. Indeed the Brechtian alienation and the metatheatrical style are among the contributions Fugard brings to bear upon material born of Kani's and Ntshona's personal lives.[21] The first twenty or thirty minutes (fourteen pages of text) is a monologue with the actor (Kani in the original performances) playing Styles taking on many roles and miming most of the action. Speaking directly to the audience, Styles makes it clear that they also have a role in the play, that the boundary between actors and spectators is being crossed. As he talks, for example, about the possible influence of China on South Africa, Styles "*Stops abruptly. Looks around as if someone might be eavesdropping on his intimacy with the audience*" and thereby makes the audience his allies against perhaps the Special Branch that might be listening to his potentially Communist comments.

As soon as the play opens and we have Styles reading aloud the newspaper headlines and commenting on the articles, we are impressed that we are in the presence of someone both literate and intelligent. As he narrates the anecdote, an actor's tour de force, about his antics on the day a member of the Ford family comes from the United States to inspect the Port Elizabeth Ford plant, we are amused by his ability to trick the doltish Afrikaner general foreman, and by his trilingual talents in English, Afrikaans, and Xhosa. But even more impressive is his ability to act out all the roles, white and black. Reminiscent of Douglas Turner Ward's comic play, *Day of Absence,* in which all the blacks in an American Southern town have disappeared but on stage all the white roles are played by black actors, *Sizwe Bansi* suggests that if blacks can play white roles convincingly on stage, they understand those roles and could easily, were the society a just one, take on those roles off stage, in real life.

In the course of the performed monologue about the Ford plant, a number of things become clear. First is Styles's recognition of a capitalist system, not merely in South Africa but everywhere, that creates classes and exploits subalterns. On stage, the lone actor playing Styles creates three players: himself, Baas Bradley, and the black factory workers (a role played by the audience). In the voice of Baas Bradley, we hear, "Say to them, Styles, that they must try to impress Mr. Henry Ford that they are better than those monkeys in his own country, those niggers in Harlem who know nothing but strike, strike." And turning to the audience as Ford workers, Styles translates: "'Gentlemen, he says we must remember, when Mr. Ford walks in, that we are South African monkeys, not American monkeys. South African monkeys are much better trained'" (7). And then when the limousines roll up with Mr. Ford and his entourage, Styles recognizes that the white plant managers are part of the same capitalist scheme as he: "The big doors opened; next thing the General Superintendent, Line Supervisor, General Foreman, Manager, Senior Manager, Managing Director . . . the bloody lot were there . . . like a pack of puppies! I looked and laughed! 'Yessus, Styles, they're all playing your part today!'" (8).

And with that last line and its theatrical image, it becomes clear that the scene is most importantly about acting and role-playing as a means for survival. In preparation for Mr. Ford's visit, the plant becomes a theatre and the managers dramatists and technicians. An artificial stage set is constructed as the dirty, unsafe plant is cleaned, painted with safety zone lines, and re-set into safe work areas. New costumes are provided for the workers, who suddenly are issued new, clean uniforms. The rhythm of the action is recast as the work line is slowed down. And a musical background is added that helps stage a picture of happy blacks singing *"Tshotsholoza"* as they work at a human pace, with new tools, and in clean clothes. But likewise, the white plant officials are also in their backstage dressing rooms brushing their hair, straightening their ties, and blacking their shoes. At the Ford Motor plant, as everywhere else in *Sizwe Bansi Is Dead,* all the world's a stage and the stage of the play is all the world.

Saying to himself, "Styles, you're a bloody, monkey, boy!" he realizes that under the system, he will remain eternally alienated, an indentured servant whose soul is owned by his employer: "Your life doesn't belong to you. You've sold it. . . . Selling most of [my] time on this earth to another man" (9). The important thing is not so much that he comes to this Brechtian anti-capitalist realization, but that he does so through observing the performance of the American capitalists, the white South African managers, and the workers on the day Mr. Ford visits Port Elizabeth. Seeing others playing their roles enables Styles to see his own situation clearly and with perspective. And this of course is for Fugard, as for any serious playwright, the very essence of theatre and the very reason for making theatre.

As an enlightened Styles resigns from Ford to become a self-employed businessman by opening a photography studio, *Sizwe Bansi*, like *Statements*, becomes a play dealing with a recurrent concern in Fugard's work: the meaning and power of photography. To obtain and then open his studio, Styles first travels a tortuous road paved with the red tape of bureaucracy, and then must act ruthlessly and pragmatically to rid himself of the cockroach colony infesting his studio. These comical anecdotes take on serious meaning as the play progresses and as they are shown to be symptomatic and characteristic of the black man's life in South Africa.

As in *Boesman and Lena,* a non-white life is a dehumanizing journey from farm to farm, employer to employer, town to town, bureaucracy to bureaucracy, whose only end is death. Likewise, the only chance for black survival is to put aside sentimentality, religion, and pride in favor of pragmatism. Styles may be an ailurophobe, but he must accept Blackie the cat if he wants his cockroaches destroyed. As Brecht's Macheath preaches, "*Erst kommt das Fressen, dann kommt die Moral,*" morals are a luxury available only after the essentials of life have been secured. And this will be the lesson learned as well by a Sizwe Bansi who pragmatically if reluctantly accepts the identity of Robert Zwelinzima in order to survive.

In *Statements after an Arrest under the Immorality Act,* written shortly after *Sizwe Bansi,* Fugard uses the idea of police photography as an invasion of personal privacy and as a way of destroying and "stilling" the dynamic of a relationship by reducing it to pornographic black-and-white still photos. In *Sizwe Bansi* the connection between photography and life is explored on a different level. Photos, as Styles explains in his continuing monologue, can be the record of the poor, the non-literate, the necessarily nomadic South African blacks. Given the wandering, unstable lives of Africans, in many cases photos will be their cherished possessions, the only record they have of family history, the only remembrance of parents, siblings, relatives, ancestors. Photos can also be posed in such a way that the subject can stage in them the life or attitude he or she might dream of having. In a central speech, Styles, looking around his photo studio, makes all this clear to the audience:

> This is a strong room of dreams. The dreamers? My people. The simple people, who you never find mentioned in the history books, who never get statues erected to them, or monuments commemorating their great deeds. People who would be forgotten, and their dreams with them, if it wasn't for Styles. That's what I do, friends. Put down, in my way, on paper the dreams and hopes of my people so that even their children's children will remember a man . . . "This was our Grandfather" . . . and say his name. Walk into the houses of New Brighton and on the walls you'll find hanging the story of the people the writers of the big books forget about. (12–13)

Clearly, this description of the photographer's craft holds as well for playwriting as Fugard sees it.[22] Like Styles's photos, Athol Fugard's plays witness the life and dreams of "the people the writers of the big books forget about." The episodes of *Sizwe Bansi* are like photo album snapshots illustrating the days in South Africa under the pass laws and recording the lives of those who suffered under those laws.[23] In a sense, then, *Sizwe Bansi* is part of a subversive historiography to remember the lives of the "others" who have been written out of the histories produced by white historians. Moreover, in his role as photographer/historiographer, Styles arranges and directs those who have come for a sitting much as the playwright and director stage-manage their actors.

Ntshona and Kani, who himself worked in the Port Elizabeth Ford plant, bring

Styles' Photographic Studio.
Positioned prominently ~~the book~~, the name-board:
"Styles Photographic studios. Reference books;
Passports; Weddings; Engagements; Birthday
Parties and Parties.
→ Prop — Styles."

Centre stage a table, with a ~~[crossed out]~~ colourful table cloth,
and a chair. Obviously a setting.
for photographs. Camera on a
tripod stands ready a short
distance away.

Another table, or desk, with ~~[crossed out]~~ odds and ends
of photographic equipment and ~~[crossed out]~~
'props' for photos.
[Underneath it a display of photographs of
various sizes.]

the Setting for this and subsequent scenes
should be as simple as possible so that
~~action can be continuous~~ ~~to facilitate the rapid changes necessary.~~

Styles walk on with a newspaper. Dapper, alert
young man, wearing a white dust-coat and
bow tie. Sits down at the table and
starts to read the paper.

9. Fugard's holograph directions for the first production of *Sizwe Bansi Is Dead.* Courtesy the Lilly Library, Indiana University, Bloomington, Indiana.

their own lives into the dramatic art they create. So, too, does Styles bring his life into the creation of his photographic art.[24] "You must understand one thing," he explains to the audience. "We own nothing except ourselves. The world and its laws, allows us nothing, except ourselves. There is nothing we can leave behind when we die, except the memory of ourselves. I know what I'm talking about, friends—I had a father, and he died." His father, he relates, served during World

War II in Tobruk and in Egypt, but after the war was stripped of his uniform, "the dignity they'd allowed him for a few mad years," and left no better off than he was before. What remains is only one photograph Styles found "in a rotten old suitcase" after his father died (16–17). That photograph is clearly what prompts Styles to be a photographer and historiographer of his people.

By using the tools of the theatre to cast the audience as black brothers and fellow sufferers of the principal characters, *Sizwe Bansi Is Dead* forcefully conveys the terrible effects of South African pass laws and the establishment of black so-called homelands. The strategy of the playwriting is such that no one can leave the theatre without knowing something of what it means to have a black skin in South Africa. As Kani and Ntshona are Fugard's conduit to the townships, so are they also the audience's.

In the Chinese box arrangement of the play, Styles tells the audience about the day Sizwe Bansi came to his studio for a photograph to send his wife, Nowetu. As principal actor in the semiotic message his smiling snapshot will convey, Sizwe Bansi, while posing for Styles, creates in his mind and for the audience the letter he will send Nowetu about his bizarre adventures in Port Elizabeth and New Brighton. What follows is a special Eastern Cape version of the "Jim goes to Jo'burg" archetype, which presents the young black man who leaves his native village to seek work in the Johannesburg mines, where he finds adventures and misadventures awaiting him. "There are so many men, Nowetu, who have left their places because they are dry and have come here to find work," Sizwe writes. But as Sizwe Bansi's story continues, the audience comes to realize that his version of a picaresque narrative lacks the upward mobility of Lazarillo's, Fielding's, Eichendorff's, or Twain's white Eurocentric picaros. For the black picaro, the journey just plods on, without social or economic rise, from Dorman Long to Kilomet Engineering to Anderson Hardware to Feltex.

On one level, *Sizwe Bansi* is about the meaningless journeys of blacks in a white-dominated society that has created the passbook to ensure that black lives are completely subject to white whims and dominated by white rules. With the substitution of *whites'* for *stars'*, Bosola's famous lines in *The Duchess of Malfi* seem remarkably appropriate: "We are merely the stars' tennis-balls, struck and bandied / Which way please them." Such seemed the philosophy guiding the South African government during the apartheid era, when it created independent homelands for Africans, carving out what were often the most infertile parts of the land and saying these are now independent black nations. Citizens of those homelands could then obtain a native identity number and enter South Africa as guest workers. In their passbooks (or *dompas*, dumb passes, as they were facetiously known) were stamped work permits and permission to remain in a particular place in South Africa if they had obtained a job.

In *Sizwe Bansi*, the title character has had his work permit revoked, as he explains to his friend Buntu, a role the actor playing Styles now takes over. Worldly wise and consequently cynical, Buntu explains that for blacks the record card in your pass is essentially your biography: "Your whole bloody life is written down on that" (24). He also explains the pointless bureaucratic journeys enforced on the Jims who come not only to Jo'burg but, like Sizwe, from King William's Town to Port Elizabeth:

> You talk to the white man, you see, and ask him to write a letter saying he's got a job for you. You take that letter from the white man and go back to King William's Town, where you show it to the Native Commissioner there. The Native Commissioner in King William's Town reads that letter from the white man in Port Elizabeth who is ready to give you the job. He then writes a letter back to the Native Commissioner in Port Elizabeth. So you come back here with the two letters. Then the Native Commissioner in Port Elizabeth reads the letter from the Native Commissioner in King William's Town together with the first letter from the white man who is prepared to give you a job, and he says when he reads the letters: Ah yes, this man Sizwe Bansi can get a job. So the Native Commissioner in Port Elizabeth then writes a letter which you take with the letters from the Native Commissioner in King William's Town and the white man in Port Elizabeth, to the Senior Officer at the Labour Bureau, who reads all the letters. Then he will put the right stamp in your book and give you another letter from himself which together with the letters from the white man and the two Native Affairs Commissioners, you take to the Administration Office here in New Brighton and make an application for Residence Permit, so that you don't fall victim of raids again. Simple. (25–26)

This farcical speech is meant to be enormously funny in the theatre, but it generates a laughter that is strongly edged by the knowledge that such is the common stupid *dompas* experience that Africans face daily and all their lives. And the irony of all the letters is heightened by the fact that the black men like Sizwe who must bear these letters from pillar to post have never been taught to read.

The laughter-inducing presentation of black existence as farce prepares the way for the play's moving and poignant analogous anecdote, which is meant to moisten the audience's eyes with tears and bring home the reality of black existence in its tragic dimension. Buntu tells the story of the lay preacher's eulogy at the graveside of old Outa Jacob, who had lived his life traveling from farm to farm in search of work. Starting with Adam, the preacher says, Man's only faithful companion is Death, but before giving himself over to Death, Outa Jacob "worked on farms from this district down to the coast and north as far as Pretoria." How Outa Jacob was buffeted from place to place is described with as much pathos as Sizwe's projected journey from government office to government office is rendered comic; and the preacher concludes:

> So it went friends. On and on . . . until he arrived there. [*The grave at his feet.*] Now at last it's over. No matter how hard-arsed the boer on this farm wants to be, he cannot move Outa Jacob. He has reached Home. [*Pause*] That's it,

brother. The only time we'll find peace is when they dig a hole for us and press our face into the earth. (28)

An existential homily, the preacher's words bring home the inevitability of death and tacitly endorse the pragmatic actions people must take to make the best of their lives and to survive. Thus the comic pragmatism of Styles's elimination of his roaches and the serious pragmatism of the passbook and name exchange that will follow are provided a philosophical context.

Always addressing the audience directly and making sure thereby that each person in the playhouse is on stage, *Sizwe Bansi* adroitly universalizes its action and ideas. This universalization is suggested as well by the allegorical tinge of the characters' names. In Xhosa, "*sizwe*" means nation and "*banzi*" broad or wide; thus "*sizwe banzi*" connotes the black nation as a whole. "*Buntu*" means humankind. Though the allegory is not that of a heavy-handed medieval morality play or that of a 1960s and '70s African American agitprop, *Sizwe Bansi* nevertheless speaks forcefully about the indignity of passbooks and their signification as the record of the demoralized lives led by blacks in South Africa.[25] With Buntu holding the passbook, Sizwe Bansi turns to the audience and plaintively exclaims, "They never told us it would be like that when they introduced it. They said: Book of Life! Your friend! You'll never get lost! They told us lies" (33). The "they," of course, are the faceless whites, the powerful and oppressive "they" who never make an appearance on stage but are the play's powerful antagonists, all the more imposing for not being embodied by visible characters.

And the lie of the passbook is replicated in the lie of the homelands, as even the unsophisticated Sizwe knows too well from firsthand experience. Addressing the audience, he says, "I must tell you, friend . . . when a car passes or the wind blows up the dust, Ciskeian Independence makes you cough. I'm telling you, friend . . . put a man in a pondok and call that Independence? My good friend, let me tell you . . . Ciskeian Independence is shit!" (31).[26] And Buntu points out the reality of the Single Men's Quarters, the housing for those who have left the starvation existence of Ciskeian independence for another form of indignity in the city: "You know what Single Men's Quarters is? Big bloody concentration camp with rows of things that look like train carriages. Six doors to each! Twelve people behind each door!" (34). The reality that emerges all too pellucidly is that whether in rural Ciskei or urban Port Elizabeth, whether bounced from farm to farm or from industrial complex to industrial complex, the life of blacks in South Africa is a pointless, demeaning, dehumanizing wandering whose only terminus is death.

In what is perhaps the play's most dramatically moving and effective moment, Sizwe, recognizing the full meaning of the passbook, homelands, and the concentration camp men's quarters, turns to the audience and, like King Lear's "Off, off, you lendings," rips off his clothes and cries out his pained interrogatives:

What's happening in this world, good people? Who cares for who in this world? Who wants who?

Who wants me, friend? What's wrong with me? I'm a man. I've got eyes to see. I've got ears to listen when people talk. I've got a head to think good things. What's wrong with me? [*Starts to tear off his clothes.*]

Look at me! I'm a man. I've got legs. I can run with a wheelbarrow full of cement! I'm strong! I'm a man. (35)

Naked and holding his genitals, Sizwe is "bare, unaccommodated man" asking himself and the audience basic questions of human existence. And the play implicitly confronts the audience with its own further accusatory question: How can this naked man be re-dressed and redressed?

Though not redressed, Sizwe becomes re-dressed in the play's simultaneously comic and tragic conclusion. Buntu goes to urinate in an alleyway and does so on what he first believes is "a pile of rubbish" and then realizes that he has relieved himself on a dead body. That a black corpse and a pile of rubbish are indistinguishable is another sad irony of South African township life. But Buntu's becomes a comically magical micturition restoring a dead soul to life because the deceased's clothing contains his valid passbook with native identification number and work permit: "*Haai!* Look at him [*the photograph in the book, reading*]. 'Robert Zwelinzima. Tribe: Xhosa. Native identification Number. . . .'" (33). To survive, Sizwe Bansi, under the supervision of comic shaman Buntu, must die and be reborn Robert Zwelinzima. The ghost of Robert Zwelinzima can inhabit the body of Sizwe Bansi because a passbook photo, that icon of a man's history and dreams produced in Styles's studio, can be removed and exchanged for another. And the reason it can be done is that for the white man, not only do all blacks look alike, they are faceless commodities, not individuals. When Sizwe Bansi balks at losing his name and asks, "How do I live as another man's ghost?" Buntu answers him with the play's tragic pragmatist wisdom:

Wasn't Sizwe Bansi a ghost?. . . . When the white man looked at you at the Labour Bureau what did he see? A man with dignity or a bloody passbook with an N.I. number? Isn't that a ghost? When the white man sees you walk down the street and calls out, "Hey, John! Come here" . . . to you, *Sizwe Bansi* . . . isn't that a ghost? Or when his child calls you "Boy" . . . you a man, circumcised with a wife and four children . . . isn't that a ghost? Stop fooling yourself. All I'm saying is be a real ghost, if that is what they want, what they've turned us into. Spook them into hell, man! (38)

The sad reality, however, is that Sizwe's exchange of identity can only be a stopgap measure because he will be caught out by the authorities if he gets into trouble and his fingerprints are checked. The tragically wise Sizwe knows: "A black man stay out of trouble? Impossible, Buntu. Our skin is trouble" (43). For the moment at least, Buntu's magic will work. As the play reverts to Styles's studio, a final snapshot of Sizwe Bansi alias Robert Zwelinzima is taken, and Robert/Sizwe can smile the smile of a man whose passbook is at least temporarily in order.

The truth of Sizwe Bansi's statement that it is impossible for a black man to stay out of trouble is immediately apparent in Fugard's next piece, *The Island* (1973), which he also created together with Winston Ntshona and John Kani.[27] *The Island* opened in June 1973 at the Space Theatre in Cape Town. As John Kani explained in an interview:

> Then it could not be called *The Island,* because the authorities would have known we were talking about Robben Island. So we decided to call it *The Hodoshe Span.* The Hodoshe means the green carrion fly. My brother spent five years on Robben Island, and there was an infamous warder who was re-ferred to as "the fly that brings death." He was so surgical in his procedures. He broke every person. You never survived Hodoshe.[28]

Like *Sizwe Bansi, The Island* had its origin in acting exercises. These seem to be-gin, as Fugard's *Notebooks* affirm, in the form of an image that grows in his con-sciousness and is then transmitted to the actors with whom he works so intimately. Such was presumably the genesis of *The Island.*[29] Fugard has explained:

> My work with the actors during one stage of the rehearsals is for both re-hearsing and improvising. With *The Island,* when I got together with John Kani and Winston Ntshona, I always came prepared with questions, ideas, provocations. This would set them up; they are both consummate personal storytellers who love acting out their lives. I fed them a constant stream of provocations relating to the idea on which we had decided.[30]

Kani has described the process more fully:

> Fugard, Winston Ntshona and myself had actually begun a process in the sixties which we called an Experiment in Play-Making, where together we would find, through trial and error, a subject that we wanted to deal with or to talk about. And then we as actors would improvise situations in the inves-tigation or exploration of the subject. And Athol would be making notes of what had happened, and at the end of the day we would discuss it. And then take it up again and try to move the story . . . it began actually by the imita-tion of space, and identifying that limited space as being that particular prison cell on Robben Island.[31]

The Island is indeed an actor's play, for acting is its central metaphor and idea: act-ing as a means for the acting out of one's life, acting as a form of survival, and act-ing as a basis for (political) *action.* As Robert Layshon, who directed a production of *The Island* in Barbados, has written, "there are very few plays which collapse the boundary between actor and character more thoroughly or more poignantly."[32]

In print, *The Island* is a short text of some thirty pages, and has been frequently presented as a double bill with *Sizwe Bansi Is Dead.* It should, however, probably best be presented alone, for its extended physical actions give it breadth and length, and the intensity of its seemingly simple complex structure gives it depth. In *The Island*, two black prisoners, John and Winston, are men whose political stands against the state have caused them to be incarcerated, sentenced without determinable end in South Africa's infamous Robben Island prison off the coast of Cape Town. There, as one commentator has noted, they are dressed in shorts "to look like the boys their keepers would make them."[33] But clearly the authorities wish them to be far, far less than boys, for the prisoners are treated with extreme brutality and are given the sorts of tasks meant to reduce them from men to beasts, to annihilate the last shreds of their humanity. Their humanity, however, remains intact, even flowers amid a situation designed to be death in life or living death.[34] And it does so because the two men continue to act as humans by using dramatic acting as the means for sustaining their humanity. Improvisation—that tool through which an actor learns to understand and practice a role—becomes the means through which John and Winston understand and practice their humanity. Acting, moreover, becomes both shield and sword to the two prisoners: a means for self-protection, for protection of the Self, and a means for taking action or acting against their captors, against the state. Fugard thus asserts that acting is no idle art, no end in itself, but the very essence of life and of being human.

On the surface, *The Island* is concerned with John's plan that he and Winston enact the confrontation of Antigone and Creon at an evening of variety entertainment to be presented for the benefit of Robben Island prisoners and guards.[35] But that classical story shares the stage with another classical story, the myth of Sisyphus. Here as elsewhere, Fugard reveals his indebtedness not merely to ancient playwrights but to Albert Camus, whose essay *The Myth of Sisyphus* is as much at the heart of *The Island* as Sophocles' *Antigone*.[36]

Although *The Island* concludes with John and Winston's presentation of their *Antigone* play, it begins with a theatrical performance of another sort. Carefully orchestrating the opening action of the play, Fugard turns the playhouse into a prison, thereby giving the audience their own brief but painful taste of what it must be like to be incarcerated on Robben Island. As the audience come into the theatre, John and Winston are already on stage asleep on the floor of their cell. There are no beds on Robben Island. A single shared blanket and bucket of water with a tin drinking cup for each prisoner are at once the extent of the stage props and the extent of what prisoners in Robben Island cells are permitted as possessions. Indeed, it is from these meager belongings that the two men—and Fugard—will fashion a play in this penal metatheatre. When the audience has been seated, a siren suddenly goes off, stage lights come on, and the two men arise dressed in shorts and showing shaven heads. At this point, an extended, excruciating, seemingly endless mime commences lasting about ten painful minutes during which the two prisoners engage in a Sisyphean labor of pointlessly digging sand at one end of the stage, filling a wheelbarrow with it, pushing the wheelbarrow to the other end of the stage, and emptying the sand. The stage directions make a point of saying, "*Their labour is interminable*" (47). The essence of *The Island* is contained between its Sisyphean beginning and its Sophoclean end, and it is concerned with the way in which the plight of Sisyphus can be connected with and transformed into the power of Antigone.

That exhausting, pointless mime serves as the play's warm-up exercise, conditioning the audience to feel the dehumanizing patterns of life in a South African prison. Ten minutes is a very long time in a theatre. And ten minutes of watching two men wordlessly cart sand from one end of the stage to the other is an eternity, especially when the audience cannot see a reason for the monotonous action. But that is the very point! The audience's restiveness and their failure to understand why actions are taking place or punishments inflicted make the theatre a microcosm of the prison world. "What am I doing here? What does all this mean?" runs through the minds of the spectators—and then they realize these are the thoughts of the prisoners who must endure the monotony and pointlessness (not to mention the physical abuse) not for ten minutes but for years without end. The audience at least knows the play will end and they will be free to leave the theatre, whereas the prisoners have no inkling of when their sentences will be over or if indeed they will ever be over.

The opening actions of *The Island* provide a painful, moving dumb show from which the drama that follows can be built. The extended mime of John and Winston's Sisyphean labors with wheelbarrow and sand brings home to the theatre audience with unusual immediacy and effectiveness the dehumanizing, pointless tedium of life on Robben Island. With the blast of a second whistle, the transfer of sand concludes and a new mime commences. This time John and Winston are handcuffed, joined at the ankles, and forced to run in tandem. Brilliantly, Fugard portrays the subhuman race with the stage directions, "*They start to run . . . John mumbling a prayer, Winston muttering a rhythm for their three-legged run*" (47). With dramatic concision, perhaps learned from Beckett, Fugard indicates how the tedium, animal degradation, and torture affect the two prisoners. Rather than reducing them to despair or turning them into tortured animals, it serves to evoke the very things that raise men above bestiality: a reliance upon the spirit, manifested in John's prayer, and a reliance upon reason, manifested in Winston's creating a rhythm so that the two men may with dignity run in unison.

At the same time, the members of the audience are rendered voyeurs, either vicariously suffering with the two prisoners or sadistically enjoying their labors, or perhaps some paradoxical combination of the two.[37] It is important, moreover, that the punishing action of the two mimes be hard physical labor for the two actors, who earn real sweat and pain. In their short traffic on stage, the actors are meant not merely to enact but to undergo what hundreds of men were undergoing every day of their lives in South African prisons. For the two actors, then, *The Island* is not merely about making theatre: every performance is an almost religious act of tribute to and remembrance for their brothers incarcerated in the lonely prison house islands throughout the land.

Finally, after the men are beaten and returned wounded to their cell, the dumb show gives way first to inchoate sounds and then to words of rage and pain. Nev-

10. John Kani and Winston Ntshona in *The Island*, Market Theatre, Johannesburg, revival 1986. Photo by Ruphin Coudyzer.

ertheless, the situation in all its physicality creates moving words and stage images of spiritual strength. Winston's pain causes John to act, to urinate and use his urine as an antiseptic to wash Winston's wounded eye. And with the consciously chosen terminology of the theatre, Fugard indicates, "*In a reversal of earlier roles Winston now gets John down on the floor so as to examine the injured ear*" (48). As the two men thus act to assuage each other's bodily injuries, Winston exclaims, "*Nyana we Sizwe*" ("brother of the land"), affirming the power of brotherhood and the indomitability of the two men's human spirit.

Later in his career—in *A Lesson from Aloes, Master Harold,* and *Playland*—Fugard will explore the ways in which the South African apartheid system is equally, perhaps even more, damaging to the psyches of whites than it is to those of coloureds and blacks. *The Island,* likewise and with great intensity, shows the backfiring of a system that wishes to rob John and Winston of their humanity by reducing them to beasts.[38] To show this, Fugard has John and Winston appear on stage constantly affirming their brotherhood. Their white guard, by contrast, is unseen. Only his irritating noises and the sting of his blows are heard. The guard is named Hodoshe (green carrion fly), and like Ben Jonson's Mosca, whose name also means flesh fly, it is the white Hodoshe who is reduced by Fugard to a character in a mean-spirited beast fable.[39] John and Winston remain triumphantly human.

Hodoshe exemplifies the prison guards whose humanity devolves into animal behavior, whereas the prisoners, Winston and John, create their humanity out of the very bestiality that has been forced on them. Their guards hail down beatings and wounds upon them; their human fastidiousness had been consciously taken from them when they were transported from Port Elizabeth to Cape Town and Robben Island (a journey of 770 kilometers, almost 480 miles) by vans, in which they were crammed and shackled to each other like animals, unable to refrain from urinating on one another as they traveled. And yet it is their care for one another's wounds that brings forth and italicizes John's and Winston's humanity, and nowhere more poignantly than when Fugard's stage direction reads, *"John urinates into one hand and tries to clean the other man's [wounded] eye with it."* The mimed stage action brilliantly portrays the transilience of inhumanity and animal function into human caring, of Sisyphus's punishment transformed into Antigone's triumph. Brilliantly, Fugard allows the very urine, the bodily function with which the oppressive powers sought to compromise the humanity of the prisoners, to become the medium for the survival of their spirit. Such triumphant humanity rising from the depths of degradation is reminiscent of the spirit that survived in Nazi concentration camps, an analogy not lost on Fugard, as his notebooks make clear.[40]

Like Fugard, Kani, and Ntshona—the devisers of *The Island*—the prisoners are not merely actors but playwrights. They forge drama, an art that is an affirmation of their humanity. And they fashion it from the basic artifacts of their prison life and from the basic resources of their imaginations. Using a few rusty nails and some string, John devises Antigone's necklace; with a precious piece of chalk he has hidden away, he lays out on the cell floor the plot of the *Antigone* skit he has created. In like manner, the two prisoners have in the past produced recreations, have recreated their spirits by taking each other to the movie theatre, creating cinema without film or screen but through the combined projections of their imaginations, narrations, and physical gestures. And in the course of the first scene, they reach out from the isolation of their island prison in Table Bay off the Cape Town shore to friends and family in Port Elizabeth. They do so by using an empty prison tin cup imaginatively transformed into a telephone receiver and employing the power of fictive imagination, rhetoric, and gesture to create a two-sided conversation (fig. 11). Through acting, in short, comes their survival. And clearly, for Fugard *acting* in the sense of making theatre and *acting* in the sense of making a commitment are two sides of the same coin.

When Winston and John begin to rehearse their *Antigone,* Fugard reveals his master's touch as a dramatist. Winston appears dressed in false wig, false breasts, and necklace, all wrought from the scraps the two prisoners have been able to find and squirrel away in their restricted, repressive, bare-essentials penal environment. Winston in his makeshift Antigone drag is ludicrous not only for John but for the audience, both of whom laugh freely at the grotesque, risible sight. But Fugard and John both know that once the audience has had its laugh at the comic figure Winston cuts, the joke will be over and they can move beyond their laughter to perceive

11. John Kani and Winston Ntshona in *The Island,* Market Theatre, Johannesburg, revival 1995. Photo by Ruphin Coudyzer.

the tragic classical Antigone, no longer a comical "drag" Winston; and to take the meaning of Antigone and *Antigone* seriously:

> This is preparation for stage fright! I know those bastards out there. When you get in front of them, sure they'll laugh . . . Nyah, nyah! . . . they'll laugh. But just remember this brother, nobody laughs forever! There'll come a time when they'll stop laughing, and that will be the time when our Antigone hits them with her words. . . . You think those bastards out there won't know it's you? Yes, they'll laugh. But who cares about that as long as they laugh in the beginning and listen at the end. That's all we want them to do . . . listen at the end! (61, 62)

What Winston does not at this point in the play realize is that the story of Antigone and his own story are congruent. He complains, ". . . this Antigone is a bloody . . . what do you call it . . . legend! A Greek one at that. Bloody thing never happened. Not even history! Look, brother, I got no time for bullshit. Fuck legends. Me? . . . I live my life here! I know why I'm here, and it's history, not legends. I had my chat with a magistrate in Cradock and now I'm here. Your Antigone is a child's play, man" (62). The audience, however, begins to realize that John and Athol Fugard have chosen the Antigone story because it is a legend that embodies the history of protest, and Winston's life is thus history and legend in one. And as he ruminates about his imprisonment on Robben Island for having burned his passbook, the obvious parallelism of his defiance of the state and Antigone's is hidden from him but understood by the audience.

The Island forces its characters and its audiences to grow. At first it is only a simple play about incarceration and about time experienced, as Fugard says in his *Notebooks*, "as a loss of Life, as a Living Death. You are no more."[41] But, to evoke the absurdity of life on Robben Island, Fugard swings his play around, moving it from a depiction of imprisonment to a consideration of the meaning of freedom: measuring freedom against the absurdity of incarceration. When John suddenly learns that his case has been reviewed and that he will be freed in a matter of months, clock time—counting the months and weeks and days—returns to him, separating him from Winston, who has only the time without end of open-ended imprisonment.

For Winston, John's forthcoming release serves to underline the pointlessness, the absurdity of his own lot. With that, his spontaneous joy for his friend is transformed into temporary jealousy and hatred that he releases through a new kind of playwriting meant at once as a self-defense and as a pointed attack on John. Whereas John and Winston's earlier creative efforts had been devised for mutual entertainment or, as in the case of their imaginary telephone calls to Port Elizabeth, had permitted joint creativity, Winston now implies his divorce from John by creating a monologue, using the same subject matter as their telephone call, but taunting John with very graphic descriptions of relationships and events that will soon be but are not yet within his reach.

Acting out a dramatic monologue about John's freedom creates heuristic experiences on several levels for Winston. He is able to give vent to his envy and purge it; he is able to punish John for his good fortune, and he is able to recognize his own absurdity. And as he comes to terms with that absurdity he also senses for the first time its power. Here Fugard adeptly brings Camus' *The Myth of Sisyphus* directly to bear on *The Island,* and he does so without a heavy hand. After concluding his dramatic monologue, Winston sees an image of himself projected in old Harry, a seventy-year-old prisoner serving a life sentence and working in the quarries:

> When you go to the quarry tomorrow, take a good look at old Harry. Look into his eyes, John. Look at his hands. They've changed him. They've turned him into stone. Watch him work with that chisel and hammer. Twenty perfect blocks of stone every day. Nobody else can do it like him. He loves stone. That's why they're nice to him. He's forgotten himself. He's forgotten everything . . . why he's here, where he comes from. That's happening to me John. I've forgotten why I'm here. (71)

The picture of old Harry, like the opening stage picture of Winston and John with the sand and wheelbarrow, is a version of Camus' picture of Sisyphus: ". . . Sisyphus is the absurd hero. He *is* as much through his passions as through his torture. His scorn of the gods, his hatred of death, and his passion for life won him that unspeakable penalty in which the whole being is exerted toward accomplishing nothing."[42]

Yet Camus argues that Sisyphus, each time he descends from the heights to find his stone and his eternal torment, gains a special consciousness:

> At each of those moments when he leaves the heights and gradually sinks toward the lairs of the gods, he is superior to his fate. He is stronger than his rock. . . . [he] knows the whole extent of his wretched condition: it is what he thinks of during his descent. The lucidity that was to constitute his torture at the same time crowns his victory. (121)

Camus concludes his description of Sisyphus saying, "The struggle itself toward the heights is enough to fill a man's heart. One must imagine Sisyphus happy" (123).[43] Elsewhere in his essay, Camus addresses the question of freedom and absurdity. And what he says there is precisely what Fugard shows as Winston's situation:

> The only conception of freedom I can have is that of the prisoner or the individual in the midst of the State. The only one I know is freedom of thought and action. Now if the absurd cancels all my chances of eternal freedom, it restores and magnifies, on the other hand, my freedom of action. That privation of hope and future means an increase in man's availability. (56–57)

In short, Winston looks with fright at old Harry who, like Camus' Sisyphus, "loves stone," but after his drama is over, Winston, as Fugard's stage direction makes clear, reflects upon his fate and for the first time understands it: *"Winston almost seems to bend under the weight of the life stretching ahead of him on the Island. For a few seconds he lives in silence with his reality, then slowly straightens up. He turns and looks at John. When he speaks again, it is the voice of a man who has come to terms with his fate, massively compassionate"* (72). The result is the repeated exultation of brotherhood and a renewed commitment, *"Nyana we Sizwe!"*—brother of the land.

In the final scene of *The Island*, John and Winston present their *Antigone* play, but it is a presentation informed on the one hand by John's and now Winston's comprehension of the Antigone legend as an archetype of resistance, and on the other by their understanding of the Sisyphus legend in much the way that Camus understood it. And in his last scene, Fugard pulls out all his stops to create a coup de théâtre that is not an end in itself but a subversive means to enlightenment and political engagement. Brian Crow astutely writes, "[T]he ability to 'act,' to assume a new identity however temporarily, is here as in *Sizwe Bansi* a form of self-protection and a strategy for survival, allowing its exponent as well as its audience (the real one as well as the imagined prison audience) to achieve an understanding and a renewed commitment to struggle in spite of the horror of the situation."[44]

Barbara Harlow posits that "[p]rison writing, whether the literary works composed by detainees during their incarceration or the works because of which they are arrested in the first place, serves as a critical and sustaining link between the prisoners inside and those struggling outside the prison walls. Writing and communication, however, function just as significantly inside those walls in establishing and maintaining a solidarity amongst the prisoners."[45] A version of this occurs as John and Winston take the stage to provide the closing performance act for the prison entertainment. We see only John and Winston on stage playing to an audience of unseen prisoners and guards. Cleverly and subversively, however, Fugard stages the scene in such a way that we, the members of the actual theatre audience, are the ones addressed as though we were the audience of guards and prisoners. And thus the connection between the Antigone story and the story of apartheid in South Africa, between the stage and life, is made immediately and stunningly clear. John's address to the audience in his role of Presenter or Prologue is one filled with the irony of the dramatic situation Fugard has created. Thus John says to the theatre audience:

> Captain Prinsloo, Hodoshe, Warders, . . . and Gentlemen! Two brothers of the House of Labdacus found themselves on opposite sides in battle, the one defending the State, the other attacking it. They both died on the battlefield . . . But Antigone, their sister, defied the law and buried the body of her brother Polynices. She was caught and arrested. That is why tonight the Hodoshe Span, Cell Forty-two, presents for your entertainment: "The Trial and Punishment of Antigone." (73)

The pause indicated in the text of the first sentence—"Captain Prinsloo, Hodoshe, Warders, . . . and Gentlemen!"—pointedly endows the prisoners with gentility while separating them from the officials of oppressive state power. Furthermore, using the word "arrested" to describe Antigone's situation raises the specter of the modern polity, and in particular the South African state. It is a word that succinctly captures the bond between the ancient Antigone legend and the events of contemporary history, fixing the Antigone story as a symbol for John and Winston's plight as well as for all who protest and resist in South Africa. This is nicely and pointedly italicized when after his exposition of Antigone's actions and subsequent arrest, John states that "*that is why*" they are presenting their play.

The conflation of ancient and contemporary, of Greek legend and the apartheid state, continues as Creon becomes the symbol for the state as well as for compliant blacks: "Creon's crown is as simple, and I hope as clean, as the apron Nanny wears. And even as Nanny smiles and is your happy servant because she sees her charge . . . your child! . . . waxing fat in that little cradle, so too does Creon—your obedient servant!—stand here and smile" (73). Creon, moreover, upholds the letter of the law of the state, as he does in Sophocles' play. Antigone upholds a higher law, but relates the issue at once to the dilemma in Sophocles as well as to that in South Africa by declaiming, "What lay on the battlefield waiting for Hodoshe to turn rotten, belonged to God. You are only a man, Creon. Even as there are laws made by

12. John Kani and Winston Ntshona in *The Island*, Market Theatre, Johannesburg, revival 1995. Photo by Ruphin Coudyzer.

men, so too there are others that come from God" (75). Antigone's defiance of the laws of the Greek state justifies the defiance of the passbook and apartheid laws of the South African state.

Antigone, like Sisyphus and like the Robben Island prisoners, knows the consequences of her deeds, knows that her defiance will cause her to be immured; but she thereby comes to know an existential, happy transcendence over tragedy. Winston playing Antigone can say to Creon, "Your threat is nothing to me" (76).

John and Winston take the Antigone story only as far as her trial (fig. 12). But with the words, "You will not sleep peacefully, Creon" (76), Winston hints at the remainder of Creon's story for Fugard's audience. As a result of his unjust treatment of Antigone, Creon's own son, Haemon, and Creon's wife, Eurydice, die; and at the close of Sophocles' drama, it is Creon who loses power and is reduced to nothingness:

> This is my guilt, all mine. I killed you, I say it clear.
> Servants, take me away, out of the sight of men.
> I who am nothing more than nothing now.[46]

The tragic nothingness awaiting the inflexible upholders of the state's laws in South Africa is obviously foreshadowed.

As Winston's Antigone leaves to be immured, she goes not to the tomb of the ancient story but to an all too familiar South African fate. Creon exclaims, "Take her from where she stands, straight to the Island! There wall her up in a cell for life, with just enough food to acquit ourselves of the taint of her blood" (77). And Antigone acknowledges that on the Island she will, like the other prisoners there, "be lost between life and death." Having said this, however, Winston moves beyond Antigone's tragedy, stepping out of his costume passionately to assert his own renewed defiance and to reaffirm his absurdity as he returns, like Antigone, to his cell and to the pointless existence he must bear for having had the courage to honor a law of mankind higher than South African civil law.

In forging the connections between ancient myths and modern history, Fugard relates the plights of Sisyphus and Antigone to those of prisoners on Robben Island. As John and Winston play Creon and Antigone, they feel the immediacy of the Greek legend. But *The Island* has another dimension, a dimension that is present at the beginning with John and Winston's names and present as well at the conclusion as the theatre audience becomes the prison audience. Fugard's actors and co-dramatists, John Kani and Winston Ntshona, themselves black South Africans, pointedly retain their own first names in *The Island,* indicating that this play in which they act—like *Antigone,* the play in which the two prisoners John and Winston act—is a metaphor. The Island is not merely Robben Island but South Africa itself, an absurd prison with absurd rules enforced by absurd officials. South Africa's citizens, be they non-white or white, are as much immured and imprisoned as either the heroine in Sophocles' play or the prisoners in Fugard's.[47]

Fugard's wife, Sheila, sheds some light on *The Island* in her poem "Robben Island":

> Seas sudden to the eye
> deliver the Island to history
> Memoirs form sandbanks
>   waves mesmerize
> The Island holds these prisoners
>   stalking the water
> Never a Christ walking
>   but as sable foxes
> Running the gauntlet of the ocean
>   learning none belong
> Neither lepers housed
>   a crucifixion of years ago
> Nor these banished counting
>   the eyes of the sea
> Stark Penelope dumbfounded
>   repeat no decade frees
> Nor lifts Afrika from the stake
>   only an Island claims
> There is no mistake[48]

The physical shape of the poem on the page brings to mind the ebb and flow of the ocean waters that separate Robben Island from the usually visible Cape Town beaches. The shape and content of "Robben Island" also combine to evoke the psychological ebb and flow, the alternate feelings of hope and despair experienced by Robben Island's inmates so clearly evident in *The Island.* Sheila Fugard's poem, moreover, shares with her husband's play the sense that the situation of the South African penal institution can be understood in terms of powerful events related in classical and biblical texts. Finally, the poem registers the solipsism of South Africa, which stands alone among nations arrogantly assured of the rightness of its policies. South Africa is also an island, and Robben Island Prison thus just a cameo replication of life in South Africa. This is a validation of John Bender's postulation that "[t]he penitentiary suspends the offender within a tightly specified topography of spectatorship which reproduces, as physical practice, an invisible masterplot that structures mental life in metropolitan society. . . . its rules are one and the same as those that govern consciousness itself."[49] In short, *The Island* is a synoptic view of Robben Island and other South African prisons, which are themselves a curiously synoptic replication of South African existence.

What *The Island* was at its initial performances is no longer what it is in post-apartheid South Africa. At the 1995 National Arts Festival in Grahamstown (6–16 July), the original actors, Winston Ntshona and John Kani, in a twenty-year tribute to the play enacted it once more and shortly thereafter in Cape Town. To see the play in South Africa in a newly post-apartheid context was a truly moving experience and gave the play itself an entirely new dramatic thrust.[50] The play has nowadays become a tribute to the suffering and endurance of those imprisoned by an oppressive regime and to those who died at its hands. One of those prisoners on Robben Island, as every South African is painfully aware, was Nelson Mandela himself. Seeing Winston Ntshona and John Kani recreate the roles they premiered twenty years earlier, one feels, too, that *The Island* in a sense is also a tribute to Ntshona and even more to Kani who have gone on to distinguished international acting careers after making their initial mark in what was then a dangerous and dangerously subversive drama. Even after the abrogation of apartheid, *The Island* continues to politicize audiences and move them deeply, but it does so by forcing them to remember and revile the realities it depicts. The lives of many political plays are coterminous with the currency of the political issues they address. This is not the case of *Sizwe Bansi Is Dead* and even less so of *The Island,* for these are works that bear witness to a specific manifestation of oppression yet touch on larger truths.

FOUR

Dimetos: *Fugard's First Problem Play*

Writing about Athol Fugard's *Dimetos* in 1985, Russell Vandenbroucke characterizes the play as "Fugard's densest and most ambitious work to date." That description continues to be apt. Dennis Walder comments, "*Dimetos*'s first audiences did not know what to make of the play" and describes the disapproval of the play by those who had come to see Fugard as an agitprop, political activist playwright.[1] Indeed, *Dimetos,* which had its world premiere at the 1975 Edinburgh Festival, was not like anything Fugard had written before. It is not set in South Africa, nor is it clearly about South African apartheid politics, as its immediate predecessors *Sizwe Bansi, The Island,* and *Statements* had been.[2] It is not about the kind of family relationships depicted in *Blood Knot, Boesman and Lena, Hello and Goodbye,* or *People Are Living There.* Not surprisingly, audiences and readers alike have had difficulty with the play, which challenges easy characterizations of Fugard as a playwright. Also not surprisingly, very little has been written about *Dimetos,* for it is a dark and recondite work that does not open itself easily to conventional literary analysis.

Dimetos can be written off neither as an aberration nor as a dramatic runt in Fugard's litter of otherwise exemplary plays. It is a haunting play that inspires rapt attention. The force of the play is one that enters our understanding through our primal ways of knowing located in our reserves of instinctive feeling rather than in our ratiocinative faculties. In this way it shares much in style and effect with plays like Pinter's *The Room* and *A Slight Ache.* Appropriately, the idea for *Dimetos* came to Fugard through his own instinctive feelings as he read a short disembodied passage in the first volume of Albert Camus' *Carnets:*

> Dimétos eut un amour coupable pour sa nièce qui se pendit. Sur le sable fin
> de la plage, les petites vagues apportèrent un jour une merveilleuse jeune

femme morte. Dimétos qui la vit tomba à genoux, éperdument amoureux. Mais il assista à la décomposition de ce corps admirable et devint fou. Ce fut la vengeance de sa nièce et le symbole d'une condition qu'il faudrait définir.

[Dimetos had a guilty love for his niece, who hanged herself. One day, the little waves carried on to the fine sand of the beach the body of a marvelously beautiful young woman. Seeing her, Dimetos fell on his knees stricken with love. But he was forced to watch the decay of this magnificent body, and went mad. This was his niece's vengeance, and the symbol of a condition we must try to define.][3]

Revealingly, Fugard describes his coming across Camus' remarks, in an interview with A. Christopher Tucker: "I read this . . . about 14 years ago, and was immediately *possessed*" [italics mine]. Likewise he says to Russell Vandenbroucke, "I was immediately *possessed* and am still acutely conscious of that moment" [italics mine].[4] *Dimetos* works as theatre by possessing the audience in much the same non-ratiocinative way that Camus' notebook entry possessed Fugard.

The play's origin in Camus' remark about a little known episode in Greek mythology, Fugard's epigraph for the play from Blake, and the fact that the play is about an artist/scientist figure have led critics to center their comments on generally useful comparisons with other writers and works. Richard Whitaker compares Fugard's Dimetos narration with Camus' and with Camus' probable source (one unknown to Fugard), Parthenius. To his study, Vandenbroucke adds an appendix, "Literary Ancestors of *Dimetos*," in which he draws connections between Dimetos and Ibsen's Solness, Goethe's Faust, Shakespeare's Prospero, Aeschylus' Prometheus, and Blake's Newton. Dennis Walder also invokes *The Tempest* as well as Nadine Gordimer's *July's People* and the generalized landscapes of J. M. Coetzee.[5]

Most of the reviews of *Dimetos* from the time of the Edinburgh Festival onward have been largely dismissive. *Dimetos* is not an easy play, and opening-night reviewers are not likely to be immediately enthusiastic about such a problematic, abstruse play when they are in search of a quick take and an immediately recognizable issue they can report the following day to their newspaper readers. Typical of opening-night reviews impatient with Fugard's style in *Dimetos* is the one by Dieter Bachmann commenting on the German-language premiere of the play in Basel: "Bitte, man kann auch von einem (weißen) Südafrikaner nicht dauernd Apartheid-Stücke erwarten. Aber muß es gerade ein solcher Mytho-Mischmasch sein?" [Even from a (white) South African one cannot, if you please, constantly expect apartheid plays. But does it *have* to be such mytho-mishmash?]. John Elsom, reviewing the play's premiere production at the 1975 Edinburgh Festival, is determined to make the play one about South Africa. He suggests, therefore, that *Dimetos,* despite its unspecified location, is "an authentic tragedy" about Afrikaners' intransigent adherence to what they regard as "the fundamental laws of life" whereby they miss "the most basic law of all, the give-and-take, the sympathy, tact and love which relate a man instinctively to his environment." When the play was staged in London a year later with Paul Scofield playing Dimetos and Ben Kingsley as Danilo, Elsom shrugged his shoulders and dismissed the play because with those British actors "South Africa has been rubbed out—and we are left with vague people in an anywhere land, doing nothing in particular except be symbolic."[6]

A few of the more thoughtful reviewers, however, sensed the power, depth, and insights of Fugard's challenging play. Reviewing the Edinburgh production, Harold Hobson called *Dimetos* "the best play I have seen in Britain this year" and commented that in an otherwise uninspired and uninspiring festival, "the authorities have discovered a new play [*Dimetos*] that is exciting, philosophically impressive, perfectly directed, and beautiful to look at." He suggested, further, that the play hinges "on the revelation that there are some matters which thermodynamics cannot reach." The best, most honest comment came from Derek Wilson, who had read the play beforehand and saw the 1981 production in which the distinguished South African actor Marius Weyers acted in the role of Dimetos. Wilson wrote, "It is indeed helpful to read this play first. . . . for the play requires—and deserves—rapt concentration. But even this does not guarantee one will understand the play completely—I still haven't quite grasped it, but it has undeniable moral and political ramifications. Essentially an abstract play, it is strong on metaphor, structurally and in the rich, powerful dialogue. Indeed, the writing is the play's prime strength."[7] Those, like Hobson and Wilson, who will let the play possess them will come closest to understanding the play. Nevertheless, it is easy to recognize that *Dimetos,* though rich in dramatic moments, is so recondite a work that it is not likely ever to find favor with most audiences or be often produced.

Fugard comments in his interview with A. Christopher Tucker that *Dimetos* "is a profound personal statement, using inner specifics in defining the condition of modern man, and is set in a remote and timeless past." He goes on to say that Freud has no influence on his writing but that Jung has, and that in *Dimetos* "[t]here are mass subconscious feelings which I have tried to define."[8] These vague and general statements nevertheless make clear that in *Dimetos* Fugard attempts no mean artistic feat: to use theatre, a visual and verbal form, to enact the ineffable, unseen, nonverbal matter of "inner specifics" and "subconscious feelings." Fugard seems eager to become like the potter Dimetos describes in the play: "In those hands the clay became something that combined the virtues of both liquid and solid. It flowed or stayed just as he wanted" (24).[9] In an interview, Fugard explained his idea of the playwright as craftsperson, talked about using "sets of tools" in his writing, and concluded, "My profession is play-wrighting—a maker of plays, like the wheelwright and all the others."[10]

In many ways, *Dimetos* goes to the heart of an essential matter that arises time and again in Fugard's work: the connection between the making of theatre and the making of life, between the art of theatrical acting and acting (politically and otherwise) on the world's stage, between understanding characters and playscripts and understanding others and life scripts. Theatre, moreover, is forged through the combination of technology (mechanics), idea, gesture, and feeling. Those same elements characterize human relationships and understanding. And it is on the interconnectedness of those matters that *Dimetos* dwells.

The first scene of the play is remarkable in its concise artistry. The opening direction reads, "*Lydia is lowered to the bottom of a well to tie ropes round a horse that has fallen down it*" (5). The notion of a horse that has fallen into a well is in itself an arresting image. What must this do to the horse's instincts of space? How does one get the horse out? How will this bizarre event affect the horse's future? What a stunning opening coup de théâtre to have a naked young woman lowered so that she is prostrate and tying ropes to a horse. While she does so, she is "*making comforting noises* [to the horse] *all the time.*" And the horse is not a live animal but is represented by a bench that, importantly, remains on stage for the duration of the play.[11]

Directed by her uncle, Dimetos, Lydia secures the ropes in such a way that a pulley system is achieved, successfully raising the horse and girl out of the well. One must remember in this play that as a teenager Fugard was the recipient of a four-year council scholarship to the Technical College of Port Elizabeth, where he studied auto mechanics and where he also discovered dramatics. It seems fortuitous that he should come to basic mechanics and basic theatre at the same time, for in *Dimetos* these two converge. And it is surely no coincidence that interleaved between the pages of his director's typescript of the play, Fugard has placed a copy of a page from a book on mechanics illustrating various kinds of pulleys (fig. 13).[12]

Indeed, underlying the physical, human, and dramatic mechanics of *Dimetos* is

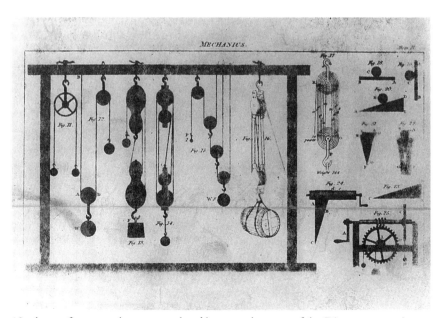

13. A page from an unknown text placed between the pages of the *Dimetos* manuscript. Courtesy the Lilly Library, Indiana University, Bloomington, Indiana.

that deceptively simple tool, the pulley, a mechanism whereby one pulls a rope in one direction making another part of the rope go in the opposite direction. It is the mechanical equivalent of the artist Dimetos most admires, the juggler who "[i]n explaining his trade to me . . . posed a paradox: 'Learn to give and take with the same action.'" (25). The pulley gives and takes with the same action; moving forward in one direction, it moves backward in the other. As *Dimetos* progresses, the pulley model becomes an important way of understanding the dynamics among the play's four characters and the way the dramatic action operates.[13]

In the second scene, Dimetos and Lydia share their understanding of what has happened. At the same time, messages are also dispersed to the audience semiotically. Dimetos opens the scene unknotting and coiling his rope, but in his typescript for the London production with Paul Scofield as Dimetos, Fugard has written that Lydia shouts, "I did it! He's free!!"[14] and that she is seen "jumping of[f] and over the bench." To go with Dimetos's opening lines, he writes in as well, "Lydia's dress. Dimetos has it over his shoulder. Tosses it to her."[15] As he does so, "*Lydia, clean and wet after a swim, dries herself with her dress and then throws it impulsively into the air*" (6). Underneath the dialogue of the first two scenes, then, is a semiotics of unspoken sexual energy. The audience as well as Dimetos are tacitly struck first by the erotic presence of a lovely, young, nude female body prostrate on the back of a horse and then by her innocent acceptance of her body when she uses her dress as a towel and then tosses it freely into the air in the presence of an adult male figure. Not sharing Lydia's innocence, the audience and Dimetos are placed in the role of adult, sexually aware, voyeurs and readers of Lydia's body as a gendered text. To understand properly the opening scenes and *Dimetos* as a whole, one must factor in these unspoken energies and the continuing on-stage presence of the bench (horse) as one hears and judges the play's spoken text.

The discussion that ensues in scene 2 seems central to the discovery of the essence of how theatre is made, which is in part what *Dimetos* seems to be about. Looking back on the rescue of the horse, Lydia imbues the animal with thoughts and feelings: "I think he was also laughing. And the way he kept shaking his head as if he couldn't believe it was true" (6). For Dimetos the engineer, by contrast, the fall and rescue of the horse has nothing to do with feelings, only with the inexorable laws of physics:

> All I saw galloping away was an obviously stupid animal that we had hauled out of a deep hole. . . . At a critical moment he found nothing under hoof and became a helpless victim of that force which attracts masses to each other. . . . It's a fact . . . mysterious! . . . but still a fact. "Every particle of matter in the Universe attracts every other particle with a force whose direction is that of the line joining the two . . ." It's called Gravity. The potential in all bodies to move or be moved. (7)

Lydia retorts, "[D]on't want any of your old facts now!" to which Dimetos's rejoinder is "They are all that matter. They'll help you understand a lot more than falling horses little one. . . . But I think I know what you want. 'Once upon a time there was a horse. He was a very happy horse until the day he noticed that the grass in the field was not as green . . .' " (7). Their friendly debate continues:

> LYDIA. Well he has got a story even if you don't care what it is, and you did give it a happy ending.
>
> DIMETOS. That happy ending was made by a system of pulleys with a mechanical advantage of five to one. Anybody who knew how to use them could have done what I did.
>
> LYDIA. But it was *you*. (7–8)

The moment is a complex one, for it is not simply a debate between narrative art and science. Lydia endows the events with meaning, suggesting the horse has feelings and an unspoken narrative; whereas using his avuncular tone, Dimetos reduces the events to a problem in an elementary physics text.

Lydia sees Dimetos as the person who thought of constructing and employing the pulleys. This makes him not merely an impersonal physicist but a playwright who uses his knowledge of mechanics in the service of a script, a drama, and the work of art that the rescue of the horse represents. At the same time, the sexual semiotics of the scene, the naked Lydia as an object of her uncle's and the audience's gaze, cue a subtextual level of erotic meaning to Dimetos's Newtonian comment, " 'Every particle of matter in the Universe attracts every other particle with a force whose direction is that of a line joining the two. . . .' " And one is reminded here of the play's epigraph from Blake: ". . . May God us keep / From Single vision & Newton's sleep!" Clearly there is also an implicit attraction of uncle for niece. What Fugard seems to understand in dramatic terms, moreover, is the work of a pulley which moves in two directions, so that as Lydia and the horse are raised from the space of the well and greeted with comic laughter, the rope of the play's psychodynamics is simultaneously pulling in an opposite direction, lowering Lydia and Dimetos into tragic disaster and a well of time. And as Danilo later says, "Man is the only animal to be trapped by time" (23).

The plot of the first act is at first glance deceptively simple. Five years before the action of the play, Dimetos, a distinguished engineer, retreated from the city to a distant rural location. He has taken with him his niece, Lydia, and his faithful housekeeper, Sophia, who has been with him since he was ten and she seventeen. They are visited by Danilo, a young man who has sought them out so that he can convince Dimetos to return to the city and use his knowledge of hydrology to help solve the city's water shortage dilemmas. Seeing that unaided he will not be able to convince Dimetos to return, Danilo hopes to do so by using his masculine charms to enlist the aid of Lydia, who may well be capable of persuading Dimetos to return to the city for her sake.

What seems like a relatively straightforward plot, however, is a basis for talking about art and about theatre and social purpose. Inflected as it is by the semiotics of erotic desire, it proves not at all straightforward. Although Dimetos is no representation of Fugard, there is some congruence between the two as Dimetos explains why he prefers the simple pleasures of his retreat. Indeed, the similarities to Fugard and his fondness for rural retreats like New Bethesda are hard to overlook. But more important, when Dimetos explains his life in the small town, he seems also to be explaining what lies behind Fugard's dramatic economies, his reasons for writing concise plays with very few characters, for using simple sets, and for building his plays from basic dramatic materials:

> . . . because life is basic. When a man needs water here he doesn't look for a tap, he digs a well. And having dug that well he must get the water to the top, and having got it there he must get it to his lands. It might all seem very obvious to you, but that is exactly what fascinates me. . . . It's refreshing, Danilo. Stimulating. (13)

This is very much like the (theatre) art of Sam in Fugard's later play *Master Harold,* in which Sam builds a kite and creates drama using the most elementary of materials: tomato-box wood, brown paper, flour, water, old stockings, and string. Here the rudiments of hydrology are akin to the rudiments of theatre. And Dimetos immediately goes on to shed light on Fugard as a social and political playwright:

> That's not to mention the further challenge of getting a new idea past the barriers of habit and prejudice. Their tools, techniques, are crude and inefficient. But they're the ones their fathers put into their hands and taught them how to use. To suggest modifying them not only demands a new dexterity of the wrist, but also of the soul. It's almost sacrilege. I haven't been all that successful, but they're learning to trust me. They've started to knock on my door when the need arises. (13)

Nowhere has Fugard or anyone else written a more eloquent statement about the art of drama as Fugard practices it. Endearingly implicit here is the playwright's love for his fellow South Africans of all color and for his fellow men who all need time to accept the new and frequently threatening and iconoclastic ideas with which the theatre and the playwright confront them.

In a similar moment, Dimetos reiterates these ideas when he discusses the joy he felt from the group efforts when he and the rustics raised Lydia and the horse from the well: "It was remarkable. At that precise moment, when we all strained in unison, it was as if our faces and names disappeared. All that mattered was what each of us, trying his utmost, could contribute. And our individual efforts brought to a simple focus by that rope. It worked" (16). This reads like Fugard's manifesto of the theatre, for this is what at its best making theatre means. And the social aim of the playwright is once more implicit, for Dimetos explains, "[T]he armoury—six mechanical powers—lever, pulley, inclined plane, wedge, screw and wheel. That's what they are. The tools and machines I've used or put into other men's hands . . .

extensions to those hands, giving them new powers in their defiance of a universe that resists us. The battle cry: Help men Defy!" (17).

Through Dimetos, Fugard suggests as well his abiding love for human beings, which enables him as a dramatist to reach beyond angry agitprop drama to the transcendent understanding and humanity we associate with such playwrights as Molière, Shakespeare, and Goethe. Dimetos says:

> Do you know what bridges that mysterious distance between head and hands, bringing them so close together that they are almost one? Caring. Not the most exciting of words is it? Almost as humble as a tool. But that is the Alchemist's Stone of human endeavour. (17)

That "caring" is also the Alchemist's Stone of playwriting. It transmogrifies the base metal of life into the gold of art.

But Dimetos claims to have lost the ability to care; and does not know himself why he has undergone a change:

> DIMETOS. Don't ask me why because I don't know. But something eroded away the habit of caring. . . . Usage blunts a tool, but when that happens you sharpen it, when it wears out you replace it. It's not as simple as that with . . .
>
> SOPHIA. The heart, Dimetos.
>
> DIMETOS. Head, hands, and heart. It's easier here only because I don't have to lie to myself, or others. . . . If I'd been my self this morning I might well have left that horse and those squabbling idiots to their predicament. (17)

On the one hand his is the cynicism and lament of every artist who cannot maintain artistic passion uninterruptedly, and feels at such times that the muse has departed, reducing him or her from caring artist to unfeeling artisan. The high-minded questions of social commitment and responsibility are one part of the pulley-cord mechanism that moves the dramatic action of the play. On the other hand, as the first act of *Dimetos* progresses, the existence of a subtextual underplot becomes clear, a subplot that is the portion of the dramatic pulley cord which moves dangerously in the opposite direction, which is not the force of social commitment and care for others but its underside, the force of selfish passions and of personal gratification.

Danilo tries in scene 5 to enlist Lydia's aid in convincing Dimetos to return to the city. Embedded in the discussion of the two young people, however, is their obvious attraction for each other. Danilo uses his personal charm not merely to work on Dimetos through his niece but also implicitly to articulate his own attraction to her. He consequently does make an appeal on behalf of the city's needy citizens, holding out the life of the city where he lives as a place to which Lydia should wish for her own sake to return. And she, talking as much about Danilo's implied courtship of her as about his attempt to woo Dimetos back to the city, initiates a dialogue rich in subtext, saying, "I think you gave up too easily. . . . Why don't you try again! . . . I'll help you. I'll tell him I want to go back. Sometimes he does things for me when he's already said no to others." To this Danilo ambiguously replies, "I can understand that. All right" (21–22). The double meaning that colors Lydia's response, moreover, marks the loss of the girlish innocence still in her possession earlier that day, in scenes 1 and 2.

Likewise, with Danilo as catalyst, the innocence of the seemingly stable triangular relationship among Dimetos, Lydia, and Sophia is abrogated. Suddenly Dimetos is no longer speaking in strictly avuncular terms to Lydia, but his language, imagery, and semiotics are replete with sensual cues:

> I saved the horse for you! [*Looks at her.*] You understand and see so much, and yet you're so blind to other things. [*Pause.*] Yes, I saved the horse for you. . . . He succumbed to you! Stood absolutely still while you straddled him and went to work. There was a moment when you were prostrate on his back, your cheek resting on his powerful neck, your hands working away quietly underneath him as you placed the slings . . . both of you covered in mud! . . . . If I was an artist I'd turn my hand to modelling that. Try to capture the contrast between the powerful contours of his helplessness and the delicacy of your determination. [*Pause. Exit abruptly.*] (28)

Dimetos's concentration on the sensuality of the experience, his comments about her blindness, and his abrupt exit, as though he were restraining himself from going further, all suggest an ineffable dark side to his comments. His comment to Sophia immediately thereafter that he is not sure he can trust his hands this night only adds to the uneasiness the audience feels. And these things suddenly evoke from Sophia a flash of conversation that lays bare some of her own desires as she asks Dimetos, "If I'm not a servant what am I? Mother? Sister? I'm not old enough for the first and I've never thought of myself as the second. There's also 'friend' 'companion' . . . if the others are too personal. How do *you* see me Dimetos? Who am I?" (29–30). It is here we begin to sense that Dimetos's feelings for Lydia and Sophia's for Dimetos are similarly edged.

Sophia's instinctive realization, moreover, that Lydia is her rival changes the nature of the relationship between the two women, a change Fugard means us to feel by contrasting the two scenes in which Sophia and Lydia play out their game of brushing hair. The first of these has Sophia with maternal indulgence brushing out Lydia's hair. The second begins with Fugard's stage direction, "*Sophia enters and starts brushing her hair. The mood between the two of them is muted and in strong contrast to their first scene together*" (30). And Lydia, beginning to lose her innocence, realizes "Something is happening to us," "Uncle is avoiding me," and that he is capable of mendacity. When Sophia stops brushing Lydia's hair, she cryptically ends the scene with an unspecific "Be careful little one" without warning her specifically about either Danilo's or Dimetos's aroused feelings, though Sophia is aware of both.

What happens next is complicated. After five days in Lydia's presence, emboldened by wine and moved by Lydia's admission that she is frightened because "it's suddenly like we've all got secrets from each other," Danilo encourages Lydia to leave, kisses her affectionately, and then attempts to force himself upon her. The stage direction reads, "*He kisses her gently. At first Lydia responds but as Danilo goes further she begins to resist him. He can't control himself. The struggle becomes violent. Her dress gets torn. She eventually manages to break free and runs away. Danilo is left alone*" (35). During this scene with Danilo, Lydia has felt the presence of a third person watching them. After her near rape and in her torn dress, Lydia runs in distress to Sophia, who in turn fears Lydia's attacker was Dimetos. Obsessed by the question of "who was it?" Sophia beats Lydia until the girl admits her attacker was Danilo. Sophia's agitation turns immediately to uncontrolled laughter in her relief that it was not Dimetos; and tells Lydia, "Don't let it upset you too much," and "To love is a position of weakness, to be loved a position of power" (36). The latter comment sheds light on Sophia's own weakness and provides an insight into the idea of love as a power relationship.

In the dazzling final scene of the first act, the stage direction reads, "Lydia, *alone and very frightened.* Dimetos *enters. He is breathless, his manner wild and disturbed. He is frightened of his hands.*" As he comforts his distracted niece, she smells the scent of lemon on his hands and realizes, "You were the man in the orchard. You were watching us. You didn't stop him." He answers confusedly, "You ran away before I needed to. I wouldn't have let him hurt you. [*Looking at his hands.*]"[16] It was so hot. the blossom made me giddy. I remember holding onto a branch . . . I must have crushed the leaves" (36). The audience and perhaps Lydia realize that Dimetos has played the voyeur watching his own illicit desires enacted by Danilo. Perhaps Dimetos has even played the role of a perverse Prospero stage-managing his own Miranda and Ferdinand, and then lewdly watching Danilo from the bushes performing the role Dimetos himself desires to play. Or perhaps Dimetos has been watching his experiment with the detached interest of a scientist (as Prospero watches Miranda and Ferdinand play chess), and would, as he alleges, have stepped in before Danilo could harm Lydia. Most likely Dimetos's gaze is imbued with a combination of both of these possibilities. In any case, the lemon scent of guilt is upon Dimetos, and the loosened moorings of his usual calm are evident. The hands of the artist and artisan, those hands that are so prominently featured throughout the first act, are now tainted.

All along, the bench representing the horse has been on stage; and throughout the first act, Dimetos has been hanging ropes and pulleys from the roof beams. Left alone on stage, Lydia addresses the horse (bench) in soliloquy and then quite unexpectedly creates her own pulley of self-destruction by climbing onto the table and using one of Dimetos's pulley ropes to hang herself. This dazzling first act curtain sends the audience into the interval bewildered, stunned, and rethinking the events of the play that have led to such a dramatic and unexpected conclusion.

The second act of *Dimetos* is drastically and impressively different from the first. It is slightly less than half as long, takes place "many years later," and is no longer set in a small village in the interior of the land but on a lonely ocean beach. The relative realism of the first act is eschewed and replaced by some scenes that are essentially interior monologues and others in which the characters seem more often to speak past one another (*Vorbeisprechen*) than to engage in true dialogue. Fugard sheds light on the style of act 2, writing in his *Notebooks,* "I have a sense that it [my 'problem'] is going to lie in finding, creating 'action' in the total 'inner dimension' which they [the characters] represent."[17] Act 2 is also played out in the context of Dimetos's and Sophia's awareness of the increasingly fetid odors emanating from the carcass of a sea mammal that has died on a nearby offshore rock. The decaying animal also bears the heady aromas of a symbolic presence, since something is also patently rotten in the state of Dimetos's and Sophia's lives and minds.

It is probably just coincidence that a year before Paul Scofield played Dimetos, he was in London playing Prospero in a revival of *The Tempest,* but this is curiously appropriate, since act 2 of *Dimetos* seems close in spirit to Shakespeare's late plays as well as to the romance element in *King Lear.* Like that Shakespearean tragedy, *Dimetos* moves from interior to seacoast. It is at the edge of civilized land, on the cliffs of Dover overlooking the untrammeled power of the sea, that the characters of *King Lear* come to grips with their profound tragedies and the destruction their actions have unleashed. It is also on that same seacoast that Cordelia forgives her father and, kissing him, says, "Restoration hang / Thy medicine on my lips," with which she brings tragedy to the borders of restorative comedy, briefly effecting the reinstatement both of Lear's physical well-being and of their father-daughter relationship. Like Lear, Timon of Athens, and Pericles, Dimetos has been stripped of affluence, the society of men, and some of his reason. Like those Shakespearean characters and like Prospero as well, Dimetos finds himself on coastal terrain, a no man's land between earth and water. He exists between the land that has been the scene of his tragedy and that has ejected him, and the powerful waters that spell another kind of irrationality and devastation. He now lives, moreover, on that sandy strip of disputed borderland that bespeaks his mental and social state, the beach that is daily claimed by the ocean at high tide and then reclaimed by the land at low tide. Sophia's comment on the state of affairs could just as well be that of a character on Dover beach in the final act of *King Lear:* "We can't go any further, you know. This is the limit. There is nowhere from here except back" (39).

For Dimetos, the tragedy that climaxes at the close of act 1 reduces the world from the integrated organism it had been and fragments it into disparate elements in act 2: "Sea. Sand. Sun. Sky. Elemental." What might once have been a structured sentence is analogously here reduced to a "sentence" of one-word nouns. Dimetos is now deprived as well of the stable space and time on which his work as engineer and artist was predicated:

> The sand underfoot is loose and heavy and when I try to ease the weight of my emptiness with handfulls of it, it spills out between my fingers as if my fists were lunatic hour-glasses, impatient to measure out what's left of my time. There are no landmarks. You walk until you've had enough. (38)

A poetic language of interior monologue here replaces the more realistic dialogue of the previous act; and Dimetos's prior engineering feats and purposefulness are succeeded by aimlessness, by motion devoid of meaning: "You walk until you've had enough."

Part of Dimetos's punishment is his confrontation with the four elements, with sea, sand, sun, and sky (i.e., water, earth, fire, air). Another aspect of the punishment is that this once admired engineer and hydrologist is now servant and victim of the sea, "a clever but mad craftsman." Like Lear, who comes to identify with the "poor naked wretches," and even more like Timon digging up roots on the seashore, Dimetos is reduced to earning his keep by selling the ocean's detritus, the seashell grit used to feed poultry. Into the typescript for the London production he directed, Fugard writes at the opening of the second act's second scene, "Shell grit emptied before dialogue. Bag on the floor."[18] The evidence of Dimetos's new occupation is thus made an inanimate actor on stage commenting on the action through its physical presence. From his pockets Dimetos empties his *collection of stones and shells onto a small table already cluttered with similar debris* (39), and we feel the difference between this table and the large one that had been cluttered with his engineer's tools in act 1, scene 3.

An older Danilo, who now seeks out Dimetos a second time, eloquently and poetically captures Dimetos's punishment and existence:

> Behind him land and a world of men he would never return to, who didn't want him any more, had in fact finally forgotten him. And ahead of him the ocean, a world he could not enter . . . unless he was tempted to act out a fanciful metaphor for the last adventure of all. . . . To all intents and purposes he had come to terms with himself in that no-man's land between the tides, collecting his sea shells. (41)

Earlier in the play, Danilo had commented, "Man is the only animal to be trapped by time." And like the horse in the first scene of the play, Dimetos is now trapped, trapped in time. His situation and punishment are that one event—the death of Lydia—has become the cynosure of his life. His psychological and human development have been arrested, trapped at that point. Fugard writes in his *Notebooks* of Dimetos and Sophia, "A sense of their lives as having been 'arrested'—both of them in a cul-de-sac—of a past, too heavy and oppressive to allow for a future—even the present is a seemingly thin and transparent reality."[19] These two are, in fact, the tragic living embodiments of the cryptic mantra an old man had once repeated to Lydia, "Tomorrow was yesterday" (34).

Undergoing punishment Dimetos certainly is. But for what? The nature of his tragic transgression is disputable. Is it that he had sexual feelings for Lydia and that he gratified those feelings as a voyeur by watching Danilo's attempted rape? Is it that he seems to have silently scripted the events that made Danilo bold and Lydia vulnerable? Is he culpable because he failed to realize that Lydia's lost innocence would result in her suicide? For any one of these offenses, Dimetos's punishment seems excessive. Dimetos's error, however, seems of a larger nature, and has to do with his total reliance upon and worship of scientific principles and facts without giving proper credence to human feelings, without granting credibility to the unscientific but palpable power of the imagination. Speaking of *Dimetos,* Fugard writes in his *Notebooks:*

> A human dilemma, but specifically that of man in the urban-industrial world of the West, a result of "single vision," of a technology and science that alienated man from a sacramental relationship to the world around him . . . a dilemma as unique to man in the twentieth century as is the artificial environment created by his science and technology.[20]

Again like King Lear, Dimetos has judged only by the externals, by Newtonian mathematical and physical laws, and must be brought to understand the full meaning of his own "O, reason not the need."

Just as the first act makes us aware that there is a subtextual underplot, so the second act teaches that tragic events flow from a combination of causes not easily separable from one another or quantifiable. This is a challenge in another key to Dimetos's insistence on inexorable cause-and-effect principles. We get a sense of this with the arrival in act 2 of Danilo, who has discovered that he was not alone responsible for Lydia's death. He explains that he had afterward returned to the city a broken man despising himself and others for what had transpired. Eventually, however, he came to see that his role been merely a function of Dimetos's crafty culpability. He exclaims, "Those five days must rank as one of your more ingenious pieces of engineering. You used us like tools and with such consummate mastery because of your passion for your niece" (44). The passage that follows is most important for understanding Fugard's point of view:

> DANILO. Because you did know what you were doing, didn't you?
>
> DIMETOS. Yes.
>
> DANILO. And you did try to stop yourself?
>
> DIMETOS. Yes.
>
> DANILO. So did I. Why couldn't we? This rational intelligence of ours, our special human capacity for anticipating, predicting pain . . . our own or another's . . . as the consequence of an action, was useless, wasn't it?

Danilo's questions bring him and Dimetos smack against the limits of reason, of physics and its laws, in accounting for human behavior. Likewise, the nature of punishment is not determinable or knowable. It is also true that not all crimes are punished. This seems to undermine the rationality of the universe:

DIMETOS. What are you trying to say, Danilo? What do you want?

DANILO. Punishment. Not just for you specifically, but as a fundamental law of the universe, and of a magnitude on a par with your gravity. Because without it our notions of justice man-made or natural, of good and evil, are the most pathetic illusions we have ever entertained. (44)

But what Danilo does not understand and what Dimetos must come to understand is that physical laws are not the only way of knowing and some punishments are also not calculable. When Danilo leaves the play on the question lines "Who knows? Who knows anything?" Dimetos is left alone and says, "Tide's turning. Mustn't get my feet wet again." This is the play's answer. To stand on the edge of the tide, to be trapped and psychologically immobilized in a cul-de-sac between the forces of ocean and earth, is Dimetos's punishment.

In this scene we recognize that Danilo and Dimetos share responsibility for what happened at the close of act 1, even if the exact percentage of their respective shares is not quantifiable. And likewise in the scene that follows, Sophia adds her share of responsibility to the tragic psychodynamics. She chides Dimetos, to whom she says accusingly, "Yours is unquestionably the most selfish soul I have ever known. Your life, your passion and now *your* guilt. . . . You understand nothing" (45). She then explains how her own jealousy contributed to Lydia's death and how it must be factored into the mix of events.

When Sophia leaves the scene reminding Dimetos and the audience of the pervasive and stifling stench from the sea mammal's carrion, Dimetos's blind devotion to science begins to crack, and he experiences mental breakdown of a special kind. He does not go mad but experiences a powerful challenge to his previously rational and purely scientific mind-set. Like a religious incantation, he recites the theorems for determining the lunar physics of tides—"Let E and M be the centres of the earth and moon respectively . . ."—but punctuating this is the increasingly loud invocation of "LYDIA" (46). What becomes clear is that time stopped for Dimetos with Lydia's death, and that in his mind, she remains strung up, not touching the ground, hanging on a rope from the ceiling. The stench Dimetos feels in his mind from her putrefying flesh is objectified by that of the dead animal on the rock outside his cottage. Her presence now breaks down the mantra of laws governing the tides and leads him "where there is no measure":

> Lydia . . . The silence chokes on your name, as if that knot will never let another sound into the world. I am going to try to let you down. That won't be easy . . . because there is no measure to the distance between your feet and the earth they never reached. (46)

Beginning to accept the immeasurables, the non-rational that Lydia stands for, Dimetos seems headed for a life transcending tragedy of the kind discovered by the principals of Shakespeare's late romances.

Sophia feels in act 2 that she has become Dimetos's fate (40–41). She actually serves more like his nemesis. Her unrequited love for Dimetos, however, made her a player in the events that led to Lydia's suicide, and she has trapped herself into a life of arrested development whose meaning is solely determined by its relation to Dimetos. Prefiguring Dimetos's escape from the well of time, Sophia enables herself to leave him by invoking Lydia and creating a story. In his typescript, after Sophia invokes Lydia's name, Fugard pens in that her narrative is "told to Lydia."[21] The story she tells is that she had an appointment and that she walked and found herself face-to-face with a woman, "her knees drawn up under her chin. Her feet misshapen . . . her hair, long and soft. . . . She keeps company with a donkey, an owl, a griffin, a bat and an old, million-year-old turtle" (50). The image is that of William Blake's 1795 color print *Hecate*.[22] The image is also that of Lydia after rescuing the horse, "*[s]itting with her chin on her knees, wide-eyed and clutching her dress*" (8). It seems relevant, too, that Hecate is generally associated with the mythology of the moon, and this seems a fictive and spiritual rejoinder to Dimetos's dispassionate concept of the moon purely as a measurable gravitational force affecting the tides. Telling her story, moreover, enables Sophia finally to speak her love to Dimetos, rediscover her laughter, and then leave the stage with her life.

Dimetos is left on stage alone babbling definitions of physical forces none of which can stop time. This Fugard equates in his typescript with the stench of the dead animal.[23] Suddenly Lydia's voice is heard. She now exchanges roles with the Dimetos of the play's first scene who instructed Lydia in the well, "Keep calm. Make sure you are comfortable." The voice of Lydia now encourages her uncle to "Keep calm. Don't be frightened" as she instructs him on how to extricate himself from the well of time into which he has fallen:

> The only tool a man can make that will help him hold time, is a story. The theory is very simple: adapting the principle of a lever of the first order we will place in exact opposition, on a common pivot, the clean edges of a beginning, and an end. (51)

Storytelling needs only three elements: "Once upon a time . . . there was . . . for ever after." Repeating those elements, Dimetos becomes comfortable with fiction and with the idea that fiction can be stronger than physics.

He creates a story, which liberates him and empowers him to confess, come to grips with himself, and reform. His restorative story tells of a voice speaking to disembodied hands, presumably Dimetos's own, saying:

> All you ever wanted to do was possess. All you've ever made were tools and machines to help you do that. It is now time for the skills you scorned. Find something and hold it. Close that powerful hand on a thing. Yours. Hold it! . . . Now give it away. Don't be frightened. Only to your other hand. . . . That was a terrible second when they were both empty. One still is. . . . Now

comes the hard part . . . so listen carefully. Each must give and take with the same action. (52)

As he listens to and acts on his own narrative, he begins to laugh and to mime juggling. He has mastered the paradoxical art of the juggler: "'Learn to give and take with the same action'" (25). What frees Dimetos from his cul-de-sac of time, what enables him, like the horse freed from the well, to gallop away into the world is a new sense of give-and-take, an acceptance of the world based on fictive narrative, dream, inspiration, and not merely on lifeless and allegedly inexorable physical laws and principles. Part of this acknowledges the human instinct to possess but tempers that with the command to let go and share. Juggling, giving and taking with the same action, can be the action that leads beyond tragedy and toward restoration. At the close of *Dimetos,* with the decaying dead sea mammal in the background and Dimetos's youthful laughter in the foreground, Fugard forges something akin to the pivotal line in Shakespeare's *The Winter's Tale,* a romance that reaches beyond the borders of tragedy into realms of restoration: "Thou mettest with things dying, I with things new-born."

The final lines of *Dimetos* add one last twist to the play's wisdom. And these lines, like Shakespeare's act-closing lines, are italicized by being delivered as a rhyming couplet. Though printed as prose in the published text (53), they are given their verse form in the *Dimetos* typescript:

> And now, because your gaiety is so great,
> the last skill of all.
> Hold them [his hands] out, and wait. . . . .[24]

The idea here is that we must simultaneously accept and surrender to others what we have in our grasp, but how and when we get what we have is part of the inscrutable adventure of living. Jerry Dickey astutely interprets the last lines: "The final image is of a new man, open and vulnerable, with hands capable of caring and with a mind possessing the double vision of scientific reason and human love."[25] And into his typescript on the page opposite these last lines, Fugard writes the dazzling comment, ". . . One of life's Cardinal mysteries. The moment when the beggar, having chosen his place in the sun, carelessly hold's [*sic*] out his hands and waits."[26]

As is abundantly evident, the thrust and feel of *Dimetos* is for me reminiscent of Shakespeare's late romances. Fugard uses the play to mark the path that is the exodus from tragedy, the exodus from the well of stopped time. It provides the means, though one is older and no longer innocent, to gallop away to freedom and back into life. At the same time, this highly parabolic play, like Shakespearean romance, is about the artist and art. It conveys what happens to art when it is mechanical or selfish, what happens to art when the artist is a taker and not also a giver. Learning to give and take at the same time is the nature of pulleys, but it is also what making art and making theatre are about. The actor and the playwright must have an understanding of people and of the world, and then give that understanding back to the audience and to society. It is also about the paradox of making theatre, in which actors, in telling a story, must subordinate themselves and their craft to the story, let the story tell itself through them. Likewise the makers, the play*wrights* must subordinate themselves to the power of the story even as they tell the story. Like the playwright or actor, Dimetos the engineer and shaper must himself be shaped, allowing himself to be a pulley that takes and lets go at the same time.

But artists—like Fugard himself, as he reveals in his *Notebooks*—experience doubts about their work and sometimes they have writer's blocks.[27] *Dimetos* is a parable about that also, about how the writer can lift himself out of the well of despond by returning to the basic tools of storytelling: in the beginning, there was, forever after. As Dimetos tells the story in the last scene of the play, it is not so much a soliloquy as it is Dimetos's partly narrating the story and then partly serving as a mouthpiece for a story that tells itself through his voice. The pulley is the simple mechanism that gives and takes at the same time, and when the playwright pulls down on his imaginative rope using the storytelling basics of "in the beginning—there was—forever after," he can be lifted up out of his artistic slump, finding himself rescued by narrative.

Dimetos stands as an anomaly among Fugard's works. It is obscure, highly poetic and parabolic, devoid of geographic specificity, and thoroughly enigmatic. Its mixed reviews and few revivals, and the paucity of commentary written about it, suggest that many are put off by *Dimetos*'s cryptic quality and difficulty. To be sure, it seems to call not for Fugard's usual popular audience but for the sort of initiate audience Yeats required for his dramas. Though *Dimetos* is not a play for every playgoer or reader, it is, nevertheless, a stunning exploration of the problems of art that Fugard ponders and of his Blakean vision of life. Certainly, too, *Dimetos* is the necessary transitional stepping stone that enables Fugard the playwright to facilitate a move from the overt, almost agitprop politics of *Sizwe Bansi*, *The Island*, and *Statements* to the new, more controlled style and the masterful psychological sensitivity he achieves in *A Lesson from Aloes*, *Master Harold*, and *The Road to Mecca*.

FIVE

The Drama as Teaching and Learning: Trauerspiel, Tragedy, Hope, and Race

The collaborative efforts with Winston Ntshona and John Kani that resulted in *Sizwe Bansi Is Dead* and *The Island,* followed by the retreat into the relative abstraction of *Dimetos,* seem to have created a kind of crucible that allowed Fugard to forge his two subsequent plays, arguably his masterpieces: *A Lesson from Aloes* (1978) and *"Master Harold"... and the Boys* (1982).[1] Nevertheless, as Russell Vandenboucke documents, *A Lesson from Aloes* was a long time in coming and was accompanied by Fugard's inner crises about running dry as an artist.[2] Perhaps the three years between *Dimetos* and *A Lesson from Aloes* was the time Fugard needed to bring together an understanding of interpersonal psychodynamics with questions of race, an amalgam that characterizes both *A Lesson from Aloes* and *Master Harold.* In *A Lesson from Aloes,* the racial matters are played off against some very specific political issues, astutely described elsewhere by Errol Durbach.[3] In *A Lesson from Aloes,* Fugard brilliantly marks out South Africa's tragic landscape as the play examines three victims of apartheid's destructive power. The damage done comes not in the form of beatings or other physical torture but as a price paid in terms of the destruction of privacy, mental stability, friendship, marital relations, community, and attachment to one's native land.

In consequence, the psychological tensions among and within the play's three characters dominate *A Lesson from Aloes,* so much so that they frequently overshadow the racial issues. This failure to focus primarily or squarely enough on race dampened the enthusiasm of some reviewers and critics.[4] But Fugard does not mean *A Lesson from Aloes* to be another agitprop drama about race in the manner of *Sizwe Bansi, The Island,* and *Statements.* Rather, he wishes to depict the ways in which South African racism brutalizes and scars all parties, whites and non-whites, descendants of the Boers and descendants of the British. Apartheid is a plague that drives some into exile, some into mental collapse, and others into seeking the most dire survival strategies. The play also suggests that, paradoxically, the strategies for survival and reform may well emerge from the Afrikaner sector of South African society, the very sector alleged to be most at fault for the country's racism and brutality.

A Lesson from Aloes is divided into two acts. In the first, Piet and Gladys Bezuidenhout wait for Steve Daniels and his family to come for a light collation a few days before that family's departure from South Africa on an exit visa to England. Steve, it is revealed, is a middle-aged coloured man who has been involved in anti-apartheid activities, has been consequently placed under a banning order, and then was imprisoned because an anonymous informer apprised the Special Branch of the police that Steve had broken his banning order. Now, out of prison, he has decided to uproot his family and leave his homeland forever through an exit visa, a euphemism for irrevocable exile. In a very deliberate and shrewd way, the first act explores the complicated relationship between Piet and Gladys, the Afrikaner husband and his wife, who is of English stock. Though South African politics are certainly present, marital and emotional psychodynamics are very much foregrounded. In the second act, when Steve arrives to pay his farewell visit, the delicate balance between Piet and Gladys is abruptly destroyed and the psychodynamics among the play's three actors propelled in new directions.

A Lesson from Aloes is very specifically located at the home of Piet and Gladys, 27 Kraaibos Street in the Algoa Park area of Port Elizabeth. As the stage set makes clear and as anyone who drives to the actual Kraaibos Street will see, the home, grandly called "Xanadu," is located in a white working-class area of trim, modest homes.

From the moment the play begins, the audience is both consciously and unconsciously made aware of the differences between husband and wife. Piet is sitting in his garden actively absorbed in identifying aloes that he is raising in tins. Gladys sits motionless. The stage directions tell us that "He is wearing spectacles, short trousers, no shirt and sandals without socks. GLADYS, behind sunglasses, sits very still on a garden bench" (3).[5] The stage image is one that is brilliantly indicative of their characters. A bare-chested Piet clad in shorts and sandals is the active Afrikaner, thoroughly open and unashamed, as signified by his lack of clothing. He is indefatigable in his project to collect and name aloes, wearing his spectacles to help him both identify the aloes and bring into focus the world around him. Gladys, by contrast, has no project. She sits in the small garden disengaged, motionless, and fully clothed. Her glasses are sunglasses meant to screen her from the outside world and its glare. Taken by itself, this interpretation might seem an over-reading of some simple stage directions, but Fugard is a master of dramaturgy, and the interpretation gains validity as the play proceeds and as who Piet and Gladys are becomes increasingly apparent.

The play opens with Piet reading from his aloe identification book in his Afrikaans-accented English, trying to name the aloe specimen he is examining. His botanic zeal and the desire to name and domesticate his unidentified aloe, moreover, link Piet to his Boer Voortrekker ancestors, who also had a need to explore, control, and domesticate the South African veld. His is an Adamic impulse, and he knows it. Examining his aloe, he says to Gladys, "Well my dear, we have a stranger in our midst. Aloe Anonymous! Because that is what it is until I know its name," and as he names the others in his jam tins, he adds, "An impressive array of names, isn't it? And knowing them is important. It makes me feel that little bit more at home in my world" (4). Later he elaborates:

> According to the Bible, that was the very first thing Adam did in Eden. He named his world. "And whatsoever Adam called every living creature, that was the name thereof." No. There is no rest for me until I've identified this. (13)

Piet's frequent employment of literary quotations for moments of heightened feeling seems another way to domesticate and thereby control his world and emotions by defining them with pre-established, pre-set phrases or apothegms from a canonical literary luminary. A love of and openness to nature are present in his physical exposure to the sun, his horticultural hobby, and his quotations early in the play from nature poems such as Keats's "Ode to Autumn" (6) and Roy Campbell's "The Snake" (14).

At the same time, he is a gregarious person, open to others. He bustles about the stage, and we learn that he has been a bus driver, has been a member of an anti-apartheid organization, and is now preparing for a supper in his garden with his friends Steve and Mavis Daniels, their three daughters and their son, Pietertjie, Piet's godson.

As soon as Gladys speaks, we recognize by her accent that hers is not Piet's Afrikaner ancestry and that she belongs to a very different South African ethnic tradition. Gladys's motionlessness and initial silence, her protective clothing and sunglasses help mark her difference. Fugard, with impressive economy, notes the significant contrasts between husband and wife that will energize the subsequent tragic action:

> PIET. Then relax, my dear. Enjoy the sunshine. . . . Just tidying up my mess.
>
> GLADYS. I hope I'm not getting too much sun.
>
> PIET. No danger of that on an autumn afternoon. This is the start of our gentle time, Gladys . . . our season of mists and mellow fruitlessness, close bosom friend of the maturing sun. On the farm there was almost a sense of the veld sighing with relief when autumn finally set in . . .
>
> GLADYS. My skin can't take it. I learned that lesson when I was a girl.
>
> PIET. Sunburn.
>
> GLADYS. Yes. A holiday somewhere with my mother and father. On the very first day I picked up too much sun on the beach and that was the end of it.

My mother dabbed me all over with calamine lotion to soothe the pain. I can remember looking at myself in the mirror . . . a frightened little white ghost. Mommy was terrified I was going to end up with a brown skin. But she needn't have worried. It all peeled away and there I was, the same as before.

PIET. The voortrekker women had the same problem. That's where the old bonnet comes from. Protection.

GLADYS. I think it was Cape Town. Not that it made any difference where I was. All I remember of the outside world was standing at a window and watching the dogs in the street go beserk when the dirt boys came to empty the bins. Heavens! What a terrible commotion that was. A big gray lorry with its mountains of rubbish, the black men banging on its side shouting, the dogs going for them savagely. (6–7)

Encapsulated here are Gladys's fragility and Piet's hardiness. Her fear of exposure is contrasted to his inherited Voortrekker knowledge of self-protection. His is an urge to keep order in the world and to have a sense of orderliness. Piet cleans up his mess (as he will in more important ways throughout the play). Growing up as he did inland, in the veld, he has a farm boy's innate sense of the seasons and their individuality, and so recognizes that sunburns are unlikely on an autumn afternoon. Without quotation marks, he allows Keats's poetic understanding to flow into and embellish his own remarks.[6] The lesson Gladys has learned is that she damages easily and has none of Piet's almost instinctive ways to protect herself. A city girl, she lacks Piet's bucolic seasonal timing; she goes to the Cape Town beaches and exposes her fair skin immoderately. Her mother's racial fears that she will look coloured are for nought, for she turns red and blisters. Her culture does not know the preventive protection of the Boer white bonnet, only the ex post facto use of calamine lotion, which soothes the sting of sunburn but does not prevent its damage. She has seen the world not as an active participant in it but through her window, not cleaning up her mess but watching those of black skin clean it up for her. And she does so without reacting to South African social injustice, symbolized by blacks' cleaning up whites' mess, but reacting only to the serenity of her enclosed world disturbed by the noise of barking dogs and banging rubbish bins.

What is learned or sensed by the audience in the short interchange quoted above is a preparation for how Piet and Gladys will act during the rest of the play. It provides an insight as well into why Piet has been able to survive the awful events that have preceded the action of *A Lesson from Aloes,* and why Gladys has been unable to identify herself with those of coloured skin and their cause, as well as into why she had her mind burned first psychologically by the Security Branch and then physiologically by shock therapy. Indeed, Gladys is, emotionally as well as physiologically, a woman with a sensitive skin, and, unlike Afrikaners like her husband, she is not able to survive that sensitivity effectively.

Names are more than just labels. Piet discusses his own name, Petrus Jacobus Bezuidenhout:

"So, would Petrus, were he not Petrus called, / Retain that dear perfection which he owns without that title?" . . . when other men say Piet Bezuiden-hout it is me they are talking about. Yes! That's what's in a name . . . "Then deny thy father and refuse thy name." Hell! I don't know about those Italians, but that's a hard one for an Afrikaner. No. For better or for worse, I will remain positively identified as Petrus Jacobus Bezuidenhout; Species, Afrikaner; Habitat, Algoa Park, Port Elizabeth, in this year of our Lord 1963 . . . and accept the consequences. (*He looks at his wrist watch*) (4–5)

His reference to the Montagues and Capulets brings to bear the divisions of the play. He, an Afrikaner Montague, has married an English Capulet, and he, a white South African, has formed an alliance with coloured adversaries. Like Romeo, he cannot finally deny his father and his name—in this case his fatherland and his Afrikaner roots. He will not, however, he implies, use subterfuge or be cowardly in his dealings, but will "remain positively identified." When the question arises later in the play as to whether Piet has betrayed his friends, the answer and Piet's innocence will already be known to the audience when they recall this speech. While he declares that he will accept the consequences of who he is, Piet looks at his watch. The stage direction is not haphazard but psychologically apposite and deftly engineered by Fugard. Simultaneously he thinks of his good name, the internecine conflicts of Shakespeare's tragedy and their South African applicability, the consequences of who he is, his current rejection by his erstwhile coloured comrades, and the imminent supper for Steve and his family. All of these things are distilled into his ruminations, and the glance at his watch suggests his anticipated reunion with Steve, the re-establishment of his friendship with Steve's family, and the possible return to the way things were.

Even more revealing than the subtext of Piet's speech about names is the pungent rejection of Piet, his political involvement, and his coloured friends implicit in Gladys's comments on their supper table arrangements. Piet provides exposition for the audience by telling her that he has invited for supper not only his old friend Steve Daniels but also the rest of the Daniels family, adding, "It's high time we saw our godson again." To this Gladys replies, "How many of them are there again?" Her vagueness about the size of their friends' family, one of whom is their very own godson, tellingly reveals her determination not to know these coloured people as intimates or peers. When Piet reminds her of the size of the family and asks whether there will be sufficient food, Gladys pointedly answers, "More than enough. That's not going to be the problem," suggesting that this visit presents other, far greater problems.

Among those problems are her memories of the great suffering that her association with Steve and his politics have brought into her life. Other problems are her resistance to sitting at table with a coloured family, and the unarticulated, unaddressed, but clearly troubled relationship between her husband and his former political comrade Steve. Facets of rejection are further subtextually revealed in Gladys's attitude about the seating arrangements:

GLADYS. I can't even remember their names, Peter!

PIET. Mavis, Lucille, Charmaine . . .

GLADYS. And then that little boy . . . !

PIET. Yes, I know. Little Pietertjie can get a bit boisterous at times . . .

GLADYS. Well . . . you can't deny we are going to be crowded.

PIET. Yes, I do. Observe. (*Placing two tables in from on the garden bench*) The festive board! (*Positioning chairs. He works hard at trying to allay* GLADYS' *anxieties*) The Lord and Lady of the Manor . . . our two honored guests . . . and then in descending order of age . . . Lucille, Charmaine, Beryl and little Pietertjie. (GLADYS *studies the seating arrangement in silence*) Does that look crowded?

GLADYS. No.

PIET. Then what's the matter?

GLADYS. You've got the little boy next to me. (8–10)

Gladys's claim to have forgotten the names of the children and her refusal to sit next to Pietertjie, their godson, named in honor of her own husband, is a pointed rejection not only of the expected visitors but of Piet himself. When she adds, "It's not that I don't like children," she brings to the fore what later becomes more clear: she and Piet are childless, will not have children, and that in her mind the consequences of Piet's connection with Steve are the reason why. Contrasted on stage are, on the one hand, Piet's busy preparations, his movements setting the table for the guests he is clearly eager to receive into his home, and on the other hand, Gladys's manner, which bespeaks something between disengagement and rejection. Gladys's determination to keep the Daniels family on the far periphery of her life coupled with a desire both to hurt her husband and to imbue him with guilt seem to make up the bitter subtext of what, on the surface, is a pedestrian conversation about the seating arrangements for seven supper guests.

A Lesson from Aloes has two playing areas: the small outdoor patio and the bedroom to which Gladys frequently retreats, to conceal her diary, to withdraw or hide from difficult situations, and to dress for the supper party. Margaret Munro sees the outside space as male and sociopolitical as opposed to the inside space which is female and psychological.[7] Though the playing spaces are hardly so schematically and inexorably divided, Munro's observation makes sense. More to the point, though, as we are made aware in the juxtaposition of the play's first two scenes, is the partially clad Piet's ease and Gladys's discomfort outdoors whereas the interior of the house is Gladys's sheltered area into which Piet enters as much as an awkward guest as a marriage partner. The subtext of scene 2, set in the bedroom, is powerful in the ways it continues to define Piet and Gladys, and their relationship. The scene begins with Piet's knocking at the bedroom door twice asking for admittance. Before she permits him to enter, Gladys desperately seeks a hiding place for her diary. When Piet enters from his bath, he does so with only a towel about his waist, and says, "I thought you might be changing"(18), to which she replies that she will change soon. He, however, proceeds unabashedly to dress on stage in his safari suit. The fact that a husband must knock before entering through the door of his own connubial bedroom lest he enter while his wife is changing speaks volumes about the relationship between this couple. And this picture of their marriage is brought further into focus by her pointedly not undressing and changing clothes while he is present whereas he walks into the bedroom with nothing but a towel and quite naturally stands naked before her (and the audience) and dresses himself. Fugard here prods his audience to learn the bases for these differences and to concentrate attention on one of the play's central inanimate actors: Gladys's diary.

The other central inanimate actors of the play are, of course, the aloes. When Piet sits like a South African Adam amid his aloes trying to give his mystery aloe a name, Gladys disparagingly remarks, "They all look alike to me. Thorns and fat, fleshy leaves" (13). The subtext pointedly implies that she declines the role of Edenic consort, that she does not share or wish to share Piet's interests and life, and that she rejects the country Piet's aloes represent. The "Notes" Fugard kept for *A Lesson From Aloes* (dated 25/1/78) read, "Her alienation from the S.A. landscape has changed into a morbid hatred of it. It threatens her."[8]

There is, moreover, surely more than botany involved, when Gladys and Piet state their views of roses and aloes:

> GLADYS. Well, they're not very pretty plants, you know. Is there a good word for something you can't and don't want to touch? That would describe them.
>
> PIET. A rose has also got its thorns.
>
> GLADYS. There is no comparison! They've got a lovely scent, they're pretty to look at and so many beautiful colors. But these . . . (*She pushes the aloe away*) No, thank you.
>
> PIET. This is not fair to them. An aloe isn't seen to its best advantage in a jam tin in a little backyard. They need space. The open veld with purple mountains in the distance. (14)

Piet's description leads him to recite the paean to the aloe in Roy Campbell's poem "The Snake"[9] and then to make clear the connection between himself and the aloes:

> A hillside covered with them in bloom! "Damp clods with corn may thank the showers / But when the desert boulder flowers / No common buds unfold." Roy Campbell. He understands them. "A glory such as from scant seed / The thirsty rocks suffice, to breed / Out of the rainless glare." And re-

member, it's a defiant glory, Gladys. That veld is a hard world. They and the thorn trees were just about the only things still alive when I finally packed up the old truck and left the farm. Four years of drought, but they were flowering once again. I'm ashamed to say it, but I resented them for that. It's a small soul that resents a flower, but I suppose mine was when I drove away and saw them there in the veld, surviving where I had failed. (14–15)

Like the aloes he catalogues, Piet wishes to be a succulent plant able to withstand long periods of hardship and drought, and like those aloes, he is seen to best advantage in his homeland veld and not in his jam tin urban flat. Piet, too, like his aloes, has a tough protective skin; yet given proper conditions he will bloom as brilliantly. The contrasting rose discussion and imagery woven into the play bespeak Gladys. The English rose is a transplant in South Africa, one which the climate and soil do not easily support. Roses, like Gladys, are fragile, able to endure neither drought nor strong sun.

The connection between Piet and the aloes is not merely one of personality, for the political ramifications of the botanic discussion are apparent as well. The survival of the aloes has not merely something but *everything* to do with Fugard's notion of the human need for survival amid the arid political and social climate in South Africa. Gladys exclaims, "Is that the price of survival in this country? Thorns and bitterness." To which Piet replies, "For the aloe it is. Maybe there's some sort of lesson for us there" (15).

The foundation for Piet's idea is manifest in the work to which he alludes, the monumental work on South African aloes, Gilbert Westacott Reynolds's *The Aloes of South Africa*, complete, as Piet reminds us, with a foreword written by General Smuts himself. Surely a playwright who writes with the economy of Athol Fugard does not drop such an allusion for nought. And when we consult Smuts's foreword to Reynolds's tome, we quickly realize the purpose of Fugard's allusion. Smuts, writing in high praise of Reynolds's endeavor, pointedly comments, "By doing so [cataloguing the aloes] he is helping to preserve the country's life blood—its living mantle, the flora on which the fauna of the land depends."[10] Indeed, Piet Bezuidenhout is the country's life blood, the flora, the aloe on which the others in the play and the others in South Africa depend if they and South Africa are to survive.

Underlying Piet's preoccupation with his aloes are several issues important to the play and its meaning. In a sense, his impulse, like that of Gilbert Westacott Reynolds, to sort out the separate forms of aloes, is the same impulse that informs the sorting out of races under apartheid. But whereas the latter stigmatizes difference, the former celebrates the individuality of each plant. It is two sides of the same coin. What becomes clear, then, in his portrait of Piet is one of Fugard's most perspicacious insights into South Africa: that the hardiness, adaptability, endurance, and interest in cataloguing the environment is what can damn or ennoble the Afrikaner. For Piet, moreover, aloes become almost religious icons, images of survival that bloom amidst drought and hardship. Thinking of their glorious survival in terms of his own privations creates a form of religious experience, wherein he both resents and worships his succulent essene saints. "It's a small soul that resents a flower," he says, "but I suppose mine was when I drove away and saw them there in the veld, surviving where I had failed" (15). The experience results not in prayer, but in the next closest thing, poetry, Campbell's own worshipful tribute to aloes. Indeed even one level of the word "lesson" in the play's title calls to mind the instructive biblical reading, the lesson of a church service, perhaps such as one might read to a Dutch Reformed congregation:

> GLADYS. Is that the price of survival in this country? Thorns and bitterness.
>
> PIET. For the aloe it is. Maybe there's some sort of lesson for us there.
>
> GLADYS. What do you mean?
>
> PIET. We need survival mechanisms as well. (15)

The passage does seem to ring faintly with the remembrances of racism and survival as might be heard in church service lessons from Exodus.

Appropriately, the play grows in intensity as it moves from the easily knowable, physiologically and psychologically open Piet to the more closely guarded inner world of the literally and metaphorically buttoned-up Gladys. Not surprisingly, Piet's is a proactive response to the current arid climate, political and otherwise, of South Africa. He is a survivor. Gladys's stance is reactive, one of a victim badly scorched by the infernal South African political climate, and now behaving like a bruised animal, lashing out, wishing to bruise others, flailing but failing to survive. Slowly the audience gleans the knowledge that she kept a diary that was then confiscated by the Security Branch during a raid, and that Piet has given her a new one so that she can begin her life and the record of her life again.

For Piet, and at one time also for Gladys, recording one's life implied that life had meaning. On their first date, he had inspired her with Thoreau's optimistic dictum, "There is a purpose to life, and we will be measured by the extent to which we harness ourselves to it" (22). And the utterance of secular faith those lines conveyed inspired her to keep a diary. Keeping such a journal of her thoughts and the events of her life bespoke a hope for the future and even seemed to provide existential sustenance in the face of her mother's unexpected death, which she recorded in words that bring to mind the opening line of Camus' *The Stranger:* "My mother died today. I haven't cried yet, and I don't think I'm going to" (23).[11]

Thus when the Security Branch invaded Gladys's inmost life, robbed her of her diary and her secrets, they robbed her as well of hope and optimism; and when, in one of the climactic moments of act 2, we learn that Gladys has given up keeping a diary, we recognize feelingly that she has lost her existential strength, that her tragedy is now to see life not merely without optimism but as a chaos and to see her own particular life as devoid of purpose and meaning, a tale told by an idiot signifying nothing. And it is more than that, for the tragedy also encompasses Gladys's desire to revenge the violation of the past by wounding others in the present. Fugard writes incisively in his unpublished notes:

> As always my sense of writing a play is not so much the organisation of facts, or the organisation of fields of energy. Thus: the S B. Raid and Gladys traumatic experience of it (Rape) is not just a fact which needs to be revealed at the right moment, but is an event in the past which generated a morbid energy seeking resolution in the present.
>
> Thus tragedy terminates the future, or put in other words . . . true tragedy terminates the flaw of a unique energy . . . Hamlet, Lear, Antigone etc.

The tragedy, however, is hardly Gladys's exclusive property, for it spills out to the others, poisoning their relationships.

Despite what has happened to his wife (and to himself), Piet remains undaunted, encouraging his wife to begin her life anew. He has presented her with a new diary inscribed, "Take this sweet soul! We'll start again" (24). As Gladys remembers the policeman reading her diaries, the psychodynamics of the Bezuidenhouts emerge once more:

> GLADYS. After all, it was in this very room. He sat down here, opened the first one, and started to read . . .
>
> PIET. I remember it very clearly, my love! I was here! With you! (*He pauses*) Maybe if we changed the room around . . . rearranged the furniture! That might help. What do you think?
>
> GLADYS. You could try.
>
> PIET. I know what it really needs, though, more light! . . . As soon as we've got a little something in the bank again I'm going to put in another window in that wall . . . And we'll change the furniture as well. (25)

To what was for Gladys a rape of her personhood by the Security Branch, Piet, unequipped and unable to address his wife's pain, can only respond pathetically but characteristically with a plan for changing the decor of her environment. This is an analogue to addressing the South African heat with an Afrikaner's pragmatic solution of a Voortrekker bonnet; but in this case, Gladys has been affected in ways that no simple practical solution, no rearrangement of either the furniture of their home or their lives, will assuage. Italicizing the ineptitude of Piet's response, there is a savage, pellucid pointedness to her "*You* could try," to his "Maybe if *we* changed the room" (italics mine). The action that he formulates as first-person plural she rejects, handing it back to him in second-person singular.

As she relives for Piet, herself, and most of all for the audience, the terrible events when her diary was impounded, when her innermost secrets were read and violated by the brutal eyes of the police, Gladys proposes her own method for dealing with the past. Piet produces from inside his Bible the police receipt for the diary that has never been returned; and she commands him, "Tear it up! Small pieces." This done, she can say, "There. I've cancelled those years. I'm going to forget I ever lived them," and derides the trust in herself and in life Piet had enjoined (27). Part of the tragedy here lies in the ineffectiveness of Gladys's and Piet's disparate responses. Hers is to destroy the past but without gesture for founding a future. His is to cope with adversity, rearrange the fragments so as to move forward into the future, but to do so without properly facing the painful past.

The exposition in act 1 goes on to tell of the loss of Piet's family farm through drought, his subsequent occupation as a bus driver, and his initiation into politics and collective action through Steve's idealism and public speaking. In this play of lessons, Piet relates, "My first lesson from Steve, and the most important one. An evil system isn't a natural disaster. There's nothing you can do to stop a drought, but bad laws and social injustice are man-made and can be unmade by men. It's as simple as that. We can make this a better world to live in" (35). A second lesson, however, comes in the form of the realities, the sheer human toll of such idealism and theoretical posturing. He has lost his friends to suspicion, he will lose his best friend Steve to an exit visa to England, and he will lose his wife by her exit to the mental hospital Fort England in Grahamstown. The lesson from aloes will be one on how to keep the optimism of the first lesson alive in the face of and despite the tragic realities of lesson number two. Trying to make Piet suffer as she has suffered, Gladys weighs in with those who would destroy Piet's optimism by deriding it:

> GLADYS. But I can remember very clearly how frightened some of the talk made me. "Overthrowing the regime" sounded very violent to me. (*With a little laugh*) Not much chance of that now, is there, with everybody . . . how did you put it? . . . crawled away into his own little shell. Snails aren't the most revolutionary of God's creatures.
>
> PIET. They weren't empty slogans, Gladys. To misquote the Bard: The weakness lay not in our ideals, but in ourselves. (39)

Piet, of course, is quoting from Shakespeare's play of governmental overthrow, *Julius Caesar;* tellingly omitting the final words of the quotation, "that we are un-derlings." Unwilling to accept either Gladys's derision or the subservience of his comrades to the sort of higher forces mentioned in the Shakespearean lines, he locates weakness of resolve in his fellow men, who are, nonetheless, as he has already acknowledged, capable of amelioration. Piet's indefatigable persistence and un-flagging belief in man's capability to improve his lot and himself can be laughable, as is his plan to move furniture, but it can also be tragic, poignant, and admirable. His mettle, however, is tried at every turn by Gladys's pessimism and her irrepress-ible desire to find his vulnerability and cause him pain as she has known it. Thus, when he reveals that his erstwhile comrades believe he may have been the informer whose treason led to Steve's imprisonment and subsequent banning order, Gladys asks, "It's not true, is it?" In this question lies her desire to wound her spouse, to violate her marriage vows with an ultimate act of disloyalty and distrust.[12] It is not that she believes it may be true, but to utter this is to strike a blow to the marriage knot after Piet's other ties of friendship have come undone. And as Piet ends the act by lighting the candles for the imminent arrival of Steve and his family, Gladys brings down the curtain with the doubting and hurtful "I'm going inside. Call me . . . if they come" (42–43).

When the curtain rises on the second act, darkness has fallen, and the dinner table stands untouched. As the much diminished candles suggest, two hours have passed since the first act, and Piet, now blowing out the candles, shows that he is at last accepting Gladys's prediction that the Daniels family will not show up. Like rain falling upon drought-stricken aloes, Steve is suddenly heard amid the darkness playing the "Marseillaise" on his harmonica, and Piet quickly replaces the crockery he had begun to remove. With Steve's arrival, conflicts and alliances among the three characters are set in motion. These are felt subtextually and through small but important touches. Almost immediately a bond of friendship and fellow feeling is established between the white and the coloured man, one that marginalizes Gladys. Both are native speakers of Afrikaans. They share similar politics and a love of their native land. Their bonhomie and special bonding is brilliantly affirmed as they recite in unison the entirety of Longfellow's "The Slave's Dream" (fig. 14), a poem hardly without resonance within the twentieth-century apartheid context. Fugard also subtly indicates their shared love of their country through the bottle of South African wine Steve has brought along. As only those who live in wine-producing regions of the world can know, pride in the local and national vintages is a signifier of national and local fealty. The marginalization of the English-speaking Gladys and her culture is made manifest as they offer her a glass of sherry, a drink traditionally identified with British society, instead of South African wine. "Here, my dear. A glass of sherry?" says Piet (55). And in the other editions of *A Lesson from Aloes*, the line is even more emphatic, for in those Piet says, "Here, my dear. A glass of *your* sherry?" (italics mine).[13]

Gladys, for her part, keeps Steve at psychological arm's length by never calling him by the friendly version of his name but always addressing him as Steven, much the way she never calls her Afrikaner husband Piet but consistently anglicizes his name to Peter. Her resistance to Steve is further made clear by her body language and the subtext of the amenities they exchange:

> STEVE. Gladys! Long time no see, hey! (*They shake hands.* STEVE *and* GLADYS *treat each other with a stilted politeness and formality*)
>
> PIET. Good to see him here again, isn't it?
>
> GLADYS. Yes, it is. I'm sorry Mavis couldn't come. Peter told me about . . . which one is it that's sick?
>
> STEVE. Charmaine.
>
> GLADYS. What a lovely name. (55)

14. Tony Amendola and James P. Phillips as Piet and Steve in *A Lesson from Aloes* at the Berkeley Repertory Theatre, Berkeley, Cal., 1983 Photo by Ken Friedman. Courtesy the Berkeley Repertory Theatre.

She here clearly rubs his nose in what she knows is his bald deception that Mavis has not come along because one of the children is ill, and forces him to give the name of the allegedly indisposed child . Her pointed response is to comment inappropriately on the child's name rather than to make the expected expression of regret, inquiry about the illness, or wish for speedy recovery. The subtextual interchange between them continues with her seemingly superficial "We'd given up hope of seeing you," and his reply, "Ja, sorry about everything" (56). Her line tries to force him to choose a level of what she says: We'd given up hope because we did not hear from you and you might have died in prison, you did not see us or make contact when you were released, or you are hours late for dinner. His answer is a parry that marks his refusal to answer any of the implicit possibilities.

She makes another attempt as she says of Piet's aloes, "Peter's new hobby, now that there's no politics left." Rather than seizing the opening, Steve carefully dodges her bullet with "I prefer flowers myself." Finally, Gladys strikes closer to the heart and to Steve's wounds as she raises the issue of Steve's exit visa and an irrevocable move to England. With a hint of sarcasm, she says, "To be leaving the country! You don't have any doubts, surely? You of all people." He again avoids the issue, pointedly deflecting the situation away from himself, refusing to expose his feelings to Gladys: "(*With an embarrassed little laugh*) Well, the children are excited, that I can say for sure." She essentially tells him she knows exactly what he is doing and exactly what the move means to him by replying, "And so they should be. It will be a marvellous experience. Travel broadens the mind" (56–57). She knows full well that an exit visa means they can never return to South Africa, that the children will grow up on foreign soil in a culture not their own. This is no travel, no happy exercise in mind broadening, but a cataclysmic change particularly for one who has been so rooted in South Africa and so involved in its politics.

For a moment, Steve seems to give Gladys an opening, as he asks, "What's it going to be like, Gladys." But rather than open up his doubts of the future, harbored in that word "it," he defines "it" as the geography and climate of England. And in so doing, he unwittingly initiates a conversation that inadvertently touches Gladys's own wounds:

> STEVE. England. All I know about it is what I've seen on the bioscope and pictures in books. They always make it look very pretty. (*She is staring at him*) Is it really like that?
>
> GLADYS. Why do you ask me?
>
> STEVE. You're from England, aren't you?
>
> GLADYS. What makes you say that?
>
> STEVE. Oh, your manners and the way you speak. Not rough and ready like Piet and myself. Sorry . . . I always thought . . .
>
> GLADYS. That's all right. In a way I suppose I am from England . . . now. (*She gives a little smile*) I've been there many times.
>
> . . .
>
> STEVE. But it's summer there now.
>
> GLADYS. (*Another smile*) Of course. It will never be anything else. (57–58)

Steve here makes the innocent mistake of assuming Gladys to be a foreigner, noting the difference of her speech and manners from his own and Piet's. Ironically, though a native of South Africa with as much claim to citizenship as her husband, she is a stranger in her own land, a hothouse English rose struggling and failing to survive in a land that demands the hardiness of aloes. Her curious smiles and replies to Steve's error arise from her own personal tragic joke that the audience will eventually understand. She is a native not of England but of Fort England Clinic. It is always summer at Fort England, for there she concentrates on one of those bland institutional waiting room framed prints of a summer garden called "Sunset in Somerset."

In act 2, Fugard gives Steve two dazzling and extended dramatic moments. In one, he recounts the savagery of the South African Group Areas Act and the ways it has affected his life and thought. In the other, he poignantly recounts his political and psychological breakdown at the hands of the Special Branch of the South African police. Steve first recounts a deeply moving anecdote about catching a thirty-pound fish with his father on Port Elizabeth's Maitland Strand. The moment is one of joy and achievement mixed with the pleasure of succeeding where the white boys with their superior tackle had failed:

> The white boys used to come past with their fancy rods and reels empty-handed, while we had Steenbras tails flapping around us on the sand. The old man had patience. That was his secret. (62)

But Steve's exultation is succeeded by a profound and angry sadness as he recalls his father's tragedy. The Group Areas Act forcibly removed the old man far from the Maitland Strand relocating him inland to Salt Lake, a body of water devoid of living things. "Fairview was declared white and that was the end of us. . . . He hadn't just lost his house and his savings, they also took away the sea. I mean . . . how the hell do you get from Salt Lake to Maitland on a bicycle?" (63). His once proud and now broken father is tragically led to lament, "Ons geslag is verkeerd," our race is a mistake. And in the performance playtext, Steve punctuates this terrible history not with revolutionary anger but with pathetic, near-tragic resignation as he tears the snapshot that has inspired the reminiscence of his father.[14] Clearly this act echoes and resonates with the earlier shredding of the receipt for Gladys's diary.

Steve's impending departure from South Africa and his father's removal from the vitality of Port Elizabeth's Indian Ocean coast links Steve with Piet, who has also been forced to leave the natural vitality of the South African veld. In Piet's case, the drought and the death of a black child from the effects of the drought led him to move to the city and abandon the Bezuidenhout family farm, *Alwynlaagte,* which, significantly, in Afrikaans means "Valley of Aloes."

The second of Steve's dramatic moments recounts his arrest after an anonymous informer tipped off the Special Branch that he was breaking his banning order. Once again movingly, Steve recalls his mental breakdown in the course of the police interrogations.[15] When he recounts his resultant mental castration and his consequent desire to emigrate irrevocably to an England he has never seen, he is suddenly revealed to the audience and to Gladys as her spiritual ally, now as much or more her fellow than he has seemed to be Piet's.

Gladys, too, has been broken by the Special Branch. In investigating possible subversives in Steve's political circle, the Special Branch made a thorough search of the Bezuidenhout house. Piet's home, named Xanadu in honor of the dreamlike city that housed the pleasure dome of Coleridge's Kubla Khan, became ironically the environment of Gladys's nightmare when the police arrived in the middle of the night and in the course of their search for political secrets and banned literature read and confiscated the diaries in which she had written her inmost thoughts and feelings. For Gladys, the moment is one of terrifying violation, a form of rape more intrusive and destructive than its sexual counterpart. Like Steve, she is broken by the traumatic events that led her not to prison as in his case but to incarceration in a mental hospital where she undergoes shock therapy and experiences thereby a form of mental castration. Here no doubt Fugard draws on the experiences of his wife, Sheila, who writes so movingly of her own shock treatments in the chilling poem "Therapy":

> You
> Who have seen me
> Convulse
> Under the shock
> Playing God
> Your hand found the switch—
> Lightning to my radiant head
> A bolt down the well of the mind
> Searing images—
> God, devil, lust
> Thrust
> Of reason, idiocy, pure delight
> All seared, scarred and twisted
> Rubble
> Where before was too bright a sun
> Myself
> Split a hundred ways
> Catapulted into prehistory
> No time
> No real world[16]

And at the end of the play, Gladys, like Steve, will voluntarily deport herself to England, but in her case it is not England the nation but Fort England, the mental hospital where she will play out what remains of her life.

Gladys and Steve are allied as well because both connect Piet with the source of their wounds and their defeat. Like his black and coloured comrades, Steve has come to suspect Piet, the white Afrikaner, as the most logical police informer. As a result, Piet has been ostracized by his former friends, Steve's wife Mavis has refused to come to the farewell meal at the Bezuidenhout home, and to some extent Steve himself has come on the evening of the play to find out whether Piet is innocent or guilty. Gladys, whose suffering has been analogous to Steve's, instinctively senses Steve's suspicions and plays with them savagely to sunder the last threads that bind Steve and Piet. And in coming to terms with what she has done, Gladys reveals Fugard's brilliant insights not merely into the biographical analogies between Gladys and Steve but into the dilemma of South Africa:

> That's my business. Yes, mine! My reason for telling you an ugly lie, which you were ready to believe! . . . is *my* business. I accept, Steven, that I am just

a white face on the outskirts of your terrible life, but I'm in the middle of mine and yours is just a brown face on the outskirts of my own story. I don't need yours. I've discovered hell for myself. It might be hard for you to accept, Steven, but you are not the only one who has been hurt. Politics and black skins don't make the only victims in this country. (74)

And as Gladys proceeds to recount her sufferings in shock therapy, she italicizes her new bond with Steve by saying, "They've burned my brain as brown as yours, Steven" (76). Theirs is a bond that she comes to comprehend only at that moment; it is only then, in her last line of farewell—"Good-by, Steve" (76)—that Gladys for the first time addresses Steve familiarly and as a comrade, as *Steve,* rather than as *Steven.* Thus with brilliant dramatic economy and with equally brilliant use of subtext, Fugard forges a new pattern of relationships. Whereas Gladys stood outside the bond of camaraderie and political commitment that existed between Piet and Steve, now it is Piet who is excluded from the new sense of spiritual bonding between Steve and Gladys.

Clearly Gladys, the white woman of British descent and sensitive skin, cannot, like the roses she adores, withstand the climate of South Africa. It blasts her, sears her, and like the strong sun in a drought beating down on a fragile rose, it turns her brown. She is a hothouse flower unadaptable to South Africa and the South African soil. She can only survive in the controlled climate and atmosphere of a sanatorium. Indeed, in this play with a botanical title, the personalities and relationships are, in part, botanically focused. Thus early in act 2, when Gladys and Steve are momentarily left alone with each other, the subject of botany and politics arises:

> GLADYS. Peter's new hobby, now there's no politics left. Aloes. He takes it very seriously. He's got a little book and he knows all their names.
>
> STEVE. I prefer flowers myself.
>
> GLADYS. That makes two of us. We tried to lay out a little flower bed here once . . . Roses! . . . But the soil is very poor. Come, let's sit down. So, Steven, you're on your way to England. I couldn't believe it when Peter told me. (56)

Like Gladys, Steve prefers flowers to Piet's succulents, and the subject of roses here naturally seems to provide a prelude to a discussion of Steve's imminent departure for England. The point that is made here subtextually, and developed as the act progresses, is that although Steve may not be a hothouse rose like Gladys he shares her lack of appreciation for the rugged odorless aloes. Unlike the aloe-like Piet, Steve, to survive the current spiritual and political drought conditions in South Africa, must escape the South African (political) climate to transplant himself and his family to the English spring, to the more nurturing landscape depicted in the pastoral "Sunset in Somerset" painting.

Steve and Gladys display their psychological wounds, wounds suffered at the hands of the Special Branch and the apartheid system. Each displays an inability to survive in the destructive biological/political atmosphere of contemporary South Africa. Further, both Steve and Gladys implicate Piet in their fates. The third victim of *A Lesson from Aloes*, then, is Piet, who is left alone at the end of the play.[17] Bereft of his wife and her love, bereft of Steve and his friendship, Piet stands personally and politically isolated as the final curtain of *A Lesson from Aloes* falls. Like the South African aloes, he remains to face the drought that is South Africa. And like those succulents, he must rely on his tough skin and on his ability to go without nurture for long periods. He is, after all, recalling again General Smuts's words in the foreword to Reynolds's *The Aloes of South Africa:* "the country's life blood . . . the flora on which the fauna of the land depends." And Fugard has said essentially of both the aloe and Piet: "I think the aloe is one of South Africa's most powerful, beautiful and celebratory symbols. It survives out there in the wild when everything else is dried. At the end of one of our terrible recurrent droughts, the aloe is still there."[18]

Piet Bezuidenhout is an Afrikaner, a Boer. When Steve derogatorily refers to the Special Branch, he calls them "those boer-boys" (68); and Gladys clearly connects Piet to the police, the most savage extension of the apartheid system and its enforcement, when she says, "He looks like one of them, doesn't he? The same gross certainty in himself! He certainly sounds like them. He speaks English with a dreadful accent" (73). What Fugard is here characterizing are those Afrikaner qualities of intense patriotism, hardiness, self-righteousness, self-possession, and ability to survive—qualities that enabled the Afrikaners to survive and tame South African wilderness and survive the onslaughts of the British during the Boer War, but that have also enabled them to institute and vigorously maintain the full apartheid system.

Used for good, these are admirable traits. But the boer-boys with their Afrikaans accents have largely been responsible for creating and enforcing the apartheid climate that castrates Steve psychologically and politically, sending him to England, and that likewise destroys Gladys, sending her to Fort England. The boer-boys have also wounded if not destroyed Piet; and yet, suggests Fugard, his very Boer hardihood will enable Piet to survive the political climate and to continue to work toward the dismantling of apartheid.[19] Like his Boer forebears, Piet has the patriotism, self-possession, hardiness, and will to survive.[20] Producing his play in 1982, Fugard suggests that these traits, which helped build and maintain apartheid, may, in the hands of people like Piet, also become that system's undoing—more so than the maneuvering of liberal English speakers or the tactics of revolutionary nonwhites. However, these unanswered questions remain at the end of *A Lesson from Aloes:* how long can an aloe survive adverse conditions, and when the long South African drought is over, will it be over due to nurturing rains or a bloodbath?

The Germans make a very important and useful distinction, one that has no proper English equivalent, between *Tragödie* and *Trauerspiel.* The first means tragedy in the best Aristotelian sense. The second translates literally as a play of grieving or mourning and describes such classic dramas as Lessing's *Emilia Ga-*

lotti or Nicholas Rowe's *The Fair Penitent* and modern works like O'Neill's *Moon for the Misbegotten* or Synge's *Riders to the Sea*. Not a tragedy in the strict classic sense, *A Lesson from Aloes* is a stellar example of the modern *Trauerspiel*, for it is very much about grieving and mourning: mourning for the three damaged souls of the play and grieving for the land that has caused their suffering. Fugard asserts in his unpublished notes, "'*Aloes*' is about three desperate people . . . and they are that from the moment we see them." In presenting their individual and joint wounds, he is reaching and finally finding that amalgam of pain and relief that characterizes much of his prior work. As Fugard writes in the notes, "What I am grasping for, still very uncertainly, is that balance between joy & pain that I seemed to have found with Hello & Goodbye, The Blood Knot, and to a certain extent also with Boesman & Lena." To this list one might add *Nongogo, People Are Living There, The Island,* and *Sizwe Bansi Is Dead.* Certainly the heart of the play can be found in the delicate balances of triangulated feeling and attitude among the three troubled characters.[21] But as much as *A Lesson from Aloes* is about three desperate people, it is also very much about the desperation and *Trauer* of South Africa in the late 1970s. Or, as Fugard said to the actors at the first read-through of his play, the aloes "are a symbol of survival in South Africa's harsh political landscape. Piet and Steve are victims of a system they have tried to resist, something man-made, whereas Gladys is God's victim."[22] *A Lesson from Aloes* reveals the separate griefs and pains that beset the characters and the country. All seem finally trapped in their situations. But the effect of Fugard's writing and theatre is a dazzling accomplishment, for in a remarkable way the drama empowers audience members, as they feel the plights and griefs of Gladys, Steve, and Piet to cross the lines of gender, race, and ethnicity; to go beyond the divisions that separate individuals and give life to apartheid; to see the larger landscape of human drought and perhaps to conquer the status quo as the characters themselves seem unable to do.

Like *A Lesson from Aloes,* Fugard's next play *"Master Harold" . . . and the Boys* (1982) is also about "three desperate people," teaching, and lessons learned or unlearned. It is a deeply disturbing, moving play about the wounds inflicted by apartheid upon three individuals. It, too, is a *Trauerspiel* that grieves for the wounded.

Fugard's casts are always small, and his spotlights here are on two black men and a young white teenage boy rather than the masses of South Africans who suffer under the apartheid regime, but Fugard's cameo of three says more about the larger portrait of South African inhumanity than it would have had he filled his stage with whole black townships. As Fugard himself (whose name is actually Harold Athol Fugard) has acknowledged, *Master Harold* stems in part from his own relationship with Sam Semela, a Basuto family servant employed for fifteen years by Fugard's mother in her various attempts to earn the family's bread by running a Port Elizabeth rooming house and later the snack bar in that city's centrally located St. George's Park.[23]

The play's apartheid context is astutely discussed in an incisive essay by Errol Durbach. Some have taken up the connection between the play and Fugard's life as well as the accusation that Fugard, as a white man with a consequently privileged position in South Africa, cannot acceptably describe South African racism and its capitalistic exploitation of blacks and coloureds. For others, the autobiographical content of the play has obfuscated rather than clarified Fugard's considerable dramatic achievement.[24] Certainly the autobiographical inflection of *Master Harold* is strong, and certainly, too, the feelings in the play have their origins in the depth of Fugard's personal and painful remembrances. Knowing the autobiographical underpinnings may add resonances to the text and enhance one's reaction to the play, but that should in no way cause one to minimize the enormous magnitude of this almost minimalist play.

Indeed, *Master Harold* may be Fugard's masterpiece. The power of *Master Harold* registered for me when I attended a Saturday matinee performance of the New York production of the play. Uncommon for a New York matinee, the theatre was perfectly still, not a shopping bag rustled. The audience groaned and wept. The applause was thunderous, the spectators, so moved by what they had witnessed, so aware of its relevance to their own American lives, that they filed out in uncommon silence.[25] They knew they had witnessed a masterpiece, a play that spoke simultaneously to their senses and their minds. And almost no one knew that the origins of the play were autobiographical. To locate the true sources of *Master Harold*'s strength, one must look not to Fugard's life or his white skin but to his dialogue and dramaturgy.

"Master Harold" . . . and the Boys is structured around the relationships among the three central characters ironically mentioned in the title. Master Harold is the young teenage Hally who befriends and teaches, is befriended by and taught by the two black men three times his age, who are in Hally's mother's employ. The irony, of course, is that South African racism elevates the teenage boy to a the role of master as it likewise reduces the two grown men to boys. These distinctions are hardly lost on an American audience, for the play is as much about racism as a global practice as it is about the specific South African variety depicted in the play. A second ironic and most important reversal in the play is that whereas in classic plays servants and blacks are at the dramatic peripheries, here the black servants are foregrounded and Hally's white parents are unseen, felt on stage only in terms of their presence at the other end of a telephone connection.

One of the central images in *Master Harold* is that of a kite which Sam years earlier fashioned for Hally. That kite comes to represent the possibilities of their relationship as well as the possibilities between their races. Hally remembers that he was convinced the flimsy kite Sam had constructed would never fly, and that he would look foolish before his peers as he attempted to make it do so (fig. 15):

> Can you remember what the poor thing looked like? Tomato box wood and brown paper! Flour and water for glue! Two of my mother's old stockings for a tail, and then all those bits and pieces of string you made me tie together so

15. Duart Sylwain, Ramolao Makhene, and John Kani as Harold, Sam, and Willie in *Master Harold*, Market Theatre, Johannesburg, 1983. Photo by Ruphin Coudyzer.

that we could fly it! Hell, that was now only asking for a miracle to happen. (29)[26]

Hally then recollects his amazement and delight as the seemingly shabby kite dazzlingly soars into the air as something remarkable and beautiful:

I don't know how to describe it, Sam. Ja! The miracle happened! I was running, waiting for it to crash to the ground, but instead suddenly there was something alive behind me at the end of the string, tugging at it as if it wanted to be free. (30)

The image is one that tells of something beautiful and free that, despite unpromising circumstances, can be achieved between black men and white boys. It is also a pointed image of Fugard's play.

Like Hally's kite, *Master Harold* is a deceptively simply construction, glued together with the most basic of dramatic materials—a triangle of characters, interacting in one space within a short, continuous time frame—and tied together with the bits and pieces of Fugard's dramatic narrative string: memories of Hally's childhood and minor current problems about a dance contest and an essay due at school.[27] Yet as miraculously as Hally's kite sailing into the sky, from those essential dramatic properties arises a stirring, profound play charting kitelike ups and downs, swooping curves of feeling for both characters and audience. For Hally, the kite Sam fashioned for him momentarily compelled him literally to look up, to see the kite and a horizon that put his personal woes into perspective. Likewise the play that Fugard fashions for the audience is one that enables us to acknowledge how art may raise the gaze of its spectators and thereby empower them to see not just with sight but with vision. "I had a stiff neck the next day from looking up so much" (31), Hally exclaims. If *Master Harold* is successful, then the audience, too, will feel the pleasurable pain of lifting its eyes from the unpleasant political and social South African present to the soaring possibilities of its future. For Fugard, playmaking like kite flying can achieve a heuristic experience from relatively unsophisticated materials.

It is almost Fugard's signature to begin with seemingly minor incidents and small issues, and use them to teach the audience about and illumine matters of great significance. And like *A Lesson from Aloes* earlier, and *My Children! My Africa!* later on, *Master Harold* is a Fugardian *Lehrstück*. In it, as in his other plays, he uses a minimum of actors—two black men and one white boy—and one playing space, the St. George's Park Tea Room, a small restaurant/snack bar providing light collations for those strolling through or playing in the surrounding park. During the whole of the play, it is raining outside, so the sound of rain on stage creates a barrier that sets off and demarcates the tea room as a special area for the drama to take place. One knows, too, that on such a rainy day, no customers will enter the tea room to influence the drama that will be played out among the three males. In short, the playing space becomes a no-man's-land isolated from the "whites only" park outside, Hally's home and the hospital where his father is ill, and the homes of Sam and Willie in Port Elizabeth's black township of New Brighton. It becomes an area in which Hally, Sam, and Willie can play out their friendship, visions, and growing pains.

At the close of *Master Harold,* Sam, reflecting on the action of the play, remarks that that afternoon "there was a hell of a lot of teaching going on . . . one way or the other" (59). Indeed on several levels this is a didactic play about teachers, teaching, and lessons learned. And the learning that takes place is as much among the audience as it is among the characters on stage. From the moment the play commences, we are in the world of teaching. Sam is teaching his fellow black servant, Willie, how to perfect his quickstep dancing in preparation for the annual Eastern Province Open Ballroom Dancing Championships. Willie's difficulty is that although he understands the physical realities of the quickstep, the actual steps of the dance, he is not getting it right because his physical steps are not graced by the ideas, imagination, and dreams that the dance is meant to embody. He has the right steps but his style lacks the ability to convey semiotically a message of harmony, as the comical dialogue between the two men makes clear:

SAM. Look happy, Willie! Relax, Willie!

WILLIE. I am relax. . . . Yesterday I'm not straight . . . today I'm too stiff!

SAM. Well, you are. You asked me and I'm telling you. . . . Try to glide through it.

WILLIE. Glide?

SAM. Ja, make it smooth. And give it more style. It must look like you're enjoying yourself. . . .

WILLIE. How can I enjoy myself? Not straight, too stiff and now it's also glide, make it smooth . . . Haai! Is hard to remember all those things, Boet Sam.

SAM. That's your trouble. You're trying too hard.

WILLIE. I try hard because it *is* hard.

SAM. But don't let me see it. The secret is to make it look easy. Ballroom must look happy, Willie, not like hard work. It must . . . Ja! . . . it must look like romance.

WILLIE. Now another one! What's romance?

SAM. Love story with happy ending. A handsome man in tails, and in his arms, smiling at him, a beautiful lady in evening dress!

WILLIE. Fred Astaire, Ginger Rogers.

SAM. You got it. Tapdance or ballroom, it's the same. Romance. In two weeks' time when the judges look at you and Hilda, they must see a man and a woman who are dancing their way to a happy ending. What I saw was you holding her like you were frightened she was going to run away. (4–6)

We then learn that Willie's dancing problem is partly the result of his domestic problems with Hilda and of his use of physical force toward her. As both dancing and domestic partner, Willie is too much given to the purely physical. There is not enough romance in his dance steps or in his treatment of Hilda. Sam tells him, "You hit her too much. One day she's going to leave you for good." Willie answers, "So she makes me the hell-in too much." Sam then tries to teach Willie at another level what he was teaching him about the dance: "Beating her up every time she makes a mistake? No, Willie! That takes the pleasure out of ballroom dancing" (7).

As teacher, Sam attempts to educate Willie and have him infuse the notion of romance, "a love story with a happy ending," into his partnership with Hilda on the dance floor and in life. As Willie then dances around the tea room singing the words of the dance tune "You're the Cream in My Coffee" (9), Hally appears. Given the racial difference between the white schoolboy and the black serving men, the words of the song of course provide an ironic edge to Hally's entrance. Carrying his schoolbooks, Hally brings the news of his day at school, and thereby introduces a discussion of education and teaching in a new key.

Hally, who has that day been punished, receiving six strokes for drawing a caricature of his teacher, complains about injustice and launches with Sam into an extended discussion of social reformers. What quickly becomes apparent is that for the past several years, Hally has been teaching his schoolwork to Sam. At the same time, however, Sam has been Hally's teacher, trying to teach Hally about life. But Hally is sometimes too young, unwilling, or unable to pick up the cues from Sam. This is lucidly demonstrated as we hear the discussion between Hally and Sam that emanates from the corporal punishment the young boy has received that day:

> HALLY. So six of the best, and his are bloody good.
>
> SAM. On your bum.
>
> HALLY. Where else? The days when I got them on my fingers are gone forever, Sam.
>
> SAM. With your trousers down!
>
> HALLY. No, He's not quite that barbaric.
>
> SAM. That's the way they do it in jail.
>
> HALLY. Really.
>
> SAM. Ja. When the magistrate sentences you to "strokes with a light cane." . . . They make you lie down on a bench. One policeman pulls down your trousers and holds your ankles, another one pulls your shirt over your head and holds your arms . . .
>
> HALLY. Thank you! That's enough.
>
> SAM. . . . and the one that gives you the strokes talks to you gently and for a long time between each one (*He laughs*)
>
> HALLY. I've heard enough, Sam! Jesus! It's a bloody awful world when you come to think of it. People can be real bastards.
>
> SAM. That's the way it is, Hally. (14–15)

Hally is Willie's opposite number. Willie understands physical punishment but has trouble making the leap to abstractions like "romance." Hally rushes to abstractions and generalizations, avoiding the painful physical information Sam relates. What Hally fails to see or wishes to avoid knowing is that Sam is not his student and is not a boy, nor is he speaking in the abstract. Clearly Sam's description of police beatings comes from personal experience, for, like many black men in South Africa, he has likely known corporal punishment and police brutality firsthand. Indeed, commenting on this speech in an interview after the first production of *Master Harold*, black South African actor Zakes Mokae, who played the role of Sam, said, "Hally doesn't know what he's talking about, he's thinking of a world that doesn't exist. Once you're oppressed, you know of things the oppressor doesn't know."[28]

Similarly, when Hally and Sam contemplate candidates for their list of great reformers, Hally fails to grasp why Sam is attracted to the history book description of Napoleon as someone who abolished the feudal system, regarding all persons as equal before the law; or why Sam was motivated to read Darwin's chapter on "The Struggle for Existence"; or why, after reading *Julius Caesar* with its overthrow of dictatorship, Sam should esteem Shakespeare; or why Sam should revere Abraham Lincoln as a man of magnitude. For Hally, Napoleon is only a figure about whom there are too many dates to memorize. *Julius Caesar* for him presents the rigors of reading Elizabethan English, not revolutionary politics. He casts Lincoln aside because slavery was abolished in South Africa before it was in the United States, but he gives no thought to Lincoln as the author of the Emancipation Proclamation.

Hally sees his relationship with Sam as one of teacher and student. He explains, "Tolstoy may have educated his peasants, but I've educated you" (23). This is true, but what Hally fails to see is that while he has been educating Sam with textbook material, Sam has also been playing the role of teacher and surrogate father, trying to educate Hally about the disparate meanings of life for whites and for blacks in apartheid South Africa.[29] Hally opens the doors of one kind of knowledge for Sam even as Sam attempts to open the doors of another kind of knowledge for Hally (as well as for Fugard's white South African and non–South African audiences).

Like many South African whites, like many whites in other countries, Hally does not see or want to see what is before his eyes and happening in South Africa. Just as he does not want to recognize Sam's obviously firsthand experience of corporal punishment at the hands of the police, he also does not want to understand the truths behind his memories of Sam and Willie's room in the servant quarters of his mother's house. Hally remembers the path to their room and what he found there:

> HALLY. I bet I could still find my way to your room with my eyes closed. . . . past the kitchen and unappetizing cooking smells . . . around the corner and into the backyard, hold my breath again because there are more smells coming when I pass your lavatory, then into that little passageway, first door on the right and into your room. How's that?
>
> SAM. Good. But as usual, you forgot to knock.
>
> HALLY. Like that time I barged in and caught you and Cynthia . . . at it. Remember? God, was I embarrassed! I didn't know what was going on at first.
>
> SAM. Ja, that taught you a lesson. . . .
>
> HALLY. A grey little room with a cold cement floor. Your bed against that wall . . . and I now know why the mattress sags so much! . . . Willie's bed . . . It's propped up on bricks because one leg is broken, that wobbly little table with the washbasin and jug of water . . . Under Willie's bed is an old suitcase with all his clothes in a mess . . . (25–26)

Unacknowledged in Hally's reverie are its underlying implications: Sam and Willie must live in a separate outbuilding; their lavatory in the yard smells because it has no plumbing; the room they share has no amenities, just a cold cement floor and a broken bed; their clothes are in suitcases because no dresser has been provided; there is also no plumbing in the outbuilding, so there is no drinking water, and a basin and jug are all that Willie and Sam have for washing themselves.

Just as important, in the course of the play, Hally fails to question why Willie and Sam no longer live with his family but in New Brighton, the black township. The time of the play is 1950, and unacknowledged by Hally is that the time he remembers in his mother's boardinghouse was before the triumph of the Nationalist Party in the 1948 elections and the subsequent institution of apartheid as a national policy. 1950 saw the institution of the Group Areas Act that remanded Willie and Sam to a separate black township on the periphery of Port Elizabeth, a sizable bus ride from their jobs at the St. George's Tea Room in the middle of a "whites only" downtown park. Hally, in short, fails to see the irony of his relationship with Sam (the irony implicit in the play's title) or the kinds of existence forced upon black men. He does not even see that the school uniform he wears and the servant uniforms worn by Sam and Willie symbolize the separateness of apartheid and the very disparate possibilities that system extends to whites and blacks.

Hally assumes the role of master even as Sam and Willie assume the role of boys. But the "boys" are in their forties; they are sexually active, and Willie has fathered children. Hally's memories are a record of his pleasant and general feelings recollecting and outlining his relationship with Sam and Willie as it appears to him. The actual grim social, physical, and political realities underlying his memories are things the young Master Harold has not yet mastered, but he will be compelled to do so before the play is quite over. Fugard for his part is making a political statement about the consequences of racism and white domination. He points, too, to the uncanny ability of whites to avoid recognizing the implications behind the facts they have called into being. And premiering *Master Harold* at the Yale Repertory Theatre, taking it to New York before it ever played in South Africa, Fugard means his message to be not just a localized one about South African racism but an essentialist one about the consequences of racism wherever it is practiced. Indeed the greatness of the play derives precisely from its ability to go beyond its immediate South African context.

Fugard's portrayal of racism in *Master Harold* is not only focused through the "master" and "boy" metaphor but also nicely projected through the relationships between fathers and sons. When Hally recalls the day Sam made a kite for him, he muses:

> Little white boy in short trousers and a black man old enough to be his father flying a kite. It's not every day you see that. . . .Would have been just as strange, I suppose if it had been me and my Dad . . . cripple man and a little boy. (31)

For Hally, Sam is a surrogate father, but one as strange as his real one. Hally's white father is physically crippled, and Sam in South African society is racially handicapped. And like all sons, Hally is caught in an Oedipal struggle that leads him at once to resent and love both his fathers as well as to harbor the younger generation's co-existent feelings of superiority and inferiority to their elders.

The equation made between Hally's two fathers enables him to translate his psychologically unacceptable feelings of helplessness and of hatred for his crippled, alcoholic father into socially acceptable manifestations of dominance practiced by white masters toward their non-white subalterns. Consequently, when he learns that his father may be returning home from the hospital, Hally sublimates his anger toward his father by turning with rage toward the innocent two black men and adopting the role of martinet. Fugard provides the stage direction: "*He struts around like a little despot, ruler in hand, giving vent to his anger and frustration*" (38).

Hally becomes, in fact, a caricature and replication of the classroom teacher he so much dislikes, transmogrifying his seemingly cordial relationship with Sam and Willie into a destructive and hierarchical power relationship. This permits him to deflect his conflicted feelings toward his father into verbal vituperation directed at Sam and into physical abuse toward Willie, giving him "*a vicious whack on the bum*" with his ruler. Deftly and subtly, Fugard here suggests the psychological underpinnings of apartheid as well as its concomitant police brutality. The whack on Willie's bum is simply the elementary forerunner to the full-scale beating from the police that Sam has implied he knows firsthand. And Hally, too, reminds us that the power relationship between teacher and student that he feels at school is part of his education, one that teaches that the world is comprised of the rulers and the ruled. Despite the fact that he despises Mr. Prentice, his teacher, Prentice is nevertheless a role model and Hally an all too apt student:

> From now on there will be no more of your ballroom nonsense in here. This is a business establishment, not a bloody New Brighton dancing school. I've been far too lenient with the two of you. (*Behind the counter for a green cool drink and a dollop of ice cream. He keeps up his tirade as he prepares it*) But what really makes me bitter is that I allow you chaps a little freedom in here when business is bad and what to you do with it? The foxtrot! (38–39)

In tones that might be Prentice's, Hally makes clear his role as the white ruler and Sam and Willie's position as the non-white ruled. By including the action of Hally's preparing his drink while scolding "the boys," Fugard adds to the picture Hally's preparation for an adult life in which he will be an affluent white *baas*, whiskey in hand, imperiously scolding the impoverished, servile black houseboys.

But Sam is a gifted and sensitive teacher who counters Hally's ugly despotism with a beautiful vision of utopia. When Hally, continuing in his despotic role, mocks their dancing and sneers, "But what really makes me bitter is that I allow you chaps a little freedom in here when business is bad and what do you do with it? The foxtrot" (39), Sam uses the occasion to launch into an eloquent defense of social dance and to teach Hally its larger significance. As Sam animatedly explains the aesthetics of ballroom dancing and the significance of the dance contest for which Willie has been practicing, both Hally and the audience realize that ballroom dancing and kite making are seemingly simple, even trivial activities that nevertheless provide a stunningly sophisticated medium of semiotic expression. In the case of ballroom dancing, that expression provides not only an escape from the imperfections and hurts of everyday life but gives physical form to political idealism. The discussion brings them to an understanding of the meaning of art as something beautiful but also as "the giving of form to the formless" (40). Certainly Fugard's dramatic art and this play itself are obvious extensions of that insight.

The warmth of Sam's description and defense of ballroom dancing and of the 1950 Eastern Province Championships suddenly strikes Hally as a shrewd topic for his 500-word essay on "an annual event of cultural or historical significance." And using a black event as one of cultural significance would, Hally is aware, be a small but pointed jab at his racist teacher. "You think we could get 500 words out of it Sam?," he asks. Sam replies, "Victor Sylvester [*sic*] has written a whole book on ballroom dancing" (43). In this line, Fugard tips his hand a bit, as he did in *A Lesson from Aloes* by mentioning General Smuts's introduction to Gilbert Westacott Reynolds's study of the South African aloe, and suggests where he has perhaps derived his idea about the significance of social dance. In the 1940s and 1950s Victor Silvester was the English-speaking world's foremost authority on ballroom dancing; and his several volumes on the subject suggest the political ramifications of the dance and its politically subversive capabilities. In his introduction to *Dancing for Millions,* for example, Silvester writes:

> The English, or Competition, style is danced in all competitions. It has won universal popularity. Certain bigwigs of world politics placed an Iron Curtain across Europe—but they could not keep the English style out. It is danced in many lands behind the Iron Curtain.[30]

Silvester's *Theory and Technique of Ballroom Dancing* begins with a verse by Winston Churchill and goes on to reveal itself as the source for Sam's earlier advice to Willie. Silvester's instructions to his aspiring ballroom dancing readers sound like Machiavellian advice to an aspiring politician:

> The reader will therefore see that although clever and attractive steps may be the ambition of the majority, they can only be made to appear attractive if the fundamental principles have been mastered. Without finish and style, the more advanced variations, and for that matter the simple ones also, look clumsy, ungainly and hard work, instead of smooth, easy and non-flamboyant, which is the stamp—the hall-mark of the good dancer.[31]

It is easy, moreover, to see how Fugard can find in Silvester a terpsichorean analogue of oppressive rule in South Africa, for Silvester writes:

> Surely it is the height of bad manners for a man to ask a girl for a dance, and then to proceed to push her around the ballroom floor for all the world as though she were a dressmaker's dummy being shifted in a big store. And, to crown it all, these shuffling shovers usually seem proud of their inability to dance. "*Never learned a step in my life*," they remark boastfully—and then resume their infliction of cruelty upon the opposite sex.
>
> The ladies are astonishingly patient and long-suffering . . . If only men who are unwilling to take the trouble to learn how to dance were to fall over, as in skating, the loss of dignity would soon cause them to take a few lessons.[32]

With *Master Harold* in mind, one can easily recognize that the egocentric, rude, shoving male dancer and the long-suffering, literally downtrodden female partner are apt analogues respectively for whites and their long-suffering, downtrodden non-white partners on the South African political dance floor.[33]

The dance contest Sam describes for Hally, however, is devoid of Silvester's shovers and their abused female partners. It is one populated rather by couples who have mastered both dance technique and mutual respect, and whose ballroom dancing style is, consequently, so integrated that it embodies an ideal, a utopian vision of the way the world should be. When Hally innocently asks whether contestants lose points if they collide with other couples, Sam laughingly illuminates the vision of the ballroom dance contest as an ideal state:

> There's no collisions out there, Hally. Nobody trips or stumbles or bumps into anybody else. That's what that moment is all about. To be one of the finalists on that dance floor is like . . . like being in a dream about a world in which accidents don't happen. (45)

Perfect dancing, Sam continues, is "beautiful because that is what we want life to be like. But instead, like you said, Hally, we're bumping into each other all the time" (46). And then master teacher that he is, Sam reveals to Hally what is merely hinted at in Silvester's books, ballroom dancing's inherent political meaning:

> SAM. None of us knows the steps and there's no music playing. And it doesn't stop with us. The whole world is doing it all the time. Open a newspaper and what do you read? America has bumped into Russia, England is bumping into India, rich man bumps into poor man. Those are big collisions, Hally. They make for a lot of bruises. People get hurt in all that bumping, and we're sick and tired of it now. It's been going on for too long. Are we never going to get it right? . . . Learn to dance life like champions instead of always being just a bunch of beginners at it.

HALLY. You've got a vision, Sam! . . . But is that the best we can do, Sam . . . watch six finalists dreaming about the way it should be?

SAM. I don't know. But it starts with that. Without the dream we won't know what we're going for. And anyway I reckon there are a few people who have got past just dreaming about it and are trying for something real. (45–46)

Hally as Sam's pupil suddenly sees the point, exclaiming, "You know, Sam, when you come to think of it, that's what the United Nations boils down to . . . a dancing school for politicians!" (47). Hally then decides to write his essay under the title "A World without Collisions" and subtitles it "Ballroom Dancing as Political Vision."[34]

Against the image of ballroom dancing as a Platonic ideal of politics, Fugard places the politics of the seriously flawed real world in which partners do not coordinate and collisions take place. This is reflected in the discordant interactions that take place within the microcosm of the St. George's Park Tea Room among the three on-stage and two off-stage characters of Fugard's drama. In the essay he proposes to write, Hally characterizes the atmosphere of the dance contest as "a relaxed atmosphere which will change to one of tension and drama as the climax is approached" (44). This description is also an apt one for *Master Harold*, which moves from the relaxed pleasantries of Sam's tutoring Willie in dance steps and Hally's warm recollections to an ending filled with tension, near tragedy, and strong emotion. It is, in fact, the disparity between the envisioned ideal climax of the dance contest and the climax of *Master Harold* that allows Fugard to show how very far from the ideal Hally's—and by extension South Africa's—situation is. The dance contest ends with the announcement of the winners. *Master Harold*'s climax announces losers.

In the midst of Hally's excited preparation of his essay on "A World without Collisions," he receives the telephone call informing him that his father will be released from the hospital and is coming home. He is overcome with a welter of emotions too great for him to handle with equanimity. His primary emotion is one of anger at having once more to face his home life marred by the acts and presence of his unemployed, crippled, and alcoholic father. At the same time he feels strongly the guilt that comes with rejecting his father and having hoped for his long-term hospitalization. What happens to Hally, as the play records, is a real-world collision so at odds with the subject of his essay that he destroys both the essay and the relaxed atmosphere of friendship he has built up with Sam and Willie over the years. The three of them had essentially been practicing to dance without collisions, had established a special world within the tea room that crossed racial and age lines, a world that might be a precursor to an ideal. In his anger and in his guilt for preferring this world to that of his home, Sam to his father, Hally brutally destroys what has built up in the tea room like a child destroying in one blow a village he has painstakingly built with blocks.

The climax of the play actualizes and foregrounds what has throughout been hovering in the background as a symbol of imperfection, failure, injustice, and waste: the arse. In the course of *Master Harold*, Fugard clearly but quietly creates a rectal theme, so that when, in the first of the play's climactic moments, Sam pulls down his trousers for Hally to view his backside, it is a surprising, dramatic moment but one that nonetheless brilliantly pulls together speeches and actions that have all along been part of the action but not italicized. During the previous action, Hally has recounted how he was punished at school with smacks on the rear administered by his teacher, and Sam has recalled the injustice of the severe floggings administered to black backsides by the South African police. Hally, disgusted with social history's progress, has commented, "One day somebody is going to get up and give history a kick up the backside and get it going again" (18). After his first telephone conversation with his mother, Hally has transferred his consternation toward his father into aggression toward Willie by giving him *"a vicious whack on the bum"* (38). One remembers, too, Hally's mention of the strong smells coming from Sam and Willie's outhouse.

The range of strong and negative emotions Hally feels when he learns his father is coming home from the hospital brings the play's rectal/anal motif to the fore. Immediately he finds scatological words for his essay and for his discussion with Sam of ballroom dancing. He calls it "bullshit" and says he does not "give a shit" about his homework. With a form of anal aggression, he smashes his father's brandy bottle in anger, thereby soiling the tea room Willie and Sam have been so industriously cleaning and mopping. Of course, true to form, it will be the blacks who have to clean up the mess the white boy makes, even as they do in the world outside St. George's Park. Hally then savagely trashes the vision of the dance floor as an ideal invoking an image of anal injury telling Sam that he has failed to include the cripples on his dance floor: "Ja! Can't leave them out, Sam. That's why we always end up on our backsides on the dance floor" (51). Furthermore, in a similarly excremental way, the winners of what Hally dubs the "All-Comers-How-to-Make-a-Fuckup-of-Life Championships" receive as their trophy "a beautiful big chamber-pot with roses on the side, and it's full to the brim with piss" (51–52).

Displacing his feelings toward his father onto Sam, his surrogate father, Hally lets Sam feel the strokes of apartheid's social caning by abrogating their friendship and insisting that the lines of apartheid be sharply drawn between them and that Sam henceforth address him only as "Master Harold." A harder stroke of the cane is administered at their relationship as Hally pointedly repeats his father's favorite joke, one which insists in more ways than one on the fundamental bases of racism: "He gives out a big groan, you see, and says: 'It's not fair, is it, Hally?' Then I have to ask: 'What, chum?' And then he says: 'A nigger's arse' . . . and we both have a good laugh" (55). The joke's nasty racism horrifies Sam and Willie, and crystallizes for the audience the connection between white oppression and black arses. The intensity of the joke is, moreover, particularly acute for a South African audience, for every South African knows that the very worst, most degrading epithet one can hurl at a black African is swartgat, which means "black arse."

As a teacher, Sam is shocked but not daunted by Hally's behavior, and he realizes that one possible way to enlighten Hally—and the audience—is to literalize Hally's insult. In a dazzling stage moment, a Fugardian coup de théâtre, Sam undoes his trousers and pulls them and his underwear down to his ankles, exposing his black backside both for Hally and the theatre audience to see and saying:

> Have a good look. A real Basuto arse . . . which is about as nigger as they can come. Satisfied? (Trousers up) Now you can make your Dad even happier when you go home tonight. Tell him I showed you my arse and he's quite right. It's not fair. And if it will give him an even better laugh next time, I'll also let him have a look. (56)

Sam is giving vent to his hurt, but he is also making an effort to help Hally see the full meaning of what he has said. It is an unforgettable moment. The audience and Hally are by turns stunned, enlightened, and shocked by both the boldness and appropriateness of Sam's action and by the sheer power of the theatrical moment, which Stanley Kauffmann aptly calls "near biblical in its strange dignity."[35]

Sam's dangerous lesson, however, is one too potent for Hally, who, in the play's second climactic moment, wheels round and spits in Sam's face. Acting like a child who turns to physical violence and tantrum in the face of frustration he cannot master, Hally dazzles Sam, Willie, and the audience by the enormity of his outburst toward his friend and teacher, and the terrifying magnitude of Sam's humiliation by this act. Knowing the seething passions beneath the outward servility of South African blacks and feeling the charged and ominously ebon atmosphere that has suddenly descended on the play like the moments before a destructive tornado, the audience anxiously awaits Hally's physical insult to be met with physical violence. Dennis Walder comments, "The tension in the theatre at this point is almost unbearable, as Sam resists the natural, expected response."[36] Indeed, Sam's restraint in the face of what Hally has done to him underscores the whole question of *fairness* in the play.[37] Hally's joke is about a black man's arse not being fair, and Sam's subsequent comment on Hally's ugly pun is that his actions have not been fair in the sense of just or decent.

But Sam's eschewing violence brings the play back to an earlier discussion of fairness in another context. One remembers that Willie accuses Hally and Sam of not playing fair when they admit that they used to let him win at checkers. Hally replies, "It was for your benefit, Mr. Malopo, which is more than being fair. It was an act of self sacrifice." (28). Fugard here problematizes the issue of fairness by raising the issue that self-sacrifice, not playing according to the rules or fairly, can also be a positive act. One can paradoxically lose in order to win. Thus Sam, in not meeting Hally's physical violence with the blow he comes close to leveling, shows a strength of another kind:

> SAM. You've hurt yourself, Master Harold. I saw it coming. I warned you, but you wouldn't listen. You've just hurt yourself *bad*. . . . (*Pause, then moving violently towards* HALLY) Should I hit him Willie?

WILLIE. (*Stopping* SAM) No, Boet Sam.

SAM. (*Violently*) Why not?

WILLIE. It won't help, Boet Sam.

SAM. I don't want to help! I want to hurt him.

WILLIE. You also hurt yourself.

SAM. And if he had done it to you, Willie?

WILLIE. Me? Spit at me like I was a dog? (*A thought that had not occurred to him before. He looks at* HALLY) Ja. Then I want to hit him. I want to hit him hard! (*A dangerous few seconds as the men stand staring at the boy.* WILLIE *turns away, shaking his head*) But maybe all I do is go cry at the back. He's a little boy, Boet Sam. Little *white* boy. Long trousers now, but he's still little boy.

SAM. (*His violence ebbing away into defeat as quickly as it flooded*) You're right. (56–57)

In the circumscribed world of the St. George's Park Tea Room, Sam rises to the level of great reformers, "men of magnitude" like Gandhi. Men who are heroically self-sacrificial, who are more than fair in not playing fairly or by the rules. And the play suggests that it is through such heroic self-sacrifice, such Gandhi-like passive rather than active resistance, that the dream of a world without collisions can move toward reality. Sam says earlier:

> Without the dream we won't know what we're going for. And anyway I reckon there are a few people who have got past just dreaming about it and are trying for something real. Remember that thing we read once in the paper about Mahatma Gandhi? Going without food to stop those riots in India? (46–47).

In 1947, three years before *Master Harold* takes place, Gandhi's policy of passive resistance enabled him to realize his dream of an independent India.[38] Sam also learns from what has happened. He learns that Hally has hurt himself more than any blows from Sam can possibly hurt him; that passive resistance, not meeting violence with violence, is the way of power, for it will allow Hally's self-inflicted wound to remain unhealed.

The climax of Hally's spitting in Sam's face and Sam's subsequent heroic restraint ushers in Hally's coming of age. Hally begins to move from boy to man, not in the way he intended. He is forced, rather, to face squarely the issues he has learned to avoid, to see clearly and perhaps for the first time the realities of prejudice and racism, for which he must, with his fellow whites of fair skin, bear the bitter guilt. Sam does not now permit Hally to avert his gaze, as he did in the earlier recollection of South African police brutality. In the final searing moments of the play Hally (and the audience) is made to realize that he and his kind are responsible for the filth and unfairness that befouls not just Sam but all people of color who are demeaned in a racist polity. Furthermore, he is forced by Sam to remember that originally, in his dire humiliation, he had turned to Sam as a father figure because his own handicapped father had to be carried out of the Central Hotel Bar drunk and begrimed with his own excrement. Sam now poignantly and movingly revises the prior happy remembrance of flying the kite he had constructed for Hally:

> If you really want to know, that's why I made you that kite. I wanted you to look up, be proud of something, of yourself. . . . If you ever do write it as a short story, there was a twist in our ending. I couldn't sit down there and stay with you. It was a "Whites Only" bench. You were too young, too excited to notice then. But not anymore. If you're not careful . . . Master Harold . . . you're going to be sitting up there by yourself for a long time to come, and there won't be a kite in the sky. (58–59)

Hally has knowledge thrust upon him and is now empowered to deconstruct things he has hitherto accepted nonjudgmentally. Perhaps he will realize that his father's comic books are a form of white supremacist pulp fiction; or that Sam and Willie work as servants in a "whites only" park and in a "whites only" tearoom with "whites only" silverware and dishes, and that that is why Hally may eat the food and have a cool drink and they may not.

Sam once and for all abrogates the racist fiction that populates the world with white *men* and black *boys*, making abundantly clear to Hally just who are the men and who is the boy in that tea room. And when he says, "You've hurt yourself *bad*," he reveals to Hally and to the audience that the teller of a racist joke or the oppressor in a racist society is as much an injured victim as the butt of the joke or the one oppressed. For Fugard, racism may well be more injurious to the perpetrators than to the victims, for it is the perpetrators who must bear the guilt. As he said in an interview when the play was first produced at the Yale Rep, "Master Harold has got to realize, that to sit on a 'whites only' bench is something as profoundly damaging to yourself as it is to do something damaging to Sam."[39] In Master Harold, the real victim, the real loser that day is Master Harold, the young white adolescent, even as whites are possibly the greatest victims of the apartheid they have called into being. Certainly this idea is already implicit in *A Lesson from Aloes* and will be most fully explored in *Playland*.

How much Hally actually absorbs of the dramatic lessons he is given at the close of the play remains unclear. He leaves the tea room saying only, "I don't know. I don't know anything anymore" (59), which has been taken by Dennis Walder to suggest the play's underlying pessimism.[40] Fugard, however, seems to abrogate a dark ending with Sam's guardedly optimistic response to Hally, a pointed one not just for Hally but also for himself, Willie, and the audience:

You are sure of that, Hally? Because it would be pretty hopeless if that was true. It would mean nothing has been learnt here this afternoon, and there was a hell of a lot of teaching going on . . . one way or the other. But anyway, I don't believe you. I reckon there's one thing you know. You don't *have* to sit up there by yourself. You know what that bench means now, and you can leave it any time you choose. All you've got to do is stand up and walk away from it. (60)

Hally leaves without responding. Indeed, for Hally to undergo a sudden reversal and enlightenment would ring dramatically false. Russell Vandenbroucke aptly points out, "Before heading home Hally begins to rise from his absolute nadir."[41] It also seems true that Hally's admission, "I don't know anything anymore," is a necessary and positive first step for re-learning. As Fugard has indicated, the dramatic sine curve of *Master Harold* signifies the oscillation between hope and despair that marks the characters of the play, Fugard himself, and South Africa.[42] For this young man, who from the beginning has been so patronizingly cocksure of himself as Sam's teacher, so adolescently imperious in his opinions, and so innocently at ease with his white privilege, admitting his essential ignorance is an admission of signal consequence. Sam's generous nonviolence and his deconstruction of the kite-flying episode break through Hally's carapace of white dominance.

Fugard is an economical playwright and *Master Harold*, like most of his works, is spare. Words and references are not wasted, and with the wavering between hope and despair at the conclusion of the play, the much earlier discussion of scalars in mathematics takes on new meaning and importance:

> In some mathematical problems only the magnitude . . . of the quantities is of importance. In other problems we need to know whether these quantities are negative or positive. For example, whether there is a debit or credit bank balance . . . whether the temperature is above or below Zero . . . All these quantities are called . . . Scalars. (16)

This definition of scalars enables us to read the end of the play as only a momentarily negative one, but one that has the possibility, like the temperature or a bank balance, of going from negative to positive. This is also an apt description of the shape of the play, its actions and emotions. Like the description of scalars, like a sine curve, the play alternates between highs and lows. This is likewise the path described by Hally's kite: "The part that scared me, though, was when you showed me how to make it dive down to the ground and then just when it was on the point of crashing, swoop it up again" (30). The relationship between Hally and Sam comes dangerously close to the point of crashing, and the play leaves open the question of whether the two can manage to "swoop it up again."

As Sam says about the afternoon, "there was a hell of a lot of teaching going on . . . one way or another." And the teaching is not just in the interactions between

Hally and Sam, for the events of the play have had their effect as well on Sam's other pupil, Willie. And his role is an important part of the play's triangulated relationship. The highly verbal and idealistic Hally is compelled to learn the physical realities that have been in front of his nose but that he either has not seen or has chosen to ignore. By contrast, the far less verbal, more physical Willie must learn to perceive the ineffable, romantic side of ballroom dancing. It is significant, then, that Hally's befuddled exit at the play's conclusion is immediately followed by Willie's reformation and enlightened vow, "Hey, Boet Sam! You right. I think about it and you right. Tonight I find Hilda and say sorry. And make promise I won't beat her no more. . . . And when we practice I relax and romance with her from beginning to end" (60). Willie has learned from Sam in a meaningful way that violence is not the answer. It only begets more hostility. And he begins to see the meaning of romance.

In the concluding moments of the play Sam and Willie go from boys to men not just because of the events that have taken place, but visually as well as they doff the waiter's uniforms that bespeak their subaltern position and put on their own street clothes as they prepare to return to the black township where they live. Willie then tries to alleviate the black mood that has settled on the tea room and on Sam. Affirming their friendship, he takes his bus fare, tosses it into the jukebox, takes Sam as his partner, and practices his dance steps one more time.

The tune Willie selects is Sarah Vaughan singing "Little Man You've Had a Busy Day." Of course this can be seen as an ironic comment on what has happened to Hally, but more important, it is a slow foxtrot, not the quickstep that Willie had been struggling to perfect as the play began. As Victor Silvester tells his readers, in order to dance the quickstep, it is necessary first to master the foxtrot.[43] What Willie does, therefore, is to return to the basics of the foxtrot, to start over and get the steps right. Surely this is what Hally is also meant to do.[44]

The play's final image of Sam and Willie in their street clothes dancing together to the strains of Sarah Vaughan emanating from the jukebox is a remarkable and remarkably moving stage picture of unity, brotherhood, and a commitment to romance. This is not without its price, as anyone who has been to Port Elizabeth will realize. Willie's bus fare has been spent for this dance. That means the two men must brave the rain that has been heard throughout the play as they return on foot to New Brighton, their black township, a substantial walk of six or seven kilometers. The bus fare has, therefore, not been offered up lightly, but it is the price they are willing to pay for dancing the dream of romance, for a world without collisions, a world in which black Willie and black Sam can share the visions of a perfect life with those white icons of perfection and a perfect world: Fred Astaire and Ginger Rogers. The effect on the audience is to stir their imagination, respect, and support, and to empower them also to dream the dream of a world without collisions and color bars. Clearly for Fugard, the audience is also Sam's pupil. "There was a hell of a lot of teaching going on . . . one way or another" is as applicable to what happens in the theatre as it is to what happens in the St. George's Park Tea Room on that rainy day in 1950.[45]

SIX

The Other Problem Plays

For many, Athol Fugard is first and foremost a political playwright.[1] He is certainly that, but running rather prominently through his work as well is an abiding concern with art, the artist, and how the artist comes to be an artist. It is there in the imaginary playwriting and acting of the two brothers in *The Blood Knot* (1961) and in the playwriting and performing of the two prisoners in *The Island* (1973), in the photography of Styles in *Sizwe Bansi Is Dead* (1972), the engineering of *Dimetos* (1975), and the ballroom dancing of Sam in *"Master Harold" . . . and the Boys* (1982). In his post-apartheid plays, Fugard focuses on a budding coloured singer in *Valley Song* (1995) and on himself as a budding writer in *The Captain's Tiger* (1998). But nowhere does he focus more centrally on art and the artist than he does in *The Road to Mecca* (1984), in which he writes a play, as his title page avers, "Suggested by the Life and Work of Helen Martins of New Bethesda" (iii).[2] Fugard, who has a house in the tiny Karoo town where Helen Martins lived, naturally identifies with her as a fellow artist and in that role can empathize with the terror she feels about her waning inspiration.[3] Although racial matters are part of the background of the play, the figure of the artist, Miss Helen, is very much in the foreground, as are her psychological struggles with her art, the local pastor, and a young teacher from Cape Town.[4] As the title suggests, *The Road to Mecca* concerns primarily a journey of a religious nature; and the title brings to mind as well another play of religious journey, August Strindberg's *The Road to Damascus*.

Strindberg's expansive trilogy *The Road to Damascus* recounts symbolically the main character's and the playwright's own journeys toward a modicum of expiation and their limited acceptance of Christianity. Fugard's *The Road to Mecca* is, by contrast, a spare drama and one that recounts a journey toward a personal vision unbounded by the constraints of conventional Christianity. *The Road to Damascus* suggests a return to Christian ideas. It strikes out in new directions dramatically as well, paving the way toward expressionist drama. *The Road to Mecca*, in contrast, is what Fugard himself describes as a "very, very orthodox" theatre experience,[5] employing a conservative dramaturgy to convey the courage necessary for finding new directions in one's art and personal life. It may be that in choosing his title and in writing his play, Fugard had Strindberg's trilogy in mind not as a model for imitation but as one to work against.

In *The Road to Mecca*, Fugard returns to the theme of the reclusive artist he began to examine in *Dimetos* and to the portrait of the persistent, indefatigable Afrikaner he outlined in his portrait of Piet Bezuidenhout in *A Lesson from Aloes*. And as in *Lesson from Aloes*, Fugard in *The Road to Mecca* keeps to one time, place, and action, limiting his drama to three characters, the third of whom does not enter until the dramatic curtain line that ends the first of the play's two acts. As always with Fugard, such simplicity is a deceptive veneer covering the richly complex fabric describing human souls in struggle.

Although in part *The Road to Mecca* is a play about art and the artist, it would be a mistake to read the play simplistically and to equate Athol Fugard with Miss Helen, the central character and eccentric creator of the bizarre cement sculptures that are so threatening to the socially and religiously conservative inhabitants of New Bethesda, her remote Karoo village. There is clearly much of Fugard as well, as the playwright himself has suggested, in the character of Elsa Barlow, the young liberal schoolteacher whose unusual friendship with Miss Helen impels her to drive for twelve hours from Cape Town to answer Miss Helen's letter of distress.[6]

One might argue that in a sense the at first unlikely friendship between Helen and Elsa embodies two sides of Fugard himself. The playwright is part Anglo-Irish and part Afrikaner. He is a city dweller raised in Port Elizabeth, and someone whose life as a playwright has taken him to the theatre environments of Johannesburg, Cape Town, New Haven, New York, London, and San Diego. At the same time, his origins are in Middleburg, a dusty Karoo town quite near the setting of *The Road to Mecca*, which he came to write after purchasing a weekend house in New Bethesda just a few doors away from Helen Martins and discovering her dazzling art. Most importantly, though, Fugard's own leanings, as illustrated in many of his plays, are at one with the politically proactive engagement of Elsa Barlow even as they are simultaneously at one with Miss Helen's reclusiveness and religious devotion to her artistic vision.

Fugard understands and knows intimately through his own life and political commitment Elsa Barlow, the young, thoroughly modern English-speaking teacher who feels strongly about the need for change in South Africa. But he also knows and understands Miss Helen, the reclusive Afrikaner sculptor who is true to her special creative vision, one that has little to do with apartheid. That these two women cling to each other in challenging symbiotic friendship bespeaks the complementary polarities of Fugard's own psyche and life even as it bespeaks the seemingly disparate but complementary extremes of South African life and culture. Anyone who has driven, as Elsa does, from the urban intensity of a Johannesburg or Cape Town, rife as they are with political conflict and stress, to the almost otherworldly tranquility of New Bethesda, with its serene Dutch Reformed Church, its quaint general store, and its dirt roads, will feel South Africa's two geographies, not merely topographical but also political and cultural. And each geography tells its own distinct truth about South African existence.

The opening moments of *The Road to Mecca* are puzzling ones for an audience. One immediately sees and is struck by what Fugard calls an atmosphere of "light and extravagant fantasy" (3). There are supple, arresting free-form sculptures working against multicolored geometric patterns on the ceilings and floors of the house, and there are walls in different colors and adorned by a wealth of mirrors.[7] One might expect to find here a flashy artist on the style of Salvador Dali, but instead there is in the midst of the dazzling artwork an elderly, sweet-visaged lady acting the role of hausfrau, laying out soap and towels. "What," the audience finds itself asking, "has this seemingly old-fashioned housewifely lady to do with the bold, rather outré setting?" Indeed what Fugard re-creates on stage and will use for his dramatic purposes is precisely what visitors to Helen Martins's "Owl House" feel as they enter what seems like an ordinary country house and find themselves stunned by the sheer density of imaginative creativity packed into the house's small rooms. Inside Martins's rooms, one suddenly leaves behind the small Karoo town of New Bethesda to find oneself remarkably, almost magically transported into a shimmering world of glass and light. It is no small feat for Fugard to create a vehicle that allows theatre spectators to transport themselves out of their own lives, cross the threshold of Miss Helen's house, and participate in Miss Helen's unique visionary world.

When Elsa, a woman in her twenties, appears on stage, one assumes that such modernistic sculptures and the room arrangement must be hers, and that perhaps the two women are mother and daughter. One quickly discovers, however, that the two are not mother and daughter but, despite their generational difference, fast friends, and that the sculptures and decor are those of the older woman. "How is it," one asks, "that these two women, years apart in age are friends? And how is it that the older woman is the creator of such contemporary and bold sculptures and of such an eccentric room?" The answers to these questions are what *The Road to Mecca* is about.

The surface issue in *The Road to Mecca* is that the citizens of New Bethesda, the conservative Dutch Reformed community in which Helen has lived all her life, have come to the conclusion that she should be removed to the Sunshine Home for the Aged, a church-run facility in Graaff-Reinet. Under the pretext of caring for the elderly widow, the local townsfolk would be quit of the eccentric old woman who offends their sensibilities, who has left her church, and who outrages their sight with the unconventional and subversive art with which she has populated her garden. They would also be thrusting her back into the arms of the church she has abandoned. But *The Road to Mecca* is no modern melodrama, for Fugard has written a script that has implications and meaning far beyond the question of whether Miss Helen will or will not be driven from her home. The question of her relocation is merely of superficial importance.

When Helen's past and present relationship with New Bethesda are introduced and discussed, and when the community's case for Miss Helen's removal to the old-age home is made with great ardor and persuasiveness by the local dominee (pastor) Marius Byleveld, one begins to sense that there are dynamics at play that go deeper than a conservative Afrikaner community seeking to still a progressive and, therefore, threatening artist in its midst. One is immediately struck by the fervor with which Marius, a man Helen's age, argues with her to give up her home and her art in exchange for the restriction of an assisted-care facility outside the community. And one wonders what it is about her art that the pastor clearly finds so distasteful and offensive.

The first act of *The Road to Mecca*'s two acts is a dialogue between the play's two women, Helen and Elsa. It is only as the curtain falls on act 1 that the dominee appears in the doorway to call on Helen, presumably to learn whether she will capitulate, leave New Bethesda and her Mecca, and retire to the Sunshine Home in Graaff-Reinet. Assuming the usual topos of melodrama, the audience may expect the subsequent act to present a struggle between Helen and Marius over her dispossession. Certainly that struggle is there, but it turns out not to be the main struggle, and the dramatic configuration is not the expected one.

As Helen fights to maintain her home, her Mecca, and her fierce independence, an issue surfaces that overshadows any agon between Helen and the community or Helen and the dominee. Soon visible beneath the surface issues, yet inextricable from them, are the vexing, central questions of the play: Of what importance are the vision of an artist and the freedom of art? What can be learned from the commitment of an artist to her vision and her art?

The Road to Mecca is a difficult play, one that resonates on many levels. Like the earlier *Dimetos* and the later *Captain's Tiger* it uses the drama to contemplate the nature of art and of the artist. It presents a particular artist and the struggle between her vision and the insensitivity of her Afrikaner community. It is, further, a work about artistic inspiration, the responsibility of the artist to her vision, the subjugation of the artist to the will of her vision, and the interaction between that enlightened vision and the conformity of the everyday world. And even though *The Road to Mecca* is not overtly about South African racial issues, as most of Fugard's prior works are, it nevertheless suggests that the answers to South Africa's vexing social problems, which are very much a product of conservative Afrikaner intransigence, will be found by marrying that very stubbornness and tenacity to an inspired vision of freedom. So often a person's greatest strength is also his greatest liability. In portraying Piet Bezuidenhout, Miss Helen, Marius, and the New Bethesda community, Fugard shows that he understands how the Afrikaner trait of dogged determination, a seeming liability, can be harnessed and made a means to achieving a better South Africa.

Throughout his career, Fugard has been under attack because his plays have not been revolutionary enough, because they have never radicalized audiences to call for unrelenting Armageddon or violent action against an inimical, oppressive regime. *The Road to Mecca* can tell us much about Fugard's position, for in many ways he identifies with Miss Helen, characterized as a "reactionary-revolutionary," who has the ability, born in part through an innate and relentless Afrikaner will, ultimately to accomplish more than Elsa, her outspoken revolutionary counterpart. Emotionally and politically engaged in the struggle against apartheid, Elsa tends to react impulsively, as she does to the coloured children in her school. An artist like Helen or Fugard, the play implies, is not simply reactive but inspired and compelled by artistic vision. Hers is not the vision of a revolutionary or iconoclast who merely wishes to destroy what is, but the constructive vision of an artist whose inspirations can move others so as to effect change without cataclysmic disturbance and bloodshed. The difference between Elsa and Helen is the difference between those visions. Fugard himself, by presenting Elsa and Miss Helen sympathetically and seeing their complementarity, enunciates the positions between which, as a politically engaged artist, he negotiates.

When the fiery Elsa attributes her political zeal and activism to her reading of Albert Camus' *The Rebel*, Helen replies, "You make me nervous when you talk like that" (26). Fugard, too, is an avid reader of Camus,[8] but he fears the bloodbath that seems likely at the close of *The Island* or *A Lesson from Aloes*, and that will begin to happen in the later play *My Children! My Africa!* The difference between the two women is well captured in how they think the insistent pastor should be handled. Elsa is angered by Helen, who plans to *ask* Marius for more time to think about moving. Elsa wants her to *tell* him in no uncertain terms that she will take whatever time she needs to make a decision. In that difference between "tell" and "ask" lies the difference between the revolutionary Elsa and the "revolutionary-reactionary" Helen; and somewhere on that continuum between "ask" and "tell" lies the political attitude of the play and its author.

There are only three characters on stage in *The Road to Mecca*, and the relationships among them are slippery and complex. These must be examined closely if the source of the play's power is to be clearly identified. As *The Road to Mecca* develops, the disparate character traits and the different approaches to problem solving of the two women, Helen and Elsa, are enunciated. Some of their differences will come out specifically in their dialogues and debates, but *The Road to Mecca*, about a sculptor, is not, surprisingly, a visual play that relies considerably on body language and semiotic messages. When, for example, Elsa arrives, she seems at first to be an energetic woman of strong opinions who has just made a long, grueling automobile journey alone from Cape Town to New Bethesda. But what we see her do on stage begins to erode that initial impression. Elsa's modus operandi is to reject, dispose of, wash away unpleasantness. Tellingly, on a prior visit she has given Miss Helen a box of scented soaps, which have gone unused by Miss Helen but which are now summoned into service by Elsa as she seeks to wash away the dirt and sweat from her drive as well perhaps as what later emerge as her personal problems. It is not for nothing that Fugard shows her concerned with having her pants and bra washed, and has her on stage with basin, facecloth, and scented soap complaining, "God, this Karoo dust gets right into your pores. I can even taste it. That first mouthful of tea is going to be mud. I'll fill up all the kettles tomorrow and have a really good scrub" (10). As she washes, she tells her touching story of the pathetic black woman to whom she had given a lift, but ends her narration incongruously yet revealingly:

> Anyway, what's the point in talking about her? She's probably curling up in a stormwater drain at this moment—that's where she said she'd sleep if she didn't get a lift—and I feel better for a good wash (16)

Her concern and momentary pity for the black woman seem peremptorily dismissed, washed away along with the Karoo dust on her body. The narrative break and the concentration on ablution seem not unrelated to her reaction to the woman and the events she has just described.

Quick rejection and abandonment characterize other observations by Elsa. Reacting to Miss Helen's remaining in the Karoo and in, to Elsa's mind, narrow-minded New Bethesda, she exclaims, "My god, you deserve a medal. I would have packed up and left at the first opportunity" (14). Commenting on the situation of Katerina, the coloured woman whose husband occasionally beats her, Elsa says, "God it makes me sick! Why doesn't she leave him?" (18). Likewise, her first reaction to her own married lover's anguish at their breakup is one filled with physical revulsion and a desire to purge herself of the unpleasantness:

> I know it's all wrong to find another person's pain disgusting, but that's what eventually happened. The last time he crucified himself on the sofa in my bedroom I felt like vomiting. (30–31)

The overall picture, the gestalt, that these things form is one of a woman who, beneath her strong exterior, is weak, who would fain reject, wash away, or vomit up unpleasantness rather than live with it or address it.

In the last moments of the play, when the most intimate secrets are revealed, the audience learns that Elsa's sexual relationship with a married man led to a pregnancy, which she has aborted. She laments to Helen, "I put an abrupt and violent end to the first real consequence my life has ever had" (105). This revelation is a surprising one only if one has ignored the hints and innuendoes with which Fugard has quietly constructed the character of Elsa. Consistent with her portrayal throughout, Elsa lacks the zeal to follow through, to see her pregnancy to term. Her heart is in the right place, but her habit of mind is to wash away, to avoid the distasteful. In that way she likely has much in common with many of her liberal, white, English-speaking peers, whose hearts are also in the right place but who avoid rather than tackle ugly and messy social problems.

Helen stands in contrast to Elsa. She looks frail and is nearly seventy, but her large, powerful cement sculptures eloquently bespeak a remarkable physical strength and a dazzling artistic vision.[9] Her sculptures, seen by the theatre audience, are imbued with visionary integrity. Clearly her large pieces, adorned with glass from bottles and automobile headlights ground down by the sculptor, require a sheer physical strength one would not at first glance attribute to the frail-seem-ing elderly woman walking in their midst. These sculptures were, likewise, not fashioned in haste or overnight. And thus whereas Elsa the city dweller wants quick solutions, Helen is characterized by the slow, painstaking, but more sure ways of her environment and her art. As she says to Elsa, "Those attitudes might be all right in Cape Town, Elsa, but you should know by now that the Valley has got its own way of doing things" (21). The contrasting personal styles of the two women are nicely captured further in the way they choose to recount to one another the current events of their lives. Elsa reports her news in appropriately staccato newspaper headlines taken from what she jestingly calls *The Elsa Barlow Advertiser.* Helen relates her own news in the more discursive form of what the two women call "village gossip." In their different ways, both women are trying to change the vision of society. So too is Fugard. In a sense, the explorations of Elsa and Helen are the explorations of how the political activist and the artist, respectively, seek to effect change. This understanding then informs a recognition of how those hy-brids—a work of political art (*The Road to Mecca*) and a political artist (Fugard)—can have a double-barreled strength.

Elsa the liberal rebel boldly tries to radicalize her coloured students but in such a way that their parents foil her efforts and complain to the authorities. The result is that she will have to back down and accomplish little or nothing. Seeming to put more trust in the artist than in the political activist, Fugard shows Miss Helen also as a rebel but one who has perpetrated her rebellion in a slow, sedulous, stubborn way. She has left the Dutch Reformed Church and, over the course of fifteen years, she has constructed her own religious vision, her own Mecca, in spite of and in de-fiance of the narrow-minded community in which she dwells. There is great truth in Elsa's statement, delivered jocularly, "I think you're history's first reactionary-revolutionary. You're a double agent" (26–27).

The contrast between the two women takes up much of the first of *The Road to Mecca*'s two acts, and its importance should not be minimized. An important con-trast that emerges is one of motion, for the two women are both journeyers. Elsa has been on the road for twelve hours driving from Cape Town to New Bethesda. Helen, though she never leaves the confines of her cottage and its garden, is a much more ambitious journeyer, for she is traveling on the road to her private Mecca. Even before Elsa herself enters the play, the audience sees on stage her symbolic prop: an overnight bag. When she does enter, she is "dressed in a tracksuit or some-thing else suitable for a long motorcar ride" (4). It is appropriate, too, that describ-ing herself, Elsa says, "I try to jog a few miles every morning" (27), for Elsa is a per-son always on the move, always in motion. She is someone whose energy can motivate students and inspire change even as it invigorates the play. Fugard seems to respect her vitality and drive, and yet it becomes clear that Elsa is also someone who moves on when she does not wish to face a situation. Her greatest asset is also her greatest liability.

Although Elsa seems to be driving to New Bethesda to rescue Miss Helen, the artist endangered by a censorious and hostile community, she also needs the stability of an overarching and ultimately rescuing vision that art and the artist provide. Elsa possesses the revolutionary spirit to motivate her students to write potentially dangerous essays about racial inequality, but she lacks the staying power to oppose the Cape Town School Board. She gives an account of how on her drive to New Bethesda she picked up and gave a ride to a black woman carrying an infant and walking to Cradock. Tellingly, she gives the woman a ride only part way, presumably dropping her at the exit on national route 9, where the road splits off one way to New Bethesda and the other to Cradock, leaving the woman another seventy kilometers of walking before reaching her destination. Elsa is moved by the woman's plight but not moved enough to ask her name or to make a fifty-minute detour to Cradock. In short, Elsa is surely the sort of person whose motivations and feelings are humane, but like most people, her energies and vision are such that she can only go or take others part way.

Consciously or unconsciously aware of her limitations, Elsa is ineluctably drawn to Miss Helen, the relentless artist and visionary, for it is the function of the artist to provide overarching vision, the insight that enables others to shape their impulses toward higher ideals. Through the example and work of artists, sublunary mortals are given the road maps to chart the routes and progress of life. And Elsa drives the roads from Cape Town to New Bethesda in part to learn from the artist how to travel the more spiritual road to Miss Helen's Mecca, for Helen is a traveler also but she travels paradoxically, without physical motion. Hers is a spiritual and visionary pilgrimage to an artistic ideal. Never leaving her cottage, she makes her pilgrimage not as a believer in a Christian ideal but as a pilgrim to Mecca; yet hers is not the Mecca of Mohammed but the Mecca of artistic idea, *das Ding an sich*. Her understanding of her art and her inspiration are a numinous journey characterized not merely by the play's title but by her description of what motivates her art:

> it was leading me . . . leading me far away to a place I had never been to before. . . . That is the East. Go out there into the yard and you'll see that all my Wise Men and their camels are traveling in that direction. Follow that candle and one day you'll come to Mecca. . . . A city of light and color more splendid than anything I had ever imagined. There were palaces and beautiful buildings everywhere, with dazzling white walls and glittering minarets. Strange statues filled the courtyards. The streets were crowded with camels and turbaned men speaking a language I didn't understand . . . And I was on my way to the grand temple . . . and that is where the Wise Men of the East study the celestial geometry of light and color. (98–99)

The lyricism of the speech italicizes the spaciousness of the mental journey from the conservative, Afrikaner, Dutch Reformed atmosphere of New Bethesda to the very source of art. Helen is more than inspired. She is possessed. And yet artists never reach the Ideal or Perfection. They can only attempt in their art to approach it asymptotically and to convey to their audience its distant skyline. Recognizing her inevitable limitations, Helen admits, "It's the best I can do, as near as I could get to the real Mecca" (99).

Helen is also the artist whose vision can provide shape and offer direction to the unruly passions of an Elsa, who explains, "She challenges me into an awareness of myself and my life, of my responsibilities to both that I never had until I met her" (90). The artist does not create art that directly brings about social change but rather art that can inspire others to become the agents of change. Elsa's statement might well be spoken by audience members who have attended a Fugard play.

The portrait of the artist in *The Road to Mecca* is made still clearer by Helen's opposition in the second act to Marius Byleveld, the Dutch Reformed dominee. Like Emily Dickinson's courtly figure of Death, Marius pays his calls on Helen. As a representative of his repressive community, he is for Helen a figure of death, of the repressive forces of darkness that stand in Manichean opposition to her world of light and artistic enlightenment: forces that would snuff out the candles of her house and the metaphorical candles of her art and life. Aware of the approaching end of both her life and her artistic vision, Helen as well associates Marius with the embodiment of Death:

> I'm frightened. And Marius can see it. He's no fool, Elsa. He knows that his moment has finally come. . . . He's been waiting a long time for me to reach the end of my Mecca. I thought I had cheated him out of it, that that moment would never come.
>
> All those years when I was working away, when it was taking shape, he was there as well . . . standing in the distance, watching and waiting. (56)

And when Marius makes his appearance in the doorway as the second act opens, he enters as an elderly, gentlemanly figure who has brought a basket of vegetables that is, according the stage directions, "the center of attraction" in the scene.

Marius's basket contains, he says, beets and tomatoes, but as the scene opens he is holding up and eulogizing the regional delicacy, "a genuine Sneeuberg potato." As he speaks of them, the vegetables for which the region is famous seem to have fallen into almost ghoulish hands. The potatoes and beets have flourished in belowground darkness, and he has dug them up for the occasion. Almost with the relish of an embalmer, he suggests that the beets, which are past their prime, be pickled and bottled. He identifies himself furthermore with "the humble potato," and, suggesting his own exclusion from Miss Helen's life, he laments, "In the old days Helen used to have a very fine vegetable garden of her own out there. But as you can see, the humble potato has been crowded out by other things. I don't think there's enough room out there now to grow a radish" (63). Her sculptures, reduced by him to "other things," have excluded the underground vegetables, even the radish. Analogously, Marius implies that Miss Helen's art has, literally and metaphorically, destroyed her roots.

As a representative of his conservative Afrikaner parish, Marius sees Helen's sculptures and art as "monstrosities" and "a nightmare," as objects to be reviled. His parishioners are threatened by Miss Helen's work and by the revolutionary inner emotions that her sculptures express. They have answered her iconoclasm by pelting rocks at her house, enacting an idol smashing of their own. Elsa understands what has happened:

> They're not only frightened of you, Helen; They're also jealous. It's not just the statues that have frightened them. They were throwing stones at something much bigger than that—you. Your life, your beautiful, light-filled, glittering life. And they can't leave it alone, Helen, because they are so, so jealous of it. (94)

Neither Marius nor the townsfolk of New Bethesda can fathom Helen's visionary statuary, which represents an individualistic, and therefore dangerous, religious experience wholly in opposition to the rote religiosity of their organized community churchgoing. Visiting New Bethesda and seeing Helen Martins's garden, one can well imagine how it alarmed and frightened her neighbors. Anne Emslie with delicious understatement recounts the reaction of the dominee and his wife who arrived in New Bethesda a year after Helen Martins's death: "In 1971, when Dominee and Mrs. Cloete took up residence in Nieu Bethesda, they were astonished to discover the existence of the Owl House behind the parsonage. 'I don't think she was really understood by the people of Nieu Bethesda,' Mrs. Cloete said. 'We couldn't really get to know her. She was such an enigmatic person.'"[10]

Helen's existence opposes darkness with light—the light of her candles, the enlightenment of her art. Hers is a vision that enables her to transcend her geographic location in the South African Karoo to perceive the outlines of her visionary ideal, the realms of her Mecca. Like his flock in New Bethesda, Marius tills the soil of the Karoo to bring forth his potatoes. His life is one of coping with defeat and sorrow, eking out his existence. Rather than oppose darkness, he serves it: on one level, by growing his tubers and roots, his humble potatoes and radishes; on another level, by affirming the restrictive attitudes of his parishioners. His is a vision that gives thanks for the routine, known, and status quo. To understand *The Road to Mecca*, it is important to acknowledge Fugard's ambivalent presentation of Marius. He does clearly appear in opposition to the spiritual freedom Helen's vision affords her; and in opposing her, Marius is marked as a figure of death, stasis, and repression. At the same time, however, he bears the markings of the pertinacious, stubborn, steadfast Afrikaner spirit that, however doggedly, accomplishes its goals. In some ways, *The Road to Mecca* is the obverse of *A Lesson from Aloes*. The Afrikaner spirit that is celebrated in Piet Bezuidenhout is what makes Marius Byleveld sinister. The psychological stress that makes Gladys Bezuidenhout destructive and sends her to Fort England mental hospital for shock treatments is celebrated as the creative force which possesses a somewhat dotty Miss Helen. Seen, moreover, in terms of what we know about Fugard's parents and what we learn from his memories in *Cousins*, one can speculate that the ability at once to admire Afrikaner steadfastness and to recognize its limitations has some of its origin in his deep respect for his mother's ability to survive, economically and spiritually, within a flawed marriage even as he sees that same ability as the trait preventing her escape from a life hopelessly always near the border of wretchedness. Likewise, Fugard seems to harbor a deep love and admiration for his father, the romantic, dashing, artistic piano player, even as he rejects him for being a cripple willing merely to collect disability payments, an alcoholic dependent on his wife's hard-won earnings, and the person responsible for marital and family hardships. Regardless of whether such biographically inspired speculations are correct, one must recognize that *The Road to Mecca* is no simple psychomachia in which Marius is a figure of evil.

Whereas Helen the artist looks to her vision of Mecca, the more earthbound Marius in his despair looks to the ground and to routine for his salvation:

> As you know, Helen, I had deep and very painful wounds in my soul when I first came here. Wounds I thought would never heal. This was going to be where I finally escaped from life . . . I was very wrong. I didn't escape life here, I discovered it, what it really means, the fullness and goodness of it. . . . all of this was going on in my head when I realized I was hearing a small little voice, and the small little voice was saying, "Thank you." With every spadeful of earth that I turned when I went down on my knees to lift the potatoes out of the soil, there it was: "Thank you." It was mine! I was muttering away to myself the way we old folks are inclined to do when nobody is around. It was me saying, "Thank you." (67–68)

His gaze is down at his own feet and at the soil from which he is digging up his Sneeuberg potatoes. His thanks are given to the darkness for its fruits. He is not a geographic traveler and progressive like Elsa, nor is he a visionary traveler like Helen. Rather he is the image of the intractable Afrikaner who glories in his pertinacity, for whom Elsa's progressive ideals or Helen's visionary art is threatening and inimical, and whose fruits of the earth gathered in his basket of vegetables challenge the fruits of the art that pervades Helen's house and covers Fugard's stage.

Typical of Marius is the moment when act 2 of *The Road to Mecca* commences, and Marius, displaying his potatoes, recounts an episode of an outsider foolishly coming to New Bethesda to sell potatoes. He concludes his remarks by asking, "What's the English expression, Miss Barlow? Coals to—where?" (61). To Marius, the enlightened and liberal-minded Elsa is a threat; here he not so subtly reminds Elsa and Helen of Elsa's alien status as an outsider and as an English speaker. The anecdote becomes a pointed parable as he implies that Elsa, like the farmer, is unwanted and wasting her time in New Bethesda, and that his aim is to send the intruder back to Cape Town. He and the town, after all, know what is best for a member of their flock who has gone astray as Miss Helen so obviously has.

Helen, it soon becomes evident, must fight for her vision, her art, and her difference by informing Marius to what extent he has become for her the repressive force of Death and Darkness standing in opposition to her life and art, to her candlelit, illuminated vision of Mecca. When Marius's wife died, he turned to darkness and the earth, and he minimalized his life by withdrawing to New Bethesda. He has tried to provide that same comfort for Helen by immuring her in her house after her husband, Stefanus, dies. Helen, however, withstands and defies Marius's wishes for her, breaking through the walls of physical and intellectual confinement to discover instead a transcendent world. And with some cruelty, she pointedly tells Marius that he was responsible for initiating her very rebellion and disobedience:

> You brought me home from the cemetery, remember, and when we had got inside the house and you . . . pulled the curtains and closed the shutters. Such a small thing, and I know you meant well by it . . . but in doing that it felt as if you were putting away my life as surely as the undertaker had done to Stefanus a little earlier when he closed the coffin lid. There was even an odour of death in here with us, wasn't there, sitting in the gloom and talking, both of us in black, our Bibles in our laps? Your words of comfort didn't help. . . .You lit one [a candle] for me before you left—there was a lot of darkness in this room—and after you had gone I sat here with it. . . . I don't know how much time passed, but I was just sitting here staring into its flame. I had surrendered myself to what was going to happen when it went out . . . but then instead of doing the same, allowing the darkness to defeat it, that small, uncertain little light seemed to find its courage again. It started to get brighter and brighter. I didn't know whether I was awake any longer or dreaming because a strange feeling came over me . . . leading me far away to a place I had never been to before. (*She looks around the room and speaks with authority*) Light the candles, Elsa. That one first. And you know why, Marius, That is the East. Go out there and you'll see all my Wise Men and their camels traveling in that direction. Follow that candle on and one day you'll come to Mecca. . . . That is where I went that night and it was the candle you lit that led me there. (96–98)

The affirmation of her life and the rejection of Marius and all he stands for is obvious in Helen's passionate account.

When Marius leaves the stage, his plans to bring Helen's art to a halt and to send her to a retirement home in Graaff-Reinet have proven abortive. After he has gone, Elsa articulates what has also become clear to the audience: "It's a very moving story. Twenty years of loving you in the disguise of friendship and professional concern for your soul" (103). Indeed, Marius the tenacious Afrikaner has never declared his love but has waited patiently and silently for Helen to free herself from what he regards as her monstrous art and to exorcise the incubus that has led her to fabricate those satanic, bizarre sculptures. Despite Helen's sharp word to him and Elsa's patent animadversion, Marius is not a melodramatic villain wishing to bind and confine Miss Helen, but a fellow sufferer, even a sympathetic one. And yet he does embody a repugnant Afrikaner conservatism that is in some of its forms, and especially as directed toward the artist figure, life-denying and a threat to creative freedom. By denying Marius, Helen rejects a form of enslavement, the restrictions imposed by Afrikaner society and its Dutch Reformed Church upon the individual, individual thought and freedom. Marius becomes the avatar of narrow-mindedness, restriction, and the bondage of social and gender roles that characterize the dark side of what Fugard presents as the Afrikaner mentality.

But, free artistic spirit though she be, Helen is herself very much an Afrikaner, silent, mulish, tied to her home, sedulously pursuing her vision, and as devout a worshiper of her Mecca as the dominee is of his Calvinist God. Who Helen is, what she is, is made manifest in the stage set. She knows the identity between herself and her house as she explains:

> You see, when I lit the candles you were finally going to see all of me . . . I mean the *real* me, because that is what this room is . . . This is the best of me, Elsa. That is what I really am, Forget everything else. Nothing, not even my name or my face, is me as much as those Wise Men and their camels traveling to the East, or the light and glitter in this room. The mermaids, the wise old owls, the gorgeous peacocks . . . all of them are *me*. (36, 37)

Helen is indeed embodied in her art and her room, yet that room is not just an otherworldly, exotic atelier but also a burgherly Karoo cottage. And that juxtaposition is truly at the heart of who Miss Helen is. It is only during the final moments of the play, when the room is dazzlingly ablaze with candlelight and when that lambent

16. Yvonne Bryceland as Miss Helen in *Road to Mecca,* Market Theatre, Johannesburg, 1984. Photo by Ruphin Coudyzer.

candlelight is reproduced exponentially in Helen's wilderness of mirrors and colored glass, that the audience achieves a momentary glimpse of Helen's transcendent vision of Mecca, of her artistic Ideal, "A city of light and colour more splendid than anything I had ever imagined" (98). Ecstatic in her brilliantly lit room, moving like a secular saint surrounded by an almost unearthly nimbus of multiplied light, the enraptured Helen exclaims, "This is my world and I have banished darkness from it" (99). Through her art she is transported from her Karoo cottage, beyond the restraints and darkness of New Bethesda to the heart of her enlightenment, to the middle of the temple in the heart of her Mecca where "the Wise Men of the East study the celestial geometry of light and colour" (98–99). And for a moment, Fugard permits the audience to travel with her to her Mecca and its temple of light.

Starting from her Afrikaner origins as a compliant, church-going wife and then widow, she begins her travels on her road to Mecca. In the course of his play, Fugard takes a seemingly simple, elderly lady in her simple Karoo cottage fussing over her towels, soaps, and housekeeping, and with quiet bravura he transforms both character and cottage to give his audience an insight into artistic inspiration and the meaning of art. From her conservative, restrictive background, Helen creates a vision of freedom, and from a seemingly simple, conservative dramatic vehicle, Fugard fashions a powerful, unorthodox visionary experience. Both Helen and Fugard in their different ways tap their conservative, salt-of-the-earth roots to bring forth into the light magnificent artistic blossoms of freedom and enlightenment.[11]

Although *The Road to Mecca* focuses on the situation of the artist, it is also rather more obliquely about the South African political and racial dilemma. After Helen has transformed her cottage into a vision of Mecca, the effects of that vision are felt by Elsa, who sees that her own road appears to lead nowhere. Returning again at the end of the play to her encounter with the black woman to whom she gave a lift, Elsa transforms the episode so it resonates with a symbolic meaning that the audience can comprehend even if it seems to escape Elsa.

> There is a little sequel to my story about giving that woman a lift. When I stopped at the turnoff and she got out of the car, after I had given her what was left of my food and the money in my purse, after she had stopped thanking me and telling me over and over again that God would bless me, after all of that I asked her who she was. She said: "My English name is Patience." She hitched up the baby, tightened her *doek,* picked up her little plastic shopping bag and started walking. . . . That baby is mine, Helen. Patience is my sister, you are our mother . . . and I still feel fucking lonely. (105–106)

"My English Name Is Patience" was the working title Fugard used as he wrote the play.[12] The black woman becomes transformed into an allegorical figure of Patience, by which Fugard does not mean resignation but undaunted progress toward a goal, and here that goal is Cradock and survival.[13] Mary Benson tells a significantly similar anecdote of Fugard, who, when he saw how downcast she was by her crippling arthritis, told her of a destitute black woman to whom he and Market Theatre director Barney Simon had given a lift in the Eastern Cape:

> Under a blazing sun she was walking "from nothing to nothing" along a Karoo road. Her husband had died and she had been evicted by a white farmer. And she was crying. "The enigma, of course," Athol said, "was the bundle on her head—an old bath, a blanket, a three-legged cast-iron pot—all that was left of her life, but not abandoned . . .
>
> "Using her as a metaphor—I think Life is asking you, telling you, to take that walk. Like her you are crying. But walk, Mary, put your life on your head and walk . . . The walk is long, bitter, barren, full of pain, but it is the only way to live."[14]

Helen, also arthritic like Mary Benson, takes that walk. Her journey to Mecca provides an example of how the individual will, without revolutionary activity, can resist submission and win its freedom. The commitment of the artist to the freedom of her art is, then, at one with commitment to freedom in the sociopolitical arena. By witnessing Patience relentlessly moving toward her goal, Cradock; by witnessing Miss Helen relentlessly journeying to her spiritual Mecca, Elsa (and the audience) can learn the lessons of perseverance. Elsa, with anti-apartheid ideals, gives up, moves on, runs away in the face of adversity. Fugard essentially tells her and us what he told Mary Benson: "The walk is long, bitter, barren, full of pain, but it is the only way to live."

The Road to Mecca ends on a note of trust and love, and for Fugard it seems obvious that patient progress, love, and trust are the nonviolent means for effecting change. It is the love and trust between Helen and Elsa that will enable Elsa to place the lesson of Helen's journey in the service of social reform. Likewise it seems that the journey to Mecca the dramatist provides for his audience will enable them to use his vision of freedom as an inspiration in reforming and curing the ills of South Africa. Elsa must learn the lessons provided by the journeys of her mother and her sister, the journeys to Mecca and to Cradock; so too must the audience.

In the 27 May 1985 edition of the *New York Times,* Fugard read the headline "Soviet Deserter Discovered After 41 Years in a Pigsty."[15] The article may have caught his eye because twenty-five years earlier he had written a play called *A Place with the Pigs,* which he submitted to Joan Littlewood, the renowned founder of London's Theatre Workshop. Of that earlier play Fugard told Russell Vandenbroucke, "It was the first of my attempts at an Immorality Act story. It centered on the reaction of a little Afrikaans community to a man who had a love relationship with a Coloured woman. I eventually tore it up."[16] After reading the *Times* piece, Fugard wrote a new play called *A Place with the Pigs,* which was not a new Immorality Act play nor even a play set in South Africa.

Premiering at the Yale Repertory Theatre on 24 March 1987, *A Place with the*

Pigs was directed by Fugard himself. It is a two-hander, based on the story of the Russian husband and wife described in the *Times* article, even using their real names, Pavel and Praskovya. Fugard himself played the role of Pavel in the Yale production and in subsequent productions in Johannesburg and Cape Town. *A Place with the Pigs* has not received the many productions, critical attention, or favorable reviews enjoyed by most of Fugard's other plays.[17] It stands with Fugard's earlier play *Dimetos* as a turbid and puzzling piece, something out of character in the Fugard canon. Fugard's comment on the reception of the Cape Town production provides a sense of the difficulty that has beset the play: "I had suffered the not uncommon fate of a writer who confounds the critics by exploring a new direction—their reviews had been savage. With the intellectual laziness that characterizes so many of them, they had sat there half asleep, waiting for me to repeat tried and tested formulas of the past, and of course had been disappointed. By the time they woke up and realised that something different was happening on stage it was too late—the play was over."[18] Stephen Gray records, "After three decades in theatre in Johannesburg . . . Fugard found all but his most faithful supporters judging *Pigs* as gruellingly self-indulgent."[19]

A Place with the Pigs, is subtitled *A Personal Parable,* a subtitle that would be equally apt for *Dimetos.* These two plays, together with the acting exercise *Orestes,* are indeed of a different order from the works specifically set in South Africa, and they should be read as such. As a "personal parable," *A Place with the Pigs* is drawn from Fugard's experiences as a human being and artist quite apart from his involvement with the politics of his country; and as a parable does, it provides a general insight open to many applications.[20] Nevertheless, *A Place with the Pigs* has none of the Yeatsian esoteric and poetic tone of *Dimetos.* It lacks as well the political punch and the epiphanous moments of sudden insights that characterize so much of Fugard's work. Though *A Place with the Pigs* is based on a real situation, the actions of its main character are often so ludicrous, his insights so paltry that this play is very likely Fugard's least successful work of theatre.

When Fugard deposited his typescript of *A Place with the Pigs* in the National English Literary Museum in Grahamstown,[21] he placed a copy of the *Times* article, marked with his underlining of particular passages, directly between the title page of the play and the first page of text. The article tells of a Red Army deserter who had lived for forty-one years in a pigsty. Fugard underlined the salient passages:

> The deserter, bearded, ragged and unwashed, now 74 years old, was found by astonished villagers only after the death of his wife, whom he had terrorized into hiding and feeding him. . . . when the terrified deserter, Pavel Navrotsky, came face to face with strangers for the first time in four decades, all he could find to say was, "Will I be punished?" . . . When his tiny village, Sarazhentsy, was liberated in 1944, Mr. Navrotsky took refuge in the pigsty attached to his wooden house. . . . In all the years since, he went out for a walk only once, late at night, dressed as a woman. . . . His wife, Praskovya,

whom he threatened to kill if she betrayed him, hid him through the years, cutting herself off from friends and relatives to maintain his secret. Whenever she left the house, the newspaper said, she locked a heavy padlock on the door.

This article seems to have offered Fugard the metaphor he needed to write a deeply personal play.

To those who think of Athol Fugard purely as a South African playwright whose work is or ought to be strictly about South Africa and apartheid, dramatizing a little human interest story from Russia is totally out of character, even inappropriate. But Fugard throughout his career has written about human relationships rather than specifically South African apartheid issues. His native South Africa happens merely to provide the setting. Such is most clearly the case with *People Are Living There, Hello and Goodbye,* and *The Road to Mecca.* And in *The Blood Knot, Boesman and Lena, A Lesson from Aloes,* and *Master Harold,* the issues are just as much or more about people's lives and about racial matters generally than they are specifically about South Africa or South African apartheid. In an interview with Gabrielle Cody and Joel Schechter during the Yale run of *A Place with the Pigs,* Fugard makes this clear, saying, "If you take the other plays done here at Yale for example, *A Lesson from Aloes, Master Harold [. . .] and the [B]oys* and *The Road to Mecca,* there is in all of them a combination of reasons for the choice of their stories. There is the personal motivation again, there is the opportunity to say something about South Africa, and about broader issues, other than just Athol Fugard. But with *A Place with the Pigs,* the focus is intensely and purely myself."[22]

As Fugard has also pointed out, *A Place with the Pigs* stands with *Orestes* and *Dimetos* as an "aberrant play" in his canon, the kind of work he seems to write about every ten years.[23] Like *Dimetos, A Place with the Pigs* centers on a character who hides himself away. In Dimetos's case it stems first from his no longer "caring" about his fellow man and then from an Orestes-like guilt. For Pavel it begins as homesickness and a one-night escape from the pressures of war but stretches to forty-one years. Fugard makes it very clear that Pavel's finding a long-term hiding place in a pigsty is related to Fugard's own history of alcohol dependence. He writes, "I made a pigsty out of a bottle of Jack Daniel's whiskey,"[24] and closes his interview with the comment:

> Two nights ago Suzanne Shepard [who played Praskovya in the Yale production] received a bunch of flowers and a note that thanked her for her wonderful performance. The note went on to say: "As the daughter of an alcoholic, I know what Praskovya is feeling." This note to Suzanne about her Praskovya, and the recognition of what Praskovya was dealing with, meant more to me than any of the complimentary notes, messages and fan mail I have received on behalf of Pavel in the course of this performance; that perceptive note came from someone who knew what the play was about.[25]

A Place with the Pigs is, finally, not a play about South Africa nor one about alcoholism but a parable "about the fact that we as human beings make and crawl into pigsties."[26]

Discussing the set of the first production of *A Place with the Pigs,* designer Susan Hilferty touches in important ways on the tone of the play. She writes, "I knew the set was too much. I knew the set was too real. I knew the world Athol was writing about was happening inside a man's brain. It didn't require anything representational. It didn't require a realistic pigsty."[27] This dissatisfaction with the realism of the pigsty in the Yale Rep production stems from the fact that the play is a parable. It is the dramatization of a real event reported in the *New York Times,* but, more importantly, it is a dramatic metaphor for destructive human strategies; it is literally played out in the Russian pigsty of the newspaper article but it is actually set "in the author's imagination."

A Place with the Pigs is Fugard's most openly comic play but it is also possibly his most classically tragic. We laugh at Pavel the buffoon who has exiled his adult life to a rank pigsty echoing with the comical grunts of unseen swine and filled with their excrement. This is hardly a place for serious matters, a far cry from Lear's heath or Oedipus's Theban palace.[28] And yet Fugard creates a delicate balance through which that noisy, noisome pigsty is nevertheless an apt enclosure for a tragic life. The foolish, capering Pavel is also a tragic figure whose life has been reduced to the graffiti that mark the passing of time. Like Macbeth, he has tragically allowed the time and meaning of his life to become measured merely as the "petty pace from day to day," which is reflected by the passing of time that he has grotesquely recorded on the pigsty walls. Susan Hilferty astutely recognizes that Pavel's pigsty graffiti emphasize the state of his mind and that they, not a realistically rendered sty, should dominate the set. These graffiti, she asserts, "should literally show the state of Pavel's mind. They are not realistic images. Unfortunately, in the gorgeous pigsty of the first production . . . they had no impact at all, when in fact they should have been BAM right in your face."[29]

The interplay of grotesquely comic and grotesquely tragic is present from the play's outset. When the play opens, Pavel, who has hidden himself away in his pigsty for the last ten years, is busy penciling down a lofty speech he intends to give when, in a few days, he will reveal himself at a ceremony honoring the war dead. His self-consciously august plea for forgiveness and his formal rhetoric are comically undercut by the punctuation of porcine sounds:

> "Comrades, Pavel Ivanovich Navrotsky is not dead. He is alive. It is he who stands before you. I beg you, listen to his story and then deal with him as you see fit. Comrades, I also beg you to believe that it is a deeply repentant man who speaks . . ." (*He can hardly hear himself above the noise from the pigs. He speaks louder.*) ". . . that it is a deeply repentant man who speaks these words to you . . ." SHUT UP! (*He grabs a stick and rushes around the sty, lashing out at the pigs.*) Silence, you filthy bastards! I want silence! Silence! Silence! (*Squeals and then a slight abatement of noise. Pavel returns to his speech.*) (55–56)[30]

Pavel laughably and pathetically composes in his head the script for his projected dramatic performance just as we all in our lives write mental scripts for our own envisioned dramatic comebacks or other imagined special moments. He is, thus, at once a bizarre living grotesquerie and a believable human being with whom the audience can identify.

Pavel's rhetoric and script writing are echoed and amplified more generally by the rhetoric and scripting of the play, for rhetorical traps are what *A Place with the Pigs* is finally about. It is striking that Fugard links *A Place with the Pigs* and *Dimetos* as his "aberrant" plays, for in important ways the one is the obverse of the other. In *Dimetos*, Fugard's eponymous character must learn to use imaginative narrative to free himself from his psychological trap, whereas in *A Place with the Pigs*, Pavel's imaginative narrative forges his trap. Well aware of Brecht's *Parables for the Theatre*,[31] Fugard creates not merely a character who writes scripts for himself but a play that tells stories. The play is divided not into acts but into four scenes, each with a heading. This is reminiscent of the titles Brecht often used to precede scenes and thus to "alienate" his audience and short-circuit Aristotelian engagement with the action. Perhaps this is what Fugard has in mind. The scenes not only have a Brechtian ring but also sound like the titles of folktales: *The Anniversary of the Great Victory, Beauty and the Beast, The Midnight Walk, Orders from the Commissar*. Subtitled "a personal parable," the title also naturally brings to mind the parable of the prodigal son (Luke 15:11–32).

Stories within stories is the rhetorical structure of *A Place with the Pigs*. Praskovya narrates, as she has clearly done time and time again, the story of Pavel's return home during a blizzard when he deserted from the army. As she tells the familiar tale, he responds like a child "*[g]reedy for still more*," with exclamations like "Yes yes yes" and "Go on" (59). And when she reaches the part about the slippers his mother made for him, he pulls them out and sentimentalizes over them much as Ibsen's Tesman laughably sentimentalizes over the slippers his aunts embroidered. But for Pavel, the slippers are also tangible artifacts that have a function in the narrative both for the past—"Every time I touch them, or just look at them . . . sometimes when I even just think about them . . . a flood of grief and guilt wrecks my soul as it did that night ten years ago" (59–80)—and for the future—"No, my conscience will not allow me to wear these until the day when I am once more a free man" (60). The first scene of the play goes on to have Pavel cite the slippers as the narrative center of his situation, for as his comrades sat in the barracks running out of other diversions, "sooner or later one of them would say in a small voice, 'Hey, Pavel, tell us about your slippers'" (68), and this would initiate their and his homesickness.

Much of the first scene is devoted to Pavel's self-consciously authoring his speech and preparing to deliver it in the grand manner. He reminds Praskovya, "Many was the time you yourself said I could have made a career of the stage if I had wanted to. . . . Today I must give the performance of my life" (62). And in the rehearsal room draft of the play, Fugard has partly typed and partly penned in at this point, "Rmember [*sic*] saying that after I had read Pushkin to you for the 1st time?"[32] Unable, however, to muster the necessary courage to reveal himself, Pavel sends Praskovya forth to tell his story at the victory celebration, where she in turn hears the political fiction of "the Russian bears who mauled the fascist mongrels" (70) and a comical marriage proposal to her from their neighbor Smetalov made, she tells Pavel, in the form of a narrative titled "The joyful vision of my pigs and his cows under the same roof" (71). Pavel proceeds to see his situation among the pigs as still another form of narrative, endowing himself with a comic place in hagiography as "St. Pavel of the Pigs" (72). And in the rehearsal room script, he imagines himself writing a "monumental study" titled *The Social History of a Pig Sty*.[33]

The stories of Pavel's return home, his slippers, his projected speech to the public, the rhetoric of the political rally, the fabulistic marriage proposal, and the comic hagiography are all constructed narratives that exist within the dramatic narrative titled "The Anniversary of the Great Victory," which is in turn a story that exists within the dramatic structure titled *A Place with the Pigs*. And sitting—pardon the expression—hamstrung in the midst of the interlocking narratives is Pavel, a captive caught in the web of his own fictions.

When the second scene of *A Place with the Pigs* begins, "A lot of time has passed" (presumably between ten and fifteen years), but Pavel has remained in the pigsty. The set, however, has become more ludicrous because the fancy slippers have nearly disintegrated, the graffiti marking the passing of days and years have escalated, and now Pavel has also begun marking the walls with the tally of flies he has killed. The stage environment is located somewhere in a limbo between the realism of an actual pigsty and the expressionist settings of Georg Kaiser's *Gas Trilogy* and Ernest Toller's *Mass Man,* or the expressionistic proliferation of numbers in Elmer Rice's *The Adding Machine*. This is appropriate, for Pavel's existence has become increasingly unreal and extravagant. The fabric of his life, like that of his embroidered slippers, has not disappeared entirely but has grotesquely fallen apart. And like his slippers, his life has become reduced to fly swatting, an activity that, located as it is amid the myriad flies drawn to the excrement in a pigsty, bespeaks the comic and tragic ludicrousness of Pavel's existence. It seems possible, too, that Fugard has in mind a grotesquely comic version of the plague in Sartre's *The Flies*.[34]

When a butterfly which has lost its way unexpectedly flies in amid the pigs, excrement, and dung flies, it is for Pavel not just a reminder of the outside world he has not seen for years but clearly also a symbol of the natural life he has forsaken:

> This is no place for a little beauty like you. Where are you? Little fluttering friend, where are you? Please . . . oh, dear God! . . . *please* don't die in here. Let me give you back to the day outside, to the flowers and the summer breeze . . . and then in return take, oh, I beg you! . . . take just one little whisper of my soul with you into the sunlight! Be my redemption! (74)

Symptomatic of *A Place with the Pigs,* Fugard makes some fast tonal shifts. This *cri de coeur* is immediately and comically undercut when the butterfly is carelessly swallowed up by one of the pigs. But the audience laughter is cut short when Pavel

17. Athol Fugard and Lida Meiring as Pavel and Praskovya in *A Place with the Pigs*, Market Theatre, Johannesburg, 1987. Photo by Ruphin Coudyzer.

jumps into the pen, knife in hand, and murders the offending pig, whose "terrible gurgles and death squeals" blend with the receding laughter. A similar tonal admixture occurs as Pavel speaks with the pomposity of, ironically and appropriately, a ham actor and Beckett's Hamm, declaiming, "I'm reaching the end, Praskovya. Those few seconds of innocent laughter might well have been the death rattle of my soul," to which Praskovya comically and deflatingly replies, "Pavel, I think I should also point out that only last week I had to let out your trouser seams because you're putting on a little weight around the waist . . . and now you've just killed a full-grown pig with your bare hands. That doesn't sound like a dying man to me" (77–78). Again, Pavel aphorizes with both truth and pomposity, "A life with nothing sacred left in it is a sullen existence, Praskovya. It is a life not worth living," but proceeds from the sublime to the ridiculous as he follows his statement with a request for a little aniseed to spice his supper of soup and dumplings (79).

The tonal dislocations recur and are intensified in the third scene, which takes place when "[a] lot more time has passed" and shows the sty now covered with even more markings indicating the tally of months, years, and dead flies, but added to these are graffiti of "obscenities and rude drawings of the pigs" (80). In this scene, Pavel, after what must be thirty or more years of hiding in the pigsty, makes his first brief foray into the outside world. He does so "disguised" as a woman, allegedly for safety's sake, and wearing one of Praskovya's dresses and a pair of her shoes. It is or could be a poignant moment, but Pavel is hardly in drag and passing, for he is rendered comical as a bearded man foolishly parading about in his wife's dress.[35]

That *A Place with the Pigs* is partially inspired by Fugard's own alcohol dependence helps one see the obvious connection between this play and Eugene O'Neill's *The Iceman Cometh*, in which a collection of alcoholics have hidden themselves away not in a pigsty but in the dingy, grimy backroom of Harry Hope's saloon.[36] Like O'Neill's Jimmy Tomorrow and all the other tomorrow denizens of Hope's backroom, Pavel talks about extricating himself from the sty, but is psychologically unable to do so. O'Neill's characters, whom Hickey pushes into the daylight and onto the street, come rushing back to the protection of the bar. Pavel, released into the outside world, exults, "You know, Praskovya, I thought that in that sty I had become some sort of moral degenerate, that my soul had rotted away in the ocean of pigshit and piss I've been swimming in since God alone knows when. But that is not true! I still have it!" To which Praskovya replies risibly and deflatingly, "Moderate your language, Pavel. That is not the way a good woman talks" (85–86). Pavel goes on to plan his escape and declares, "I'd rather die in a ditch beside the road, under the stars with a clean wind in my hair, than return to that sty and die of suffocation from a pig fart" (87). But like O'Neill's characters, return he does to his place with the pigs when Praskovya goes back to the house saying she will not accompany him if he leaves.

Nicely revealed in this "Midnight Walk" scene is Praskovya's co-dependence. Pavel's hiding has defined a role for her as his hider and protector. And yet there is a sense that she realizes his humanity will not be restored if he merely runs away. In a highly histrionic gesture, Pavel re-enters his place with the pigs, attempts to transfer blame for his own self-loathing onto Praskovya, Lear-like tears off his clothes, and flings himself naked into one of the pens:

> . . . you have finally come to believe that this is where I belong. My Home!
> . . . So what does that make me? A pig? Some sort of superior pig that God endowed with language and rational thought? Your favorite, your pet pig?
> . . . (PAVEL *leaves* PRASKOVYA, *wanders around the sty and then steadies himself for a final declaration*) . . . I am broken. These are the last words that you will ever hear from me. I abandon my humanity! From now on, Praskovya, feed me at the trough with the others.
>
> *He tears off his clothes and throws himself naked into one of the pens with the pigs.* (89–90)

With this, she fetches Pavel's pig-herding crook and uses it to flagellate him back into humanity. The scene closes on *"Pavel alone—naked, covered in mud and hurting—a picture of abject misery"* (92).

A few hours pass between the third and the final scene. Pavel appears *"still naked and dirty, but now wrapped in one of his blankets"* and launches into a manic monologue; shouts like Lear, "Crack crack crack crack crack crack crack" (94); emerges from his lunacy; and opens the doors to the pens and the sty, releasing the pigs into the world. Clearly their release is also his own, and he tells Praskovya, "I *had* to do something, and that was all I could think of" (98). It is significant, however, that the man whose fictions trapped him in a pigsty now, like Dimetos in his final action, uses fiction to extricate himself from his hiding place. Pavel says in dialogue with himself:

> I'll tell you a story, Pavel. Are you listening? Once upon a time, in a small village, there was a very very stupid man who woke up one morning and decided that he wanted to be a pig.
> Oh shut up!
> Don't you want to hear the rest of it? It's got a very funny ending, Pavel. His feet turn into trotters, his nose becomes a snout . . .
> I said shut up! (93)

In the schizoid psychomachia and Armageddon that dominate the play's final scene, the Pavel who has hidden away for forty-one years is finally subdued by the Pavel who yearns for liberation. The victorious Pavel can now erase the graffiti that in the course of the play have increasingly taken the shape of a prison inmate's pathetic markings on his cell wall; at once like a prisoner on the day of his release and like a bridegroom accepting a new life, he dons his black wedding suit. The play then ends on a comic note as Pavel begins to script his confession. Praskovya suggests he surrender at the police station, to which Pavel, offended, replies, "I'm not just a common criminal, Praskovya. As I remember it, the *Military Manual* listed desertion as one of the most serious offences a soldier could commit. I'll hand myself over at the military barracks. Come . . . let's go" (100).

Seen as a dramatization of a newspaper article and a story about a Russian deserter who hides away for forty-one years, *A Place with the Pigs* is trivial. Seen as a parable, it is profound. What Fugard evokes is the comic, tragic, and pathetic aspects of what Ibsen portentously called our "life lies," and what for Fugard are the fictions we use upon ourselves to defer and hide from the projects we at once want and don't want to undertake ("I was going to paint the kitchen this year, but my aging mother broke her hip and needed me"), from the resolutions we do and don't want to keep ("I must start losing weight, and I'll do it after I eat this last piece of cream pie"), from the truths we do and don't want to see ("my daughter needs to be financially independent but she'd look so wonderful in this expensive dress I'm buying for her"). And this holds true for the hiding places for more destructive fictions such as those, as Fugard knows from personal experience, that alcoholics tell themselves and their loved ones. And if one wished to extend the parable to South African politics—and one can certainly do so, though this does not seem to have been Fugard's intention in writing the play—one might say it is tantamount to whites' hiding away in the sty created by their fictions of racial supremacy.

Though it is an anomaly in the Fugard canon, *A Place with the Pigs* is an impressive play that teaches and dramatizes in parabolic form important perceptions about human denial strategies and their consequences. Through Pavel, we see both the ludicrous and serious consequences of hiding and the fictive strategies we employ to keep ourselves hidden. It is hardly surprising, then, that audiences will find *A Place with the Pigs* Fugard's funniest play but that they will also react feelingly, as did the daughter of the alcoholic who identified so strongly with Paskovya in her fan letter to Suzanne Shepard.

SEVEN

Writing to Right: Scripting Apartheid's Demise

In a curious way, writing the anomalous and parabolic *Dimetos,* treating the madness of the title character, seemed to free up Fugard so that he could go on to write of both individual and racist madness in new ways in the plays that followed: *A Lesson from Aloes, Master Harold,* and *The Road to Mecca.* A little more than ten years after *Dimetos,* Fugard wrote another anomalous piece, *A Place with the Pigs.* As with *Dimetos,* audiences were thrown off balance because this play did not square with the Fugard they knew.[1] Again like *Dimetos, A Place with the Pigs* seemed to liberate Fugard, as his character Pavel is also liberated, to move ahead with his life; and in Fugard's case to move ahead in such a way that he could write new plays imbued with the future tense. In large part, Fugard's dramas before *A Place with the Pigs* deal either with the past of remembered incidents or with the painfulness of the present. With *My Children! My Africa!* (1989), however, there is a recognition that apartheid's days are numbered and that a new generation of young people, black and white, stand on the threshold of the future. They will soon throw off the shackles of racism either to turn South Africa into a bloodbath or to forge a new society never envisioned by their parents.

The years since *A Place with the Pigs* have seen South Africa undergo rapid and remarkable political and social change. Fugard's sensibility and personal history enable him to identify at once with both the older and the younger generations, and his skill as a playwright enables him to move an audience so that they can also simultaneously empathize alike with young and old, to hope for a bright future even as they fear the possibly destructive legacy of an history of oppression. *My Children! My Africa!* (1989), *Playland* (1992), *My Life* (1994), and *Valley Song* (1995) are an eloquent record of Fugard's adjustments to the changes in South Africa and to his role as an artist. Implicitly and explicitly in his 1990s plays, he faces the dilemma of being an older-generation artist in a young South Africa. What is his proper role as an established white playwright in a new, post-apartheid multiracial society, a society whose changes he has helped to bring about? Indeed, in many ways Fugard's plays can be regarded as "the abstracts and brief chronicle" of his time. For the critic, however, they pose a dilemma, for they must be judged on their effectiveness as theatre as well as for their contribution to contemporary South African political discourse.

Fugard, like novelist and short-story writer Nadine Gordimer, sets most of his work in South Africa, and like her (and this cannot be emphasized often enough) he is not writing exclusively about South Africa, for his plays tackle common world problems: letting go of the past, finding paths to the future, and cherishing what is good from the past amid the frenzy of iconoclasm and of rapid and radical change. Although Fugard's plays are set in his native land and are often redolent with Eastern Cape and Karoo regionalism, they are as much about transcendent, eternal human issues as are Trollope's Barsetshire, Hardy's Wessex, Faulkner's Yoknapatawpha County, or Narayan's Malgudi novels. On his stage, moreover, the accents of Fugard's small community regionalism serve as backdrop to and heighten, in another key, the drama of the on-stage small communities of learning that exist among just two or three characters.

A Lesson from Aloes (as its title suggests) and *Master Harold* are both plays about teaching. *My Children! My Africa!, My Life,* and *Valley Song* are also overtly teaching plays, but in them pedagogy and learning are presented and interrogated in new ways. To recognize the difference between the teaching and heuristic aims of the earlier plays and those of later ones is to comprehend how Fugard moves in new directions after the writerly breathing space he takes through *A Place with the Pigs.* Fugard's plays of the 1970s (for example, *A Lesson from Aloes*) are dark plays. In them an end to apartheid, South African injustice, the omnipresence of wrongfully incarcerated prisoners in South African prisons, and the existence of the Special Branch all seem to be near impossibilities in the playwright's or the audience's lifetime—as much as did the breaking of the Berlin Wall to Germans.

By the late 1980s, however, the dismantlement of apartheid seemed imminent. Fugard, therefore, went from writing about how decent human beings (like John and Winston, Buntu and Sizwe, Piet Bezuidenhout, and Sam and Hally) can survive during a long period of oppression to how people of all races must prepare for the soon-to-occur demise of apartheid. He enjoins his audiences as well to reflect on how they will address the terrible legacy of more than four decades of apartheid and an even longer history of oppression, racism, and exploitation. What, Fugard conjectures through drama, will become of the lost generation born into apartheid and thus ill-prepared for the new, democratic, multiracial South Africa about to happen? What will the old order leave in its wake and what new issues will political and social change bring? Fugard's plays after *A Place with the Pigs* are in large part his ruminations on these questions.

The first of those plays, *My Children! My Africa!* (1989), was "forged . . . from within the cauldron of the violence in the Eastern Cape,"[2] and it is set in 1984 during the time of school boycotts protesting Bantu education.[3] In this play, Fugard examines the issue of how a new generation will achieve freedom and at what cost. As the lights go up on the first scene of *My Children! My Africa!*, "[a] lively interschool debate is in progress. Everyone is speaking at the same time." The din is silenced by the first words of the play spoken by Mr M, a teacher at a black South African township high school: "Order please!" (135).[4] As the play progresses, those initial words resonate with increasing and punning meaning, for *My Children! My Africa!* is at once about the keeping order in contemporary South Africa and about the rise of a new black order in that country.

One spare set, a classroom at Zolile High School in an Eastern Cape black township, serves as the backdrop for *My Children! My Africa!*, and with such a set, Fugard is clearly cuing his audience that his play, like most plays set in schoolrooms, is going to be about teaching and learning, and will probably be didactic.[5] His three-hander begins with the staging of a special and unique event at Zolile High: a debate between Thami Mbikwana, the flashy and articulate top debater at the black township school, and Isabel Dyson, the composed and astute top debater from the town's all-white Camdeboo Girls High School. The two debaters, a black male and a white female, are in the process of making their concluding arguments on the topic of full rights for women.

Perhaps not for the unseen, off-stage Zolile High School debate audience but surely for the theatre audience, which is also cast in the role of debate audience, the congruence between the gender issue arguments and those of race will be immediately apparent. More remarkable still will be the novel picture, for South Africa, of Thami, a black male, and Isabel, a white female, contending against each other on the level playing field of debating team competition, trading quip for quip, argument for argument, and adhering to the same rules of play. They meet as well as equals gender to gender and race to race. Theirs is not a combat of physical aggression and violence but of reasoned verbal contention. And school debate, one might argue, is the paradigm and prolegomenon for real-life political negotiation. And who better to practice such racial rapprochement and such pointed verbal repartee than Thami and Isabel, the members of the next generation, who will likely be called upon to argue the issues and forge South African life after the dismantling of apartheid?

The use of debate in *My Children! My Africa!* is significant in another and related way, for debate is a performance and an analogue of theatre as Fugard and his model, Bertolt Brecht, craft it. Like debate, the theatre of *Lehrstücke* requires acting out and arguing a position, basic conflict, verbal sparring, and performance art. The Brechtian theatre also provides no easy solutions, no easy partisan propaganda, but forces the audience to ponder the issues and judge for themselves. A literary descendant of Horace and of Ben Jonson as well as of Brecht, Fugard creates in *My Children! My Africa!* drama based on agon, on conflict, that is *utile dulce*, instructive as well as pleasurable. This is likewise an apt description of the school debate we see on stage. The Zolile High School debate, like Fugard's theatre, places Isabel and Thami on an equal footing in terms of race and gender; and debate, like theatre, is but a dress rehearsal for life outside the playhouse.

With Fugard's brand of Brechtian political theatre in mind; and with the critical, violent, and potentially explosive racial situation in South Africa in mind as well, the words of *My Children! My Africa!*'s black schoolmaster, Mr. M, about the nature of debate resonate with meaning:

> I think it is necessary for me to remind you all exactly what a debate is supposed to be. My dictionary defines it as follows: "The orderly and regulated discussion of an issue with opposing viewpoints receiving equal time and consideration." Shouting down the opposition so that they cannot be heard does not comply with that definition.
>
> Enthusiasm for your cause is most commendable but without personal discipline it is as useless as having a good donkey and a good cart but no harness.
>
> We are running out of time. (135–136)

These cautions could easily serve as Fugard's dictum for meaningful theatre. Indeed, for Fugard, debate, theatre, and politics seem to require both the presentation of differing viewpoints and the marriage of enthusiasm for a cause with discipline or order. *"Master Harold" . . . and the Boys* used the semiotics of dance and kite-flying as metaphors for such a marriage. *My Children! My Africa!*, whose central inanimate actor is Mr. M's dictionary, forges that union through language.

Both *Master Harold* and *My Children! My Africa!* are *Lehrstücke*, plays of and about teaching. The learners are the characters of the drama plus the audience. The triangular on-stage relationships in both plays focus on the teachers—Sam in the former and Mr M in the latter—and on the ways those teachers come to learn from their respective students. In its alternately critical and loving, accusing and sentimental portrait of Mr M, *My Children! My Africa!* celebrates the strengths and decries the liabilities of the old pedagogical order and curriculum, and of South Africa's colonized black teachers who accepted that country's racialism as a given, and sought empowerment for blacks through mastery of white, European, hegemonic culture acquired via traditional Eurocentric schooling.

In the course of the play, the valuation of Mr M has as many reversals as a Beaumont and Fletcher tragicomedy, for it bespeaks the ambivalence in postcolonial societies about the Western cultural baggage that shaped colonial pasts and continues to play a significant role in the shaping of postcolonial futures. Nowhere in Fugard's work does that ambivalence about the role Western culture plays in a non-Western colonized land come to the fore as sharply as it does in *My Children! My Africa!*, in which, after the spirited debate between Thami and Isabel, Mr M obtains permission to enter the two debaters as what will likely be South Africa's first integrated team in the nationwide English literature quiz bowl competition. Thus the play begins with Thami, Mr M, and Isabel aligned—an optimistic dramatic syzygy that will prove tragically evanescent.

But before Thami and Isabel are brought together by Mr M as a team, there is a significant interaction between them during the aftermath of their debate. Left alone with one another on stage without adult or teacherly supervision, the two young people awkwardly but successfully try to eke out a common space for friendship and mutual understanding. In a dialogue that foreshadows the exchanges among the five teenage girls in *My Life* (1994), Isabel and Thami briefly exchange their biographies and their feelings about schooling. An earnest Isabel, who sees herself as a dissident liberal, responds straightforwardly to Thami, whose cordiality is laced with the ironic hostility of township experience toward the privileged but naive white girl primly attired in her school uniform.

When Thami half-jokingly concludes his battery of questions with "What did you have for breakfast this morning?," she laughingly and banteringly replies, "Auntie, our maid, put down in front of me a plate of steaming, delicious Jungle Oats over which I sprinkled a crust of golden, brown sugar, and while that was melting on top I added a little moat of chilled milk all around the side. That was followed by brown-bread toast, quince jam and lots and lots of tea" (142). Her affable and charmingly ingenuous answer, however, serves sharply to characterize the difference between her life and his. For her, her breakfast is an unremarkable meal, but for a township resident like Thami it is a cornucopia of extraordinary plenty containing the exotic (quince jam), the limitless (lots and lots of tea), and the products of an electrified home (chilled milk and toasted bread). To the artless Isabel, it does not occur to her that such an ordinary meal would be unknown and extraordinary to Thami. Nor does she recognize the colonial irony of the white girl feeding on a breakfast cereal called Jungle Oats. And most important, she takes for granted the role of Auntie in her household: Auntie, deprived of her African name; Auntie who travels to the Dyson home from Thami's township; Auntie waiting on a teenage mistress who need only sit down at her breakfast table and accept its riches. Fugard does not condemn Isabel for her innocence or her role, but he neatly pinpoints and italicizes the small things that bespeak the vast differences that will eventually need to be encountered and bridged by blacks and whites in a post-apartheid South Africa.

Isabel Dyson and Thami Mbikwana join forces to prepare for the national competition because, tellingly, Mr M has invited Isabel to do so and, in his patriarchal manner, told Thami he *will* do so. The deferential manner toward the white girl and the imperative manner toward the black boy allow the audience to feel one of many examples of how students, black and white, are colonized and taught their respective roles, and to realize that this is done even by black teachers who are themselves products of an educational system meant indelibly to inscribe the lessons and code of apartheid. The two young people, Thami and Isabel, however spiritedly combine forces and, in a lively scene, prepare themselves for the English literature contest by boning up and testing each other in the area of nineteenth-century English poetry.

At first they compete by challenging one another with biographical information about the Romantic poets and swap famous lines from Wordsworth, Coleridge, and Southey. They do so using the metaphor of a tennis competition. The irony, of course, is that in apartheid South Africa, these two young people would never meet on the same tennis court, so what they are unwittingly doing is role-playing some rather transgressive, revolutionary behavior. As they proceed, it becomes clear that Thami's favorite poets are Lord Byron and Shelley. He asks Isabel:

> What poet was born with deformed feet, accused of incest and died of fever while helping the Greeks fight for freedom? "A love of liberty characterises his poems and the desire to see the fettered nations of Europe set free."

And then he quotes from *Childe Harold* (canto 4, verse 78):

> "Yet, Freedom! yet thy banner, torn, but flying,
> Streams like the thunder-storm *against* the wind." (163)

As soon as this is spoken, one realizes the relevance of Thami's preference for Byron. The applicability to the lamentable situation in contemporary South Africa of Byron's paean to Freedom in *Childe Harold* and of his personal heroism in the cause of the Greeks is almost painfully obvious.

Likewise revealing, along similar lines, are two sonnets the young scholars have memorized and about which they are both extremely enthusiastic. The first is John Masefield's "Sea-Fever," the second Shelley's "Ozymandias." These works take on new meanings when read in the context of South African apartheid and the realities of black townships. Both "Sea-Fever" and "Ozymandias" in their construction reflect Mr M's requirement for proper debate and Fugard's implicit requirement for progress: the union of enthusiasm and discipline.

The first, "Sea-Fever," exemplifies that union in its untrammeled enthusiasm for life at sea expressed through the formal discipline of a sonnet; it exemplifies as well the combination of feeling with the formal poetic devices of alliteration, rhythm, and rhyme. Its famous celebration of the free individual spirit, the "vagrant gypsy life," projects a romantic freedom unknown to those whose lives are constrained by the strictures of apartheid rule.

Even more striking in its resonances for contemporary South Africa is Shelley's "Ozymandias," which, when read in a South African context, becomes an ironic commentary on the ultimate fate of white apartheid policy and rule. After Isabel and Thami take turns reciting the lines of Shelley's ominous sonnet, Isabel significantly comments to Thami and Mr M that Ozymandias was not a figment of Shelley's fictive imagination but the Egyptian king, Ramses II, about whom, she says, *The Everyman's Encyclopedia* comments, "his oppressive rule left Egypt impoverished and suffering from an incurable decline." The point is driven home when Thami responds with his remembrance of Ramses:

> THAMI. I had a book of Bible stories when I was small, and there was a picture in it showing the building of the pyramids by the slaves. Thousands of

them, like ants, pulling the big blocks of stone with ropes, being guarded by soldiers with whips and spears. According to that picture the slaves must have easily outnumbered the soldiers one hundred to one . . .

ISABEL. What are you up to, Mbikwana? Trying to stir up a little social unrest in the time of the pharaohs, are you?

THAMI. Don't joke about it, Miss Dyson. There are quite a few Ozymandiases in this country waiting to be toppled. And with any luck you'll live to see it happen. *We* won't leave it to Time to bring them down. (165–166)

My Children! My Africa! could be criticized for its overt and even flat-footed didacticism, and certainly there is nothing subtle about the points being made here. But that lack of subtlety is precisely Fugard's point.

It is immediately clear that the Romantic and Victorian writers Isabel and Thami study and memorize resonate with ironic social and political meaning for contemporary South Africa. But it is important to see that Fugard does not stop here. Instead he turns the play around in such a way that we begin to realize that there is something very much amiss about the use of canonical English texts to define an African, non-Western situation. And there is something very much amiss about a South African national literary contest that is based entirely on British writers. Toward the end of the contest practice session scene, therefore, Thami rebels against the old order, against the old-fashioned, colonized mentality of Mr M that privileges European poetry and culture over that of Africa. And Fugard nicely juxtaposes to the scene in which Thami and Isabel recite Wordsworth, Coleridge, Southey, Masefield, and Shelley, a scene which begins with African lyricism, with Thami chanting a Xhosa poem about school. This registers as well Thami's defection from Mr M and from the Eurocentric, colonizing culture Mr M's teaching valorizes. In the play's crucial turn, Thami changes from compliant disciple to interpellating adversary, and Mr M must face the unpleasant truth all teachers face: the students they educate may come to use their education against the very teachers that taught them.

Thami's rebellion includes his comments on the education fostered by whites, an education that seeks to erase black culture and history by replacing them with beatified white versions. Addressing the audience, Thami lashes out against the educational program of Oom Dawie (Uncle Dave), the deceptively unthreatening sobriquet for the regional Inspector of Bantu Schools. The education that Oom Dawie and his colleagues foster is essentially one that teaches the facts of white civilization and fosters an image of a world controlled by whites, defined by white Eurocentric culture. Even Oom Dawie's avuncular name enforces the recognition that his relation to black students and their teachers is one of adult to children, kindly white master but white master nonetheless to those of subaltern race. Thami exclaims passionately and powerfully to the audience:

Do you understand now why it is not as easy as it used to be to sit behind that desk and learn only what Oom Dawie has decided I must know? My head is rebellious. It refuses now to remember when the Dutch landed, and the Huguenots landed, and the British landed. It has already forgotten when the old Union became the proud young Republic. But it does know what happened in Kliptown in 1955, in Sharpeville on 21st March, 1960, and in Soweto on the 16th of June, 1976. Do you? Better find out because those are dates your children will have to learn one day. We don't need the Zolile classrooms any more. We know what they really are . . . traps which have been carefully set to catch our minds, our souls. (175)

If the audience has not already questioned the racist underpinnings of the national contest for which Mr M is preparing his two star students, Thami's singing of the Xhosa lyric and this speech will make them do so. They may also ask why a black teacher is encouraging their participation in a contest whose very subject matter denies the rich cultural heritage of the nation's black majority and replaces it with a valorized, foreign, Eurocentric poetry that represents the cultural heritage of only a relatively small handful of the South African population.

My Children! My Africa! is an extraordinarily deceptive play. A teaching play set in a school, it smacks of heavy-handed didacticism. Yet to see the play this way is to misunderstand Fugard's brilliant craftsmanship and insight. Yes, the play teaches, but its lessons become increasingly complex and difficult. Likewise, our understanding of the characters and the characters' understanding of one another grows, develops, and becomes increasingly faceted. The first, obvious, and elementary lesson is about integration. The audience shares Mr M's pleasure at seeing the intellectual and social power generated when the white and the black student work together successfully as a team. The pleasure of liberal feelings is given vent as a deprived black teenager shows that as a debater and as an understander of English poetry he can match wits and skills with an advantaged white. In the mind of the audience members, Mr M receives accolades as a teacher for seeming to foster integration and interracial teamwork.

With Thami's withdrawal from the canonical literature contest, the tables turn and the lesson gets a bit harder as the insidious and subversive aspects of the educational system become manifest. Suddenly the canon and integration are instruments of enslavement and things to be reviled and rejected in favor of Afrocentric culture, resistance, and violent revolution in the form of school boycott. Mr M becomes not the black township "teacher of the year" but a traitor to his students and his people, a racial quisling whose treason ultimately makes him worthy of execution.

A programmed product of white supremacist brainwashing, Mr M informs the authorities about the rebellious activities of his students and is consequently murdered by the very students whose intellectual lives he has sought to foster. Richard Hornby regards Mr M as "a classically tragic hero, bringing about his own downfall by acting according to a set of genuine but ultimately limited ideals."[6] The intermediate-level lesson of the play is thus about the oppression of blacks and the devaluation of their lives and culture by white South Africans. But importantly, Thami and his revolutionary comrades replace the authority of Mr M, the lover of words and language whose most treasured possession is his English dictionary, with a new authority of physical discipline and physical violence. Thami exclaims, "The struggle doesn't need the big English words you taught me how to spell," to which Mr M rebuts, "Stones and petrol bombs can't get inside those armoured cars. Words can" (p. 183).

In its final and advanced lesson, *My Children! My Africa!* teaches its difficult truth, a truth that is as applicable to education and social change as it is to theatre: mere words devoid of actions or feelings are empty rhetoric; mere actions devoid of words or reasoned thought are mayhem.[7] Words by themselves produce artful but unproductive debates. Actions by themselves result in destruction and mindless killings. Just before his murder, Mr M stands in his schoolroom holding his dictionary in one hand and a rock that has been thrown through his window in the other (fig. 18).[8] Each symbol by itself represents a worthless approach to problem solving and more particularly to South African problem solving. Together, the play suggests, the two—action and words—can educate and spur reform even as Fugard's own playwriting can educate and suggest reform through its combination of dialogue and physical action. The theatrical space is a site where social issues can be debated and acted upon, providing the model and a dress rehearsal for the space beyond the playhouse.

18. John Kani as Mr M holding the rock and the dictionary on the set of *My Children! My Africa!*, Market Theatre, Johannesburg, 1989. Photo by Ruphin Coudyzer.

At the conclusion of *My Children! My Africa,* after Mr M dies, Isabel and Thami take stock of Mr M and what he stood for. The result is that Thami decides to leave South Africa, go north, and use his mind to become a strategist for the black rights movement instead of remaining a member of the mindless mob. Isabel ends the play with a eulogy that posits her as one of Mr M's children and suggests she, in her role as a now enlightened white South African, will work from the inside for social reform. Importantly, what the final moments of the play, with their revaluation of Mr M and what he taught, do is to revalorize the canon but in a new key. Byron and Masefield and Shelley may be white Eurocentric writers who should not be the centerpieces of African education, but they are not to be rejected out of hand and they are not irrelevant anachronisms from another cultural system. Colonial oppression is not unique to South Africa or to people of black skin. Thami's spirited recollection of the enslavement of the Israelites by the Egyptian pharaohs reminds us of that. And Europeans, like Byron's Greeks, have also fought oppression. There are, consequently, things to be learned from other cultures and their literatures. Fugard here takes a stand with which not all his audience will agree. For him, by implication, the British literature Thami and Isabel study should not be the privileged literature, but it should also not be disregarded, for it can be, as it is in *My Children! My Africa!,* a first lesson and a means for placing South African struggles in a wider context. After all, how different is Byron's idea of Freedom from the Xhosa word for freedom, *Amandla,* which Thami shouts as the play's first act curtain line?

In the last few years, much ink has been spilled over that neologism "canonicity." In its way, *My Children! My Africa!* engages the debate within the academy about so-called canonical literature, the allegedly privileged literature of dead white Eurocentric males. Fugard's play suggests that canonical literature does have an important place. When invested with exclusive authority, as it is in the beginning of *My Children! My Africa!,* it can be an instrument of cultural tyranny and oppression. When annihilated, it falls victim to another equally lamentable tyranny and oppression. Productive multicultural integration (and Mr M as a black Confucian implies that the cultures need not be just African and European) seems to be the play's *ultima Thule.*

What is needed is not the artificial window-dressing integration of a black and a white student teaming up for a school contest or on a tennis court, but the more difficult integration of cultures, art, and insight in the service of humanity—an integration in the best sense of that word, not a power struggle in which one culture seeks mastery over another. That lesson is neither easily learned nor easily accomplished, but it is clearly the challenge Fugard has set for himself as a white playwright writing about black and coloured South Africa and as a playwright who in many of his plays compels black and white actors to create art and meaning on stage together. It is that same challenge that he has set for his characters, Thami and Isabel, working as young people who may accomplish a multiracial society in their country. It is likewise the challenge that he has set for his audience, whom his theatre educates and empowers to make South Africa and the world a place in which the cries for Freedom and Amandla will be obsolete.

As Nick Visser points out, productions of *My Children! My Africa!* received standing ovations in South Africa; he reads these as the white liberal audience's own self-congratulatory applause. He writes of how they reacted with hoots and applause to the satirical picture of a black schoolboy protester unsure how to spell "Liberation" or "Education" for his school-boycott placard. And Visser recounts as well the feeling of audience satisfaction that "castigations of political action" are spoken by a black character, Mr M, "whose chief dramatic and ideological function is to act as a ventriloquist's dummy, uttering as if with his own voice what are actually the anxieties and perceptions and aspirations of middle-class white South Africans."[9] Along similar lines, Jeanne Colleran argues that with *My Children! My Africa!* (and *Playland* thereafter) Fugard takes advantage of "this period of incredible political flux to resuscitate his political voice, position, and vision." She then criticizes him for what she regards as his political nonalignment.[10] These are important charges that go to the heart of the serious issues raised in *My Children! My Africa!* and in *Playland.*

Fugard is the first to acknowledge the inseparability of his theatre from South African politics. "The notion that there could be such a thing as an apolitical South African story is a contradiction in terms," Fugard averred at the 1990 University of Witwatersrand graduation ceremonies, when he received an honorary doctorate.[11] And as a playwright who uses the political and social dilemmas of apartheid and post-apartheid South Africa as the environment for most of his dramas, Fugard is judged from differing standpoints. Seeing his work as dramatic art is not always the top priority of those who write about Fugard's theatre. Thus those who, like Visser and Colleran, are largely focused on Fugard's engagement or lack of what they see as appropriate engagement with a progressive 1990s political and social South African reform discourse take a dim view of Fugard's political stance in *My Children! My Africa!* and *Playland.* Likewise, there are those who will applaud merely because the sentiments of one character or another echo their own. As Visser and Colleran point out, many members of the audiences who responded so enthusiastically to *My Children! My Africa!* may have done so because they saw Mr M as affirming their own smarmy liberal politics and not because they were taken with the playwright's theatrical art. Writing seven years prior to *My Children! My Africa!*, Mel Gussow wisely explained, "Fugard is an artist of intense integrity and moral commitment, but he is seldom an activist. . . . and [he decided] that the emphasis [of a play] should be on the political effects of the work of art itself rather than on the effectiveness of public protest."[12]

There are of course dangers in equating the playwright with one of his characters. Mr M may revere words as Fugard does, and surely there is much of the older-generation playwright and director in the older-generation teacher, but Mr M is no more a stage representation of Fugard than the Shavian-looking and -sounding Captain Shotover is of Bernard Shaw. It is, moreover, useful whenever possible to separate judgment of a work's politics from judgment of its use of art in the presentation of ideas, regardless of whether we agree with those ideas. Brecht's *Good Woman of Setzuan* or Shakespeare's *The Merchant of Venice* are estimable works of theatre even if we do not agree with the Marxist agenda of the one or the stance toward Jews of the other. The strength of *My Children! My Africa!*, moreover, is precisely that Fugard does not take sides, even though the audience Visser saw may have. Indeed, the power of the play is that Fugard makes us understand the anger of Thami and his peers, and makes us understand, too, that anger without words, without discussion leads to senseless violence and a reign of terror. At the same time that Fugard may share Mr M's reverence for words, love of literature, and hope for peaceful solutions, he recognizes that Mr M has accepted the subaltern position imposed upon him by the system, that he is an assimilationist, and that his politics will not result in major social changes or relieve the plight of his fellow black South Africans. And Isabel's earnest, naive liberalism is also at once esteemed and satirized. There are no villains or heroes in *My Children! My Africa!*, but rather the play lays bare for the audience the complexities, the intricate knot, that apartheid has wrought; and it suggests with both fear and hope what might happen when that knot is finally unraveled.

The majority of Athol Fugard's plays are premised on a society based on apartheid, on the separation of races and the tensions that thereby result. Indeed, one might well say that Fugard's plays are about "separation anxiety," a term that seems peculiarly appropriate for describing plays like *My Children! My Africa!*, *Master Harold*, and *A Lesson from Aloes*, plays which portray apartheid's power to keep South Africa racially divided and to prevent people from knowing each other as human beings across racial lines. But in February 1990, President F. W. de Klerk began the process of dismantling apartheid and Nelson Mandela was released from Robben Island prison, and to all it seemed clear that the days of apartheid rule were fast drawing to a close and that a new epoch in South African life and history was close at hand. But could the wounds of forty-two years of apartheid rule heal overnight and a new South Africa commence without bloodshed? And what does a writer like Fugard write about when his long-desired goal of racial equality is at last achieved and he is robbed of his recurrent subject matter?

Playland (1992) is Fugard's first post-apartheid play, and in it the "separation anxiety" of his previous dramatic output is replaced by what one might aptly call "suppuration anxiety," for *Playland* centers on the festering psychological wounds, the running sores, engendered by decades of apartheid and by the racial divisions and racism that reach back not merely to 1948 but to the first white settlements in South Africa. In the course of *Playland*, South Africa's infected ulcerations ooze forth their pus, forcing audiences to feel the ravages of racism and to realize the many years it will take for the infections of history to drain and the reparative scar tissue to form before the deep wounds of the past properly heal.

Like so many of Fugard's works, *Playland* is parabolic. Set in Playland, a mobile amusement park that travels through the Karoo and Eastern Cape, and which Fugard knew in Port Elizabeth as a boy,[13] the play presents the post-apartheid confrontation of a black man and a white man, each in need of healing and repentance. Like Edward Albee's *The Zoo Story*, with which it has some marked affinities, *Play-*

land marries realistic detail (in this case the well-known Karoo amusement park and the personal histories of its two characters) to more abstract, Beckettian existential confrontations. Fugard's drama calls not merely Albee's Peter and Jerry to mind but also Beckett's Hamm and Clov, and Didi and Gogo. Fugard's amusement park, his Playland, furthermore becomes not just a symbolic image of South Africa on the brink of dismantling apartheid but of any population recovering from severe ethnic, racial, religious, or political division.

Though written in 1992, *Playland* takes place on New Year's Eve 1989. Myles Holloway reminds us that that time was an interregnum period just a few weeks "before the announcement of the release of Nelson Mandela on 2 February 1990 and the unbanning of dissident organizations. . . . Not only are the characters (and the audience) faced with the prospect of a new decade, but they stand at the brink of tremendous significance in which the past must be accounted for and the future shaped."[14] Similarly, in his preface to the play, Mannie Manim, who produced *Playland* at the Market Theatre, explains that "Athol has fashioned a tale about repentance, forgiveness and reconciliation at a time when our country and the world desperately need to consider these things. He gives us another of his parables about people finding new understanding and appreciation of each other in a world that holds more than just our individual catastrophes, hurts, regrets and sadness; in a world where God is alive."[15]

What Holloway's and Manim's comments underscore is that although *Playland* is a specifically South African work conceived at a critical moment in contemporary South African history, it is, nevertheless, also a dramatic work whose parable extends well beyond South African borders. But *Playland* does not sit well with all critics. Jeanne Colleran, for example, is uneasy with *Playland* and *My Children! My Africa!*, which she finds works exemplifying what she labels "Fugard's liberalism," a liberalism that, she argues, "permits and approves uprooting historical context." Discussing *Playland*, she takes Fugard to task for equating the trespasses of the play's two characters—white Gideon le Roux and black Martinus Zoeloe—and for suggesting "fantasy worlds of utopian race relations" whereby oppressed blacks do not receive retribution but "are compelled by their abusers to act the role of therapist, salving tormented psyches."[16] Holloway's and Manim's praise and Colleran's disapproval curiously have the same point of origin, and arise because *Playland*'s greatest strength is also its greatest liability: the creation of a larger parable within a specific sociopolitical South African context.

For those who hope for post-apartheid rapprochement among South Africa's races and ethnicities, *Playland* provides an optimistic and useful, though idealistic, parabolic exemplum that could likewise provide an image and way of healing for white Americans and African Americans, Catholics and Protestants in Northern Ireland, North and South Koreans, Israelis and Palestinians, or Serbs and Croats. For those, however, who would have Fugard write plays that fix blame on South African whites and demand reparations to blacks and coloureds for the past injuries and inhumanities they have endured, Fugard's plays from *My Children! My Africa!* to the present will fall far short of the mark and may even seem blameworthy for their failure to be congruent with a particular critic's political points of view.[17] There are surely those who feel a South African reign of terror is called for. Fugard is clearly not one of these. Writing four years after *Playland* (26 March 1996), he remarks:

> South Africa was, and still is, involved in a heated and passionate debate about the formation of a Commission for Truth and Reconciliation—a commission that will be empowered to investigate and expose the crimes of our Apartheid era and, in so doing, hopefully create a spirit of reconciliation in the country. Because without that spirit of reconciliation, unless we face up to and come to terms with the lies behind us, no healing of the terrible wounds of our Apartheid past will take place.[18]

With this statement he places himself in the political spectrum in ways that illumine where he stood when he wrote *Playland.*

The inevitable liability for drama with a political background or for political theatre is that the work is judged not on the merits of its effectiveness as drama and its ability to convey insights but on whether or not it massages the agendas of partisan politics. In short, without ignoring the political issues Colleran and like-minded critics raise, one must nevertheless ask whether *Playland* is successful theatre and whether it convincingly conveys Fugard's parable for South Africa and for other global areas emerging from bloody epochs of civil division, oppression, and combat. The answer will not be a universally affirmative one, for *Playland* often has more the feel of an oratorio than an opera. The climate of dramatic debate Fugard achieved in *My Children! My Africa!* is sacrificed for two characters standing on stage talking at each other rather than interacting. As a work of theatre, *Playland* often comes dangerously close to the static dramatic style of Milton's *Samson Agonistes.* It requires a talented actor like Kevin Spacey, who played the role of Gideon in the New York production, to save the play from being mere talking heads.

As he does in *The Island, Master Harold,* and *My Children! My Africa!,* Fugard employs for *Playland* a unique, carefully circumscribed setting in which the parabolic action of the drama can be staged. The aptly named amusement park is a *play* land in which Gideon and Martinus, the play's two characters, can act out and play out their guilt and interpersonal dynamics.[19] It is also a setting in which Fugard can posit a microcosmic dramatic landscape representing the macrocosm of South Africa and of damaged societies more generally. As the audience enters the theatre, they see on stage a corner of an amusement park before it has been lighted and open to the public. Prominently featured is a broken car from one of the rides. Soon after the action begins, therefore, the audience recognizes that *Playland* is set behind the scenes and amid the underside of a familiar but grotesque world. The broken carnival ride suggests as well that the play will concern itself with matters in need of repair.

Playland opens with something like the formulation of two sides of an equation.

19. Lou Ferguson and Gary
Cole as Martinus and Gideon in
Playland at Steppenwolf Theatre
Company, Chicago, Ill., 1995.
Photo by Michael Brosilow.
Courtesy Steppenwolf Theatre
Company.

A white Gideon le Roux and a black Martinus Zoeloe enter simultaneously from opposite sides of the stage. Perhaps indicative of his façade of white confidence, Gideon's entry is a sauntering one.[20] Not noticing Gideon's presence, Martinus enters soliloquizing aloud and summoning up, in tones reminiscent of the allegorical Porter in *Macbeth,* images of Judgment Day, hellfire, and an omniscient God:

> Ja! Ja! Go on. Laugh as much as you like but I say it again: I'll see all of you down there in Hell. That's right. All of you. In Hell! And when you wake up and see the big fires and you start crying and saying you sorry and asking forgiveness, then it's me who is laughing. . . . You tell lies and cheat and drink and make trouble with the little girls and you think God doesn't know? He knows! He sees everything you do and when the Big Day of Judging comes he will say to you, and you, and specially you . . . (5–6)

When Gideon makes his presence known by applauding Martinus's expostulation, the two characters do not converse but rather talk at each other without truly connecting. Although Gideon seems eager to forge a relationship, he is offered little opportunity to do so by Martinus's terse replies. This turns Gideon's speech into a kind of manic and insistent monologue (7–10).

In a number of aspects, *Playland* revisits three decades later the dramatic world of *Blood Knot.* [21] Like the earlier play, *Playland* brings together two men of different skin color who are, in curious ways, brothers. Like the earlier play, too, *Playland* forges a dramatic environment that is at once realistic and allegorical, whose characters are men with realistic histories yet with extra-realistic existences, and whose language falls somewhere between natural and artificial. Gideon's opening speeches place the location squarely in the Karoo amid towns like Middleburg, Cradock, Colesburg, and De Aar. The time is precisely New Year's Eve 1989. We learn something of Gideon's family background, the pigeons he and his father kept, and that he has served in the South African armed forces during the Border War. At the same time, the Playland backdrop with its advertisements for rides like "The Ghost Train," Martinus's bizarre opening monologue about hellfire, and the silences that punctuate the initial speeches between the characters suggest a drama that is something other than realistic or one played within clearly definable abscissas and ordinates of space and time. In short, *Playland* is an amalgam of realistic, specifically South African, localized detail and symbolic location. The white Afrikaner and black night watchman confront each other separated by a vast interpersonal and dialogic void indicative of the geographic and spiritual no-man's-lands that have separated people from one another under apartheid rule.

The temporal setting of *Playland,* in the hours preceding 1990, reminds the audience that in South Africa 1990 was not only the end of a decade but the beginning a new era. Gideon and Martinus are apartheid's scarred, moribund human leftovers in need of renewal and new directions. A hint of new beginnings and reform comes as Gideon contemplates his New Year's resolutions exclaiming, "No bloody miseries next year! I don't care how I do it, but 1990 is going to be different. Even if it kills me, I'm going to get things going again" (9). For Gideon it seems that his new start has something to do with effecting a comradeship between himself and Martinus.

Gideon's initial attempts to communicate with Martinus are abortive as he seems compulsively to pour forth information about his life. What does, however, form the space for their first connection is not, significantly, based on linguistic dialogue but on their shared love of nature in its South African manifestation, in their shared response to a politically uncharged event: "*Both men stare at the horizon where a Karoo sunset is flaring to a dramatic climax*" (10). What this black man and this white man clearly share, what here implicitly South Africans of all color seem to share, is a love of their country, not its politics but its landscape, its natural beauty. One remembers here Piet's similar love of South African vegetation amid political ugliness in *A Lesson from Aloes.* And for both Gideon and Martinus, the brilliant last summer sunset of the decade is an image of eschatological last things: for Gideon, it is the mushroom cloud of an atom bomb exploding on the nearby Karoo town of De Aar; for Martinus, it is "the fires of Eternal Damnation" (12).

As Martinus and Gideon speak, and as the play progresses, Playland is seen as a grotesque and unreal space to which people frantically flee in order to deny the truths of their existence and to escape the record of their deeds:

Playland is Happyland! Pretty lights and music. Buy your ticket for the Big Wheel and go round and round and forget all your troubles, all your worries. . . . they pray for rain but they wait for Playland and the happiness machines. And when we switch on the lights and the music, they come. Like moths they come out of the night. . . . They all come to play because they all want to forget. . . . You can try to forget as hard as you like but it won't help, because all the things you did are written down in the Big Book, and when the day comes you will stand there and *He* will read them to you. (13)

Surely Playland is an image of the land that is the setting for most of Fugard's plays. It is the falsely and grotesquely happy South Africa determined to assert its well-being despite its bloodshed and riots, and despite the harsh notes that sound from its townships, locations, and so-called homelands. The forced gaiety of Milly in *People Are Living There* is here enacted on a grand scale, but with seemingly similar results in the offing.

Indeed, all is not well in Playland, for in recent weeks it has, tellingly, been having generator troubles, and for a while it is doubtful whether on this night the power will work, permitting the lights to go on and the rides to turn. The symbolic value of this breakdown, the weakening viability of a way of South African life, is clear. The rides and honky-tonk sounds of the amusement park take on an ominous and sinister value in *Playland* as they become an increasingly grotesque background for what appears to be the inevitable and possibly disastrous confrontation between black and white in the foreground, a confrontation replete with references to sin, murder, and destruction.

In the course of the opening scene, Gideon strives with near-manic determination for a personalized relationship with Martinus, but to little effect. Martinus for his part, either unable or unwilling to pick up Gideon's desperate cues for attention, asserts rather than speaks to him of Judgment Day, Hell, and the Sixth Commandment ("Thou shalt not kill"). The two are thus talking *at* rather than *with* each other. From Gideon's dialogue it is clear that he has come to Playland seeking more than amusement and that he has likewise sought out Martinus as Albee's Jerry seeks out Peter, for some sort of confession and purgation. Appropriately, the stage directions call for him to be visibly agitated when the Playland generators momentarily fail and there is a threat that the park may have to close down for the night. And for the audience, therefore, there is something unsettling and dangerous at the conclusion of the scene when the lights of the park come on again, for Martinus does more than rebuff Gideon's overtures. He reduces him to a racial "other," sends him out onto the fairway: "Look! Listen! Pretty lights and music! Go forget your troubles white man. Playland is open and waiting for you" (18).

Presided over by "Barking Barney" Barkhuizen, its faceless and unseen ruler or deity, its Wizard of Oz, Playland is a microcosm filled with its own minor events of fortune (free meals to be won at the local Happy Rustler Steakhouse or free perms at Maison Capri) and misfortune (announcements of lost property and lost children). Glaringly lit and resounding harshly with a succession of loud pop music and Afrikaner Boeremusiek amplified over old and scratchy loudspeakers, the tawdry amusement park contains its own grotesque versions of birth and death. By turns the birthdays of patrons, lost children, and the lure of rides called The Whip and The Wall of Death are announced over the static-filled loudspeakers. In the background, moreover, are the shrieks of terror and screaming laughter emanating from the rotating Big Wheel, another grotesque representation of a bizarre world spinning on its axis.

Aimlessly reeling amid Playland's circumscribed, artificial carnival world, a world without significant problems, is Gideon, who is out of sync and out of place *"trying too hard to have a good time. He tells jokes, tries to sing along with the music, and wisecracks about the PA announcements, creating an image of forced and discordant gaiety"* (20). But the conventional distractions and amusement park anodynes seem to provide no relief for his evident but as yet unspecified psychological bruises. Gideon drunkenly wandering about the fairway trying to create his own "forced and discordant gaiety" renders the play's second scene a choreography of alienation.

When Gideon leaves the carnival while it is still in progress to return to Martinus, his determination to have a friendship with Martinus is intensified not merely by the brandy he imbibes but by a desperation born of Playland's evident failure to relieve his malaise. This is italicized by the false gaiety of the paper hat he has donned and the noisemaker he brandishes. The desperation and tenacity of Gideon's need are evident, too, in the lyrics of the song he sings as he enters:

> ". . . baby don't you know I love you so
> Can't you feel it when we touch
> I will never let you go
> I love you Oh so much." (20)

The audience recognizes the inevitability of Gideon and Martinus's ultimate confrontation, but its nature is shadowy. And that inevitability seems heightened and implicit if the audience remembers that Gideon's lyrics are taken from the song "Save the Last Dance for Me."[22]

As the intensity and persistence of Gideon's pursuit of Martinus's friendship heighten in the third scene, we recognize that the secret Gideon is teasing out of himself has something to do with his military experience fighting the SWAPO (South West African People's Organization) forces on the South African border:

> Your old friend Corporal Gideon le Roux. . . . Two stripes. But listen, forget about the rank. Just call me Gid. I been thinking about it you see and what do you say we must just let bygones be bygones? I want us to be buddies. Me and you. Gid and Marty? Okay? (21)

At the same time, he is teasing out Martinus's secret, which has something to do with his belief in Hell, eternal damnation, and Commandment Number Six. When Gid realizes that Martinus has a murder in his past, he excitedly exclaims,

"It was Number Six wasn't it? The Big One. You killed somebody hey. That's why the Big Baas is so the hell in with you" (26). Pleased that he may now have the chance to alter the power balance between himself and Martinus and to coerce Martinus into a relationship, Gideon attempts to assume the role of counselor or therapist: "I'm only trying to help. All I want is to help you deal with your problems" (27). When Martinus does not accept this bait and sends Gideon back to Playland and "back to your own people" (27), Gideon makes a new attempt to gain his confidence by dissociating himself from the whites in the amusement park and forging an analogy between his and Martinus's ideas of Hell:

> GIDEON. While that crowd of fat arses were having joyrides in Playland we were in Hell. Ja! For your information you don't have to wait for Judgment Day to find out what that word means. Hell is right here and now. I can take you to it. It's called the Operational Area and it's not everlasting bonfires either. It's everlasting mud and piss and shit and sweat and dust. And if you want to see the devil I can show you him as well. He wears a khaki uniform, he's got an AK-47 in his hands.
>
> MARTINUS. SWAPO. (27–28)

But instead of having Martinus lay bare his problems, Gideon begins to lay bare his own.

The result of Gideon's confession is not Martinus's capitulation but his empowerment. With an edge of triumph, he exults, "Number Six! You also. Number Six! I'll see you in Hell Corporal Gideon le Roux." And he goes on to rebuff Gideon, pushing him to the edges of racial conflict: "The secrets in my heart have got nothing to do with you or anybody else. So go. There is nothing for you here. This is my place." (28). Suddenly that "place" for the audience and for Gideon is not merely Playland with Martinus's night watchman's location on its fringes but also that other playland, white South Africa, which is also fringed with black locations. Martinus continues, "This is the night watchman's place. I am the night watchman. You go somewhere else." And Gideon replies with sentiments that surely echo those felt by many whites in 1990 as they could see the dismantlement of apartheid distinctly in the near future: "Don't you tell me to go! This is still a free country. You people haven't taken over yet" (28–29).

As the midnight hour comes and a new year, a new decade, and new era begin, Fugard deftly contrasts two points of view. As 1989 draws to a close and the sun sets, Gideon calls up an image of nuclear holocaust as he compares the sunset-tinged clouds to an atomic mushroom cloud after a bomb has been dropped on De Aar. The terrible ravages of Hiroshima and Nagasaki are brought to mind along with a sense that the "New South Africa" could be initiated with just such destruction in its wake. But the ushering in of 1990 is placed by Fugard into the voice and unseen presence of the Playland's *genius loci*, "Barking Barney" Barkhuizen, the carnival owner and barker. Significantly, he replaces Gideon's atomic holocaust with an image of Playland as a space shuttle being launched into a pacific era, "Playland's 1990 Orbit of Happiness." And his words clearly sound not merely the end of a year but the end of the South African nightmare that began in 1948:

> The tension is unbearable ladies and gentlemen as the countdown clock ticks its way through the last seconds of 1989. On everybody's lips, the same whispered prayer. Thank God it's over. . . . We have a launch! We have a launch! Yes, ladies and gentlemen, Playland has lifted off into 1990. (29–30)

As optimistic as this sounds, Fugard nonetheless well knows that an "orbit of happiness" is not achieved so instantaneously or without purgation and unsteady new beginnings.

That purgation and the shaky start of a new footing between Martinus and Gideon are the subject matter of the last and climactic scene, toward which the dramatic action has palpably been building both for the characters and for the audience. Perhaps *Playland* is lacking in subtlety, but if it is so, it is so in the way of *Endgame* or *Zoo Story,* in each of which it is certain that all is leading to a final confrontation between the two principal characters. What is uncertain, what forms the dramatic suspense, is the form that confrontation will take. In *Playland,* that dramatic anxiety is heightened, for one knows the issues are not merely those of Gideon and Martinus but also those of white and black in South Africa. And they will, moreover, be Fugard's insight into whether the wounds of ethnic and civil division are fatal or how they might be remedied—be they those of South Africa, Ireland, Korea, the Middle East, or elsewhere.

When the New Year is reached, the grotesquely artificial daytime world of Playland comes to a halt. The fairway is locked up and put to rest until the next day, and the nightwatch of black Martinus Zoeloe commences. But on this night, Gideon is unwilling to go home with the others of his race or to disconnect from Martinus. The time has come, he asserts, for confrontation and engagement:

> GIDEON. Don't think you can just switch off the fucking lights and tell me to go home, because I'm telling you it's not over.
>
> MARTINUS. It is, white man. Look! There's nobody left. I tell you Playland is finished for tonight.
>
> GIDEON. Fuck Playland! I'm talking about you and me. That's what it's all about now. You and me. Nice and simple. No complications. You and me. There's things to settle between us, and now is the time to do it. Right now . . . right here. (32)

When the hostile tone of Gideon's language escalates, he physically blocks the way of the exiting Martinus and pugnaciously calls the black man "SWAPO" in response to being called "white man" by Martinus, the atmosphere scintillates with impending danger and possibly the shocking conclusion of Edward Albee's *Zoo*

Story or the racial violence of Paul Slabolepzy's *Saturday Night at the Palace*.[23] The stage directions tell us that "*The two men are on the brink of real physical violence*" (33), and a personalized version of South African racial Armageddon seems nearly inevitable.

It is Martinus who moves the situation away from the brink of disaster by exclaiming, "Gideon le Roux! I say your name." In naming the name, Gideon casts aside the racial generalization and opens the door for a man-to-man relationship across the barriers of race and individual racially inflected histories. The use of personal names as a means for crossing or enforcing barriers appears with significance elsewhere in Fugard's work. Name change is the central act of *Sizwe Bansi Is Dead*, for it allows Sizwe Bansi to cross the border from joblessness to survival. It is Piet Bezuidenhout who marks his unflagging opposition to the racial generalizations of apartheid by identifying the specific individual botanical names of his aloes. His wife, Gladys, pointedly marks a new kinship with her husband's coloured friend, Steve Daniels, when she finally calls him Steve instead of Steven. And it is Hally who, by rescinding his informal name and insisting that he henceforth be called "Master Harold," abrogates his personal relationship with Sam, reducing his friend once more to a racially subaltern position. The invocation of Gideon's name signifies as well Martinus's willingness to reveal to this white man his own darkest secret: the murder of Andries Jacobus de Lange, a white Afrikaner, and his lack of remorse for that murder. For Martinus to reveal this to Gideon, himself a white Afrikaner recently returned from killing black insurgents on the South African border, is a truly remarkable act, one that implicitly offers to bridge their separate personal and racial histories. And it is all the more remarkable that this cue for connection and possible friendship comes from the mouth of one who has been oppressed and whose oppression in the play betokens that of his race.

The psychodynamics that follow are the crux of the drama. Martinus recounts the white man's rape of Thandeka, Martinus's woman; how he murdered de Lange, who had returned to rape again; that the court gave no credence to the rape story because the victim and the murderer were black; and how, after fifteen years of imprisonment for a justifiable homicide, he has never found Thandeka again. Fugard makes the audience feel the grievous pain of Martinus's injuries and of his life. One might well expect Gideon to identify with such feelings and to reach out with a sincere friendship that supersedes the hollow heartiness of his prior alleged camaraderie. But the audience gasps and Martinus is stunned when Gideon's harsh retort is:

> You killed that poor bugger just for that? Just for screwing your woman? (*Laughter*)
> You people are too funny. Listen my friend, if screwing your woman is such a big crime, then you and your brothers are going to have to put your knives into one hell of a lot of white men . . . starting with me! . . . We've all done it. And just like you said, knocked on that door in the backyard, then drag her onto the bed and grind her arse off on the old coir mattress. That's how little white boys learn to do it. On your women!

And you want to know something else, Swapo? They like it from us! Your woman was crying crocodile tears. I bet you anything you like she had a bloody good time there with the baas humping away on top of her. (36)

The stunning dramatic effect of this speech is akin to that of Hally's spitting in Sam's face, and the result is the same: "*Martinus rigid, every muscle tense as he tries to control the impulse to throw himself at Gideon.*"

Before either Gideon or the audience can recover, a whole new recognition of what the action of the play has been about suddenly becomes apparent. Gideon, the audience and Martinus realize, has come to Playland seeking out a black man. Since the first moments of the play Gideon has been stalking Martinus hoping that he can goad him into violence, into ending the guilt-ridden life Gideon has not himself had the courage to end by his own hand. Limpidly revealing his self-loathing, he prompts Martinus, "Now do you understand what I'm saying? If you want to kill that white man again, now's your chance. He's standing here in front of you" (36). There is also an ironic reminder here, as there was in *Master Harold,* that the role of South African blacks has been to clean up the mess that whites have made. Gideon cannot commit suicide, cannot clean up the mess of his life without black agency.

And *Playland* virtually reeks of the mess that South African racial policy has made in the lives of both white and black South Africans, for Fugard not only suffuses the play with fecal language but centers his main theme and the play's climactic statement on defecation. How he does this is clearly reminiscent of the ways he allowed passing anal references in *Master Harold* to lead up to Sam's baring his backside to Hally. Like a musician, Fugard has small hints of his theme early in his composition, allowing those hints to develop slowly to a dramatic crescendo. In *Playland,* the fecal theme enters the play in scene 3 with Gideon's passing recollection of how his father's cabbages brought on "a good cabbage fart from my dad" (24). Soon thereafter, Gideon derides with scatological graphicness Martinus's belief in an unseen God:

Real is what you can believe because you can touch it, and see it, and smell it . . . with your eyes wide open. Next time you sit there in the bush and have a boskak, have a good look at what you leave there on the ground, because that is what real means. When you can show me Heaven and Hell like I can show you shit, then I'll listen to the dominees and believe all their Bible stories. (25–26)

At the end of the scene, Martinus sends Gideon back to the whites on the Playland midway, and Gideon retorts, "My people? Shit!" calling them "fat arses" and then explaining that while these whites were enjoying themselves in Playland, he was on the South African border in a hell on earth "called the Operational Area and it's not everlasting bonfires either. It's everlasting mud and piss and shit and sweat and dust" (28).

In the final and climactic scene of the play, matters come to a head between the two men when Gideon asserts, "Listen Swapo, there's a lot of shit we got to clean up" (34). While trying to push Martinus into murdering him, Gideon is overpowered by his own narration, and he falls into the intensity of a patient making a breakthrough in therapy, laying bare the source of pain. Indeed, Gideon's near-manic narrative is the core of the play's breakthrough, reaching as it does to the noisome defecation that Fugard sees as the foundation on which South African life has been constructed. Written in that Beckettian and Albeesque limbo between realism and symbolism, *Playland* endows Gideon's confession with several levels of meaning. It is at once his personal horror, the infernal underside of South Africa, and the hellishness that accompanies civil strife more generally. Speaking of the black men he has killed on the border, Gideon's confession graphically brings together and concretizes the references to feces, flatulence, and stench that have to this point merely peppered the dialogue:

> Those brothers of yours were full of shit, and I don't mean their politics. I mean the real stuff. They started stinking even before the sun had cooked them up a bit, because when that happened, when they'd been in the oven for a couple of days, as we used to say, then I'm telling you, you didn't eat meat for a week. (37)

Moreover, Gideon's recollection, of counting the dead bodies redolent with the stench of decay, draws on and makes meaningful the much earlier mention of his father's counting his cabbages and his "cabbage farts."

Gideon's speech is one of purgation. On the eve of South Africa's new era, it is a confession that, in more than one sense, reveals the human waste generated by decades of apartheid rule. Here Fugard suggests strongly that the muck of his country must be acknowledged and as much as possible removed before the post-apartheid era can properly commence and succeed. Gideon's long monologue permits him to excrete his personal muck and thereby evoke and face his demons at last. By extension, Fugard exhorts South Africa to do likewise.

In the play's poignant dramatic turn, Martinus eschews the role of assassin into which Gideon would cast him, becoming instead Gideon's father confessor and therapist. Having spewed forth the shit of his life, Gideon, as the stage directions tell us, "*is left totally defeated*" (38), and Martinus can then ask the therapist's rhetorical questions that will elicit the wellsprings of Gideon's malady and guilt:

> What is the matter with you white man? What is it you are doing tonight? You come here to me, but I don't want you. . . . You try to make me kill you and now you tell me you are laughing at dead men but I can see it is a lie. Why? Why are you telling me that lie? Why are you trying so hard to make me believe it? . . . What is the true feeling inside you? (39)

Early in the play, we recognize that Gideon is in a rut, his life hardly progressing. "Some days at work," he says, "it was so bad I use to think my watch had stopped" (8).

Playland suggests that only when he can peel away the layers of his defenses and anger to expose the heart of his darkness can Gideon's life move forward.

This he does as he recalls his dehumanization in the military and his ability to shoot down, robot-like, twenty-seven members of SWAPO. The stench of their bodies, reeking with decay as he tosses them in a hole like so many animal carcasses, awakens him so that he recognizes them not as mere targets but as murdered human beings. And the old woman watching him becomes, like Niobe weeping for her sons, a powerful symbol conveying the enormity of what he has done.[24] Recollecting how as a child he had recoiled at the live roe inside fish he had caught and cut open, Gideon sees his actions on the South African border as a remembrance of that childhood traumatic experience: "What I had done was a sin. You can't do that to a mother and her babies. I don't care what it is, a fish or a dog or another person, it's wrong!" (43).

With great psychological shrewdness, Fugard alters Gideon's narrative from first to second person, allowing Gideon to dissociate from himself and see his situation with a kind of objectivity. Connecting his childhood experience with his present one, he wishes to confess to and seek absolution from the old black woman who had watched him toss bodies into a mass grave. He wishes to tell her, moreover, that he knows the men were human and not inanimate objects of color. Having lost the old woman and unable to play out his remorse, he has, on the eve of the new decade and in this "playland," sought out Martinus as her surrogate. Suddenly Martinus understands the full extent of the role Gideon has scripted for him, and he feels unable to act as the agent of forgiveness for a damaged white man who is also an image of the white oppressor. Bringing Fugard's message home, Gideon exclaims to Martinus, "The whole world is me and you. . . . Forgive me or kill me" (44). Clearly there is an echo here of Beckett's Didi exclaiming to Gogo, "To all mankind they were addressed, these cries for help still ringing in our ears! But at this place, at this moment of time, all mankind is us. Whether we like it or not."[25] The moment likewise affirms the working idea for the play: "A meeting between two desperate men. Each other's fate."[26]

The dilemma for Martinus is that if he forgives Gideon, he must also forgive the rapist de Lange and ask God's forgiveness for himself; "and then," he painfully ruminates, "what is left? Nothing! I sit here with nothing . . . tonight . . . tomorrow . . . all my days and all my nights . . . nothing!" (44). This is the critical moment. But for one influenced by the existentialism of Sartre and Camus, as Fugard is, that moment of nothingness is the positive starting point for a new concept of life, relationships, and way of being. It is the nothingness experienced by Hally and Sam at the conclusion of *Master Harold;* but whereas in that play the characters are left suspended in their nothingness, in *Playland* the light of the new day, year, decade, and era radiates onto the stage and the men come to a positive understanding.

Martinus encourages Gideon to revive his interest in a pigeon coop. At the beginning of *Playland*, Gideon had related how the pigeons he had kept had been killed one night, likely by a wildcat, how they were "dead as fucking freedom fighters" with their body parts littered about. Connecting the pigeons to the SWAPO

20. Frankie Faison and Kevin Spacey as Martinus and Gideon in *Playland* at Manhattan Theatre Club, New York, N.Y., 1992. Photo by Gerry Goodstein.

forces Gideon has killed, Fugard suggests that breeding pigeons will be an act of contrition and renewal; nor will the similarity between the pigeons and the doves of peace be lost on an audience. Martinus goes on to say that when he returns the following year, he hopes to "look up in the sky, watch the pigeon-birds flying and drink my tea and laugh" (47).

Like Sam and Hally looking skyward to their homemade kite, Martinus projects a time of hope, optimism, and good feeling for himself and Gideon. This is what Mary Benson calls "their break from the prison of the past" and Mannie Manim characterizes as "a kind of exorcism of both their lives."[27] Fugard reveals that he has been influenced by Wilfred Owen's poem "Strange Meeting" (which he incorrectly calls "The Enemy"), in which the narrator meets in Hell an enemy soldier he has killed. The men discover, like Martinus and Gideon, that they are two faces of the same coin: "Whatever hope is yours, / Was my life also." Having revealed themselves to one another, one says to the other, "Let us sleep now." For the conclusion of *Playland* Fugard alters Owen's line to "Let us live now."[28]

Projected, too, at the close of *Playland* is Fugard's own optimism for the future of South Africa. Indeed, in the foreward to his collected plays, he writes "And then at the end of the decade, South Africa's famous political miracle. I saw it coming and I knew that the extraordinary opportunity to build a just and decent society would depend on our capacity for Truth and Forgiveness. *Playland* is my recognition of that."[29]

Certainly *Playland* is close to allegory in its simplicity, but it is not simple-minded. Fugard clearly knows that the past cannot be erased and forgotten. Gideon will continue to be haunted by "that hole outside Oshakati" and Martinus will never regret his murder of de Lange, but both of them have, as Mary Benson astutely realizes, actually *listened* to each other for the first time, and that is something of a beginning.[30] The car from one of Playland's rides remains broken and Gideon's car is still disabled, but these two characters who entered the stage separately leave together to give the car the push it needs to get it going. Clearly, too, the separation, the apartheid that has kept the people of different races apart, will come undone not merely when the laws say so but when people begin to *listen* to one another as human beings, not as essentialized members of different races. Only then will the vehicle that is South Africa have the requisite push to drive forth into the future.

EIGHT

Where Do We, Where Do I, Go from Here?
Performing a New South Africa

The need to listen, of which Mary Benson spoke when she described Fugard's ideas in *Playland* (1992), is a need that forms the very basis of Fugard's subsequent two works, *My Life* (1994) and *Valley Song* (1995). On 8 July 1994, at the annual Standard Bank National Arts Festival in Grahamstown, Athol Fugard launched his first new work staged in and for the "new" post-apartheid South Africa, *My Life*. Produced by the gifted Mannie Manim, *My Life* went from Grahamstown to play at the Johannesburg Civic Theatre. It is hard to know what to call *My Life*, which Fugard did not write but rather called into being with the help of Rebecca Waddell, his young American-educated South African assistant. Fugard and Waddell, themselves at a loss for exactly what to call *My Life*, have called it "a recital."[1]

My Life records autobiographical narratives from five South African young women. According to Fugard's program note in the playbill for the Johannesburg production, he and Waddell handpicked these five from among many male and female teenagers who auditioned. After selecting five, who all chanced to be female, Fugard and Waddell told them "to start keeping diaries of their day-to-day lives." The diaries that Fugard collected at a later date were filled with personal matters, but all reflected the work of "natural storytellers" eager to relate their lives.[2]

The young women Fugard and Waddell chose were Riana Jacobs (age 15), who is coloured; Sivagamy Govender, or Gamy (age 17), a Tamil Indian; Reshoketswe Maredi, or Shoki (age 21) and Eleanor Busi Mthimunye, or Busi (age 20), both of whom who are black; and Heather Leite (age 17), who is white. Since Fugard had selected his candidates from specific institutions—Fuha (Federated Union of Black Artists), the Performing Arts School, the Market Theatre Laboratory, and two senior schools in Eldorado Park and Lenasia—some of the five women chosen were presumably aspiring actors and performers.[3] Clearly all of them were given the opportunity of a lifetime: having Athol Fugard, arguably the most distinguished living English-language playwright, stage their narratives and direct their performances. What emerged was not a Fugard play, indeed not a play at all, but a *performance* that Fugard essentially called into being and shaped. The text belongs to the girls. The arrangement of the texts, the juxtaposing of one girl's statements to another's, the movement on stage, and the work's length belong to Fugard. Consequently, *My Life* has the spontaneity of a performance rather than the feel of an enacted playtext.[4]

And since *My Life* is a performance vehicle, the "text" that has been published has its uses,[5] but far less so than a formal playtext, for it can never properly capture the performance dynamic of the work. It is important to recognize, furthermore, that *My Life* is rather different from Fugard, Kani, and Ntshona's earlier workshopped plays, *The Island* and *Sizwe Bansi Is Dead.* Those plays drew from the life experiences of actors John Kani and Winston Ntshona, and emerged from improvisation exercises and workshop discussions.[6] Kani, Ntshona, and Fugard are listed as authors in the published versions. In a *Star* [Johannesburg] interview with Adrienne Sichel, Fugard explains the important distinctions between those earlier works and *My Life:*

> [*My Life*] taps into the same source of energy but "My Life" stops short of being, finally, artifice. I got hold of John and Winston's raw material and I was quite ruthless with it. I've tried to be totally respectful of this material and tried not to make it a vehicle for myself. That's the difference.[7]

Although there are certainly affinities with the earlier plays, *My Life* is written in a South Africa very much changed or changing from the South Africa that provided the context for *The Island* and *Sizwe Bansi.*[8] Accordingly it is a new kind of work for Fugard, who is eager to change and grow with the times.

My Life was first performed at the 1994 National Festival in Grahamstown, an appropriate venue for a piece celebrating a new nationalism, and happily a video recording filmed by Basil Mills of that Grahamstown performance does exist at NELM. With some appropriateness, the Grahamstown production was staged in the not very well-appointed or acoustically excellent gymnasium of the Victoria School for Girls, the very sort of school the young actors might themselves have been attending. The videotaped production, moreover, provides a great deal of insight into what Fugard was about in *My Life* and why he chose to stage such a vehicle at this point in his theatre career.

Negative reviews can often be enlightening, and in this regard one of *My Life* written by Mary Jordan in *Business Day* [Johannesburg] is useful in pointing up objections to the piece and its style. In her review, "Dear Diary, Today We Saw an Awful Show by Fugard," Jordan asserts, "Fugard has mistaken for reality something that is an image only in his own mind. He sees purity where there is prissiness and a desire to please, and he interprets girlishness as goodness."[9] She deplores the play's naïveté, calling it "an adolescent journey that is like the worst sort of school play—workshopped Enid Blyton." She goes on to argue that none of the five girls can act, and she deplores the lack of "a critical and dispassionate feminist overview." But what Jordan cites as flaws are precisely among the work's strengths. It is knowingly unsophisticated, it knowingly uses amateur actors, and it knowingly has, to its great credit, no *a priori* agenda about sexuality, feminism, or gender imposed by Fugard upon either the women or the text they create. It also, one might add, does not attempt to give a panorama of South African youth. There are no males, no white Afrikaners or speakers of Afrikaans, no Cape coloureds, no Muslims, no Jews, and no speakers of the several indigenous South African languages.

Veronica Bowker, defending Fugard from potential attackers, raises and ponders potential issues stemming from the interrogations of theoreticians like Gayatri Spivak on the subject of who can speak for whom. She asserts that Fugard, after all, does have authorial control over *My Life,* choosing the actors, shaping their texts, and directing the piece as a whole. And rhetorically she asks, who is he as a privileged, white South African male to control a work that presents women in a multiracial South Africa? Like a lawyer for a seemingly guilty client, Bowker offers proof, from her interview with the actors, to convince her jury of readers that Fugard has been falsely charged with supporting patriarchy.[10] One might, however, argue here that Fugard is actually not in need of defense, for he is not only eschewing the role of Prospero for his five Mirandas but is initiating, rather than creating, an event in a theatre space in which he (together with Mannie Manim and Ruth Waddell) is as much a participant as Gamy, Heather, Busi, Riana, and Shoki.

In a sense, Fugard's role in *My Life* parallels and bespeaks his role as a member of an older white generation in South Africa, a generation that is surrendering control of but not surrendering participation in a new society of equals, a society in which different races, ethnicities, and age groups can learn from one another and act in concord. Fugard himself says that he created *My Life* because in the changing political climate of his country, "I felt the one voice that was not being heard was that of young South Africans, and dammit all, they are the future."[11]

"The three things theatre starts out with—an actor, a story, and an audience," Fugard claims, are the three ingredients of *My Life.*[12] And, as is so often the case in Fugard's theatre works, the definitions of "acting" in its theatrical, social, and political senses are intimately connected. Perhaps the most eloquent record of this work is Mary Benson's. She explains that Fugard saw *My Life* "as a chamber quintet for which he would interweave their stories." She goes on to recall Fugard's comment to her and his unrestrained joy in this unique work: "'The girls came on as complete strangers to each other. And I thought, this is fascinating, I am being led into the future by five young people and we are going to be able to explore the racial dynamics of South Africa.' His laughter rang out."[13]

My Life is Fugard's attempt to stage a barometric reading of the lives and thoughts of the next generation, the one that will populate and shape postapartheid South Africa. The members of Fugard's generation have fought the battles and recorded the often bitter history of life in South Africa since 1948, when apartheid was first instituted as a government policy. Fugard's generation has been shaped and scarred by apartheid, and certainly much of Fugard's work has been a record of the festering wounds inflicted by South African racialism. One thinks immediately of *Statements, The Island, Sizwe Bansi, A Lesson from Aloes,* and *Master Harold . . . and the Boys* as well as the earliest works, *No-Good Friday* and *Nongogo.* More recently, however, in *Playland,* the work he completed just prior to *My Life,* Fugard records the coming together of two grown men, one white and one black, finally reaching out to one another at the end of the apartheid era, but each continuing to bear the residual anger, guilt, and damage of the past. Likewise, *Valley Song,* the play which follows *My Life,* celebrates the new opportunities for young people as they break free to forge the paths for their lives in a post-apartheid world.

An important perspective on the origins of *My Life* comes in an eight-page faxed typescript in the Fugard archives at Indiana University's Lilly Library. On the last page of that fax (onto which is written at a later date in pencil and in Fugard's handwriting: "Notes from Rebecca Waddell. FUGARD'S Assistant Director"),[14] Waddell writes:

> Miracles do happen. In 1994, a country called South Africa, transformed. A white dove emerged from the ashes of Shame, and a nation was born again. The world watched, the world waited. Two thousand years ago, a man had walked on water, could a nation really do the same? Yes, but we didn't know that then. Until Nelson Mandela's inauguration, we didn't trust anything. Ofcourse [*sic*], we hoped and prayed, but we also doubted and feared. And we had reason to. There were people in our land, who wanted to destroy everything. Imagine the damage, a single bomb at a single polling station, could have caused our timid novitiate? Change is really an act of faith. We believed, but would that be enough?

She then goes on to explain how the actors for *My Life* were chosen and how the performance came about. And she says, "None of us, not even Athol Fugard, knew what to expect. Our only clue to the work that lay ahead of us was Athol Fugard's intent. 'I made an act of faith. I said to myself "I'm going to get these five young women to lead me into my country's future."' Beyond that we knew nothing."[15] Waddell's participation in the creation of *My Life,* reflected in her statements, also plays a role in the meaning of the work, for Waddell is the granddaughter of Harry Oppenheimer, the former head of De Beers Consolidated Mines, Ltd., and the Anglo-American Corporation, and possibly the richest man in South Africa.[16] Thus it is not just Fugard, the artist of lower-middle-class origins, but also Waddell, as white upper class as it possible to be, who join forces to turn over the legacy and future of South Africa to all its people, all its races.

My Life uses theatrical space to uncover, discover, and record the feelings of still relatively innocent and unscathed, certainly unsophisticated inheritors of South African social reform. The articulation of the five aspiring actors is aided and enhanced by the very vehicle they have, as it were, co-authored. The actors are helped as well by Fugard as the theatrical *eminence grise* whose wisdom can teach them how to act and perform not merely on the theatrical stage but in the next stages of their lives. These girls will become women who will perform the acts that will mark and make the South Africa to come. Fugard may serve as enabler, but it is their show, and they must teach *him* even more than he teaches *them*. Waddell records a touching moment when one of the girls said to Fugard that she will open the door to her life and allow him to enter, and he replied, "I will be sure to wipe my feet before I come in."[17] Certainly as the stager of *My Life*, Fugard is not passive, but he is also not a controlling, authorial, or authorizing force. The work itself is meant as a democratic space with no single controlling authority. It is a performance of mutuality and one that, moreover, performs and celebrates Fugard's passing of authority and authorial control to the young, even as the young will, at the end of the piece, include the audience within the realm of authority.

The verbal text of *My Life* is not what the piece is about at all, for it is a performance text and what is being performed is the emergence into adulthood of five young people and the breaking down of barriers among them. When Fugard was beginning his career, his 1961 play *The Blood Knot* was considered radical and problematic for it presented on one stage a white and a black actor. At that time, having actors of different races—and certainly audiences including different races—in the same room was unusual and eventually not permissible. As Russell Vandenbroucke explains, ". . . the production itself was a milestone, since it had been traditional in South Africa for whites in blackface to play the roles of blacks and Coloureds. Mokae's performance challenged this custom. Four years later such mixed casts were prohibited."[18] In part, then, *My Life* celebrates the fact that in 1994, more than thirty years after *The Blood Knot*, actors of various races and background can perform with ease on the same stage and share their lives. And as they do so, each provides for the other four and for the audience an access to her family, home life, and social development; the things that have led her to the brink of maturity, to the place where she can assume her role as an actor performing (in) a new South Africa.

These young women, then, are seen as actors in a performance piece whose loose performing directions are not only those of *My Life* but, far more importantly, those being sketched out by President Mandela and the new post-apartheid politics of South Africa. Only months before the production of *My Life*, these five young women and the members of their audience would all have been confined to individual Group Areas. Certainly the girls would not have met as neighbors and friends, not have met at the theatre, not have participated jointly in the staging of their country's future. In *My Life*, the doors of five very different homes and lives in what were racially demarcated, totally separate Group Areas swing open and we are welcomed into them.

Of course the stories the five adolescents tell—stories of their relationship to parents and siblings, stories of personal adventures and misadventures, Sivagamy's explanation of her belief in Hindu gods and of her reverence for and subservience to her family, or Riana's hopes and dreams for her future—are all likely to sound trite and have the familiar rhetorical ring of those told in teenage magazines. But

Fugard is clearly after just that quality, for with familiarity comes demystification.[19] Their finally banal revelations, aired in the performance or recital of *My Life*, are a true breakthrough within a society whose members have been trained to be ignorant across racial lines and to distrust those of other colors and languages. They give voice to who these girls are, and do so with authenticity rather than with the shaping and controlling of a white male playwright many years their senior.

The discovery that emerges from Fugard's performance piece is that behind those apartheid barriers were people who were not so very different from one another, people whose similar stories of family relations and individual aspirations connect them in ways that the racial separation of apartheid rule had not allowed them to realize. At the beginning of *My Life* there appear on stage five teenage girls, five different voices, from what seem like vastly different backgrounds. By the end there is a chorus of five burgeoning women and friends unafraid of one another and prepared to work together in a new society. Clearly they perform for an audience what is possible in South Africa, and as such they offer a model performance script for the audience themselves to enact. Mannie Manim expresses this notion of *My Life* in an interview:

> Many people got very excited about it, and said, This is the theatre of the New South Africa! This is us telling our story! This is Uhuru.
>
> I think, maybe, yes, this *is* the story of the New South Africa. I don't know that that was a great work of art. I think it was a beginning. The first scribbling of New South Africa, saying what was going on to them during that pre-election time and after the election. And also talking about how all of this did or did not touch their lives.[20]

My Life is, as Manim affirms, not great art, but it is certainly a sign of change at a critical moment in South African history.

The style of *My Life* is an appropriately easygoing one, but one that Fugard has shaped to his purpose. The girls are not wearing costumes but are dressed in their everyday clothes: jeans, blouses, T-shirts. In the recorded Grahamstown production, Busi is even wearing a carmine sweatshirt that reads "Great American." The stage is bare except for two benches on which the girls sit, except when one of them stands to recite her narrative. The backdrop is a black wall with five hooks holding the girls' jackets, which they hang up at the start of the performance and don as they go off at the conclusion. In light of the content and style of *My Life*, it seems, moreover, that performing it in an unadorned and acoustically rude school gymnasium during the Grahamstown Festival was even more appropriate than performing it a few weeks later at the far more formal Gesson Theatre at the Johannesburg Civic Theatre.

Although Fugard cedes the traditional authorial control over his text to become a citizen in a performance democracy, to be an enabler rather than a dramatist, *My Life* is neither random nor improvisational. The performance staged in *My Life* is engineered by its participants to assure us that what is presented is genuine. The lives presented are neither cosmeticized nor costumed. The piece is, furthermore, constructed so that five girls appear at the opening in a kind of brief aerobic dance exercise (fig. 21); then each of them launches, one at a time, into a soliloquy derived from the diary she kept. These diaries are filled with family, racial, ethnic, class, gender, and age matters. And yet despite their describing widely disparate lives, lives that have been separated by the strictures of apartheid, the diary contents have a ring of familiarity to all on stage and in the audience, so that the commonalities among the five women quickly become clear. This is italicized when Heather begins her recital with a traditional jump rope rhyme common to children regardless of race or class. Thus, the narratives discover the lines of connection among the women, the lines across which they can begin to know each other.

In a second phase, the five girls interact with one another, question each other, worry about each other's values (such as the familial devotion and timidity of Sivagamy), and join as a chorus to sing South African songs. In performance, their singing can include the audience; and as a performance, it invokes and turns to joyful music a common harmony and unity of spirit that stands in staunch opposition to the racist and separatist world of South Africa that has existed since the appearance of white men in that country, even before a more draconian apartheid policy codified that country's racialism. The individual voices of the five women unite as one voice whereas under apartheid rule the songs of each racial group tended to be sung solo and to tell of protest.

Explaining the purpose of the *My Life* project and his role in it, Fugard has written:

> Our [his and Rebecca Waddell's] responsibilities then became very obvious: to facilitate and coach them [the five actors] in the craft and to select and organise the material. In making our choices we have tried our best, given the limited scope of this project, to reflect and celebrate the cultural diversity and contrasts of our South African reality while at the same time trying to capture something of the unique quality of each of the five personal voices.[21]

At the conclusion of the piece, that celebration of cultural diversity moves from the stage to the audience as Heather and the four other actors of *My Life* turn to them asking, "What do you think? . . . You must have been judging us . . . I didn't know other people's lives were full and full of life."[22] The performance here recognizes that the audience has all along been directly involved as part of the performance process, even as that same audience is likewise directly involved in the performance of a new society. Fugard and Waddell have thus positioned the audience to join the actors in order to "*celebrate* the cultural diversity and contrasts," the very things that until recently were the differences demonized by apartheid policy.

My Life is Fugard's affirmation that he and the older generation of South Africans, whatever their color, now must listen to the country's new voices. In his earlier plays, Fugard had rendered the voices of the apartheid South Africa he knew. But the voices of the new South Africa are not those of Fugard's generation.

21. Sivagamy Govender, Elleanor Busi Mthimunye, Heather Leite, Reshoketswe Maredi, and Riana Jacobs (left to right) in *My Life*, Market Theatre, Johannesburg, 1994. Photo by Ruphin Coudyzer.

If, however, Fugard is to remain vital as a playwright, he must listen to and attune his work to the new generation of South Africans, to the multicultured and many-ranged voices of the young so nicely embodied by the five women of *My Life*. Theirs are the voices to which he and we must listen, and we must respect them if we are to allow the young people of South Africa to lead themselves and their land into adulthood and into the future. Finally, Fugard, Waddell, the five girls, and the audience participate in a celebratory performance of connected regenerations: Fugard as a playwright, South Africa as a country, South African young people as future citizens and leaders, and ourselves as citizens of the world.

One might feel that *My Life* is an ephemeral piece belonging only to the five young actors on whose lives it is based, that they alone can play themselves and now that they have grown older, the piece can only exist in its vestiges, in the form of published script and the NELM videotape. A summer 1997 performance of *My Life* at the Lankershim Arts Center in North Hollywood, California, how-ever, showed that this is not the case. Directed by Peter Grego, the production cast young American actors in the roles of the South African women (fig. 22). The mes-sage of the performance piece was as clear as it was with the original cast. It re-vealed, moreover, that the piece's celebration of diversity and contrast, and its de-mand that the older generation let go so as to foster rather than control the young, are matters that cross national boundaries, that reach far beyond the borders of

22. Alyssa Lobo, Margaret Kemp, Felice Parish, Michelle Crosby Jones, and Ilene Bergelson (left to right) in *My Life,* The Lankershim Arts Center, North Hollywood, Cal., 1997. Photo by Attica Mann. Courtesy Synthaxis Theatre Company.

South Africa. In short, although *My Life* performs a new South Africa, it has as well the power to perform change and celebrate diversity well beyond South African borders.

The "my" in *My Life* refers to the lives of the piece's five protagonists, and surely it refers to the past and new life of South Africa as well. But the title arguably also includes the life of its creator, Athol Fugard, who seems to recognize that the end of apartheid and the welcome, for him, coming to power of a new, young multiracial generation all herald a new direction in his life both as South African citizen and writer. For nearly five decades, some of the most important white South African writers honed their literary energies so that their readers, international and South African, could not bury their heads in the sand while the injustices and atrocities of apartheid were daily taking place. The white skins of these writers often gave them opportunities to be heard and published that were not available to most of their fellow writers of color. As Helen Suzman did in the political arena, writers such as Nadine Gordimer, André Brink, Breyten Breytenbach, J. M. Coetzee, and Athol Fugard in the literary sphere gave voice to the oppressed. But what happens to such writers when the battle is won and they need no longer write about the dire situation that has been at the core of their writing for so many years? Breyten Breytenbach's *The Memory of Birds in Time of Revolution* (1996) is a collection of essays by a writer who went into exile and who seems unwilling now to relinquish the role of irascible outsider criticizing his native country. André Brink's *Imaginings of Sand* (1996) and Nadine Gordimer's *The House Gun* (1998) are novels that look back to the years of apartheid and what they wrought. And J. M. Coetzee, usually a fiction writer with a turn for the allegorical and a man frequently private about his own life, writes what seems to be a personal memoir, *Boyhood: Scenes from Provincial Life* (1997), in which the protagonist, John, is either Coetzee himself or a fictional persona whose life is often congruent with that of the author. All of these important writers seem understandably hard pressed to let go the South African apartheid of the past and to address the new South Africa and its future.

Doubtless for Athol Fugard, almost all of whose works have been directly or indirectly about South African apartheid, a new South Africa without apartheid must hold some angst for him as a writer. Like his fellow distinguished white South African literary peers, Fugard, in his sixties, suddenly needed to find a new voice and new issues for his writing: no easy matter. In *My Life*, Fugard seems to find at least one role for himself: as an enabler of the new generation and the new South Africa. Although that work is about the lives of its five protagonists and about the life possibilities of a new South Africa, Fugard is also using the piece to say that his life, too, is now changing in a post-apartheid society; and producing *My Life* is the signifier of that change. The playwright, however, remains behind the scenes in *My Life*, providing a theatrical and integrational opportunity for his five-woman cast as he (depending on one's view) massages or manipulates their material.

Valley Song (1995), Fugard's first proper post-apartheid play, goes an important step beyond *My Life*, for the script is entirely Fugard's, and in significant ways he writes himself into the script as both character and actor. Ultimately, although *Valley Song* foregrounds the life and choices of its central character, Veronica, it is also about Fugard's new life in his post-apartheid country.[23] And, of course, more largely it is about the changes that must occur in South Africa after apartheid; or, as Fugard said in an interview, "But this is a play that straddles the present, with one foot in the past and one foot in the future, and that is where South Africa is right now."[24]

A deceptively simple play, *Valley Song* is a two-hander with three characters. It begins with Fugard's showing the audience some pumpkin seeds and explaining that if the conditions are right these can yield hundreds of beautiful large pumpkins. That thought is meant to hold true for both the events in this modest-seeming play and for its young main character. It is also a lovely metaphor for Fugard's dramatic art: the modest seeds of *Valley Song*'s plot are nurtured in the course of the play, eventually giving rise to large and meaningful concepts about human, artistic, and South African national growth.[25] Part of the growth registered in *Valley Song* is one that enables people to break through old boundaries in order to understand the lives of others. It can enable them as well to find and act new roles for themselves. Even as the five young girls and the audience in *My Life* are able to cross the rigid boundaries that apartheid had previously drawn and enter one another's lives, so, too, in *Valley Song* there are important boundary crossings.

Valley Song begins with a border crossing. It transgresses the traditional boundary between an unseen playwright and the audience, for the playwright (or an actor playing him) comes on stage and addresses his audience directly in his own person (or persona), a privilege that narrators of fiction have long enjoyed. In the first performances in Johannesburg (August 1995), Princeton (October 1995), New York (December 1995), and London (January 1996), the role of Fugard was played by Fugard himself. At a subsequent mounting of the play in New York (May 1996), South African actor Marius Weyers played the role of Fugard. In both cases, the audience found itself confronted, as it rarely does in drama, with the playwright himself as a character within the plot of the drama and as its narrator. But Fugard plays two parts in *Valley Song*, so in a turn that is at first surprising, the playwright steps into the dramatic action to act not merely himself but the role of Abraam Jonkers (nicknamed Buks), the coloured grandfather, as well.

Fugard has played coloured figures before, most notably in *Boesman and Lena* and in the first production of *A Lesson from Aloes*, but the facile movement back and forth between the white and coloured roles sans makeup and costume in *Valley Song*, is at once impressive and significant. Both Fugard and Weyers effected those transitions simply by donning and doffing a fisherman's knit woolen cap when they became, respectively, Jonkers and Fugard. And Fugard is careful to insist in his "Author's Note" for the play that "[t]he role of the Author and Abraam Jonkers must be played by the same actor" (xix).[26] Thus, in addition to blurring the line between stage and audience, the author/actor consciously conveys through the actor's body a post-apartheid fluidity that not only permits but endorses the abrogation of color lines. This is surely an important step beyond *The Blood Knot*, a play about illicit crossing of the color line, in which a coloured man passing for white is enacted by a white actor (Fugard himself in the original production) passing for coloured. In *Valley Song*, the same actor is now empowered to play white and coloured in the same play. In a perhaps less important but complementary way, Fugard stretches age limits as well, for the same actor embodies the playwright in his sixties and the coloured farmer in his seventies. As Fugard has explained, "Playing both roles creates the theatrical effect of seeing each character through the other. There's a kind of a parallel between the characters—they are very like heads and tails of the same coin."[27]

Most of Fugard's previous works are dark, psychologically complex, and frequently parabolic. They force the audience and the characters themselves to face the intricacies of race, interpersonal dynamics, and the impact of the former on the latter. *The Blood Knot, Boesman and Lena, Statements, The Island, A Lesson from Aloes,* and *Master Harold* all explore the tragic and existential lessons of life in South Africa and of human interactions more generally. By contrast, *Valley Song*, as its title suggests, is filled with music. Its thrust is comedic and optimistic. *Valley Song* is an uncharacteristically upbeat, "feel good" play conveying its author's (some would say unwarranted) ebullience at the bright prospects for young people in South Africa.[28]

Since *My Life* was seen by so few, his rather radical change of style in *Valley Song* was new to most Fugard audiences, who could nonetheless recognize in it the genuine (though guarded) enthusiasm for the new horizon in South Africa now that the low ceilings erected by the racially claustrophobic apartheid rule have been removed. For Veronica, a figure of youthful optimism, the sky's now the limit, and young people of all races can feel empowered to reach for the stars. Their possibilities are limited only by the extent of their imaginations, an insight nicely articulated in *Valley Song* when a young, aspiring Veronica, dreaming big dreams for herself, belittles the wish of her friend, Alfred Witbooi, to obtain a used bicycle. Were Veronica to dream of a bicycle, she would envision a "big, black, shiny new bicycle with loud ringatingaling bell and all that" (21), but Alfred, still dreaming the restricted dreams prescribed by apartheid, merely envisions purchasing a secondhand bicycle. Fugard plays devil's advocate and hints that the raised post-apartheid ceiling may be made of glass. He suggests that perhaps Alfred is simply being realistic. To this Veronica heatedly retorts:

> If he dreams properly he'll get it. . . . You must see it and believe it. Alfred must see the bicycle like he is watching it on TV, he must see himself sitting on it and riding around the Village ringing the bell and waving at everybody and then he must believe that is what is going to happen. He must believe that as hard as he can. (21)

For Veronica, dreams are goals, and without them the status quo will continue regardless of South Africa's new laws. Dreams provide the images of the desired future. *Valley Song* is about such dreams, and the lyrical mode Fugard employs in this drama is unusually well suited to his subject.

The setting Fugard employs for *Valley Song* is the remote, postage-stamp Karoo town of New Bethesda (or Nieu-Bethesda) that also served as the setting for *The Road to Mecca*. In his "Notes" to the play (sometimes reprinted in playbills), Fugard tells his readers that New Bethesda has a white population of 65 and a coloured population (living in what was the coloured location) of 950. Nowadays, one of those 65 whites is Fugard himself, who, as becomes apparent in the play, has in recent years purchased and renovated a New Bethesda house in which he and his wife reside for part of each year. The town is located in a relatively fertile valley formed by the Sneeuberg Mountains and known for its vegetables and fruits (one remembers the specialness of the Sneeuberg potatoes in *Road to Mecca*). The fertility of the valley is important to the meaning of the play, as is the Karoo setting: the South African Karoo is the partial desert where the traces of a great prehistoric lake and many dinosaur remains have been found. Thought by paleontologists to be the likely setting for the origin of life on this planet, it is thus an ideal setting for presenting the origin of a new human existence in South Africa.

At the heart of that newness is Veronica, who, like the five young women in *My Life*, is the embodiment of the new post-apartheid generation constructing its identity and newly empowered to write and sing their own new songs. *Valley Song* is filled with music, and much of it consists of the joyous tunes and verses composed and sung by Veronica, which contain a mixture of her environment and her dreams. It is, after all, that combination of personal roots and personal aspiration that is the necessary ingredient for human growth. Veronica, like the vegetables her grandfather Buks grows, is rooted in New Bethesda, but she longs to go to the big city, Johannesburg, to realize her dream and become a singer and celebrity. She has, however, never left her village, and other than what she has seen while covertly standing on an apple crate and peeking through Mrs. Jooste's window to watch the shows on the television set she has left on, Veronica knows nothing of the city and its perils; she has no knowledge of what it takes to break in to the music and entertainment industries. But, impelled by her dreams of success and stardom, she is saving her coins to make what she knows must be the inevitable break from the confinement of New Bethesda, where her fate would be to repeat her grandmother's life as a servant to white families, and to try her fortune in Johannesburg.

Impressively Veronica's desire is the 1990s revised version of the "Jim goes to Jo'burg" trope of South African literature, in which black characters from a rural region go to Johannesburg only to be exploited in the mines and become shebeen queens (like Xuma and Leah in Peter Abrahams's *Mine Boy)* or turned into criminals and prostitutes (like Absalom and Gertrude Kumalo in Alan Paton's *Cry, the Beloved Country).* This is indeed the very story of Veronica's own mother, Caroline, who ran away from New Bethesda, disappeared from the lives of her grieving parents, only to be found in Johannesburg dying in childbirth after what is presumed to be a dissolute life, and leaving behind her illegitimate daughter Veronica for her parents to raise. "Jim goes to Jo'burg," like all clichés, has a great core of truth, a truth for non-whites before racial equality. What Veronica seeks is not, as her grandfather dreads, a replication of her mother's story, but the positive white version of that story, a version Fugard knows quite well, for it is also his own.

Rooted in Port Elizabeth with a hard-working mother whom he adored and a crippled, alcoholic father, Fugard, had he remained at home, could easily have become just another Port Elizabeth worker and led an empty, unfulfilled life. Surely Johnnie in *Hello and Goodbye* is an image of what Fugard could have become had he not followed his dreams of writing and success. Instead, Fugard left Port Elizabeth, hitchhiked his way to North Africa, and, as he celebrates in *The Captain's Tiger,* got a position on a steamer, where he began his career as a writer. Not the son of educated or literary parents, Fugard pursued an idea of himself formed by his imagination, an idea that, because he is white, was unrestricted. Happily for him, his combination of creative imagination and the South African realities he knew within his family and within his native environment somehow combined to create his acclaim and success. Before the dismantling of apartheid, such a scenario was possible mainly for whites. Nowadays it is open to Veronica and her peers regardless of race. She may well not become the celebrity she dreams of, but in the 1990s hers is a permissible dream for someone of color, and it need not end with her being exploited or dragged into the world of shebeens, brothels, dissolution, and crime as it might well have a few years before. What happened to Caroline Jonkers will likely not happen to her daughter, and Veronica has the personal energy so that she may even make a mark in the entertainment world not dissimilar to Fugard's own.

The comparison between Fugard and his character is likewise appropriate in another key, for one of the theatrical breakthroughs in *Valley Song* is the intrusion of the nonfictional playwright into his fictional world, including Fugard's dialogues on stage with his fictional characters. In this way, the play celebrates a new freedom and direction not merely for the Veronicas of South Africa but also for Fugard as an artist. With the abrogation of the apartheid barriers, he seems to feel free to write comedy and to abrogate the usual barriers between playwright and audience, between playwright and characters. Thus Fugard's role within his own fictive plot presents the fusion of the real and the imaginative which likewise forms the substance of dreams and of art. *Valley Song* in this way makes us feel once more the truth of Shakespeare's lunatic, lover and poet speech in *Midsummer Night's Dream.*

As much as Fugard's play is a heartwarming story of Veronica Jonkers's and South Africa's coming of age, it is also a parable about artists and art. It is a lyrical drama, which one reviewer called a tone poem, containing Veronica's songs, Buks's remembrance of a Verdi aria he learned from an Italian soldier, and the hymns Veronica and Buks sing together.[29] Yet it is only in the play's fiction that the young Veronica has written her songs, for it is Fugard the dramatist, of course, who has actually written the song lyrics (DiDi Kriel composed the music), and so the play becomes his own "valley song" as much as it is Veronica's.

The underlying idea of fiction and reality, as a basis for human development and for art, is articulated at the very beginning of the play, when Fugard comes on stage to show the audience the handful of pumpkin seeds that can grow into beautiful pumpkins and "delicious eating." Describing the pumpkins and holding up a seed for the audience to see, Fugard asserts, "Anyway, this is how they start out . . . one of these together with a little prayer for rain in a hole in the ground, and in a good year, when you get that rain, this little handful could easily give up to a hundred of those beauties" (1). Even for the most elementary vegetative growth and productivity, then, the equation must bring together the earthly realities—ground and rain—and the poetically transcendent—prayer. This homely truth is the thread that in the deceptively simple *Valley Song* binds together a complex weave of analogous ideas encompassing the growth and development of vegetables, adolescents, the nation, the artist, and art itself.

In the tale Fugard tells in *Valley Song*, seventeen-year-old Veronica has been raised by her seventy-year-old oupa (grandfather), Buks, a coloured man who has spent his entire life working in New Bethesda as a tenant farmer, planting and harvesting his *akkers* (acres), except for a brief time during World War II when he was a member of a coloured regiment and stationed in the Transvaal, where he guarded Italian prisoners of war. The length and breadth of his life are New Bethesda and its coloured location where he has always lived, his fruit and vegetable tenant farming on the *akkers* owned by whites, and his church. His time among the Italian prisoners in the army and his patchy remembrance of a song one of the Italians taught him are the remaining fragments of a now almost unreal dream that nevertheless continues to tint his life. The Italian song he remembers as "Lac donder mobili" and whose words he doesn't understand is the aria from Verdi's *Rigoletto* "La donna e mobile"—women are fickle, an idea that has some ironic applicability to Veronica.

Buks does not see, as Fugard's audience does, that Veronica is becoming a woman and growing restless in New Bethesda with its spatial and occupational confinement:

> VERONICA. There's no good mischief left in this place. I've used it all up. . . .
>
> BUKS. I see. So what are you looking for then?
>
> VERONICA. Adventure and Romance! . . .
>
> BUKS. I don't know how much of that you are going to find around here.
>
> VERONICA. So then what Oupa? . . . What is there for me? I'm bored . . . Always just the same old story. Nothing happens here Oupa. (7)

Buks, moreover, fears that if Veronica ever leaves his sight and rural New Bethesda, she will be corrupted and prostituted by urban life as her mother was. Consequently, the further dramatic irony of Buks's singing "Lac donder mobili" is that Verdi's tragic story of Rigoletto and Gilda narrates the very fate Buks fears for himself and Veronica, and that the song he unwittingly and unknowingly sings is the aria sung by the cynical and lecherous Duke.

For Verdi, describing a society based on class distinctions and aristocratic privilege, the court or city was a place of danger. For the writers of "Jim goes to Jo'burg" fictions and for those who, like Buks, have known South Africa as a land of racial distinctions, the city is regarded as the site of racial exploitation and urban corruption for non-whites. What Fugard celebrates through Veronica, however, is that in a new South Africa this need no longer obtain.[30] He is not, of course, so naïve as to believe that the dismantling of apartheid has meant a 180-degree turn, that suddenly a move to the city is danger-free, but he does endorse a vision that the city can now contain scenarios of success for citizens of all colors and need not necessarily be a geography either for Verdi's Gilda or for Paton's Absalom. The dissonance between the disparate views Veronica and her grandfather hold emerges when she sings her newly composed "Railway Bus" song:

> Railway Bus O Railway Bus
> Why don't you come no more
> I want to travel fast
> On the smooth tar road
> Far away, Far away.
>
> Railway Bus O Railway Bus
> I want to climb on board

I want to see Big Cities
And strange places
Far away, Far away (9–10)

Buks is visibly distressed by the song, for it recalls for him the daughter who ran off to Johannesburg and died there giving birth to her illegitimate daughter. He laments, "If that Railway Bus hadn't been there and made it so easy for her, who knows? Maybe she would still be alive and sitting here with us today. That is how she ran away" (11). Buks's fear and his desire to keep Veronica from harm are as understandable as Veronica's need to leave the close confinement of her New Bethesda nest and try her wings in Johannesburg. And this is where Fugard steps in.

As the character of Author in his play, Fugard acts the role of enabler and devil's advocate for Veronica, warning her that things may go amiss for her and for her dreams. Clearly, however, his intent is not to discourage her but to test her mettle, strengthen her resolve, and encourage her not to lose sight of those goals and dreams:

> VERONICA. You don't know what is going to happen to me.
>
> AUTHOR. That's true. I don't. But what I do know is that dreams don't do well in this Valley. Pumpkins yes, but not dreams—and you've already seen enough of life to know that as well.
>
> Listen to me Veronica. Take your apple box and go home, and dream about something that has a chance of happening—a wonderful year for your Oupa on his akkers with hundreds of pumpkins. Or dream that you meet a handsome young man with a good job . . .
>
> VERONICA. You're wasting your breath.
>
> AUTHOR. Okay, let's leave it at that. But for your sake I hope you don't remember tonight and what I've said to you, in ten years time, if like all the other women in the Village you are walking barefoot into the veld every day with a baby on your back to collect firewood.
>
> VERONICA. Never!
>
> AUTHOR. Because you know what you'll be dreaming about then don't you . . . that I've given you a job scrubbing and polishing the floors of my nicely renovated old Landman house.
>
> VERONICA. Never! Now you listen to me. I swear on the Bible, on my Ouma's grave, that you will never see me walk barefoot with firewood on my head and a baby on my back—you will never see me on my knees scrubbing a whiteman's floor. (16–17)

The dialogue here is nicely orchestrated so that Veronica, who begins by answering the Author in brief sentences or with a word, comes to find her voice, cuts the

Author off, and takes control of the argument and of her life. The Author's prompts for Veronica's growth work in this scene like fertilizer on her development. She stomps out after the lines above and returns without a break, imbued with new determination not merely to talk about her dreams but to make them reality. We see her move without pause from arguing with Fugard to singing her songs for tourists in order to earn enough coins to pay for her ticket to Johannesburg.

By including psalms and the hymns Buks and Veronica sing in church, Fugard makes us aware that his valley songs are not just those composed by Veronica or Verdi. Veronica sings her song "Wake Up and Dream Properly Alfred Witbooi," which is followed directly by recitation of Psalm 24 by the Author; the psalm is immediately succeeded by Buks and Veronica together singing the Afrikaans hymn "Die Heiland Is Gebore." What happens here is that the play lets us feel the importance of religion and church in the New Bethesda coloured community, but it also brings to bear the biblical archetypes that inform *Valley Song*. Psalm 24 is a psalm of David, a rural shepherd boy who composed his own valley songs, like this one, of hope, salvation, and celebration of the land. In I Samuel, moreover, we read of David, a callow boy with big dreams who is allowed by Jesse his father to go to the court of King Saul; who strikes down Goliath, the enemy of the land; and who reaches the pinnacle of society by succeeding Saul and becoming King of Israel. The analogy with Veronica, her songs and her aspirations, is obvious. Moreover, and once more with dramatic irony directed toward Buks, the hymn Buks and Veronica sing at church is one of the angels singing joyfully, announcing the Savior's birth and celebrating God sacrificing his son for a higher good, the gift of salvation and peace for mankind. The celestial image of the Father sacrificing his offspring for a higher good is likewise a song that speaks to the situation of Buks and Veronica.

Buks fails to see the analogies, so that he and Veronica enter into a generational agon, wherein he expects her to remain in New Bethesda to clean houses as though the South African elections never happened and the social limitations of apartheid were still intact, and she cries out:

> Isn't it supposed to be different now. . . . Our lives and . . . everything. Isn't that why there was an election. Oupa mos voted in it . . . and all that talk that was going on about how things was going to change and be different from now on. Well this doesn't look like it. Here we are carrying on and talking like the "klomp arme ou Kleurlinge" [bunch of poor coloureds] we've always been, frightened of the whiteman, ready to crawl and grateful if we can scrub his floors. . . . (28)

Veronica's rebellion, as her references to the initiation of a new order in South Africa and of elections with multiracial suffrage suggest, is more than occupational. She is also rebelling against the paternalism of the two men in the play, presumed racial/gender roles, and the art of an older generation that includes Fugard himself. Or, to put it more positively, she is simultaneously constructing her identity as a human being, woman, and artist; and she thereby embodies one version of South Africa's new construction of its own national, racial, and political identity.

Valley Song is a manipulative play encouraging the audience to take comedy's conventional stance by favoring the trajectory of youth against the older generation's blocking character(s). Along with that, one is allowed the comfort of knowing, long before it happens, that Veronica will successfully mollify her grandfather, leave the Karoo, seize her chance for professional success in Johannesburg, and forge a life as a vital young person—not female, not coloured, but just a person—in South Africa. The nature of comedy is, moreover, imbued with the spirit of optimism, one that denies the tragic fate of a Gilda or of an Absalom and a Gertrude Kumalo.

Part of the play's sensitivity, however, lies in its understanding of Buks, who is not rendered as a foolish pantaloon with the mind of an eternal servant but as an old man who has known only the life of an uncomplicated, church-going coloured tenant farmer tied to his *akkers* in a remote Karoo village. His fears and anxieties for Veronica as well as his inability to comprehend the political and social ramifications of the post-apartheid social order are both understandable and even heartwarming. Softening the binaries of old order–new order in this way, Fugard returns the audience to his vegetative metaphor, one that serves as *Valley Song*'s theme. The pumpkin seeds that will grow into new plants and fine eating have come from the bowels of old pumpkins; similarly, Veronica is not rejecting her grandfather and her valley but merely planting its seeds in new earth elsewhere. She expresses this idea by vocalizing, "I'll sing your songs / Valley that I love / So that people will know / How beautiful you are" (56).

More complicated are the stands Veronica and the play itself take toward Athol Fugard the writer. On the one hand, Fugard can identify warmly with Veronica, since he, too, in his youth broke free from his parents and his limited Port Elizabeth background to become a world-class artist. On the other hand, however, Fugard can identify with Buks's contentment with the status quo and with his fear of change. For Fugard there is the dual pull of wanting to cheer for Veronica and for the new South African order and of simultaneously dreading the idea of being left behind, a relic of some older precursor generation of writers whose works gather dust in libraries, are relegated to footnotes, and go unproduced or unread. By purchasing a house in the Karoo, where he was born, has Fugard returned and retired to his origins to be buried there? He confesses:

> Do you believe in ghosts? I'm not sure if I do or if I don't. I must admit I get a little scared when I walk around late at night. I almost imagine I can see them—at the windows of the old houses—pale, frightened white faces looking out at a world that doesn't belong to them anymore. I'm going to be one of them one day. (35)

This is not made any easier when Fugard suggests to Veronica that she is merely dreaming about her future, and, with the cruelty of youth, she retorts:

23. Lisa Gay Hamilton and Athol Fugard in *Valley Song* at McCarter Theatre, Princeton, N.J., 1995. Photo © T. Charles Erickson.

> That's right, and that life isn't over yet like yours maybe is. If your dreams didn't come true that's your bad luck not mine. Maybe you are ready to be a ghost, I am not. You can't see into the future. You don't know what is going to happen to me. (36)

At the conclusion of *Valley Song*, it is not only Buks who must bless Veronica as she leaves New Bethesda to find her future but also Fugard who makes a triste speech, laying hands on Veronica, identifying with her yet identifying as well with her oupa:

> I am also jealous. Your youth. Your dreams. The future belongs to you now. There was a time when it was mine, when I dreamt about it the way you do, but not anymore. I've just about used up all of the "Glorious Future" that I once had. But it isn't something you give up easily. I'm trying to hold onto it the way your Oupa wanted to hold onto you. (58)

In stating it this way, Fugard enables the members of his audience to transcend the barriers of age to identify both with the energetic hope of youth and with those nearing retirement who feel threatened by the new ways and new ideas of their young successors. Fugard here shrewdly allows his audience to draw on their acquired understanding in the relatively uncharged area of age bias and generational friction so as to apply their insights to the far more emotionally and politically charged ramifications of the new policies of nondiscrimination in the post-apartheid revisionings of South African life during the Mandela era.

The close of the play boldly moves its center from Veronica to Fugard himself as white South African and as writer. This is not some act of authorial egoism but an honest admission that as both citizen-landowner and writer it is, paradoxically, difficult to surrender the world that he has worked so hard to alter:

> Like your Oupa, I don't want to see you go. It means the Valley is changing and that selfish part of me doesn't want that to happen. It wants it to stay the unspoilt, innocent little world it was when I first discovered it . . . You see the truth is that I am not as brave about change as I would like to be. It involves letting go of things and I've discovered that that is a lot harder than I thought it was. (58)

Using a consciously simple vocabulary and the homely situation of Veronica and her oupa, Fugard here brilliantly uncovers large and paradoxical truths of parenting that provide insight into his position as a white man and as an aging white writer. We work hard so that our children will have advantages in life we did not enjoy and so that their lives will be an improvement on ours, and then we have a niggling resentment when they leave our parental control and perhaps actually find that better life for which we have sought to equip them.[31]

Perhaps the most astonishing thing about *Valley Song* is that, as we immerse ourselves in its three characters and their disparate points of view, we forget that a magisterial playwright stands behind the script understanding, and helping us to understand, the boundless aspirations of young Veronica, an embodiment of the new South Africa; the mind and fears of her coloured peasant grandfather, whose life has been spent accepting unquestioningly the ceiling imposed on him by apartheid; and the position of the playwright himself, now in his sixties, saying farewell to the system he hated but uneasy about what lies ahead for him as a writer. Has he spent all the bows in his quiver? He answers the question in the last moments of the play in his imaginary conversation with the old man:

> Think of it Buks. Another spring has come and we are still here! Still strong enough to go out there and plant!
>
> Tell me now Buks, think back to your young days and tell me . . . Did a woman ever smell as good as Karoo earth after a good rain? Or feel as good? (*A sly laugh*)
>
> Ja, the ground is soft and wet and waiting. And look what I've got for you! (*A handful of shiny, white pumpkin seeds*) Pumpkin seeds! Imagine it Buks. An akker full of shiny, Flat White Boer pumpkins as big as donkey-cart wheels!
> *The Author laughs; starts to leave.* (60)

Fugard becomes in one voice the two characters he has enacted in the play, and he addresses Buks not as a master speaking to a servant but as a fellow lover of the earth. Fugard's sexual imagery combines with his almost Mephistophelian tempting of Buks to plant the new seeds and thereby remain virile, potent and young. There is as well a male bonding between the two men, endowing both with a recaptured youthfulness and a new innocence.[32] Thus at the end of the play, they stand together alive and facing a new world. Their lives are not over, but they are yielding to the temptation to start anew, to plant their pumpkin seeds, whether those seeds are the actual thing or the seeds an author plants in the minds of an audience. There are always new seeds for Buks to plant, and that is just as true for Fugard the playwright. Appropriately, then, *Valley Song* ends on a note of laughter, the sound of comedy, the genre that affirms life and the future tense.

The Port Elizabeth *Evening Post* of 3 July 1954 featured an article, "Caught in a Typhoon in the Pacific," by a twenty-two-year-old lad, Athol Fugard by name. Above the headline is written, "A young Port Elizabeth man who served as a deckhand in [*sic*] a tramp steamer to see the world describes a terrifying experience." In colorful and dramatic terms, the article describes a frightening typhoon during which the ship on which Fugard was serving has a near collision with another, the damage done to the ship by the storm, the death of a sailor during the storm and the sailor's subsequent burial at sea.[33] Looking back on that article now and knowing what we do of what was to become of its young writer, one can recognize the richness and vivid detail of the writing even then. Forty-four years later, Fugard returns once more to that steamer, the SS *Graigaur*, to write *The Captain's Tiger* (1998). This time he recounts not a storm at sea but the tempest within himself as a young writer aboard ship struggling to write a novel in tribute to his mother and based on her coming of age as a young woman.

However, *The Captain's Tiger* is not so much about the Port Elizabeth adventure that propels Fugard's mother into adult life as it is about the shipboard adventure that launched Fugard himself as a writer. The play is also about a kind of death—not that of the young sailor whose body is given up to the sea but that of Fugard's manuscript about his mother, which he commits to the waves. What Fugard said in the 1954 newspaper article of his shipmate's death also now rings curiously true for the climactic moment in *The Captain's Tiger* when the writer gives up his prose to the sea: "Death strikes a hollow disturbing note at sea. For the issues, the questions you've ignored so long are laid out with the corpse, a cold fact that can no longer be avoided."

The manuscript Fugard destroys aboard the SS *Graigaur* about his mother, Betty, and how she came to meet his father, undergoes a double dying in *The Captain's Tiger*. It dies first for the twenty-two-year-old Athol Fugard, for whom its destruction implies acknowledging hitherto ignored questions of race and politics. It dies a second time for Fugard the established playwright in 1998, this time bringing to the fore the tabled and/or previously suppressed questions about his relationship with parents. At the same time, there is also about *The Captain's Tiger* a feeling of restoration, of Shakespearean romance as the characters drowned in 1954 are, thanks to the pen of the writer, revived, alive once more and ready for mature consideration four decades later. Like Thaisa and Marina in *Pericles,* Betty Fugard has not been lost at sea after all nor has her story drowned, for Fugard is able through his art to effect the resurrection of his pages from the brine and make the ink on those once destroyed pages fresh once more. In the process, more than an aborted old story is being recaptured, for Fugard also seems to be reviving himself, a playwright for whom the end of apartheid may initially have seemed a death knell for his writing. By writing *The Captain's Tiger,* Fugard is imbuing his art and life with new directions.

More correctly, perhaps, one might say *The Captain's Tiger* takes Athol Fugard in his maturity back to an abandoned direction of his youth. Here again one is reminded of Shakespearean romance—*The Winter's Tale, Pericles, The Tempest*—in which characters with wrinkled complexions return, with their hard-won knowledge of life's vicissitudes, to the time when they were young, when the signs of age had not yet been scripted on their visages. This notion has also been employed recently by playwright David Henry Hwang, who, in the prefatory remarks to his play *Golden Child* (1998), speaks of himself as a young boy writing down the stories his dying grandmother recounted to him of her life in China. Hwang writes, "Almost three decades later, in early 1995, I returned to my manuscript as a middle-aged man, and began to collaborate with my ten-year-old self to create a new play. At ten, could I have known that my adult self would one day return to this work? Probably not. But something at that young age did compel me to record these stories . . ." (vi).[34] Hwang's words ring true and resonate as well for Fugard, who in *The Captain's Tiger* is a playwright in his sixties collaborating with his twenty-year-old self. This is pointedly evoked on stage by having one actor play both the gray-bearded Fugard and Fugard the youth. And in the initial South African and American mountings of the play that actor was Athol Fugard himself.

The Captain's Tiger records the moment when Fugard made a decision to scuttle one path of literary endeavor, the story of his mother and father, and choose another. The new path he then chose has arrived at its destination: the abrogation of apartheid and the birth of a new South Africa. In *The Captain's Tiger* Fugard appears to return to the path he abandoned more than forty years before on the SS *Graigaur* to see where it will now lead him. This is not to say that he has not written autobiographically before. His *Hello and Goodbye* is a subjunctive play recording condition contrary to fact: Johnnie Smit is surely who Fugard would have become had he not left his family and home, gone to sea, and found his metier as a writer. Certainly *Master Harold* is the story of Fugard the teenager and serves as a prequel to *The Captain's Tiger*. During most of *Hello and Goodbye,* the Smits' father is seemingly in the next room but is never seen. Likewise Hally's father and mother are very much present at the other end of a telephone connection but they never appear in person in *Master Harold.* Fugard's parents do appear in the narrative of his memoir *Cousins,* but it is not until *The Captain's Tiger* that Fugard manages to give physical life to his mother. And then it is his mother before her marriage, constructed through authorial fiction, as the lives of all our parents before we are born are fictions constructed in our imaginations largely through anecdote, hearsay, and old photographs. When his father is about to enter significantly into the fictional-ized life of his mother, Fugard, perhaps knowing that no happy ending will come of this, literally and figuratively aborts his writing, tossing it overboard.

Fugard's father's alcoholism and early occupational disability; the hard lot of his mother, who ran cafés and rooming houses like those depicted and described in *Master Harold;* and other painful family issues are matters Fugard repressed or shelved over the years. Recently, however, they seem increasingly ready to erupt. Indeed, Fugard appears to be particularly reluctant to write about his father, his feelings toward whom are apparently mixed and unresolved. *Hello and Goodbye* suggests the emotionally crippled life Fugard might have led had he remained at home and taken care of his father. Importantly in that play, the father is never shown but is only a strongly felt presence allegedly in the next room. *Master Harold* strikes closer to home, showing Hally's deeply ambivalent feelings toward his again un-seen father. Revealing, too, is the title page of the original typescript for that play. There, after the title, Fugard types in "for Sam." He then prints in brown ink "and my father," but crosses out "my father" and replaces it with "H.D.F."[35] The initials here are as close as Fugard seems able to come in facing his father.

Certainly *Master Harold* is strong in autobiographical matter, but it is fiction, not memoir. In *Cousins,* Fugard approaches a personal memoir obliquely and in-directly; allegedly writing about his cousins Johnnie and Garth, he writes about himself, implying that the disparate sides of his own makeup are to be located in the distinctive personalities of the two cousins whose lives colored his boyhood. With *The Captain's Tiger,* he puts his fingers still nearer to the flame of family.[36] It seems quite possible that, like Eugene O'Neill, a playwright who also went to sea and whose work was likewise colored by alcohol and the tortured ghosts of his childhood, Fugard is on the verge of writing his own version of *Long Day's Jour-ney into Night,* the drama which O'Neill characterized as "this play of old sorrow, written in tears and blood," about which he wrote that he was able "to face my dead at last and write this play—write it with deep pity and understanding and forgiveness."[37]

Although speculations about where *The Captain's Tiger* may be leading its author are tempting and appropriate, it is more important to consider what he actually does and does not accomplish in what is for him a unique and uncharacteristic play. One thing Fugard obviously does not accomplish or reproduce in *The Captain's Tiger* is the kind of straightforward, traditionally constructed, thesis play we have come to expect from his pen. As a result, many of the reviews were respectful but measured and unenthusiastic. These are instructive. For example, comparing *The Captain's Tiger* to *Long Day's Journey into Night,* reviewer Laurie Winer describes Fugard's play as "just an amiable exercise in nostalgia"; Andrew Wilson calls it "es-sentially untheatrical theatre"; Peter Marks comments, ". . . the play itself is a bit of a letdown. It founders in the effort to achieve the kind of narrative force and effortless grace of Mr. Fugard's earlier plays"; and Raeford Daniel complains, "What is lacking is any tangible evidence of conflict."[38] The point made by these tepid and generally consistent reviews of the play is that it fails to exhibit the expected rising action–climax–dénouement structure of traditional drama and of Fugard's prior work.

Noteworthy is John Simon's acerbic and derisive review of the New York production, in which he asserts that *The Captain's Tiger* reaches a new low for boredom in the theatre. Without apartheid, Simon writes,

> the man is reduced to purveying ditch water. . . . One wonders why Fugard chose the theatre as the medium for this memoir of his youth, which would have done better as a novella. That's what it still is, narrated for at least four fifths of the text by himself. . . . And except for 100 minutes of trivial and pointless palaver, there is no play.[39]

Although his tone is much harsher, Simon is really raising the same issues as his more circumspect colleagues: that *The Captain's Tiger* lacks punch and is not truly a play because it does not have a traditional play structure; that it is merely dramatized memoir. Simon's intention may be to lambaste Fugard and his play, but he has unwittingly stumbled on the very things that set *The Captain's Tiger* apart and mark it as a new departure point for Fugard as dramatic artist. Certainly this play is *not* a moving or profound piece of theatre in the ways that *Boesman and Lena*, *The Island*, *A Lesson from Aloes*, and *Master Harold* are. Certainly, too, it does not grapple with the powerful political issues addressed in many of Fugard's previous works for the stage. But that does not mean *The Captain's Tiger* is "trivial and pointless palaver" or that it lacks theatrical power, for *The Captain's Tiger* is moving in other ways, striking out in relatively untrodden dramatic directions, shaping new possibilities in theatre.[40]

For a writer who has dedicated himself, as Fugard has, to a political and social cause, the achievement of the desired ends may bring with it the fear that there is no longer a topic to write about and that one has come to the end of one's artistic career. In *My Life* and *Valley Song*, Fugard comes to grips with and supersedes that fear; in *The Captain's Tiger* he suggests that as a playwright he may have found a new direction and a new freedom. Indeed the very sets of *Valley Song* and *The Captain's Tiger* underscore that new freedom. Many of Fugard's prior plays are characterized by small, enclosed spaces: the small rooms of *Hello and Goodbye*, *The Blood Knot*, *People Are Living There*, and *The Road to Mecca;* the prison cell of *The Island* and the prisonlike hut of *A Place with the Pigs;* the enclosed patio of *A Lesson from Aloes* and the cramped township schoolroom of *My Children! My Africa!;* and the small empty dining area walled by the sheets of rain outside in *Master Harold.* By strong contrast, *Valley Song* and *The Captain's Tiger* convey an almost heady freedom and authorial empowerment. The characters of the former are seen outdoors, surrounded by the vast and open expanse of the Karoo. This is conveyed to the audience not merely through mention of the landscape but by the paradoxically vast emptiness of a small but unadorned stage area.

Similarly and even more extensively, the set of *The Captain's Tiger* does not construct a realistic tramp steamer on stage but places the characters within a nearly blank playing space that conveys at once the vastness of the open sea, the limitless expanse of a writer's imagination, and the open-endedness of the life adventure the young Fugard commenced aboard the SS *Graigaur.* The sets or lack thereof for *Valley Song* and *The Captain's Tiger* thus italicize not artistic enclosure but the artistic liberation a seasoned Fugard in his sixties has gained as a consequence of his country's liberation from apartheid. As a writer, he can now move beyond the important and compelling but nevertheless confining anti-apartheid agenda to which he has given so much of his playwriting and political energy. He has not come to the end of his artistic tether; quite the contrary, he is now free to write about whatever he wishes, including subjects that he may have previously put aside in deference to the more pressing demands of dismantling South African racism. He articulated this new freedom in an interview with David Richards of the *Washington Post:*

> The huge changes that have taken place have obviously involved an extraordinary liberation for South Africans, and as an ordinary South African, I've been dealt into that liberation. . . . But as a writer, there has also been the most extraordinary payoff. I have been able to jettison my very guilt-ridden liberal conscience. I feel free to take on the telling of personal stories, which I would have considered a gross indulgence in the older South Africa. There was a moral imperative then that someone bear witness to what the hell was going on in that society and you couldn't ignore it, but now I'm free.[41]

Interestingly, as Fugard jettisons his anti-apartheid agenda, he pulls from the sea the personal stories and manuscript he jettisoned four decades earlier.

In his barbed review quoted above, John Simon complains that memoir is not a fit subject for drama. Here again, Simon puts his finger not, as he thinks, on a weakness but on a strength of *The Captain's Tiger.* As part of his new-felt, post-apartheid artistic freedom, Fugard explores in *The Captain's Tiger* the possibilities of the theatre for the writing and presentation of autobiographical memoir. He does not use the standard play form to contain autobiographical material as he did in *Master Harold,* but forges a new dramaturgy in which the narrator appears on stage to serve, as he might in a standard published autobiography or a memoir like *Cousins,* as a medium or middleman negotiating between present and past self.

Perhaps Fugard has picked up some of his dramaturgy from plays like Tennessee Williams's *The Glass Menagerie,* Gardner McKay's *Sea Marks,* Hugh Leonard's *Da,* or Brian Friel's *Dancing at Lughnasa,* in which a narrator talks to the audience, setting scenes and remembrances of his younger self. But those plays, though seemingly autobiographical, are fictions narrated by a fictional character. Fugard goes the next step: actually having one actor (himself) narrating Fugard's own personal memoir and negotiating between his twenty- and sixty-five-year-old selves. *The Captain's Tiger* thus hybridizes the arts of theatre and autobiography to allow the writer literally to enact his young self, to portray and inscribe both innocence and experience in one actor's body. As a dramatist, Fugard here pushes the envelope of theatre, successfully employing it as a medium for life writing. He creates a hybrid stage genre that offers possibilities of narration and self-enactment beyond those traditionally available in the purely print genres (e.g., autobiographies, journals, memoirs, diaries, letters). In this regard, *The Captain's Tiger* should be esteemed as a modest but significant theatrical milestone.

Like *Valley Song*, *The Captain's Tiger* is not a hard-hitting play. It lacks the dramatic magnificence of the heart-stopping moments when Sam drops his trousers to show Hally "a real Basuto arse" and when Hally without warning spits in the face of the older black man. It lacks the force of John and Winston enacting the Antigone story for their cell block on Robben Island, or of the fiercely searing triangulated emotions that erupt from Piet, Gladys, and Steve's truth telling. As the reviewers in one way or another recorded, *The Captain's Tiger* lacks dramatic edge. If the young Fugard's tossing his manuscript overboard serves as the play's high point, it is a moment, one must acknowledge, that is not a dramatic arête. There is only the modest frisson derived from reaching a hilltop. But heady dramatic climaxes are not necessarily the stuff of memoir.

Must one say, then, that memoir and drama are incompatible? That *The Captain's Tiger* is not a proper play? I think these are the wrong questions to ask. More appropriate questions are these: How does Fugard combine the disparate arts of memoir and drama? To what ends? With what success?

Commenting on *The Captain's Tiger* in *The Sowetan*, Elliot Makhaya writes that Fugard "has opted to use some of his most intimate memories to give voice to his relationship with his country, his fellow beings and his art."[42] This is exactly what Fugard's dramatic memoir is about. Looking back in the 1990s on his development as a writer, Fugard sees his experience at sea as the onset of his life's journey and the sea as an image of the tabula rasa of his life, "It used to be one of life's epic moments wasn't it—the start of a long and perilous voyage to unknown lands. Just about impossible now but that is what it felt like then. . . . I was twenty years old. My future was as wide open and blank as the oceans we were going to sail across" (ms. 3 and 4).[43] He places himself, moreover, amid other notable modern English-language writers connected with the sea, explaining, "But here we are! And we're in good company you know. Melville, Conrad, Hemingway, Faulkner, Twain. . . . they all did it. Cut loose and took their chance with fate. There's no other way. You can't play it safe if you want to be a writer" (14).

What *The Captain's Tiger* gives us is a perceptive insight into the drama of being a writer. This is not theatre's usual tragic struggle between protagonist and antagonist or its comic contention between young lovers and blocking characters. Nor is it the dramatics of the modern thesis play. Rather, at precisely the post-apartheid moment when Fugard is examining his revised role as a playwright, *The Captain's Tiger* dramatizes and provides insight into both the craft and mission of a writer. The play does contain dramatic struggle but it is an internal writerly psychomachia, the paradoxical conflict between Fugard the writer and his own imagination, personal memories, and characters. It is also dramatizes the ways a writer becomes a body on which old experiences and new ones do battle with one another to enscript themselves and claim a place of privilege in the authorial imagination. Indeed, in

The Captain's Tiger the young Fugard is the site of two competing scripts: one is the novel he is trying to write about his mother, and the other that of his new experiences—friendship with the black Donkeyman, carnal knowledge, and distance (geographic and psychological) from family and country.

After an initial brief scene in which the playwright sets the stage and gives the audience some expositional background, the play begins in earnest, and almost immediately several disparate issues surface. The playwright reads aloud a letter, signed "your ever loving son," to his mother explaining how he obtained his position as a captain's tiger (the captain's personal steward), where the SS *Graigaur* is headed, and the nature of his ambitions as a writer. The letter is pointedly not also addressed to his father, though he does say, "Tell Dad to get a map, a red pencil and a ruler and to draw straight lines joining up all the places I mention in my letters. That way he can follow me on all my travels and adventures . . . How is he, by the way?" (5). It takes no brilliant psychologist to recognize that Fugard's strong "ever loving" feelings for his mother are not equally felt for his father, whom he keeps at a distance and only approaches through maternal mediation.

Fugard's ambition, he admits to his mother, is to undertake a major work of fiction that will star his mother and in which he, through his creative authority, will give her the romantic, happy ending her life should have had:

> No more short stories and poems, I'm going for the big one—a novel *à la* Tolstoy—and it's going to be about a beautiful young Afrikaner girl in a white dress in a small Karoo town. Recognize her? That's right! It's the photograph of you when you were a girl that's hanging in your bedroom. That's going to be my inspiration. I'm going to weave together all the stories you've told me about your life and what you wanted to do with it, only this time all those dreams you had are going to come true. (5)

Precisely which failed dreams Fugard is trying simultaneously to rectify and deny is left vague. In the original manuscript, however, they are made somewhat, and more poignantly, specific:

> I've got another special memory of you in that bedroom. I think it's a few years later. My mother is sitting at the edge of her bed in an awful old pink flannel nightie, fighting for breath, for her life. She's in the middle of a really bad asthma attack—and there is nothing I can do to help her. I'm just standing there . . . useless. I want to put my fingers in my ears to stop me hearing that ugly raw sound she makes as she tries to suck in air. I want to close my eyes because she looks terrible. So I look at the wall instead and there you are again, where you've always been, looking at me just the way you are looking at me now. Do you see it? You . . . young, beautiful, innocent . . . and on the bed that tired, defeated old body with its flabby breasts and frightened eyes . . . the same life! the beginning and end of the same life! Brilliant isn't it. A perfect metaphor for the drama of destiny, the enigma of fate. (ms. 12–13)

This passage, (wisely?) excised in production and in the published playtext, adds a personal dimension that reveals the palliative and restorative power of narrative to deny and thereby eviscerate pain. The written word becomes Prospero's magic through which a youthful but bruised Fugard can reinscribe himself and his mother with utopian life texts. Fiction here becomes an analogy to the dancing in *Master Harold*, which is posited as a way of embodying the idea of life as a world without collisions. Fictional narrative is likewise a version of Sam and Hally's kite, which serves to direct the gaze skyward and away from the pains of reality. And it resembles as well the Edenic vegetative world Piet Bezuidenhout creates to oppose the hellish events in the background of *A Lesson from Aloes*.

The photograph of the youthful Betty that entranced him as a child has talismanic power for Fugard, enabling him to call into being the fictive image of his mother.[44] The play enables us to understand the fiction-writing process by reminding us that, as for Fugard, the picture we have of our parents and their lives before our births, before we knew them, is a construction whereby the past, imbued with present feelings and family lore, becomes an imagined world peopled with our parents but transformed by us into their fictionalized personae. The confusion between Fugard's actual mother and the fictional construction of Betty that Fugard creates is immediately apparent. The young Betty of Fugard's imagination, the character he creates based on his mother and on her photographic self, appears to Fugard on stage as someone vying with Fugard for textual authority. She reminds him of forgotten details and, asserting an independent consciousness, informs him how she has watched him mooning over her photo: "I've watched you grow up, standing there in front of me . . . staring . . . staring. You left quite a few grubby fingerprints on the glass to prove it. You mean you don't remember?" And Fugard answers, "No, of course I do. I can even remember the very first time I saw you . . . really saw you . . . I was alone in the house and I had sneaked into my parents' bedroom . . ." (7). The immediacy of the dialogue between Fugard and Betty becomes distanced when he unconsciously speaks of "my parents' bedroom." She is then not his mother but a maternal character who can be told of his mother. The effect is to illuminate for the audience how fiction comes to be.

The young Fugard basks in an abundance of strong filial and authorial emotions, transforming the prosaic Elizabeth Magdalena Katerina Potgieter into a romantic Betty Le Roux, about whom he evidently plans to write a saccharine novel, assuring her, "If it all works out the way I've planned it, there's a happy ending in store for you" (11). Shrewdly, however, Fugard shows Tiger (his youthful self) suddenly compromised in the midst of his authorial enthusiasm by the intrusion of Donkeyman, a black crew member from Kenya. Donkeyman's very presence, social class, and race call into question young Fugard's enterprise of writing some twentieth-century white colonial version of Fanny Burney's *Evelina*.[45] One is reminded of André Brink's *A Dry White Season*, whose narrator is a writer of popular ladies' fiction and whose central character is a conventional white Afrikaner schoolteacher. Unexpected events thrust the latter into the world of another race and cause the former to write for an entirely new audience. Similarly, the appearance of Donkeyman on the scene as Fugard begins his romantic novel and the black man's continuing presence as the unanticipated audience of that novel bring about a new direction for Fugard's life and writing.

Setting out from South Africa, the twenty-year-old Fugard, we learn, has hitchhiked to Sudan, where he has managed to get a position as a captain's tiger on a tramp steamer. To him it seems a beginning. He writes to his mother, "So there Mom. First Africa, now the world! The great adventure continues," and he tells the audience, "The voyage had begun. I was twenty years old" (5, 3). In the manuscript, an additional line reads, "My future was as wide open and blank as the oceans we were going to sail across" (ms. 4). The words "wide open and blank" in this simile make almost explicit what is implicit in the final published text: that to him his future and the blank pages he is about to fill with the text of his novel are connected.

The beginning of the young writer's "great adventure" at sea is echoed by Betty, who is once his mother in her girlhood photograph, his unruly muse, and his anxious romantic heroine:

> BETTY. I'm nervous.
>
> TIGER. Of what?
>
> BETTY. The Big Adventure.
>
> TIGER. Why?
>
> BETTY. I don't know. It just makes me nervous.
>
> TIGER. That's perfectly natural. We can even use it . . . But don't worry. If it all works out the way I've planned it, there's a happy ending in store for you. (10–11)

With a certain male confidence he assumes that he is in unchallenged and unchallengeable control of his literary text and of Betty's future, her "Big Adventure." Furthermore, like a ship's captain, he also assumes he is steering the vessel of his own big adventure, his epic journey into life and the vocation of writer.

When Fugard asks Betty if, when he describes her, he should dab her with some of the English lavender cologne his mother favored, she answers meekly, "If you say so," to which he asserts with autocratic arrogance:

> That is . . . simply brilliant. That is what it is going to be all about isn't it . . . If I Say So!
>
> Creative authority. That's what you've put your finger on young lady. The freedom and authority of the creative artist to go in any direction his imagination chooses. Theoretically I can do anything I like with you. It's a hell of a responsibility you know. (8–9)

Echoed here are the despotic tones of Hally, the image in *"Master Harold"... and the Boys* of Fugard some seven or eight years younger than he is in *The Captain's Tiger*. And as in the earlier play, the drama here centers around reversals whereby the main character's tyranny is challenged and overthrown by those he assumes are his subjects and inferiors: his parents and black men. In both plays, his is the confidence that presumes the younger generation can always outsmart and control the older. And far more important, his is also the confidence of the racial script that posits the oxymoron of white boys' paternalistic supremacy over subaltern, inferior non-white men. Tellingly he writes home, "The officers are white and the sailors a real bag of liquorice all sorts . . . black, brown and yellow" (5). The metaphor of children's candy speaks volumes.

The drama of *The Captain's Tiger* emerges from Fugard's increasing awareness of where his attitudes toward parents and the dark-skinned Donkeyman are leading him. The on-stage juxtaposition, moreover, of Betty and Donkeyman is at the core of the internal dramatic agon that the play stages (fig. 24). Indeed, shorn of its allegory and its Good versus Evil essentialism, the simple dramatic structure Fugard effectively employs is nothing more than that of *Everyman* or *The Castle of Perseverance* with the author himself as the central character beset by conflicting forces. His aim is to assert his "creative authority" and write a novel about his mother, but quickly he finds himself in a battle for authorial power with his own created character, who takes on a life and will of her own. And he finds himself as well joined by a strong co-author, the illiterate "reader" or listener to whom he is reading his prose. Fugard admits:

> Donkeyman help Tiger plenty plenty. When Donkeyman watch Tiger andika [write], Tiger feel strong. When Tiger read story and Donkeyman listen, Tiger feel more strong. This one . . . [*He puts his hand on his manuscript*] . . . Tiger and Donkeyman andika this one together. You and me. (28)

Ultimately, unlike Everyman and Humanum Genus, Fugard as Tiger does not choose one over the other but jettisons his manuscript in order, paradoxically, to free himself of both while incorporating the claims of both in his future writing.

In the course of *The Captain's Tiger*, employing articulate and frequently florid language, Tiger tries to come to terms with his mother, about whom (with Olive Schreiner's *The Story of an African Farm* in mind) he is writing the white bourgeois novel *Betty Le Roux: The Story of a South African Woman*. His aim is to depict "the Karoo woman as Hero . . . which is what my mother would have been if life had given her half a chance" (35). With his father, he is not coming to terms at all. As he writes his purple prose enshrining his mother, he increasingly falls under the sway of the Donkeyman, who is soon no longer seen as a piece of licorice candy but emerges as a sentient, individuated human being.

The force of the black sailor's power is such that Fugard finds himself departing from the linguistic plane of literary narrative and attempting to meet his comrade

24. Jennifer Steyn, Owen Sejake, and Athol Fugard in *The Captain's Tiger*, PACT production, South Africa, 1997. Photo by Ruphin Coudyzer.

on Donkeyman's own linguistic turf: first by speaking pidgin English and then by learning some functional Swahili vocabulary. This linguistic adjustment is an important and noteworthy step for a white South African youth, whose culture has taught him that blacks and coloureds must learn Afrikaans and/or English, but whites need learn no indigenous African languages.

As the influence of Donkeyman upon Tiger grows, Tiger is framed on stage by two very different and opposing forces: on the one hand, Betty Le Roux, prim, often clothed in white, with the scent of English lavender emanating from her body, and speaking perfect English; on the other, the black, sweaty, bare-chested, shabbily dressed Donkeyman marked by his terse, monosyllabic mixture of English, pidgin, and Swahili. By extension, and likewise in comic opposition, are the romance fiction of idealized love which Fugard projects for Betty in the pages of his novel, and the frankly physical and very real copulation of Donkeyman's "jig-jig" with prostitutes in each port.

In Fugard's authorial relationship with Betty, the tension escalates between young author and his created mother as he writes himself into the untenable corner of witnessing what is for him the distasteful primal scene between his parents. He must come to terms with the fact that even more than projecting his mother as

Karoo heroine, Fugard's aim in writing his novel has been to re-script his mother's life (and by extension, his own) through eliminating from the novel his real and handicapped father, and replacing him with the idealized romantic one his mother should have married (and he should have had). The scene reeks with blatantly Oedipal content. First Betty taunts her son/author with the waves of her sexual desire as she awaits a sexual encounter with the man destined to become Fugard's father: "I'm lying there on my bed in my nightgown. It's a warm summer's night. My young body is hot and sweating, my heart's throbbing" (46). As she wrests authorial control from Fugard, she becomes his Oedipal nightmare, jeering at him for his own sexual inadequacy, inexperience, and consequent inability to write knowledgeably about desire: "The Captain's Tiger is still a whelp. . . . You had the nerve, the conceit, the male arrogance to think that in spite of your ignorance about the most basic drive in human nature you could write about me?" (48). Finally, to his horror, she articulates his Oedipal lust:

> BETTY [*teasing*]. Oh come on, Mr Author. Don't make me blush. Surely I don't have to spell it out? [*She slides into bed beside him.*] Use that famous imagination of yours. And for heaven's sake stop shivering! Look at me. I'm not frightened. And I know you want it every bit as much as I do.
>
> TIGER [*in a panic*]. For God's sake no. Do you realise what you're doing? You're based on my mother. This is as good as incest! Donkeyman! Donkeyman! [*He breaks through his paralysis and escapes* BETTY.](49)

She has taken over writing the text, and his impassioned cry for Donkeyman signals his need to be rescued and guided by Betty's opposite number.

As he turns to his black companion, using him to arrange his coital initiation, Fugard essentially turns away from an unruly and increasingly distasteful parental white script to a new script of color with the black-skinned Donkeyman as new mentor and muse. Fugard's first sexual experience on the Niigata waterfront, moreover, is with a woman of color, a Japanese prostitute:

> Her name was Aiko. She was neither young nor pretty, but she made up for that in other ways. With infinite patience and exquisite tact she gave me my first lessons in that most ancient and personal of all the arts: how to touch another human being. (52)

Thus, curiously and importantly, the incipient white playwright comes to learn, in more than sexual ways, from his non-white teachers, Donkeyman and Aiko, the secret ingredient of successful art, "how to touch another human being." And in large part, Athol Fugard throughout his life has learned from non-white teachers the lessons that inform his plays and enable them and him to touch audiences. Indeed, for him, the calligraphy he receives from Aiko proves predictive: "All Life is Learning."

The new experiences of friendship with Donkeyman and sexual desire with Aiko disconnect the captain's tiger from his romantic manuscript and the disconcerting directions it had begun to take. The SS *Graigaur* is becalmed and the young writer is likewise in the doldrums, unable to resume his racially white story of Betty Le Roux. Instead he begins to contemplate writing about his Kenyan companion and his Japanese coital partner, saying to Donkeyman:

> To work, to work, perchance to write! Japan too much good time . . . Concentration not so good at the moment . . . But by God, it was worth it. And I owe it all to you. That could be another story you know, me and you, our Niigata nights! Certainly a chapter in the memoirs. (56)

Not recognizing that he has begun to replace Betty in the writer's imagination, Donkeyman, as audience for Fugard's novel manuscript, berates the author for his writerly sloth. In response, Fugard, handing him the pen and confronting Donkeyman with his illiteracy, angrily retorts, "Stop looking at me like that. If it means so much to you, go write your own bloody novel!" (58–59).

The dramatic climax of *Master Harold* occurs in two rapidly connected parts: the first when Sam exposes his "real Basuto arse" and the second when Hally spits in Sam's face. Similarly, *The Captain's Tiger* reaches a double climax. The first of these comes when Tiger attempts and fails to construe a romantic ending for Betty. The handsome piano player is meant to rise from his instrument, take her in his arms, dance with her, and lead her off to the land of happily ever after. Fugard realizes, however, that he cannot use his writing to avert the truth, for Betty confronts him with realities:

> TIGER. You wanted real happiness, well here it comes. Striding to meet you across the dance floor. This is where you finally meet.
>
> BETTY. You don't understand.
>
> TIGER. Yes I do. . . .The band stops playing, everybody looks around to see what's going on . . .
>
> BETTY. No no no. You don't understand . . . He can't come "striding to me across the dance floor," and he can't dance because he's a cripple. (68–69)

With great emotion the voice of the twenty-year-old Tiger seems to blend with that of the sixty-five-year-old Fugard in a near-tearful admission of his parents' unfortunate ever after:

> She's . . . sitting on the side of her bed . . . her tired old nightie clammy with sweat, the sweat of desperation . . . clutching her asthma spray with one hand, scratching her greying head with the other. She's trying to work out how she can make the few quid she's got in her bag pay the café rent, and the

boys' wages, and the baker, and the cooldrink man, and the Cadbury's man, and all the other bloody parasites that feed off her life.

　. . . she'll never have enough. Her once beautiful eyes are little pools of anxiety and fear. (72)[46]

Before him he sees his indolent father sponging on his wife and reading comic books: "Those wonderful blue eyes are still unclouded . . . his fine, aristocratic features and complexion smooth and unlined . . . they have the repose of a death mask" (73). Turning to Betty and his manuscript, Tiger has his highly dramatic and near-tragic moment of insight, acknowledging, "There's no escape . . . for me or for you [*indicates his manuscript*]. I thought I could at least give you one on paper, but even that won't work. I can't make a happy ending out of my Dad" (73).

With that, he tosses his novel into the Pacific, effecting at once the second part of the climax and the murder of Betty, who laments, "The ink is already running, the words starting to blur and drift off the pages. It's like bleeding to death . . . after all, it was my life. I can feel it ebbing away. A few more seconds and there won't be a word of it left" (73–74). And he murders as well his friendship with the horrified Donkeyman, who sees the destruction of the manuscript as Fugard's betrayal of him as audience.

In one stroke, Fugard loses both Betty and Donkeyman, text and reader, the two contending forces of his writing. But in a brilliant last-scene turn, Fugard, now speaking as present-day Author and not as Tiger, recognizes that their loss has been a paradoxical but remarkable gain. Through the years, the image of Donkeyman remains with him to remind Fugard the playwright of his responsibility to his audience and of his mission to answer Gayatri Spivak's important question, "Can the subaltern speak?"[47] The lesson of his friendship with Donkeyman has taught Fugard that his purpose as a writer must be to write and speak for those, like Donkeyman, who cannot do so for themselves:

> I wouldn't go so far as to say he haunts me, but sometimes when I'm working I get a quiet feeling that I'm being watched, that someone is sitting there watching me while I write. . . . He reminds me that I and my writing belong to a world where a lot of people can't put words on paper and tell their stories. (76–77)

And putting their words on paper, telling their stories, is perhaps Fugard's greatest achievement as a playwright.

At the same time, Fugard has also been haunted by his mother and by Betty Le Roux, both of whom he surrendered to the waves. And yet that betrayal of them he now recognizes as his empowerment as a writer: "Failing to tell your story is my Original Sin as a story-teller. All the others I've told since that night in Fiji when I threw you to the sharks, every one of them was just an attempt at penance" (78). Clearly, too, the loss of the manuscript allowed Fugard to gain mastery of his art and of his subjects, to free himself from the kind of artistic thralldom imposed in their separate ways upon him by Betty and by Donkeyman. The play ends as it began with the striking of the ship's eight bells, an appropriate gesture, for the end of the play marks its beginning. A seasoned Fugard now in control of his writer's magic cannot erase his Original Sin, but can pull his manuscript from the deep and bring it to life once more as he has just done in *The Captain's Tiger*.

Betty tempts Fugard to end his career: "Aren't you tired? Don't you want to make my story your last one? Your first failure, your last great success" (78). Fugard rebuffs her and now sees her as the spirit that challenges him to write:

> AUTHOR. If I knew there were only one story left to tell, I'd be too frightened to tell it. I'd feel like a condemned man who has reached his last day.
>
> BETTY. Well, I'm not going to give up you know.
>
> AUTHOR. Please don't. You've become my muse. Your visits keep me going. (78)

One can now only speculate where exactly Fugard is going and whether he is on his way to telling, and coming to terms with, the real story of his mother and, far more challenging, the painful story of the threatening Dad who still remains carefully marginalized in the script of *The Captain's Tiger*.

The more than four decades of Athol Fugard's playwriting career mark his growth as a playwright and chart his ability to take on the racial and social issues that have been the bitter products of racism and apartheid rule. Impressively, he has been successful in shaping those domestic issues into issues of international significance. In Fugard's dramas, South African problems become larger global problems. Although South African audiences are certainly moved by Fugard's theatre, audiences around the world feel the issues in their hearts, debate the issues in their minds; they are not disengaged viewers merely observing another culture, like so many visitors peering at glass-enclosed exhibits at an anthropology museum. Plays like *Boesman and Lena, Sizwe Bansi Is Dead, The Island, A Lesson from Aloes, Master Harold,* and *My Children! My Africa!* have made the world responsive to South Africa even as they have italicized racial issues and racism elsewhere.

Race and apartheid, however, are just one aspect of Fugard's work. His great achievement is to see into the depths of the human mind and soul, portraying the force of human interactions in their often tragic dimensions. Fugard writes of his characters—even those who offend—with love, understanding, and tolerance, thereby teaching us how to be better and more generous than we are. Always a man of the theatre, Fugard turns stage acting into social action, stage performance into the performance of life. At bottom, all of his plays are about the power of art and more specifically the art of theatre to touch and diagnose the ills and problems humans and societies are heir to.[48] When the passions, fears, and venom in mankind and in cultures is made manifest on stage by a playwright with Fugard's talent and wisdom, they become known, comprehensible, and capable of being either fruitfully employed or exorcised. Certainly Fugard is a man of his time charting the history of his country during the second half of the twentieth century, but he is also a playwright for all time addressing those things that make us fallible and, consequently, human.

NOTES

INTRODUCTION

1. Athol Fugard, *Notebooks: 1960–1977*, ed. Mary Benson (Johannesburg: Ad. Donker, 1983), and Mary Benson, *Athol Fugard and Barney Simon: Bare Stage, a Few Props, Great Theatre* (Randburg: Ravan Press, 1997).

2. Russell Vandenbroucke, *Truths the Hands Can Touch: The Theatre of Athol Fugard* (New York: Theatre Communications Group, 1985), and Dennis Walder, *Athol Fugard* (London and New York: Macmillan and Grove Press, 1985). Both of these studies do provide some analysis of the plays, but the emphasis in Vandenbroucke's important study, as his title suggests, is Fugard as a theatre practitioner. Likewise Walder's cogent and very readable book, which became part of the Grove Press Modern Dramatists series, was meant, as the editors to the series (Bruce and Adele King) state, to be a general introduction to Fugard.

3. [Robert Kavanagh] Mshengu, "Political Theatre in South Africa and the Work of Athol Fugard," *Theatre Research International* 7 (Spring 1982): 171. Less vitriolic in tone but along similar neo-Gramscian lines is the criticism leveled by Martin Orkin, *Drama and the South African State* (Manchester, New York, and Johannesburg: University of Manchester Press and Witwatersrand University Press, 1991), pp. 146–147.

4. Dennis Walder, "Resituating Fugard: South African Drama as Witness," *New Theatre Quarterly* 8 (November 1992): 343–361.

5. Mshengu, p. 178.

I. EARLY WORK AND EARLY THEMES

1. John Elderfield, ed., *Henri Matisse: A Retrospective* (New York: Museum of Modern Art, 1992), pp. 24–26, 88–97.

2. See Mel Gussow, "Profiles: Witness," *New Yorker,* 20 December 1982, pp. 47–94, an excellent portrait of Fugard, as well as the useful biographical chapters in Russell Vandenbroucke, *Truths the Hand Can Touch: The Theatre of Athol Fugard,* pp. 1–16, and Dennis Walder, *Athol Fugard,* pp. 19–32. See also the useful chronologies in Stephen Gray, ed., *Athol Fugard* (Johannesburg: McGraw-Hill 1982), pp. 3–14; Temple Hauptfleisch, Wilma Viljoen, and Céleste van Greunen, eds., *Athol Fugard: A Source Guide* (Johannesburg: Ad.

Donker, 1982), pp. 14–17; and John Reed, ed., *Athol Fugard: A Bibliography* (Grahamstown, South Africa: National English Literary Museum, 1991), pp. 5–8.

3. A vivid description of how *No-Good Friday* was created and staged is given in Sheila Fugard, "The Apprenticeship Years," *Twentieth Century Literature* 39 (Winter 1993): 394–408.

4. Russell Vandenbroucke, *Truths the Hand Can Touch: The Theatre of Athol Fugard,* pp. 14–15.

5. Here and elsewhere I use the term "coloured" to indicate those in South Africa of mixed race. Similarly, I use "non-white" not in a pejorative way of talking about "the other," but as a phrase for indicating black, mixed-race, and Indian peoples in South Africa.

6. Loren Kruger astutely sees the liabilities of *No-Good Friday* in her essay "The Drama of Country and City: Tribalization, Urbanization and Theatre under Apartheid," *Journal of Southern African Studies* 23 (December 1997): 577–579.

7. Some of the criticism leveled against Fugard and Paton is made clear in Loren Kruger, *The Drama of South Africa* (London and New York: Routledge, 1999), pp. 88–90.

8. Athol Fugard, *Dimetos and Two Early Plays* (Oxford: Oxford University Press, 1977). The text of *No-Good Friday* appears in this collection. All references to *No-Good Friday* are from this edition. The page numbers in parentheses refer to this edition.

9. Dennis Walder also notices this in his *Athol Fugard,* p. 47.

10. Athol Fugard, *Dimetos and Two Early Plays.* The text of *Nongogo* appears in this collection. All references to *Nongogo* are from this edition. The page numbers in parentheses refer to this edition.

11. Russell Vandenbroucke sees *Nongogo* as merely a "thin slice of township life" (in *Truths the Hands Can Touch,* p. 23) and as "a conventional story of a woman with a past she tries to hide—as in *Lady Windermere's Fan* and *The Second Mrs. Tanqueray*—and of the prostitute with a heart of gold" (p. 24).

2. THE PORT ELIZABETH PLAYS

1. Athol Fugard, *Cousins: A Memoir* (Johannesburg: Witwatersrand University Press, 1994), p. 83; Robert L. King, "The Rhetoric of Dramatic Technique in *Blood Knot*," *South African Theatre Journal* 7 (1993): 40–49; and Russell Vandenbroucke, *Truths the Hand Can Touch: The Theatre of Athol Fugard,* p. 48.

2. Dennis Walder, "Crossing Boundaries: The Genesis of the Township Plays," *Twentieth Century Literature* 39, no. 4 (1993): 411.

3. Loren Kruger usefully fills in background on other plays of the period that deal with racial difference, like *Kimberley Train* and *Try for White,* in *The Drama of South Africa,* pp. 103–110.

4. Pp. 47–48.

5. *The Blood Knot* had a somewhat different feel when it was revived twenty-four years later, in 1985, first at the Yale Repertory Theatre and then on Broadway with Fugard and Mokae playing the roles they originated in 1961. A useful discussion of the changes made in the revival of *The Blood Knot* is Kim McKay, "*The Blood Knot* Reborn in the Eighties: A Reflection of the Artist and His Times," *Modern Drama* 30 (December 1987): 496–504.

6. In the BBC 2 "Theatre 625" filmscript (directed by Robin Midgley) of *The Blood Knot* (12 June 1967), p. 20, a decision was made to eliminate the ambiguity of the playtext by having Morris say, "Different fathers but the same mother, and that's what counts . . . brothers." A copy of this filmscript is held by the Lilly Library at Indiana University and the National

English Literary Museum in Grahamstown. Since Fugard played the role of Morrie in that production, he was, one presumes, willing to have this clarification in the filmtext. At the same time, however, the 1960 entry in Fugard's *Notebooks* containing the germ of *The Blood Knot* clearly states, "It was the same mother! It was the same father!" See Athol Fugard, *Notebooks 1960–1977*, p. 10. The differences among the playtext, filmtext, and notebooks concerning the biological parentage of Morrie and Zach are, finally, unimportant except that they serve to indicate that the brotherhood between the two characters is something far larger and far more significant than biology or genealogy.

7. Curiously, in Holland a couple taking fertility pills recently had twin sons, named Teun and Koen. The *New York Times* reported, "Little Teun is as white and blond as his father and mother and little Koen is black." See Marlise Simons, "Uproar over Twins, and a Dutch Couple's Anguish," *New York Times*, 28 June 1995, p. A3, cols. 1–4

8. Athol Fugard, *Cousins*, pp. 70–71.

9. In a Pretoria newspaper interview shortly after the opening of *The Blood Knot*, Fugard told the interviewer, ". . . the greatest influence on me has been Beckett. I've been very much influenced by the attitudes underlying his work." J.D.F.J., "Athol Fugard Talks about His Play," *Pretoria News*, 8 December 1961. See also Dennis Walder, *Athol Fugard*, p. 55. The influence of Beckett on Fugard has become a commonplace of those who discuss Fugard's theatre. One should note, however, Martin Orkin's disagreement. In his desire to claim Fugard as a Marxist, Orkin denies the Beckettian qualities of *The Blood Knot* in order to stress an alleged anti-industrial, anti-capitalist agenda. See Martin Orkin, *Drama and the South African State*, p. 98.

10. The Beckettian quality of the play and the power relationships between the brothers is the theme of R. J. Green, "South Africa's Plague: One View of *The Blood Knot*," *Modern Drama* 12 (February 1970): 331–345.

11. All quotations from *The Blood Knot, People Are Living There, Hello and Goodbye*, and *Boesman and Lena* are from Athol Fugard, *Boesman and Lena and Other Plays* (Oxford: Oxford University Press, 1978). Parentheses after quotations refer to this edition.

12. It is worth noting that in the letter to Ethel, Zach writes his favorite quotation, "[T]oo many cooks spoil the broth" (32), but that Fugard's original choice, which would perhaps have too heavy-handedly invoked a theme of the play, was "Blood is thicker than water." See original typescript of *The Blood Knot* at the Lilly Library at Indiana University. A copy is held by the National English Literary Museum (NELM).

13. Amy Robinson, "It Takes One to Know One: Passing and Communities of Common Interest," *Critical Inquiry* 20 (1994): 715–736. Robinson argues, "In the many textual incarnations of passing, a triangular event appears with conspicuous regularity. Three participants—the passer, the dupe, and a representative of the in-group—enact a complex narrative scenario in which a successful pass is performed in the presence of a literate member of the in-group. As a standard feature of the passing narrative, such a triangle poses the question of the passer's 'real' identity as a function of the lens through which it is viewed" (724ff.).

14. It is of course possible to argue that the race question is always implicitly if not explicitly in the background of every South African play, for the characters, their lives, and their actions are shaped by a society and polity based on racial separation.

15. In his typescript, Fugard divided the play into acts and scenes. In the published version, the scene divisions were eliminated. See typescript at the Lilly Library (Indiana University), p. 24.

16. Samuel Beckett, *Waiting for Godot* (New York: Grove Press, 1954), p. 57a.

17. Athol Fugard, *Cousins*, p. 22.

18. A stimulating reading of the play, and one very different from the one that will follow here, is given by Martin Orkin, who reads *Hello and Goodbye* as a critique of Afrikaner Calvinist values. *Drama and the South African State,* pp. 129–138.

19. *Cousins,* p. 81.

20. Loren Kruger also speaks of the Beckettian influences on *Hello and Goodbye* in *The Drama of South Africa,* pp. 111–112, as does R. J. Green, "Athol Fugard's *Hello and Goodbye,*" *Modern Drama* 13 (September 1970): 139–155.

21. Athol Fugard, *Hello and Goodbye,* in *Boesman and Lena and Other Plays,* pp. 173–177.

22. See Albert Wertheim, "The Modern British Homecoming Play," *Comparative Drama* 19 (Summer 1985): 151–165.

23. Barney Simon's marked typescript of the play is part of the Simon archive at NELM. Pp. 1–8v, NELM acquisition no. 95.11.1.39.

24. Athol Fugard, *Notebooks: 1960–1977,* p. 118.

25. In his *Notebooks,* Fugard records, "I read my first Proust (*Swann's Way*) and realise how far I have yet to go in my understanding the implications of Hester 'finding her own self' in the suitcases and boxes from her father's room. Provoked by this realisation, particularly by the incident of the piece of madeleine soaked in tea which ends the 'overture' of Swann's Way" (102).

26. In her provocative essay, Marcia Blumberg points out another important dimension of Hester's unpacking: "As she enacts the multiple subject positions of a lonely, poor woman, prostitute, family outcast, fighter, and schemer, the play makes visible societal structures and concomitantly marks audience members as partially complicit in their positioning, in this theatre context, as silent spectators." Marcia Blumberg, "Re-Staging Resistance, Re-Viewing Women: 1990s Productions of Fugard's *Hello and Goodbye* and *Boesman and Lena,*" in Jeanne Colleran and Jenny S. Spencer, eds., *Staging Resistance: Essays on Political Theatre* (Ann Arbor: University of Michigan Press, 1998), p. 124.

27. Marcia Blumberg argues that an understanding of Hester's role demands some contextualization of women's roles in South Africa. Her comments on *Hello and Goodbye,* its feminism, and the impact of particular productions are useful and incisive. See Blumberg, "Re-Staging Resistance," pp. 128–130.

28. Fugard, *Cousins,* pp. 82–83, and Russell Vandenbroucke, *Truths the Hand Can Touch,* p. 51. In his *Notebooks,* Fugard writes, "*Hello and Goodbye*—a dedication: 'To my father, who lived and died in the next room,'" p. 121.

29. Russell Vandenbroucke, *Truths the Hand Can Touch,* p. 66; Dennis Walder, *Athol Fugard,* p. 55; Chris Wortham, "A Sense of Place: Home and Homelessness in the Plays of Athol Fugard," in Malvern Van Wyk Smith and Don Maclennan, eds., *Olive Schreiner and After: Essays on Southern African Literature in Honour of Guy Butler* (Cape Town: David Philip, 1983), pp. 174–175; Craig W. McLuckie, "Power, Self, and Other: The Absurd in *Boesman and Lena,*" *Twentieth Century Literature* 39 (Winter 1993): 423–429; Errol Durbach, ". . . No Time for Apartheid: Dancing Free of the System in Athol Fugard's *Boesman and Lena,*" in *South African Theatre as/and Intervention,* ed. Marcia Blumberg and Dennis Walder (Amsterdam: Rodopi, 1999), pp. 61–74; and Mel Gussow, "Fugard's Humanism," *New York Times,* 2 February 1977, reprinted in *Athol Fugard,* ed. Stephen Gray (Johannesburg: McGraw-Hill, 1982), pp. 94–95.

30. In his *Notebooks,* Fugard fleshes out the timetable and circular travels of Boesman and Lena amid the towns that ring Port Elizabeth, p. 169.

31. Martin Orkin reads the play entirely in light of its criticism of the South African gov-

ernment and its policy of apartheid. See Martin Orkin, *Drama and the South African State,* pp. 142–145.

32. Stanley Kauffmann, *Persons of the Drama: Theatre Criticism and Comment* (New York: Harper & Row, 1976), 205–206; Walder, *Athol Fugard,* p. 71.

33. Kauffmann, *Persons of the Drama,* p. 204.

34. Kauffmann, *Persons of the Drama,* p. 204.

35. Marcia Blumberg, "Languages of Violence: Fugard's *Boesman and Lena,*" in James Redmond, ed., *Violence in Drama* (Cambridge: Cambridge University Press, 1991), p. 242. See also Blumberg, "Re-Staging Resistance," pp. 136–142.

36. The power of such denigrating words should not be underestimated. Mary Benson relates the moving moment when exiled black jazz musician Dudu Phukwane attended the Royal Court production of *Boesman and Lena.* Phukwane, "on hearing Boesman's vicious 'Swartgat' [literally, black arse] aimed at Outa, rushed from the theatre." See Mary Benson, *Athol Fugard and Barney Simon,* p. 90.

37. In the holograph version of the play at Indiana University's Lilly Library (a copy of which is at NELM), Fugard has crossed out the following lines, but bracketed them and marked them "stet?": "It's a long time since we had somebody with us. If we had wine we could have celebrated properly. . . . but I had to buy you a place at the fire," I-22, NELM acquisition no. 139.

38. Fugard, *Notebooks,* p. 173.

39. Monica Meinert, "Dramatiker Athol Fugard," *Allgemeine Zeitung* [Windhoek], no. 4 (7 January 1970).

40. Fugard, *Notebooks,* p. 171.

41. Brook, *The Empty Space,* p. 11.

42. For a full and perspicacious examination of Lena's dance and its meaning, see Errol Durbach's excellent essay ". . . No Time for Apartheid: Dancing Free of the System in Athol Fugard's *Boesman and Lena.*"

43. Sheila Fugard, *Threshold* (Johannesburg: Ad. Donker, 1975), p. 34.

3. "ACTING" AGAINST APARTHEID

1. Dennis Walder, *Athol Fugard,* p. 92; Russell Vandenbroucke, *Truths the Hands Can Touch,* p. 138.

2. Elsa Joubert, "'Immorality Drama': Review of *Statements after an Arrest under the Immorality Act,*" *Rapport* [Johannesburg], 2 April 1972; reprinted and translated [by Josandra Janisch] in *Athol Fugard,* ed. Stephen Gray (Johannesburg: McGraw-Hill, 1982), p. 85.

3. David Coleman, "After 10 Years the Flaws Are Showing," *Natal Mercury* [Durban] 133, no. 36908 (12 October 1984), p. 4.

4. Robert Cushman, "'The Naked Truth': Review of *Statements after an Arrest under the Immorality Act,*" *The Observer* [London], 27 January 1974; reprinted in *Athol Fugard,* ed. Stephen Gray, pp. 87–88.

5. Fugard is actually working a three-way pun in Philander's name. In addition to the idea in the name of philanderer, there is the knowledge for a South African that Philander is a very common, typically coloured name. And then the linguistic root of "philander" is "lover of an other"; of course Philander's love for Frieda is that both in the sense of another person and of a racial other.

6. The adultery and crossing of racial barriers in *Statements* may perhaps be tinged with Fugard's sense of himself. His description of himself as a person of the theatre in an inter-

view with Michael Coveney has obvious similarities with Errol Philander. Fugard says, "I have a fairly adulterous relationship with theatre in South Africa. I work with white actors, I work with black actors. Maybe that's why I feel tired; adultery is not easy! Serpent Players is one of the very meaningful relationships I've had for a long time, a group of black actors in my home town, Port Elizabeth." Michael Coveney, "Challenging the Silence: Athol Fugard Talks to Michael Coveney," *Plays and Players* 21, no. 2 (November 1973): 35.

    7. All quotations from *Statements after an Arrest under the Immorality Act, Sizwe Bansi Is Dead* and *The Island* are from Athol Fugard, *Statements* (Oxford and New York: Oxford University Press, 1974). Parentheses following quotations refer to this edition.

    8. Charles Lyell, *The Principles of Geology,* vol. III (London: John Murray, 1833), p. 385.

    9. John Murray, "Colour-Bar Romance," *To the Point* [Johannesburg] 8, no. 26 (29 June 1976): 46.

    10. Lyell, vol. II, p. 62. The heading does not appear in this edition but does so in later editions such as Charles Lyell, *Principles of Geology,* vol. I (Philadelphia: James Kay, Jun. Y Brother, 1837), p. 525.

    11. Robert Baker-White, "Authority and *Jouissance* in Fugard's *Statements after an Arrest under the Immorality Act,*" in *Text and Performance Quarterly* 12 (1992): 228–244, offers a complex and sensitive discussion of the disjunction in style between the two halves of the play as well as an explanation of how the audience is brought closer in the second half to the dynamics of the play.

    12. Athol Fugard, *Notebooks,* p. 200.

    13. Fugard's rehearsal notes are among the materials on this play housed at Indiana University's Lilly Library (formerly at NELM, acquisition no. 1342/6); *Notebooks,* p. 199.

    14. Baker-White, p. 239.

    15. Dennis Walder, "Crossing Boundaries: The Genesis of the Township Plays," *Twentieth Century Literature* 39, no. 4 (Winter 1993): 417.

    16. A sense of these exercises can be gained from Fugard's published description of *Orestes* and the published text of *The Coat.* Athol Fugard, *Orestes,* in *Theatre One: New South African Drama,* ed. Stephen Gray (Johannesburg: Ad. Donker, 1978), pp. 81–93; and Athol Fugard, *The Coat* (Cape Town: A. A. Balkema, 1971). These acting exercises are discussed in Russell Vandenbroucke, *Truths the Hand Can Touch,* pp. 101–103, 111–114. See also Robert J. Green, "The Drama of Athol Fugard," in *Aspects of South African Literature,* ed. Christopher Heywood (London: Heinemann, 1976), p. 170; and Patrick O'Sheel, "Athol Fugard's 'Poor Theatre,'" *Journal of Commonwealth Literature* 12 (1978): 67–77.

    17. See Brian Crow, with Chris Banfield, *An Introduction to Post-Colonial Theatre* (Cambridge: Cambridge University Press, 1996), pp. 103–108, for a useful discussion of how *Sizwe Bansi Is Dead* emerged from workshop exercises.

    18. Michael Coveney, "Challenging the Silence," p. 35.

    19. Fugard succinctly recounts the genesis of *Sizwe Bansi Is Dead* in "The Art of Theatre VIII: Athol Fugard," ed. Lloyd Richards, *Paris Review* 31, no. 111 (Summer 1989): 148–149. This is the transcript of a public interview of Fugard at the Poetry Center of the 92nd Street YMHA on 13 October 1985. The interview was conducted by Lloyd Richards, the artistic director of the Yale Repertory Theatre.

    20. For the newspaper reading scene, there are, for example, separate notes in Fugard's hand, marked p. 1 and appended to his corrected typescript of the play, that offer alternate headlines to those in the text. These read, "Gathering charges withdrawn. Charges against 25 students. . . . Ag!" and "'Japanese Express in tunnel Horror. 28 killed in train blaze.'. . . . Lucky its in Tokyo . . . 80% would have been my people." See NELM, acquisition no.

1338/12 at Indiana University's Lilly Library. Similarly in the Kani-Ntshona production of the play filmed at the University of Miami, there are references to Richard Nixon. See the video recording of *Sizwe Bansi Is Dead,* produced and directed by Andrew Martin (Chicago: Films Incorporated, c. 1978).

21. For the sake of simplicity, the discussions of *Sizwe Bansi Is Dead* and *The Island* will refer to the plays as Fugard's even though they are very much the joint creations of John Kani, Winston Ntshona, and Athol Fugard.

22. This is not the view of Hilary Seymour in "'Sizwe Bansi Is Dead': A Study of Artistic Ambivalence," *Race and Class* 21 (Winter 1980), 273–289. She takes a very dim view of the play, and in her estimation, Styles encourages "the delusions and self-delusions of the black working class," providing them with fantasies that "serve to maintain a system of economic and racial exploitation" (278). There is also a stimulating discussion of *Sizwe Bansi Is Dead* and Seymour's view in Piniel Viriri Shava, *A People's Voice: Black South African Writing in the Twentieth Century* (London and Athens, Ohio: Zed Books and Ohio University Press, 1989), pp. 132–135.

23. Like Styles's photos, *Sizwe Bansi* records a history that many whites would nowadays like to bury or destroy. In this regard, volumes are spoken in the acerbic remarks of a post-apartheid reviewer commenting on the 1991 Johannesburg revival of *Sizwe Bansi:* "The timing of this particular revival is, however, perfectly wrong. The once and future king of apartheid plays should be in hibernation, basking in its past glory and gathering noble dust for the future. Right now SA is moving into the unknown—giant steps and all that—and theatre should be, and in many cases is, reflecting contemporary concerns. We are looking ahead, and any drama based on the notorious dompas, unless it is jazzed up with a sudden spurt of inspirational flair, is temporarily as dead as mutton." John Michell, "An Untimely Resurrection," *Business Day* [Johannesburg], 9 April 1991, p. 8.

24. John Kani worked in the Port Elizabeth Ford plant, and explains how his experiences there helped him create the auto plant scenes of the play. See Rolf Solberg, *Alternative Theatre in South Africa: Talks with Prime Movers since the 1970s* (Pietermaritzburg, South Africa: Ravan Press, 1999), p. 226. See also Dennis Walder, *Athol Fugard,* p. 84.

25. Martin Orkin effectively reads *Sizwe Bansi Is Dead* in these terms. *Drama and the South African State,* pp. 160–163.

26. When *Sizwe Bansi* played in the Transkei, this remark resulted in John Kani and Winston Ntshona's detention there for several days.

27. Versions of the discussion of *The Island* that follows appeared as "Political Acting and Political Action: Athol Fugard's *The Island,*" *World Literature Written in English* 26 (1986): 245–252, and "The Prison as Theatre and the Theatre as Prison: Athol Fugard's *The Island,*" in J. Redmond, ed., *Themes in Drama,* vol. 9 (Cambridge: Cambridge University Press, 1987), pp. 229–237.

28. Rolf Solberg, *Alternative Theatre in South Africa,* p. 223.

29. Athol Fugard, *The Island,* in *Statements* (Oxford: Oxford University Press, 1974), p. 45. All quotations are from this text. The genesis of *The Island* is described by Russell Vandenbroucke in *Truths the Hands Can Touch,* pp. 126–128.

30. Lloyd Richards, "The Art of Theatre VIII: Athol Fugard," pp. 147–148. This is the transcript of a public interview of Fugard at the Poetry Center of the 92nd Street YMHA on 13 October 1985. The interview was conducted by Lloyd Richards, the artistic director of the Yale Repertory Theatre.

31. Rolf Solberg, *Alternative Theatre in South Africa,* pp. 223–224.

32. Robert Leyshon, "Laughing in the Beginning a Listening at the End: Directing Fu-

gard in Barbados," in *South African Theatre as/and Intervention*, ed. Marcia Blumberg and Dennis Walder (Amsterdam: Rodopi, 1999), p. 78.

33. Russell Vandenbroucke, "Robert Zwelinzima Is Alive," reprinted in *Athol Fugard*, ed. Stephen Gray (Johannesburg: Ad. Donker, 1982), p. 193.

34. See Athol Fugard, *Notebooks*, p. 212.

35. Loren Kruger, *The Drama of South Africa*, p. 157, reminds us, "The reenactment of *Antigone* derived from a performance on Robben Island, with Nelson Mandela as Creon." Errol Durbach provides an excellent discussion of *Antigone* and the Sophoclean tradition in "Sophocles in South Africa: Athol Fugard's *The Island*," *Comparative Drama* 18 (1984): 252–264. See also Deborah D. Foster, "*The Blood Knot* and *The Island*," in *Athol Fugard*, ed. Stephen Gray, pp. 202–217, and an earlier monograph version of that essay under the same title in Occasional Paper no. 8 of the African Studies Program, University of Wisconsin (Madison, 1977). Fugard's use of Sophocles can be usefully compared with the way contemporary South African playwright Guy Butler uses Euripides in his anti-apartheid play *Demea*. See Albert Wertheim, "Euripides in South Africa: *Medea* and *Demea*," *Comparative Drama* 29 (Fall 1995): 334–347.

36. Fugard has also written an acting exercise called *Orestes*, and he draws on Camus for his central idea in *Dimetos*. See also Jerry R. Dickey, "The Artist as Rebel: The Development of Athol Fugard's Dramaturgy and the Influence of Albert Camus" (Ph.D. dissertation, Indiana University, 1987).

37. An extended examination of the relationship between fiction and audience on the one hand and prisons and citizens on the other is given in John Bender's shrewd but (unnecessarily) abstruse study, *Imagining the Penitentiary* (Chicago: University of Chicago Press, 1987). See especially the chapter on "The Aesthetic of Isolation as Social System."

38. Michel Foucault suggests a version of this idea when he writes, "The Panopticon is a royal menagerie; the animal replaced by man, individual distribution by a specific grouping and the king by the machinery of a furtive power." Michel Foucault, *Discipline and Punish: The Birth of the Prison*, trans. Alan Sheridan (New York: Vintage Books, 1977), p. 203.

39. The importance of prisoners' assigning special names to their guards is discussed in Barbara Harlow, *Resistance Literature* (New York and London: Methuen, 1987), p. 128.

40. Athol Fugard, *Notebooks*, p. 209.

41. Athol Fugard, *Notebooks*, p. 212.

42. Albert Camus, *The Myth of Sisyphus and Other Essays*, trans. Justin O'Brien (New York: Alfred A. Knopf, 1969), p. 120. Parentheses following quotations from Camus refer to pages in this edition.

43. See Germaine Brée, *Camus* (New Brunswick, N.J.: Rutgers University Press, 1959), p. 202.

44. Brian Crow, "Athol Fugard," in *Post-Colonial English Drama*, ed. Bruce King (New York: St. Martin's Press, 1992), pp. 157–158.

45. Barbara Harlow, *Resistance Literature*, pp. 127–128.

46. Sophocles, *Antigone*, trans. Elizabeth Wykoff, in *The Complete Greek Tragedies*, ed. David Grene and Richmond Lattimore (Chicago: University of Chicago Press, 1959), vol. 2, ll. 1319–1321.

47. Relevant here is Barbara Harlow's assertion, "In prison memoirs of political detainees, the 'power of writing' is one which seeks to alter the relationships of power which are maintained by coercive, authoritarian systems of state control and domination" (Harlow, p. 133).

48. Sheila Fugard, "Robben Island," in *Threshold* (Johannesburg: Ad. Donker, 1975), p. 45.

49. John Bender, *Imagining the Penitentiary,* p. 228.

50. See my article "The 1995 Grahamstown Festival," *South African Theatre Journal* 10 (May 1996): 94–100.

4. DIMETOS

1. Russell Vandenbroucke, *Truths the Hands Can Touch,* pp. 150–151; Dennis Walder, *Athol Fugard,* pp. 98–99.

2. Fugard does, however, reveal his mental location of Dimetos's house: "We've got a house in the mountains, about four and a half hours' drive from Port Elizabeth. It's where you find Dimetos in the first act. There's nothing there, just rock, and silence." See Mel Gussow, "Profiles: Witness," p. 87.

3. Albert Camus, *Carnets,* vol. 1 (Paris: Gallimard, 1962), p. 163; Albert Camus, *Notebooks: 1935–1942,* trans. Philip Thody (New York: Modern Library, 1965), p. 136.

4. A. Christopher Tucker, "Athol Fugard," *Transatlantic Review* 53/54 (February 1976): 88; Russell Vandenbroucke, *Truths the Hands Can Touch,* p. 149.

5. Richard Whitaker, "Dimoetes to Dimetos: The Evolution of a Myth," *English Studies in Africa* 24 (March 1981): 45–59; Russell Vandenbroucke, *Truths the Hands Can Touch,* pp. 209–212; Dennis Walder, *Athol Fugard,* pp. 96, 100.

6. Dieter Bachmann, "Der hohle Klang der letzten Fragen: Fugards *Dimetos* in Basel," *Frankfurter Allegemeine Zeitung,* 6 November 1980; John Elsom, "The True and False Pilgrim," *The Listener,* 4 September 1975, pp. 311–312; John Elsom, "Atonement," *The Listener,* 2 June 1976, p. 712.

7. Harold Hobson, "A Play to Remember," *Sunday Times* [London], 7 September 1975, p. 37; Derek Wilson, "Powerful Fugard Play Gets Deserved Airing," *Argus* [Cape Town] supplement, 28 December 1981, p. 3.

8. A. Christopher Tucker, "Athol Fugard," pp. 88–89.

9. All quotations from *Dimetos* are taken from Athol Fugard, *Dimetos and Two Early Plays* (Oxford: Oxford University Press, 1977). Page numbers given parenthetically after quotations are from this text.

10. "Athol Fugard: An Interview," in *Momentum: On Recent South African Writing,* ed. M. J. Daymond, J. U. Jacobs, and Margaret Lenta (Pietermaritzburg, South Africa: University of Natal Press, 1984), p. 22. Curiously, the name of the interviewer is not given.

11. In an e-mail communication (22 February 1997) replying to my inquiry about how the opening scene of *Dimetos* was staged, Athol Fugard wrote, "I have a very special relationship with that play. My staging of the opening moments was very simple . . . Lydia, naked, isolated in pool of light, astride a four-legged bench with ropes coming down from the flies . . . one around her waist and the other to tie around the horse (bench). Dimetos was to one side, in the dark, and all we knew of him at first was his powerful and authoritative voice instructing her in the knots she had to tie. When she had done that and the horse was secured, she leapt off the bench and went skipping around the stage in celebration of its rescue while Dimetos coiled up the ropes. The bench itself was NOT hauled away . . . all was left to the imagination of the audience. That bench became the centrepiece of all the scenes that followed . . . a very bare and essential staging, like Valley Song."

12. Athol Fugard, *Dimetos* typescript, at Indiana University's Lilly Library, NELM acquisition number 1342/1. The illustration with the pulleys is placed between pages 28 and 29.

13. Mel Gussow notes, "Though he [Fugard] did not pursue a career as a mechanic, the

school [Port Elizabeth Technical College] gave him a grounding in aptitudes that he retained into adulthood: as an artist, he is mechanically minded." See Mel Gussow, "Profiles: Witness," *New Yorker,* p. 56.

14. These words are added in Fugard's hand to the typescript, and they are included in the later published version of the play.

15. *Dimetos* typescript, p. 2v-3.

16. Fugard's typescript of the play for the London production reads, "[Smells his hands.]," p. 51.

17. Athol Fugard, *Notebooks 1960–1977,* pp. 215–216.

18. *Dimetos* typescript, p. 63v.

19. *Notebooks,* p. 216.

20. *Notebooks,* p. 220.

21. *Dimetos* typescript, p. v.

22. Whitaker, p. 59, note 17, suggests that this is not the print at the Tate Gallery but the one at the National Galleries of Scotland. It seems likely that Fugard may have seen the Blake print there before the play's initial performance at the Edinburgh Festival.

23. *Dimetos* typescript, p. v.

24. *Dimetos* typescript, p. 76.

25. Jerry R. Dickey, "The Artist as Rebel," p. 255.

26. *Dimetos* typescript, p. 75v.

27. *Dimetos* typescript, p. 199.

5. THE DRAMA AS TEACHING AND LEARNING

1. The discussion of *A Lesson from Aloes* is an expanded and much revised version of an earlier essay, "The Lacerations of Apartheid: *A Lesson from Aloes,*" in *Text and Presentation,* ed. Karelisa Hartigan (Lanham, Md.: University Press of America, 1988), pp. 211–221.

2. Russell Vandenbroucke, *Truths the Hand Can Touch,* pp. 168–169.

3. Errol Durbach, "Surviving in Xanadu: Athol Fugard's 'A Lesson from Aloes,'" *Ariel* 20 (January 1989): 5–21.

4. Walder's and Vandenbroucke's remarks are indicative. See Dennis Walder, *Athol Fugard,* pp. 117–118, and Russell Vandenbroucke, *Truths the Hand Can Touch,* p. 175.

5. Unless otherwise noted, all references to the play are from Athol Fugard, *A Lesson from Aloes* (New York: Random House, 1981). Parentheses indicate page numbers in this edition.

6. This is true in the Random House edition and in the version of the play published in *Theater* 11 (1980): 7–23. In the acting edition, however, Piet adds, "Keat's Ode to Autumn." See Athol Fugard, *A Lesson from Aloes* (New York: Samuel French, 1981), p. 8.

7. Margaret Munro, "The Fertility of Despair: Fugard's Bitter Aloes," *Meanjin* 40 (December 1981): 476.

8. Fugard's twenty-seven handwritten pages of notes for this play (dated 25/1/78) are held by Indiana University's Lilly Library (a photocopy at NELM: number 87.25.13.16.8). There is no pagination.

9. Roy Campbell, "The Snake," in *The Collected Poems of Roy Campbell,* vol. 1 (London: The Bodley Head, 1949), pp. 55–58.

10. Gilbert Westacott Reynolds, *The Aloes of South Africa* (1950 reprint, Cape Town and Rotterdam: A. A. Balekma, 1974), p. ix.

11. The impact of Camus on Fugard cannot be underestimated. Although this passage is not cited in Dickey's study, the impact of Camus on Fugard is the subject of Jerry R. Dickey,

"The Artist as Rebel: The Development of Athol Fugard's Dramaturgy and the Influence of Albert Camus" (Ph.D. dissertation, Indiana University, 1987).

12. Michel Foucault's incisive comments on state-controlled discipline are instructive here for understanding the system of state-run discipline that has permitted the confiscation of Gladys's private diary, has left her psychologically incapacitated, and has likewise given rise to suspicions that Piet is a paid informer. See Michel Foucault, *Discipline and Punish*, pp. 213–216.

13. See the text of the Samuel French acting edition of the play, p. 47; the version of the play printed in *Theatre*, p. 18; and in Fugard's typescript at Indiana University's Lilly Library (a photocopy at NELM) for the November 1978 production at the Market Theatre (NELM 87.25.13.10.1), p. 46.

14. This appears only in the Samuel French edition, p. 53.

15. Indeed, Steve's narrative sounds very much like an appropriate case study for Elaine Scarry's comments on the nature of torture in *The Body in Pain* (New York and Oxford: Oxford University Press, 1985), p. 29.

16. Sheila Fugard, *Threshold*, p. 22.

17. Theodore F. Sheckels, Jr., suggests that the "lesson from aloes is survival": *Lion on the Freeway: A Thematic Introduction to Contemporary South African Literature in English* (New York: Peter Lang, 1996), p. 117.

18. Lloyd Richards, "The Art of Theatre VIII: Athol Fugard," pp. 133–134. This is the transcript of a public interview of Fugard at the Poetry Center of the 92nd Street YMHA on 13 October 1985. The interview was conducted by Lloyd Richards, the artistic director of the Yale Repertory Theatre.

19. Sheila Roberts's reading is more skeptical than mine, and is very persuasive. She recognizes that Piet is identified with his hardy aloes, but notes that they are not out in the veld but confined to tins. She writes, "Certainly Piet faces his life of increasing isolation with courage and gentleness and, more importantly, with a stable sense of self and a consequent tolerance of the weakness of others. Yet there is in him an inflexibility too, a stubborn resolution to remain in his own political and social 'jam tin.'" See Sheila Roberts, "'No Lessons Learnt': Reading the Texts of Fugard's *A Lesson from Aloes* and *Master Harold . . . and the Boys*," *English in Africa* 9 (October 1982): 29.

20. Fugard writes in his unpublished notes, "Piet—Sanity in its most meaningful sense."

21. The importance of the balance among the characters is made clear in a marvelously illuminating, little-known Ross Devinish film (originally filmed for BBC 2) about the creation of *A Lesson from Aloes* and Fugard's direction of the Market Street Theatre's production of the play: *A Lesson from Aloes*, 16mm. Double system print, copy owned by Pacific Film Archive at the University of California, Berkeley.

22. Mary Benson, *Athol Fugard and Barney Simon*, p. 115.

23. Athol Fugard, *Notebooks: 1960–1977*, pp. 25–26; and Mary Benson, *Athol Fugard and Barney Simon*, p. 122–124.

24. Errol Durbach, "*'Master Harold' . . . and the Boys*: Athol Fugard and the Psychopathology of Apartheid," *Modern Drama* 30 (March 1987): 505–513. An anonymous paper distributed at the July 1982 Conference on South African Culture and Resistance, held in Gaborone, Botswana, skewered Fugard as a white author for presuming to portray the suffering of non-whites. That paper as well as the autobiographical aspect of the plays is discussed in Rob Amato, "Fugard's Confessional Analysis: 'MASTER HAROLD' . . . and the Boys," in *Momentum*, ed. M. J. Daymond, J. U. Jacobs, and Margaret Lenta (Pietermaritzburg, South Africa: University of Natal Press, 1984), pp. 202–203. Margarete Sei-

denspinner reduces the play to "Fugard's 'atonement' for his own racist attitudes of the past" in *Exploring the Labyrinth: Athol Fugard's Approach to South African Drama* (Essen, West Germany: Die Blaue Eule, 1986), pp. 274–275. See also John O. Jordan, "Life in the Theatre: Autobiography, Politics and Romance in *'Master Harold'... and the Boys*," *Twentieth-Century Literature* 39 (Winter 1993): 461–472.

25. Reviewing the South African premiere of the play in Johannesburg, Joseph Lelyveld wrote that "it left its multiracial audience at the opening night performance here on Tuesday visibly shaken and stunned." "'Master Harold' Stuns Johannesburg Audience," *New York Times*, 24 March 1983, p. 22. Mel Gussow relates similar emotions among the actors rehearsing for the play's premiere in New Haven: "The actors were stunned, and after a few moments of silence, they and the playwright broke into tears." See Mel Gussow, "Profiles: Witness," pp. 47–48.

26. Athol Fugard, *"Master Harold"... and the Boys* (New York: Alfred A. Knopf, 1982). All quotations refer to this edition.

27. See also Russell Vandenbroucke, *Truth the Hands Can Touch*, pp. 186–187.

28. Alisa Solomon, "'Look at History': An Interview with Zakes Mokae," *Theater* 14 (Winter 1982): 28.

29. David E. Hoegberg makes some astute points as he usefully compares the relationship between Hally and Sam with that between Prince Hal and Falstaff in Shakespeare's *Henriad*. See *"Master Harold"* and the Bard: Education and Succession in Fugard and Shakespeare," *Comparative Drama* 29 (Winter 1995–96): 415–425.

30. V. Silvester, *Dancing for the Millions: A Concise Guide to Modern Ballroom Dancing* (London: Oldhams Press, 1950), pp. 11–12.

31. V. Silvester, *Theory and Technique of Ballroom Dancing* (London: Herbert Jenkins, 1948), p. 9.

32. V. Silvester, *Dancing for the Millions*, p. 13.

33. See Albert Wertheim, "Ballroom Dancing, Kites and Politics: Athol Fugard's *Master Harold and the Boys*," *SPAN* 30 (1990): 148–149, and David Hoegberg, "*'Master Harold'* and the Bard," pp. 429–430.

34. An unusually astute essay on dance and *Master Harold* is J. Ellen Gainor's "'A World without Collisions': Ballroom Dance in Athol Fugard's *'MASTER HAROLD'... and the Boys*," in *Bodies of the Text: Dance as Theory, Literature as Dance*, ed. Ellen W. Goellner and Jacqueline Sheila Murphy (New Brunswick, N.J.: Rutgers University Press, 1994), pp. 125–138.

35. Stanley Kauffmann, *Theatre Criticisms* (New York: Performing Arts Journal Publications, 1983), p. 157.

36. Dennis Walder, *Athol Fugard*, p. 124.

37. I make a comparison with a similar South African play in which the author allows the stage to become a scene of physical violence. Albert Wertheim, "Triangles of Race: Athol Fugard's *'Master Harold'... and the Boys* and Paul Slabolepzy's *Saturday Night at the Palace*," *Commonwealth* 20 (Autumn 1997): 86–95.

38. Gandhi and General Smuts, who is invoked in the lines that follow the one quoted, may have been in Fugard's mind because while he was writing *Master Harold*, Fugard was acting the role of Smuts in Richard Attenborough's film *Gandhi* (1982).

39. Heinrich von Staden, "An Interview with Athol Fugard," *Theater* 14 (Winter 1982): 42.

40. Dennis Walder, *Athol Fugard*, p. 124.

41. Russell Vandenbroucke, *Truths the Hands Can Touch*, p. 190.

42. Heinrich von Staden, "An Interview with Athol Fugard," p. 43.

43. V. Silvester, *Dancing for the Millions,* p. 19.

44. Theodore F. Sheckels, Jr., also sees the Sarah Vaughan song as a sign of optimism in *Lion on the Freeway,* p. 176.

45. Sheila Roberts offers a more pessimistic view in her article "'No Lessons Learnt,'" pp. 32–33. She feels that at the play's conclusion there is no reconciliation, and that Hally's turning away is a rejection of Sam and of what he teaches.

6. THE OTHER PROBLEM PLAYS

1. The discussion of *A Road to Mecca* that follows is an expansion of an earlier version: "The Darkness of Bondage, the Freedom of Light: Athol Fugard's 'The Road to Mecca,'" *Essays in Theatre* 5 (November 1986): 15–25.

2. Athol Fugard, *The Road to Mecca* (New York: Theatre Communications Group, 1985). Parentheses following quotations refer to page numbers in this edition.

3. Lloyd Richards, "The Art of Theatre VIII: Athol Fugard," pp. 138–139. This is the transcript of a public interview of Fugard at the Poetry Center of the 92nd Street YMHA on 13 October 1985. The interview was conducted by Lloyd Richards, the artistic director of the Yale Repertory Theatre.

4. Marcia Blumberg's stimulating essay on *The Road to Mecca,* however, argues compellingly that questions of race and gender are very much in the foreground. See Marcia Blumberg, "Women Journeying at the South African Margins: Athol Fugard's *The Road to Mecca,*" *Matatu* 11 (1994): 39–50.

5. Laura Ross, "A Question of Certainties," *American Theatre,* September 1984, p. 6.

6. Gitta Honegger, Rassami Patipatpaopong, and Joel Schechter, "An Interview with Athol Fugard," *Theatre* 16 (Fall/Winter 1984): 35. Elsa Barlow seems modeled on Jill Wonman, who came from Cape Town several times to visit Helen Martins and who corresponded with the artist regularly. A photo of Jill Wonman and Helen Martins appears in Anne Emslie, *The Owl House* (London and New York: Viking Penguin, 1991), p. 18.

7. There are stunning photographs by Roy Zetisky of Helen Martins's house and garden in Anne Emslie, *The Owl House.* For photos of the house's interior, which Fugard hoped to re-create on stage, see the photos on the unnumbered photo pages between pp. 16 and 17.

8. Jerry R. Dickey, "The Artist as Rebel: The Development of Athol Fugard's Dramaturgy and the Influence of Albert Camus," Diss. Indiana University, 1987.

9. Anne Emslie, *The Owl House,* pp. 32–35.

10. Anne Emslie, *The Owl House.* This quotation appears below the remarkable photo of Miss Helen's garden among the series of unnumbered plates between pp. 48 and 49.

11. Mary Benson writes, "I realized she [Helen] was himself." Mary Benson, *Athol Fugard and Barney Simon,* p. 126.

12. Gitta Honegger et al., "An Interview with Athol Fugard," pp. 38–39.

13. Thomas H. Arthur argues that Elsa, Helen, and Patience form an allegorical family based upon mutuality rather than race, in "Looking for My Relatives: The Political Implications of 'Family' in Selected Works of Athol Fugard and August Wilson," *South African Theatre Journal* 6 (September 1992): 5–10. See also Marcia Blumberg, "Women Journeying at the South African Margins," pp. 47–48.

14. Mary Benson, *Athol Fugard and Barney Simon,* p. 25.

15. Seth Mydans, "Soviet Deserter Discovered after 41 Years in a Pigsty," *New York Times,* 27 May 1985, p. 2, cols. 3–4.

16. Russell Vandenbroucke, *Truths the Hands Can Touch*, p. 26. See also Margarete Seidenspinner, *Exploring the Labyrinth*, p. 124. She erroneously calls the play *A Place for Pigs*.

17. For a an overview of what newspaper reviewers and critics have said, see Stephen Gray, *File on Fugard* (London: Methuen, 1991), pp. 64–67.

18. Athol Fugard, *Cousins*, p. 89. Typical of the attitude about which Fugard complains is exemplified by Michael Chapman, "The Liberated Zone: The Possibilities of Imaginative Expression in a State of Emergency," *English Academy Review* [Johannesburg] 5 (1988), pp. 34–35. Even a positive and sensitive review of the Cape Town production takes the stance of defending Fugard from other reviewers, asserting that Fugard has "been unnecessarily slammed by some overseas critics" for writing a play not about South Africa. See Marianne Thamm, "Fugard Breaks Free with New Captive Drama," *Cape Times*, 7 April 1987, p. 21.

19. Stephen Gray, "'Between Me and My Country': Fugard's 'My Children! My Africa!' at the Market Theatre, Johannesburg," *New Theatre Quarterly* 6 (February 1990): 25.

20. I obviously differ here from the interpretation of Jeanne Colleran, "*A Place with the Pigs:* Athol Fugard's Afrikaner Parable," *Modern Drama* 33 (1990), pp. 82–92. Colleran's intelligent piece sees the play as *specifically* about Fugard's attempt to deal with his disconcerting position as an Afrikaner whose anti-apartheid views caused him to be seen by whites on the one hand as "a traitor in the laager" and on the other hand by blacks "as a self-appointed and presumptuous spokesman." I do not think the play has any such specific application in mind. It is not *A Lesson from Aloes* replayed as a parable.

21. Athol Fugard, *A Place with the Pigs: Rehearsal room draft [third draft.]*, Indiana University's Lilly Library (photocopy at NELM acquisition no. 97.5.3).

22. Gabrielle Cody and Joel Schechter, "A Interview with Athol Fugard," *Theater* 19 (Fall/Winter 1987): 70.

23. Athol Fugard, *Cousins*, p. 89.

24. Athol Fugard, "Some Problems of a Playwright from South Africa," *Twentieth Century Literature* 39 (1993): 388. See also Lloyd Richards, "The Art of Theatre VIII: Athol Fugard," p. 144. This is the transcript of a public interview of Fugard at the Poetry Center of the 92nd Street YMHA on 13 October 1985. The interview was conducted by Lloyd Richards, the artistic director of the Yale Repertory Theatre.

25. Cody and Schechter, "An Interview with Athol Fugard," p. 72.

26. Athol Fugard, "Some Problems of a Playwright from South Africa," p. 388.

27. Susan Hilferty, "Realizing Fugard," *Twentieth Century Literature* 39 (1993): 481.

28. In the Cody and Schechter interview, pp. 71–72, Fugard comments on the highly comic and Chaplinesque quality of the play.

29. Hilferty, "Realizing Fugard," p. 481.

30. All quotations from *A Place with the Pigs* are from Athol Fugard, *Playland and A Place with the Pigs* (New York: Theatre Communications Group, 1993). Parentheses following quotations refer to this edition.

31. Cody and Schechter, "An Interview with Athol Fugard," p. 70.

32. Athol Fugard, *A Place with the Pigs: Rehearsal room draft [third draft.]*, p. 11.

33. Athol Fugard, *A Place with the Pigs: Rehearsal room draft [third draft.]*, p. 23v.

34. Vandenbroucke notes Fugard's interest in Sartre, *Truths the Hands Can Touch*, p. 5.

35. A photograph of a bearded Fugard playing the comically cross-dressed Pavel appears in the playtext published in *Theater* 19 (Fall/Winter 1987): 62. That photo also shows the graffiti on the pigsty walls.

36. Fugard acknowledges O'Neill as one of the major influences on his development as a playwright. See *Cousins*, p. 49.

7. WRITING TO RIGHT

1. Nowadays, Fugard delights in that audience befuddlement. See Fugard's televised interview, "A Tribute to Athol Fugard," SATV, 10 June 1992.

2. Mary Benson, *Athol Fugard and Barney Simon*, p. 134.

3. In Paul Allen, "Interview with Athol Fugard," *New Statesman and Nation* 3, no. 17 (7 September 1990): 38, Fugard reveals that the play "was inspired by actual political characters. The central provocation was a new item on the back pages of my local Port Elizabeth newspaper, reporting the death by way of necklacing of a school teacher, a man who had stayed at his desk in spite of a call for a boycott of his school and all classes."

4. All quotations from the play are from the text printed in Athol Fugard, *My Children! My Africa! and Selected Shorter Plays*, ed. Stephen Gray (Johannesburg: Witwatersrand University Press, 1990). Numbers in parentheses indicate page numbers in this edition.

5. See Stephen Gray, "'Between Me and My Country': Fugard's 'My Children! My Africa!' at the Market Theatre, Johannesburg."

6. Richard Hornby, "Review," *Hudson Review* 45, no. 1 (1990): 126, reprinted in *Mad about Theatre* (New York: Applause, 1996), p. 118.

7. I differ here from Nicholas Visser, who argues that "[t]he view that words are the only weapons in social and political conflict clearly lies close to the center of Fugard's thinking." See "Drama and Politics in a State of Emergency: Athol Fugard's *My Children! My Africa!*," *Twentieth Century Literature* 39 (1993): 492.

8. Richard Hornby remembers that the audience gasped at this dramatic and symbolic moment. Hornby, "Review," in *Hudson Review*, p. 127, and *Mad about Theatre*, p. 118.

9. Visser, "Drama and Politics in a State of Emergency," pp. 486, 493, and 494.

10. Jeanne Colleran, "Athol Fugard and the Problematics of the Liberal Critique," *Modern Drama* 38 (1995): 394.

11. Athol Fugard, *Playland . . . and Other Words* (Johannesburg: Witwatersrand University Press, 1992), p. 66.

12. Mel Gussow, "Profiles: Witness," p. 48.

13. Athol Fugard, *Cousins*, p. 30. Mary Benson also relates that Fugard took his daughter, Lisa, to Playland, where he had seen a black attendant from whom the character of Martinus springs: *Athol Fugard and Barney Simon*, p. 140.

14. Myles Holloway, "*Playland:* Fugard's Liberalism," *UNISA English Studies* 31 (April 1993): 38.

15. Mannie Manim, "Producing Fugard," in Athol Fugard, *Playland . . . and Other Words* (Johannesburg: Witwatersrand University Press, 1992), pp. xiii–xiv.

16. Jeanne Colleran, "Athol Fugard and the Problematics of the Liberal Critique," *Modern Drama* 38 (1995): 393, 402.

17. The tensions between Fugard's partisans and detractors remarkably foreshadow the tensions that continue in assessing what "reconciliation" can mean as South Africa's post-apartheid Truth and Reconciliation Commission carries out its tasks. See Antjie Krog, *The Country of My Skull: Guilt, Sorrow, and the Limits of Forgiveness in the New South Africa* (New York: Random House, 1998), pp. 142–149.

18. Athol Fugard, in his introduction to Emily Mann, *Testimonies: Four Plays* (New York: Theatre Communications Group, 1997), p. xi.

19. In the original typescript for *Playland,* the character of Gideon is named Vincent. Athol Fugard, *Playland,* Indiana University's Lilly Library (photocopy at NELM, acquisition no. 96.32.2).

20. In the South African original edition stage directions, Fugard called for the two to walk on. But in the American edition and in what seems like a telling revision, he calls for Gideon to *saunter* on. Athol Fugard, *Playland . . . and Other Words*, pp. 8–9, and Athol Fugard, *Playland and A Place with the Pigs* (New York: Theatre Communications Group, 1993), p. 5. All quotations and page references are from the latter edition.

21. An entry in Fugard's 1990 additions to his *Notebooks* reads, "Useful comparison with the innocence of the two brothers in *The Blood Knot*. Morrie and Zach face the *threat* of violence. Martinus and Gideon live with the *consequences* of violence . . . which in a sense is the story of South Africa during the 35 years of my writing career." See Athol Fugard, "Recent Notebook Entries," *Twentieth Century Literature* 39 (Winter 1993): 534. The connection between these two plays is also noticed by Mary Benson, *Athol Fugard and Barney Simon*, p. 141.

22. The title of the song is not in the published playscript, but Fugard handwrites it into the typescript, p. 23.

23. For a discussion of violence in Slabolepzy's play, see Albert Wertheim, "Triangles of Race: Athol Fugard's *'Master Harold' . . . and the Boys* and Paul Slabolepzy's *Saturday Night at the Palace*."

24. Fugard points out "the huge significance" of this nameless black mother in his "Recent Notebook Entries," p. 533.

25. Samuel Beckett, *Waiting for Godot* (New York: Grove Press, 1954), p. 51.

26. Fugard, "Recent Notebook Entries," p. 527.

27. Benson, *Athol Fugard and Barney Simon*, p. 141, and Rolf Solberg's interview with Mannie Manim in Rolf Solberg, *Alternative Theatre in South Africa*, p. 255.

28. Fugard, "Recent Notebook Entries," p. 536. For the text of Wilfred Owen's "Strange Meeting," see Wilfred Owen, *The War Poems*, ed. Jon Stallworthy (London: Chatto & Windus, 1994), pp. 35–36.

29. Athol Fugard, *Plays One* (London: Faber and Faber, 1998). pp. vii–viii.

30. Benson, *Athol Fugard and Barney Simon*, p. 141.

8. WHERE DO WE, WHERE DO I, GO FROM HERE?

1. Adrienne Sichel, "Fugard's Novel 'Recital'," *The Star* [Johannesburg], 14 June 1994, p. 10, and Rebecca Waddell, "How It Came Together," in Athol Fugard, *My Life and Valley Song* (Johannesburg and London: Hodder & Stoughton and Witwatersrand University Press, 1996), p. xii.

2. See copy of the program for *My Life* held by the National English Literary Museum (NELM) in Grahamstown.

3. "The Genesis of *My Life*," in Athol Fugard, *My Life and Valley Song*, pp. ix–x.

4. The five girls tell something of the process as they perceive it in their interview with Veronica Bowker and Mary West, "An Interview with the Cast of *My Life*, 20 August 1994," *Current Writing: Text and Reception in Southern Africa* 7 (1995): 54–59.

5. Fugard deposited a copy of a text (as opposed to *the* text) of *My Life* at NELM. It is now at Indiana University's Lilly Library. NELM holds a photocopy. The "frozen" text has been published in Athol Fugard, *My Life and Valley Song* (London and Johannesburg: Hodder & Stoughton and Witwatersrand University Press, 1996).

6. See Russell Vandenbroucke, *Truths the Hand Can Touch*, pp. 116–118, 126–127.

7. Adrienne Sichel, "Confessions of a Passionate Patriot," *The Star*, 21 June 1994, p. 9. See also Veronica Bowker, "Fugard's Experimentation in *My Life:* The Practice of Repre-

sentation and the Representation of Practice under Scrutiny," *Current Writing: Text and Reception in Southern Africa* 7 (1995): 49.

8. At the 1995 National Arts Festival in Grahamstown, a year after the opening of *My Life*, Kani and Ntshona performed in the twentieth anniversary production of *The Island*. They did so in a post-apartheid South Africa and to an audience that saw the play as a document from the recently troubled but nonetheless concluded past. In 2000, they performed a twenty-fifth anniversary revival in London.

9. Mary Jordan, "Review: *My Life*," *Business Day* [Johannesburg], 22 July 1994, p. 27.

10. Veronica Bowker, "Fugard's Experimentation in *My Life*," pp. 48–53.

11. Athol Fugard, "The Genesis of *My Life*," p. vii.

12. "The Genesis of *My Life*," p. viii.

13. Mary Benson, *Athol Fugard and Barney Simon*, p. 141.

14. The fax was sent on 6 August 1994 (a month after the Grahamstown opening) by Mary Slack, Rebecca Waddell's mother, to an unknown recipient, perhaps to Fugard himself, who deposited the fax at NELM. The original is now at Indiana University's Lilly Library. A photocopy is at NELM.

15. Ibid., p. 1.

16. See the article in Afrikaans on Waddell and her grandfather, Barrie Hough, "Praat nie met my van geld, sê Harry O-kleinkind," *Rapport* (Johannesburg), 24 July 1994, p. 12.

17. Rebecca Waddell, "How It Came Together," p. xv.

18. Russell Vandenbroucke, *Truths the Hands Can Touch*, pp. 47–48.

19. Mark Gevisser astutely writes, "[T]he voices of the young women are theirs and theirs alone; not even Fugard could capture so perfectly that querulous adolescent mix of bravado and timidity, of awakening and romance. If these were Fugard's own words, he would have excised the banality that makes them so charming and replaced them with his own acute and elegant poetic formulations." See "Truth and Consequences in Post-Apartheid Theatre," *Theatre* 25 (1995): 13.

20. Rolf Solberg, *Alternative Theatre in South Africa*, p. 256.

21. See The Civic Theatre playbill, held by the National English Literary Museum in Grahamstown.

22. This quotation is taken from the videotape, held by NELM, of the Grahamstown performance. A slightly different version appears in Fugard, *My Life and Valley Song*, p. 29.

23. In her shrewd essay, Marcia Blumberg argues that "*Valley Song* is situated on the threshold within the space of the in-between: between interregnum and the so-called post-apartheid era, between decaying structures of oppression and the uncertainty of a fledgling democracy, between the stifling entrapment of old ways and the energy and enthusiasm of youth." "Negotiating the In-Between: Fugard's *Valley Song*," *Journal of Literary Studies* 12 (December 1996): 456–469. In other ways, Dennis Walder sees *Valley Song* as "a new move in the acting-out of a personal history tied up with the national history in profound and complex ways." See "Questions from a White Man Who Listens: The Voices of *Valley Song*," in Marcia Blumberg and Dennis Walder, eds., *South African Theatre as/and Intervention* (Amsterdam: Rodopi, 1999), pp. 101–112.

24. Patrick Pacheco, "His 'Song' of Hope," *Los Angeles Times*, 26 December 1995, p. F1.

25. The simplicity of Fugard's play is misunderstood by John Simon, who asserts that Fugard's "simpleminded metaphor is worked into the ground, so to speak." Simon, who seems more intent upon sparking his own acerbic repartee than on understanding Fugard's play, reveals an important short-sightedness that prevents him and perhaps others, who wish Fu-

gard to take a skeptical position about the new South Africa, from seeing why in *Valley Song* Fugard has written the kind of play he has. See "Falling Apartheid," *New York,* 9 January 1996, p. 48. Simon is by no means alone, for Toby Silverman Zinman likewise sees the play as "preachy and saccharine, providing little to look at and less to listen to." See *"Valley Song: Fugard Plays It Again,"* in *South African Theatre as/and Intervention,* ed. Marcia Blumberg and Dennis Walder (Amsterdam: Rodopi, 1999), pp. 93–100.

26. The text referred to is the American text, Athol Fugard, *Valley Song* (New York: Theatre Communications Group, 1996). This text has Fugard's opening remarks expanded and contextualized for American audiences. Readers should be aware of two other texts in which the first moments, geared for British and South African audiences, of the play are slightly different and more spare. See Athol Fugard, *Valley Song* (London: Faber & Faber, 1996), and Athol Fugard, *My Life and Valley Song* (Johannesburg: Witwatersrand University Press and Hodder & Stoughton, 1996).

27. Fugard is quoted in Douglas J. Keating, "Playwright Finds His Way in a New South Africa," *Philadelphia Inquirer,* Sunday, 22 October 1995, p. G1. Fugard makes a similar statement in a London interview with Matt Wolf, "Write Angles," *Time Out* (31 January– 7 February 1996), p. 20.

28. While Fugard was still writing *Valley Song,* he was quoted in *The New York Times* as saying that Veronica and her father, "could be construed as metaphors for the reality we face at the moment: a past we've got to turn our back on and a future we've got to embrace. We're pulling off a political miracle here . . . We're going from the last great odious, racist society of the 20th century overnight into what's turning into a genuine democracy." Donald G. McNeil, Jr., "On Stage, and Off," *New York Times,* 13 January 1995, p. B2.

29. Vincent Canby, "Athol Fugard's Salute to the New South Africa," *New York Times,* 9 May 1996, p. B3.

30. A discussion of *Valley Song* as Fugard's postcolonial play of racial reconciliations can be found in Kristina Stanley, "Athol Fugard's Theatre of Intervention and Reconciliation in *Valley Song,"* in *South African Theatre as/and Intervention,* ed. Marcia Blumberg and Dennis Walder (Amsterdam: Rodopi, 1999), pp. 85–91.

31. In a stimulating essay, Jeanne Colleran puts a very different spin on the play from mine, for she sees *Valley Song* as (willfully?) ignorant of the material circumstances that have created Buks's life, patriarchal, and guilty of "re-inscription, despite its concern for the emergence of a new South Africa, of the liberal/colonialist paradigm." See "Lessons from a Fair Country," in *South African Theatre as/and Intervention,* ed. Marcia Blumberg and Dennis Walder (Amsterdam: Rodopi, 1999), pp. 113–123.

32. It is appropriate that the British and South African editions of the play in the final stage direction above have "Devil" where the American edition has "Author."

33. Athol Fugard, "Caught in a Typhoon in the Pacific," undated publication, presumably *Port Elizabeth Evening Post,* c. July 1954. See also Athol Fugard, "Life aboard a Tramp," *Port Elizabeth Evening Post,* 3 July 1954.

34. David Henry Hwang, *Golden Child* (New York: Theatre Communications Group, 1998).

35. Typescript for *"Master Harold" . . . and the Boys* (Indiana University's Lilly Library; photocopy at NELM, acquisition no. 87.25.14.3).

36. In a *New York Times* article about Fugard and *The Captain's Tiger,* reviewer and Fugard aficionado Mel Gussow writes, "His father's story is one of Mr. Fugard's many unkept appointments, a play he has yet to write." Mel Gussow, "From a Discarded Novel to Fugard's New Play," *The New York Times,* 5 January 1999, p. B3.

37. Eugene O'Neill, *Long Day's Journey into Night* (New Haven, Conn.: Yale University Press, 1956), p. 7.

38. Laurie Winer, "Athol Fugard: The Writer as 'Tiger' Cub," *Los Angeles Times,* 14 July 1998, p. F8; Andrew Wilson, "Voyage Back to the Start," *Johannesburg Mail & Guardian,* 21 August 1997, p. 4; Peter Marks, "A Rite of Passage, with Excess Baggage," *New York Times,* 20 January 1999, p. B4; Raeford Daniel, "Fugard in Retrospect," *The Citizen* [Johannesburg], 7 August 1997, p. 25.

39. John Simon, "'The Captain's Tiger' Has No Bite," *New York Magazine,* 1 February 1999.

40. Fugard himself has some awareness of this. In an interview with Simon Lewis, editor of the journal *Illuminations,* Fugard explained that he has abandoned overtly political theatre, saying, "I'm certainly not likely to go down that path again. I just can't. My direction has changed as a writer. . . ." See "Athol Fugard: An Interview," *Illuminations,* Summer 1998, p. 81.

41. David Richards, "A 66-Year-Old White Dramatist Breaks Free of Apartheid," *Washington Post,* 13 September 1998, p. G1.

42. Elliot Makhaya, "Fugard Finishes New Play," *The Sowetan,* 1 May 1997, p. 16.

43. Athol Fugard, *The Captain's Tiger.* The quotations cited come from an unpublished typescript Mr. Fugard sent to me via electronic mail on 27 May 1997. It varies from the published edition. When pertinent, this edition will be quoted and will be cited in parentheses as "ms." with page numbers. Otherwise, numbers in parentheses refer to the published edition of the play: Athol Fugard, *The Captain's Tiger* (Johannesburg: Witwatersrand University Press, 1997). A copy of that typescript received via e-mail is on deposit at Indiana University's Lilly Library.

44. The actual photograph prefaces the published text, p. v.

45. In his *New Yorker* profile of Fugard, written sixteen years prior to *The Captain's Tiger,* Mel Gussow recounts what Fugard related to Gussow about his time on the SS *Graigaur.* According to that article, the donkeyman was Sudanese and not, as in the play, Kenyan. One can only speculate why Fugard has taken authorial license to make the donkeyman more essentially African. See Mel Gussow, "Profiles: Witness,"

46. This speech appears in the manuscript, p. 116, but is very much like the already quoted speech in the manuscript, which occurs early in that text, pp. 12–13 . Obviously in the published and performance text, Fugard eliminated the first portrait of his mother scarred by her life to heighten the dramatic effect of the play's climax.

47. Gayatri Chakravorty Spivak, "Can the Subaltern Speak?" in *Marxism and the Interpretation of Culture,* ed. C. Nelson and L. Grossberg (Basingstoke: Macmillan Education, 1988), pp. 271–313.

48. It seems likely that Fugard will continue his examination of art and the creative artist, for, in a personal communication to me, he writes, "As for myself dear friend, a rough working draft of a new opus is now nearing completion. Title: 'The Abbess. Suggested by an episode in the life of Hildegard of Bingen'" (e-mail 16 January 2000). One wonders whether "The Abbess" will have affinities to that other quasi-religious play, *The Road to Mecca.*

WORKS CITED

Allen, Paul. "Interview with Athol Fugard." *New Statesman and Nation* 3, no. 17 (7 September 1990).

Amato, Rob. "Fugard's Confessional Analysis: 'MASTER HAROLD' . . . and the Boys." In *Momentum: On Recent South African Writing*, edited by M. J. Daymond, J. U. Jacobs, and Margaret Lenta, pp. 198–214. Pietermaritzburg, South Africa: University of Natal Press, 1984.

Arthur, Thomas H. "Looking for My Relatives: The Political Implications of 'Family' in Selected Works of Athol Fugard and August Wilson." *South African Theatre Journal* 6 (September 1992): 5–10.

Bachmann, Dieter. "Der hohle Klang der letzten Fragen: Fugards *Dimetos* in Basel." *Frankfurter Allgemeine Zeitung*, 6 November 1980.

Baker-White, Robert. "Authority and *Jouissance* in Fugard's *Statements after an Arrest under the Immorality Act*." *Text and Performance Quarterly* 12 (1992): 228–244.

Beckett, Samuel. *Waiting for Godot*. New York: Grove Press, 1954.

Bender, John. *Imagining the Penitentiary*. Chicago: University of Chicago Press, 1987.

Benson, Mary. *Athol Fugard and Barney Simon: Bare Stage, a Few Props, Great Theatre*. Randburg, South Africa: Ravan Press, 1997.

Blumberg, Marcia. "Languages of Violence: Fugard's *Boesman and Lena*." In *Violence in Drama*, edited by James Redmond. Cambridge: Cambridge University Press, 1991.

———. "Negotiating the In-Between: Fugard's *Valley Song*." *Journal of Literary Studies* 12 (December 1996): 456–469.

———. "Re-Staging Resistance, Re-Viewing Women: 1990s Productions of Fugard's *Hello and Goodbye* and *Boesman and Lena*." In *Staging Resistance: Essays on Political Theatre*, edited by Jeanne Colleran and Jenny S. Spencer. Ann Arbor: University of Michigan Press, 1998.

———. "Women Journeying at the South African Margins: Athol Fugard's *The Road to Mecca*." *Matatu* 11 (1994): 39–50.

Blumberg, Marcia, and Dennis Walder, eds. *South African Theatre as/and Intervention*. Amsterdam: Rodopi, 1999.

Bowker, Veronica. "Fugard's Experimentation in *My Life:* The Practice of Representation and the Representation of Practice under Scrutiny." *Current Writing: Text and Reception in Southern Africa* 7 (1995): 47–53.

Bowker, Veronica, and Mary West. "An Interview with the Cast of *My Life,* 20 August 1994." *Current Writing: Text and Reception in Southern Africa* 7 (1995): 54–59.

Brée, Germaine. *Camus.* New Brunswick, N.J.: Rutgers University Press, 1959.

Brook, Peter. *The Empty Space.* Harmondsworth, England: Penguin Books, 1972.

Campbell, Roy. "The Snake." In *The Collected Poems of Roy Campbell,* vol. 1. London: The Bodley Head, 1949.

Camus, Albert. *Carnets.* Vol. 1. Paris: Gallimard, 1962.

———. *The Myth of Sisyphus and Other Essays.* Translated by Justin O'Brien. New York: Alfred A. Knopf, 1969.

———. *Notebooks: 1935–1942.* Translated by Philip Thody. New York: Modern Library, 1965.

Canby, Vincent. "Athol Fugard's Salute to the New South Africa." *New York Times,* 9 May 1996.

Chapman, Michael. "The Liberated Zone: The Possibilities of Imaginative Expression in a State of Emergency." *English Academy Review* [Johannesburg] 5 (1988).

Cody, Gabrielle, and Joel Schechter. "An Interview with Athol Fugard." *Theater* 19 (Fall / Winter 1987): 70–72.

Coleman, David. "After 10 Years the Flaws Are Showing." *Natal Mercury* [Durban] 133, no. 36908 (12 October 1984).

Colleran, Jeanne. "*A Place with the Pigs:* Athol Fugard's Afrikaner Parable." *Modern Drama* 33 (1990): 82–92.

———. "Athol Fugard and the Problematics of the Liberal Critique." *Modern Drama* 38 (1995): 389–407.

———. "Lessons from a Fair Country." In *South African Theatre as/and Intervention,* ed. Marcia Blumberg and Dennis Walder, pp. 113–123. Amsterdam: Rodopi, 1999.

Colleran, Jeanne, and Jenny S. Spencer, eds. *Staging Resistance: Essays on Political Theatre.* Ann Arbor: University of Michigan Press, 1998.

Coveney, Michael. "Challenging the Silence: Athol Fugard Talks to Michael Coveney." *Plays and Players* 21, no. 2 (November 1973): 34–37.

Crow, Brian. "Athol Fugard." In *Post-Colonial English Drama,* edited by Bruce King. New York: St. Martin's Press, 1992.

Crow, Brian. "'A Truly Living Moment': Acting and the *Statements* Plays." In *Theatre and Change in South Africa,* edited by Geoffrey V. Davis and Anne Fuchs, pp. 13–24. Amsterdam: Harwood Publishers, 1996).

Crow, Brian, with Chris Banfield. *An Introduction to Post-Colonial Theatre.* Cambridge: Cambridge University Press, 1996.

Cushman, Robert. "'The Naked Truth': Review of *Statements after an Arrest under the Immorality Act.*" *The Observer* [London], 27 January 1974. Reprinted in *Athol Fugard,* edited by Stephen Gray, pp. 87–88 (Johannesburg: McGraw-Hill, 1982).

Daniel, Raeford. "Fugard in Retrospect." *The Citizen* [Johannesburg], 7 August 1997.

Davis, Geoffrey V., and Anne Fuchs, eds. *Theatre and Change in South Africa.* Amsterdam: Harwood Publishers, 1996.

Daymond, M. J., J. U. Jacobs, and Margaret Lenta, eds. *Momentum: On Recent South African Writing.* Pietermaritzburg, South Africa: University of Natal Press, 1984.

Dickey, Jerry R. "The Artist as Rebel: The Development of Athol Fugard's Dramaturgy and the Influence of Albert Camus." Ph.D. dissertation, Indiana University, 1987.

Durbach, Errol. "*'Master Harold' . . . and the Boys:* Athol Fugard and the Psychopathology of Apartheid." *Modern Drama* 30 (March 1987): 505–513.

———. ". . . No Time for Apartheid: Dancing Free of the System in Athol Fugard's *Boesman and Lena.*" In *South African Theatre as/and Intervention,* edited by Marcia Blumberg and Dennis Walder, pp. 61–74. Amsterdam: Rodopi, 1999.

———. "Sophocles in South Africa: Athol Fugard's *The Island.*" *Comparative Drama* 18 (1984): 252–264.

———. "Surviving in Xanadu: Athol Fugard's 'A Lesson from Aloes.'" *Ariel* 20 (January 1989): 5–21.

Elderfield, John, ed. *Henri Matisse: A Retrospective.* New York: Museum of Modern Art, 1992.

Elsom, John. "Atonement." *The Listener,* 2 June 1976.

———. "The True and False Pilgrim." *The Listener,* 4 September 1975.

Emslie, Anne. *The Owl House.* London and New York: Viking Penguin, 1991.

Foucault, Michel. *Discipline and Punish: The Birth of the Prison.* Translated by Alan Sheridan. New York: Vintage Books, 1977.

Foster, Deborah D. "*The Blood Knot* and *The Island.*" In *Athol Fugard,* edited by Stephen Gray, pp. 202–217. Johannesburg: McGraw-Hill, 1982.

———. "*The Blood Knot* and *The Island.*" Occasional Paper no. 8 of the African Studies Program, University of Wisconsin, Madison, 1977.

Fugard, Athol. *Boesman and Lena and Other Plays.* Oxford: Oxford University Press, 1978.

———. *The Captain's Tiger.* Johannesburg: Witwatersrand University Press, 1997.

———. "Caught in a Typhoon in the Pacific." Undated publication, presumably *Port Elizabeth Evening Post,* c. July 1954.

———. *The Coat.* Cape Town: A. A. Balkema, 1971.

———. *Cousins: A Memoir.* Johannesburg: Witwatersrand University Press, 1994.

———. *Dimetos and Two Early Plays.* Oxford: Oxford University Press, 1977.

———. *A Lesson from Aloes.* New York: Random House, 1981.

———. *A Lesson from Aloes* in *Theater* 11 (1980): 7–23.

———. *A Lesson from Aloes.* New York: Samuel French, 1981.

———. "Life aboard a Tramp." *Port Elizabeth Evening Post,* 3 July 1954.

———. *"Master Harold" . . . and the Boys.* New York: Alfred A. Knopf, 1982.

———. *My Children! My Africa! and Selected Shorter Plays.* Edited by Stephen Gray. Johannesburg: Witwatersrand University Press, 1990.

———. *My Life and Valley Song.* Johannesburg and London: Hodder & Stoughton and Witwatersrand University Press, 1996.

———. *Notebooks: 1960–1977.* Edited by Mary Benson. Johannesburg: Ad. Donker, 1983.

———. *Orestes.* In *Theatre One: New South African Drama,* edited by Stephen Gray, pp. 81–93. Johannesburg: Ad. Donker, 1978.

———. *Playland and a Place with the Pigs.* New York: Theatre Communications Group, 1993.

———. *Playland . . . and Other Words.* Johannesburg: Witwatersrand University Press, 1992.

———. *Plays One.* London: Faber and Faber, 1998.

———. "Recent Notebook Entries." *Twentieth Century Literature* 39 (Winter 1993): 526–536.

———. *The Road to Mecca.* New York: Theatre Communications Group, 1985.

———. "Some Problems of a Playwright from South Africa." *Twentieth Century Literature* 39 (Winter 1993): 381–393.

———. *Statements.* Oxford: Oxford University Press, 1974.

————. *Valley Song.* New York: Theatre Communications Group, 1996.

————. *Valley Song.* London: Faber & Faber, 1996.

Fugard, Sheila. "The Apprenticeship Years." *Twentieth Century Literature* 39 (Winter 1993): 394–408.

————. *Threshold.* Johannesburg: Ad. Donker, 1975.

Gainor, J. Ellen. "'A World without Collisions': Ballroom Dance in Athol Fugard's 'MASTER HAROLD' . . . and the Boys." In *Bodies of the Text: Dance as Theory, Literature as Dance,* edited by Ellen W. Goellner and Jacqueline Sheila Murphy, pp. 125–138. New Brunswick, N.J.: Rutgers University Press, 1994.

Gevisser, Mark. "Truth and Consequences in Post-Apartheid Theatre." *Theatre* 25 (1995): 8–18.

Gray, Stephen. "'Between Me and My Country': Fugard's 'My Children! My Africa!' at the Market Theatre, Johannesburg." *New Theatre Quarterly* 6 (February 1990): 25–30.

————. *File on Fugard.* London: Methuen, 1991.

Gray, Stephen, ed. *Athol Fugard.* Johannesburg: McGraw-Hill, 1982.

Green, R. J. "Athol Fugard's *Hello and Goodbye.*" *Modern Drama* 13 (September 1970): 139–155.

————. "South Africa's Plague: One View of *The Blood Knot.*" *Modern Drama* 12 (February 1970): 331–345.

Green, Robert J. "The Drama of Athol Fugard." In *Aspects of South African Literature,* edited by Christopher Heywood. London: Heinemann, 1976.

Gussow, Mel. "From a Discarded Novel to Fugard's New Play." *New York Times,* 5 January 1999.

————. "Fugard's Humanism." *New York Times,* 2 February 1977. Reprinted in *Athol Fugard,* edited by Stephen Gray, pp. 94–95 (Johannesburg: McGraw-Hill, 1982).

————. "Profiles: Witness." *New Yorker,* 20 December 1982, pp. 47–94.

Harlow, Barbara. *Resistance Literature.* New York and London: Methuen, 1987.

Hauptfleisch, Temple, Wilma Viljoen, and Céleste van Greunen, eds. *Athol Fugard: A Source Guide.* Johannesburg: Ad. Donker, 1982.

Heywood, Christopher, ed. *Aspects of South African Literature.* London: Heinemann, 1976.

Hilferty, Susan. "Realizing Fugard." *Twentieth Century Literature* 39 (Winter 1993): 479–485.

Hobson, Harold. "A Play to Remember." *The Sunday Times* [London], 7 September 1975.

Hoegberg, David E. "*Master Harold*' and the Bard: Education and Succession in Fugard and Shakespeare." *Comparative Drama* 29 (Winter 1995–96): 415–425.

Holloway, Myles. "*Playland:* Fugard's Liberalism." *UNISA English Studies* 31 (April 1993): 36–42.

Honegger, Gitta, Rassami Patipatpaopong, and Joel Schechter. "An Interview with Athol Fugard." *Theatre* 16 (Fall / Winter 1984): 33–39.

Hornby, Richard. *Mad about Theatre.* New York: Applause, 1996.

————. "Review." *Hudson Review* 45, no. 1 (1990).

Hough, Barrie. "Praat ni met my van geld, sê Harry O-kleindind." *Rapport* [Johannesburg], 24 July 1994, p. 12.

Hwang, David Henry. *Golden Child.* New York: Theatre Communications Group, 1998.

J.D.F.J. "Athol Fugard Talks about His Play." *Pretoria News* (8 December 1961).

Jordan, John O. "Life in the Theatre: Autobiography, Politics and Romance in 'Master Harold' . . . and the Boys." *Twentieth-Century Literature* 39 (Winter 1993): 461–472.

Jordan, Mary. "Review: *My Life.*" *Business Day* [Johannesburg], 22 July 1994, p. 27.

Joubert, Elsa. "'Immorality Drama': Review of *Statements after an Arrest under the Immorality Act.*" *Rapport* [Johannesburg], 2 April 1972. Translated by Josandra Janisch and reprinted in *Athol Fugard,* edited by Stephen Gray (Johannesburg: McGraw-Hill, 1982).

Kauffmann, Stanley. *Persons of the Drama: Theatre Criticism and Comment.* New York: Harper & Row, 1976.

———. *Theatre Criticisms.* New York: Performing Arts Journal Publications, 1983.

Keating, Douglas J. "Playwright Finds His Way in a New South Africa." *Philadelphia Inquirer,* 22 October 1995.

King, Robert L. "The Rhetoric of Dramatic Technique in *Blood Knot.*" *South African Theatre Journal* 7 (1993): 40–49.

Krog, Antjie. *The Country of My Skull: Guilt, Sorrow, and the Limits of Forgiveness in the New South Africa.* New York: Random House, 1998.

Kruger, Loren. "The Drama of Country and City: Tribalization, Urbanization and Theatre under Apartheid." *Journal of Southern African Studies* 23 (December 1997): 565–584.

———. *The Drama of South Africa.* London and New York: Routledge, 1999.

Lelyveld, Joseph. "'Master Harold' Stuns Johannesburg Audience." *New York Times,* 24 March 1983.

Lewis, Simon. "Athol Fugard: An Interview." *Illuminations* (Summer 1998): 75–81.

Leyshon, Robert. "Laughing in the Beginning and Listening at the End: Directing Fugard in Barbados." In *South African Theatre as/and Intervention,* ed. Marcia Blumberg and Dennis Walder (Amsterdam: Rodopi, 1999).

Lyell, Charles. *The Principles of Geology.* Vol. II. London: John Murray, 1833.

Makhaya, Elliot. "Fugard Finishes New Play." *The Sowetan,* 1 May 1997.

Manim, Mannie. "Producing Fugard." In *Playland . . . and Other Words,* by Athol Fugard. Johannesburg: Witwatersrand University Press, 1992.

Mann, Emily. *Testimonies: Four Plays.* Introduction by Athol Fugard. New York: Theatre Communications Group, 1997.

Marks, Peter. "A Rite of Passage, with Excess Baggage." *New York Times,* 20 January 1999.

McKay, Kim. "*The Blood Knot* Reborn in the Eighties: A Reflection of the Artist and His Times." *Modern Drama* 30 (December 1987): 496–504.

McLuckie, Craig W. "Power, Self, and Other: The Absurd in *Boesman and Lena.*" *Twentieth Century Literature* 39 (Winter 1993): 423–429.

McNeil, Donald G., Jr. "On Stage, and Off." *New York Times,* 13 January 1995.

Mda, Zakes. "Politics and the Theatre: Current Trends in South Africa." In *Theatre and Change in South Africa,* edited by Geoffrey V. Davis and Anne Fuchs, pp. 193–218. Amsterdam: Harwood Publishers, 1996.

Meinert, Monica. "Dramatiker Athol Fugard." *Allgemeine Zeitung* [Windhoek], no. 4 (7 January 1970).

Michell, John. "An Untimely Resurrection." *Business Day* [Johannesburg], 9 April 1991.

Mshengu, [Robert Kavanagh]. "Political Theatre in South Africa and the Work of Athol Fugard." *Theatre Research International* 7 (Spring 1982): 160–179.

Munro, Margaret. "The Fertility of Despair: Fugard's Bitter Aloes." *Meanjin* 40 (December 1981): 472–479.

Murray, John. "Colour-Bar Romance." *To the Point* [Johannesburg] 8, no. 26 (29 June 1976).

Mydans, Seth. "Soviet Deserter Discovered after 41 Years in a Pigsty." *New York Times,* 27 May 1985.

O'Neill, Eugene. *Long Day's Journey into Night.* New Haven, Conn.: Yale University Press, 1956.

Orkin, Martin. *Drama and the South African State.* Manchester, New York, and Johannesburg: University of Manchester Press and Witwatersrand University Press, 1991.

O'Sheel, Patrick. "Athol Fugard's 'Poor Theatre.'" *Journal of Commonwealth Literature* 12 (1978): 67–77.

Owen, Wilfred. *The War Poems.* Edited by Jon Stallworthy. London: Chatto & Windus, 1994.

Pacheco, Patrick. "His 'Song' of Hope." *Los Angeles Times,* 26 December 1995.

Reed, John, ed. *Athol Fugard: A Bibliography.* Grahamstown, South Africa: National English Literary Museum, 1991.

Reynolds, Gilbert Westacott. *The Aloes of South Africa.* (1950, Reprint, Cape Town and Rotterdam: A. A. Balekma, 1974).

Richards, David. "A 66-Year-Old White Dramatist Breaks Free of Apartheid." *Washington Post,* 13 September 1998.

Richards, Lloyd. "The Art of Theatre VIII: Athol Fugard." *Paris Review* 31, no. 111 (Summer 1989).

Roberts, Sheila. "'No Lessons Learnt': Reading the Texts of Fugard's *A Lesson from Aloes* and *Master Harold . . . and the Boys.*" *English in Africa* 9 (October 1982): 27–33.

Robinson, Amy. "It Takes One to Know One: Passing and Communities of Common Interest." *Critical Inquiry* 20 (1994): 715–736.

Ross, Laura. "A Question of Certainties." *American Theatre* 1 (September 1984): 4–9.

Scarry, Elaine. *The Body in Pain.* New York and Oxford: Oxford University Press, 1985.

Seidenspinner, Margarete. *Exploring the Labyrinth: Athol Fugard's Approach to South African Drama.* Essen, Germany: Die Blaue Eule, 1986.

Seymour, Hilary. "'Sizwe Bansi Is Dead': A Study of Artistic Ambivalence." *Race and Class* 21 (Winter 1980): 273–289.

Shava, Piniel Viriri. *A People's Voice: Black South African Writing in the Twentieth Century.* London and Athens, Ohio: Zed Books and Ohio University Press, 1989.

Sheckels, Theodore F., Jr. *Lion on the Freeway: A Thematic Introduction to Contemporary South African Literature in English.* New York: Peter Lang, 1996.

Sichel, Adrienne. "Confessions of a Passionate Patriot." *The Star,* 21 June 1994.

———. "Fugard's Novel 'Recital.'" *The Star* [Johannesburg], 14 June 1994.

Silvester, V. *Dancing for the Millions: A Concise Guide to Modern Ballroom Dancing.* London: Oldhams Press, 1950.

———. *Theory and Technique of Ballroom Dancing.* London: Herbert Jenkins, 1948.

Simon, John. "'The Captain's Tiger' Has No Bite." *New York,* 1 February 1999.

———. "Falling Apartheid." *New York,* 9 January 1996.

Simons, Marlise. "Uproar over Twins, and a Dutch Couple's Anguish." *New York Times,* 28 June 1995. A3, cols. 1–3.

Smith, Malvern Van Wyk, and Don Maclennan, eds. *Olive Schreiner and After: Essays on Southern African Literature in Honour of Guy Butler.* Cape Town: David Philip, 1983.

Solberg, Rolf. *Alternative Theatre in South Africa: Talks with Prime Movers since the 1970s.* Pietermaritzburg, South Africa: Ravan Press, 1999.

Solomon, Alisa. "'Look at History': An Interview with Zakes Mokae." *Theater* 14 (Winter 1982).

Sophocles. *Antigone.* Translated by Elizabeth Wykoff, in *The Complete Greek Tragedies,* vol. 2, edited by David Grene and Richmond Lattimore (Chicago: University of Chicago Press, 1959).

Spivak, Gayatri Chakravorty. "Can the Subaltern Speak?" In *Marxism and the Interpretation of Culture,* edited by C. Nelson and L. Grossberg, pp. 271–313. Basingstoke: Macmillan Education, 1988.

Stanley, Kristina. "Athol Fugard's Theatre of Intervention and Reconciliation in *Valley Song.*" In *South African Theatre as/and Intervention,* edited by Marcia Blumberg and Dennis Walder, pp. 85–91. Amsterdam: Rodopi, 1999.

Thamm, Marianne. "Fugard Breaks Free with New Captive Drama." *Cape Times,* 7 April 1987.

Tucker, A. Christopher. "Athol Fugard." *Transatlantic Review* 53/54 (February 1976): 53–54, 87–90.

Vandenbroucke, Russell. "Robert Zwelinzima Is Alive." *Yale/Theatre* 7 (1975), 116–23. Reprinted in *Athol Fugard,* edited by Stephen Gray. Johannesburg: Ad. Donker, 1982.

———. *Truths the Hands Can Touch: The Theatre of Athol Fugard.* New York: Theatre Communications Group, 1985.

Visser, Nicholas. "Drama and Politics in a State of Emergency: Athol Fugard's *My Children! My Africa!*" *Twentieth Century Literature* 39 (Winter 1993): 486–502.

von Staden, Heinrich. "An Interview with Athol Fugard." *Theater* 14 (Winter 1982): 41–46.

Waddell, Rebecca. "How It Came Together." In *My Life and Valley Song,* by Athol Fugard. Johannesburg and London: Hodder & Stoughton and Witwatersrand University Press, 1996.

Walder, Dennis. *Athol Fugard.* London and New York: Macmillan and Grove Press, 1985.

———. "Crossing Boundaries: The Genesis of the Township Plays." *Twentieth Century Literature* 39, no. 4 (Winter 1993): 409–422.

———. "Questions from a White Man Who Listens: The Voices of *Valley Song.*" In *South African Theatre as/and Intervention,* edited by Marcia Blumberg and Dennis Walder, pp. 101–112. Amsterdam: Rodopi, 1999.

———. "Resituating Fugard: South African Drama as Witness." *New Theatre Quarterly* 8 (November 1992): 343–361.

Wertheim, Albert. "Ballroom Dancing, Kites and Politics: Athol Fugard's *Master Harold and the Boys.*" *SPAN* 30 (April 1990): 141–155.

———. "The Darkness of Bondage, the Freedom of Light: Athol Fugard's 'The Road to Mecca.'" *Essays in Theatre* 5 (November 1986): 15–25.

———. "Euripides in South Africa: *Medea* and *Demea.*" *Comparative Drama* 29 (Fall 1995): 334–347.

———. "The Lacerations of Apartheid: *A Lesson from Aloes.*" In *Text and Presentation,* edited by Karelisa Hartigan, pp. 211–221. Lanham, Md.: University Press of America, 1988.

———. "The Modern British Homecoming Play." *Comparative Drama* 19 (Summer 1985): 151–165.

———. "The 1995 Grahamstown Festival." *South African Theatre Journal* 10 (May 1996): 94–100.

———. "Political Acting and Political Action: Athol Fugard's *The Island.*" *World Literature Written in English* 26 (1986): 245–252.

———. "The Prison as Theatre and the Theatre as Prison: Athol Fugard's *The Island.*" In

Themes in Drama, vol. 9, edited by J. Redmond, pp. 229–237. Cambridge: Cambridge University Press, 1987.

———. "Triangles of Race: Athol Fugard's *'MASTER HAROLD'. . . and the Boys* and Paul Slabolepzy's *Saturday Night at the Palace*." *Commonwealth* 20 (Autumn 1997): 86–95.

Whitaker, Richard. "Dimoetes to Dimetos: The Evolution of a Myth." *English Studies in Africa* 24 (March 1981): 45–59.

Wilson, Andrew. "Voyage Back to the Start." *Johannesburg Mail & Guardian,* 21 August 1997.

Wilson, Derek. "Powerful Fugard Play Gets Deserved Airing." *Argus* [Cape Town] supplement, 28 December 1981.

Winer, Laurie. "Athol Fugard: The Writer as 'Tiger' Cub." *Los Angeles Times,* 14 July 1998.

Wolf, Matt. "Write Angles." *Time Out,* 31 January–7 February 1996.

Wortham, Chris. "A Sense of Place: Home and Homelessness in the Plays of Athol Fugard." In *Olive Schreiner and After: Essays on Southern African Literature in Honour of Guy Butler,* edited by Malvern Van Wyk Smith and Don Maclennan. Cape Town: David Philip, 1983.

Zinman, Toby Silverman. "*Valley Song:* Fugard Plays It Again." In *South African Theatre as/and Intervention,* edited by Marcia Blumberg and Dennis Walder, pp. 93–100. Amsterdam: Rodopi, 1999.

INDEX

Page numbers in italics refer to illustrations. Some note references include a chapter number in parentheses, if necessary.

"Abbess, The," 257n48

Abrahams, Peter, 215

acting, 89, 207; projection of self, 60–61, 88; self-transformation, 28, 55, 80, 180, 185; theatrical as political, vii, ix, 3, 92, 102–103, 205, 237

acting out, 32, 63, 102–103, 179

adolescence, 203–12, 255n19

adultery, 70–79, 243n6

African Music and Dance Association, 44

African Theatre Workshop, 2, 17

Afrikaners, 44, 51, 154–56, 161; spirit of, 124, 134, 162–65

Afrocentrism, 184

age bias, 221, 232

agitprop, 100, 107, 116

agon, 156, 179, 219, 232

Albee, Edward, 193, 199; *The American Dream,* 51; *Zoo Story,* 188

alcoholism, 143, 146, 169–70, 174–76, 215, 225

alienation, 80, 171, 194

allegory, 202. *See also* metaphors; parables

Amato, Rob, 249n24

Amendola, Tony, *129*

anti-apartheid activities, 118

anti-apartheid views, 224, 227, 252n20

Antigone, 76, 89, 90, 93, 228

Antigone (Sophocles), 89–98, 246n35

apartheid, 29, 76, 142, 188, 206; end of, ix, 178, 255n23; politics, 100, 166, 187, 242n31; witness of, 69, 188–89, 206

arias: Boesman, 66; Errol, 78; Hester, 49; Milly, 41; Miss Helen, 41; Morris, 22, 27; from Verdi, 216, 217; Zachariah, 27

art, 115–16, 160, 165, 227; inspiration, 107, 153; power of, 15–16, 159, 161, 237. *See also Captain's Tiger, The; Dimetos; Road to Mecca, The*

audience, 152, 227, 236, 253n1

audience participation, 76, 80, 96, 209

authority, 63, 207; creative, 231, 232

autobiographical narratives, 135–36, 203, 224, 226

Bachmann, Dieter, 101

Baker-White, Robert, 78

barriers, 197

Bates, Kathy, xii

Beckett, Samuel, 41, 43, 189; *Endgame,* 35, 39; humor, 35, 41; influence, 1, 241n9; insight, 27, 39; *Krapp's Last Tape,* 44; minimalism, xii, 2, 10, 44; models, 57, 173, 200, 242n20; space, 32, 45, 56, 199; style, 19, 20; *Waiting for Godot,* 44

Bender, John, 99

Benson, Mary, vii, 201, 202, 203, 205
Bentley, Eric, ix
Bergelson, Ilene, *211*
birthright, 47
Blake, William (*Hecate*), 101, 105, 114, 116
Blood Knot, The, 17–32, 44, 192, 240n5(2), 240n6(2), 254n21; crossing the color line, 43, 207, 213; Ethel (*The Blood Knot*), 23, 24–25, 29, 30–31, 57; Morris, 19–32, 56–57, 240n6(2), 254n21; Zachariah, 19–32, 56–57, 241nn6,12, 254n21
Blumberg, Marcia, 60, 242nn26,27, 251nn4,13, 255n23
bodily odors, 110, 141, 147, 157–58
bodily wastes, 34–35, 46–47, 141, 147, 150, 198–99
body language, 27–28, 60–61, 65–66, 68, 157
Boesman and Lena, 43; Boesman, 55–68, *59,* 75, 243n36; Lena, 55–68, *59,* 75
boundaries, 212–13
Bowker, Veronica, 205
Brecht, Bertolt (*Parables for the Theatre*), 14, 29, 80, 81, 179
Breytenbach, Breyten, 211
Brink, André, 211
brotherhood, 19, 95, 152, 241nn6,7
Bryceland, Yvonne, xii, 79, *165*
Busi (*My Life*), 203–12
Byron, George Lord (*Childe Harolde*), 182, 186

Campbell, Roy, 119, 123, 125
Camus, Albert: *Carnets,* 100; existentialism, 7–8, 35, 42, 50, 200; *The Myth of Sisyphus,* 89, 94–95, 248n11; *The Rebel,* 157; *The Stranger,* 125
canonicity, 186
capitalism, x, 80–81
Captain's Tiger, The, 156, 223–37, *233;* Betty Le Roux, 230–37; Donkeyman, 229–37, 257n45; and the SS *Graigaur,* 1, 215, 257n45
casts, mixed, 17, 19, 180, 207
Christianity, 153–54
Ciskeian Independence, 86

clocks, 31, 32, 34, 37, 67. *See also* time
Cody, Gabrielle, 169
Coetzee, J. M., 101, 211
Cole, Gary, *191*
Colleran, Jeanne, 187, 189, 256n31
coloureds, 57, 60, 64, 67, 240n5(1)
comedy, 216, 220, 223; restorative, 110; Roman, 46; and tragedy of errors, 24, 35
coming of age, 149–52, 207
Commission for Truth and Reconciliation, 190, 253n17
compensation, 50–51, 52–53
Cousins (memoir), 79, 162–63, 224–25; excerpt, 19, 20, 33, 41
Coveney, Michael, 80
Creon, 89, 96–98, 246n35
cross-dressing, 36, 76, 92–93, 173–74; racial, 22–23, 26–27, 29–30, 31
Crow, Brian, 95, 244n17
Curry, Bill, *59*
Cushman, Robert, 70

dancing, 209, 235; in *"Master Harold" . . . and the Boys,* 138–39, 143–46, 152, 180, 250n34
Daniel, Raeford, 225
de Klerk, F. W., 188
debate, analogue of theatre, 179
Dickey, Jerry, 115, 246n36, 248n11
Dimetos, x, 10, 100–16, 156; Danilo, 102, 105, 107–109, 111–13; Dimetos, 102–16; Lydia, 103–16; vs. *A Place with the Pigs,* 168–71; Sophia, 107, 108, 113, 114; staging of, 247n11
discipline, 249n12
disengagement, 29, 49–50, 118, 121–22
domestic violence, 60, 66, 158
Durbach, Errol, 117, 136, 243n42, 246n35

Eden, 71–72, 119, 123
Elsom, John, 101–102
Emslie, Anne, 162, 251nn6,7
enslavement and freedom, 12, 16, 164–65
Eurocentrism, 180, 182–83
evolution, 72, 75, 77

existence, meaning of, 44, 48
existentialism, 189, 200; Camus, 7–8, 35, 42, 50, 200; fear, 42, 55; questions, 37, 56, 213; strength, 7–9, 54, 125

Faison, Frankie, *201*
family, 20, 100; allegorical, 251n13; issues, 48–49, 122, 146, 147, 225
fantasies, 245n22
Ferguson, Lou, *191*
fiction, 216, 230, 246n37
Fordsburg Native Commissioner's Court, 2
forgiveness, 66, 189, 200, 202
Foucault, Michael, 246n38, 249n12
freedom, 15, 64, 94, 95; art, 156, 226, 231; Byron, 182, 186; enslavement, 12, 16
Fugard, Athol, *viii, 18*, 154; born, 1; criticism of non-apartheid work, x, 169, 225–26, 252n18; education, 2, 103–16, 187, 247n13; employment, 2; hitchhiking, 1, 215, 231; marriage, 2; on stage, *173, 221, 233;* roles, 2, 19, 42, 44, 168, 241n6, 250n38, 252n35, 257n40; white writing of non-whites, x, 136, 178, 205, 249n24
Fugard, Harold (father), 1, 223, 234, 256n36; alcoholism, 162–63, 225
Fugard, Lisa (daughter), 17
Fugard, Sheila Meiring (wife), 2, 35, 68, 98, 240n3(1); "Lena," 68; "Robben Island," 98–99; "Therapy," 132

Gainor, J. Ellen, 250n34
Gamy (*My Life*), 203–12
Gandhi, 79
Gandhi, Mahatma, 149, 250n38
gender roles, 75, 145, 205, 251n4; female, 60, 179, 219–20, 242n27; male, 56, 234
Gevisser, Mark, 255n19
ghettoized authors, ix–x
Gordimer, Nadine, 101, 178, 211
Govender, Sivagamy, 203–12, *210*
Gramsci, Antonio, x
Gray, Stephen, 168
Greek mythology, 101
Greek tragedy, 9, 10
Green, Robert J., 241n10, 242n20, 244n16
Grego, Peter, 210

Grotowski, Jerzy, 79
Group Areas Act, 70, 130–31, 142
Gussow, Mel, 187, 239n2(1), 247nn2,13, 250n25, 256n36, 257n45

Hamilton, Lisa Gay, *221*
Harlow, Barbara, 95–96
Hauptfleisch, Temple, 239n2(1)
Hello and Goodbye, 33, 43–55, 215, 225; Hester Smit, 44–55, *54*, 242n25; Johnnie Smit, 44–55, *54*, 215, 224
Hildegard of Bingen, 257n48
Hilferty, Susan, 170
Hobson, Harold, 102
Hodoshe Span, The. See *Island, The*
Hoegberg, David, 250nn29,33
Holloway, Myles, 189
homecoming plays, 46
Honegger, Gitta, 251nn6,12
hope, 43, 125–27, 151, 201–202, 213–14, 221
Horace, 179
Hornby, Richard, 253n8
Huxley, Julian, 72
Hwang, David Henry, 224

Ibsen, Henrik, 35, 101, 171, 175
imagination, 3, 20, 215
Immorality Act, 25, 70, 73, 75, 79, 167
individuality, 124
injustice. See oppression
inspiration, waning, 153, 220, 221
integration, 145, 180, 184, 186, 212. See *also* multiracial society
Island, The, 68, 88–99, *91, 93, 97*, 245n21, 255n8; Hodoshe, 91–92, 96; John, 89–99, 178, 228; Winston, 76, 89–99, 178, 228
Ivanek, Zeljko, 49–50, *54*

Jacobs, Riana, 203–12, *210*
Jews, 187–88
Jones, Michelle Crosby, *211*
Jonson, Ben, 91, 179
Jordan, John O., 249n24
Jordan, Mary, 204–205
Joubert, Elsa, 69
Jung, Carl, 102

Kaiser, Georg, 172
Kani, John, ix; co-creator, 68, 79, 117, 204,
    245n21; *The Island*, xii, 88, 255n8;
    roles, 80, *91, 93, 97, 137, 185; Sizwe
    Bansi Is Dead*, 82–84, 245n26
Kauffman, Stanley, 56, 57, 148
Keats, John, 119, 120
Kemp, Margaret, *211*
Kente, Dambisia, *12*
King, Robert, 240n1
Kingsley, Ben, 102
kites, 136–38, 142, 144, 150–51, 180
Kliptown, 184
Kriel, DiDi, 216
Kruger, Loren, 240nn6(1),7,3(2), 242n20,
    246n35

Layshon, Robert, 88
learning, 117–52, 234
Lehrstücke(e), 138, 179, 180
Leite, Heather, 203–12, *210*
Lesson from Aloes, A, 117–35, *129*, 154, 162,
    192; Gladys, 118–35, 162, 197, 228,
    249n12; Piet, 118–35, *129*, 197; Steve
    Daniels, *129*, 228
Library Theatre (Johannesburg), 43–44
life, 58, 172, 175, 234; affirmation, 62,
    164; disillusionment, 52, 199–200;
    laws, 101–102, 104–106; origin, 77,
    214
Littlewood, Joan, 167
Lobo, Alyssa, *211*
Longfellow, Henry Wadsworth, 128
love of country, 192
Lyell, Charles, 72

Machiavelli, Niccolò (*La Mandragola*),
    79
madness, 130–32, 177
Makhaya, Elliot, 228
Makhene, Ramolao, *137*
Mandela, Nelson, 99, 188, 189, 206, 207,
    246n35
Manim, Mannie, 189, 201, 203, 205, 208
Maredi, Reshoketswe, 203–12, *210*
Market Theatre (Johannesburg), 44, 72,
    167, 189
Marks, Peter, 225

Martins, Helen, 153, 154, 162
Marxism, 187–88, 241n9
Masefield, John, 182, 183, 186
"Master Harold" . . . and the Boys, 27, 106,
    135–52, *137*, 198, 224–25; end, 200,
    235; Hally, 136–52, *137*, 178, 197,
    250n29, 251n45; Sam, 106, 136–52,
    137, 180, 197, 198, 250n29; Sam's arse,
    27, 198, 228, 235; Willie, 137, 138–52
McCarter Theatre (Princeton), xii, 50, 55
McKay, Kim, 240n5
McLuckie, Craig, 242n29
meaning, struggle for, 35, 44, 56, 63,
    66–67, 90, 125
Meinert, Monica, 62
Meiring, Lida, *173*
messes, cleaning up, 120, 147
metaphors, 98, 102, 229, 256n28
Miller, Arthur, 35
Modisane, Bloke, 2
Mokae, Zakes, ix, 2, 10, 79, 140; *The Blood
    Knot*, xii, 17, 19, 207
Molière, 107
monologues, 22, 94; interior, 27, 110,
    170–71, 229. *See also* arias
Mshegu, Robert Kavanagh, x
Mthimunye, Eleanor Busi, 203–12, *210*
muckheap, 20, 42, 43, 199. *See also* rubbish
    imagery
multiracial society, 178, 186, 205, 219. *See
    also* integration
Munro, Margaret, 122, 248n7
My Children! My Africa!, 178–88, *185, 189*;
    Isabel Dyson, 179; Mr M, 179–88, 184,
    185; Thami Mbikwana, 179
"My English Name Is Patience," 166
My Life, 181, 203–12, *210, 211*, 255n8;
    Heather, 203–12

names, 147, 197; *A Lesson from Aloes*, 119,
    122, 133; *Sizwe Bansi Is Dead*, 82,
    86–87
National Arts Festival (Grahamstown), xii,
    99, 203, 204, 255n8
Navrotsky, Pavel, 168–69
Navrotsky, Praskovya, 168–69
New York Times, 167, 168–69, 170
Nkonyeni, Nomhle, *59*

Nkosi, Lewis, 2, 3–4
No-Good Friday, vii, 1, 3–10, 17; Father
  Higgins, 2, 3–4; Guy, 5–6, 7, 8; Pinkie,
  5–6, 7; Shark, 4–9; Tobias, 4–5, 7, 8,
  14; Van Rendsburg, 5–6; Watson, 7–8;
  Willie, 3–4, 7–9, 14
non-apartheid plays, 101, 154, 169, 226
nondiscrimination, 221–22
Nongogo, 1, 10–16, *12;* Blackie, 10, 13, 16;
  Johnny, 10, 14–16; Queeny, 10–16, *12*
non-white, 240n5(1), 249n24; Sam, 10–16
Notebooks (memoirs), 57–58, 77, 94, 111,
  112
nothing, 37–38, 50, 200
Ntshinga, Norman, 79
Ntshona, Winston, ix; co-creator, 79–80,
  117, 204, 245n21; *The Island,* xii, 88,
  255n8; roles, 68, *91, 93, 97; Sizwe
  Bansi Is Dead,* 82–84, 245n26

objectivity, 2, 200
Oedipal complex, 142–43, 170, 234
O'Neill, Eugene, 1, 17, 252n36; *The Ice-
  man Cometh,* 10, 39, 174; *Long Day's
  Journey into Night,* 225
Oppenheimer, Harry, 206
oppression, 186, 200, 211; of blacks, 6,
  140, 184, 197; lessons, 61, 177
order, 179, 180
Orkin, Martin, 20, 239n3, 241n9,
  242nn18,31, 245n25
O'Sheel, Patrick, 244n16
Outa (*Boesman and Lena*), 57, 58, 61–67,
  79, 243n36
Owen, Wilfred, 201

parables: eulogy for Outa Jacob, 85–86; Joe
  and his horse, 15; *A Place with the Pigs,*
  170, 252n20; *Playland,* 189; potato
  farmer in New Bethesda, 163; *Valley
  Song,* 216
Parish, Felice, *211*
Parthenius, 101
passbooks, 2, 84–86, 87, 94
passing as white, 19, 22, 25, 28–29,
  173–74, 213, 241n13
Paton, Alan, 3, 217
Patrick (*Nongogo*), 13

People Are Living There, 10, 32–43, 40, 100,
  193; Ahlers, 35–39; Don (*People Are
  Living There*), 34; Milly, 34, 193;
  Shorty, 34; Sissy, 36
pessimism, 43, 127–28, 150–51
Phillips, James P., *129*
photography, 72, 77, 81, 82, 153
Phukwane, Dudu, 243n36
Pinter, Harold, vii, ix, xii, 46; *The Birthday
  Party,* 77; *The Room,* 100; *A Slight Ache,*
  100
Place with the Pigs, A, x, 167–76, *173;* vs.
  Dimetos, 168, 170–71; old version, 167;
  Personal Parable, 168; Pavel, 168–76,
  173; Praskovya, 168–76, *173*
Playland, 188–202, *191, 201,* 254n20,
  254n21; "Barking Barney," 193, 195–96;
  Martinus, 189–202, *191, 201,* 254n21
playwrights, 92, 106–107, 153, 216; Dimetos, 105, 109; Gideon, 189–202, *191,
  201,* 253n19, 254n21; Johnnie, 53;
  Johnny, 15–16; Lena, 63; Milly, 34, 36;
  Morris, 22, 24; Zachariah, 26, 27
Pogrund, Benjamin, 2
police brutality, 125–27, 131–32, 140, 141,
  143, 147, 149–50
Port Elizabeth plays, 17–68
possession, 101, 102, 160–61
post-apartheid concerns, 99, 206, 220, 227,
  245n23
post-apartheid works, 43, 153, 203–38,
  255n8
Potgeiter, Elizabeth (mother), 1, 223–37
power, 62, 64, 75, 109, 195
prisons, 95–96, 246n37, 246n47
problem plays, 110–16, 153–76
prostitution, 50, 52, 234
Proust, Marcel, 51, 242n25
pulleys, 102–105, *103,* 109, 115, 115–16
punishment, nature of, 112
purgation, 46–47, 51, 193, 196, 199

race relations, 189, 205, 256n30
racial classification, 57, 60, 64, 67,
  240n5(1)
racial roles, 29, 179, 198, 219–20, 243n6,
  251n4; power, 75, 145, 232; teaching,
  181, 234

racism, 117–18, 125, 136, 147, 150, 237, 241n14; consequences of, xi, 142

Ramses II, 182–83

rape, 14, 75, 126, 131–32, 197

rapprochement, 189–90

recognition play, 46

reconciliation, 189, 190, 251n45, 253n17, 256n30

Reed, John, 239n2(1)

Rehearsal Room, 44

reign of terror, 190

rejection, 121–22

religious experiences, 62, 112, 124–25, 153–67, 173

renewal, 201

repentance. *See* forgiveness

retirement, 220, 221

revenge play, 36

reviews: *The Blood Knot,* 18; *The Captain's Tiger,* 225–26; *Dimetos,* 101–102; *My Life,* 204–205; *Statements,* 69, 70, 72–73

revolution, 7–8

Reynolds, Gilbert Westacott, 124

Rhodes Theatre (Grahamstown), 44

Riana Jacobs (*My Life*), 203–12

Rice, Elmer, 172

Richards, David, 227

Richards, Lloyd, ix

Road to Mecca, The, 22, 153–67, 165; Elsa, 154, 157–58, 159–60, 251n13; Marius Byleveld, 156, 161; Miss Helen, 41, 153–67, *165,* 251n13; Patience, 166–67, 251n13

Robben Island, 88–99, 188, 228, 246n35

"Robben Island" (Sheila Fugard), 98–99

Roberts, Sheila, 249n19, 251n45

Robinson, Amy, 241n13

rubbish imagery, 20, 34–35, 58, 64, 67, 87

sacraments, 62, 112

Sartre, Jean Paul, 172, 200

scenery, as message, 170, 175, 190

Schecter, Joel, 169

Schreiner, Olive, 232, 242n29

Scofield, Paul, 102, 104

Seftel, Mollie, 44

segregation, 23, 27, 70, 130–31, 142, 208

Seidenspinner, Margarete, 249n24, 252n16

Sejake, Owen, *233*

self-definition, 44, 52–53, 56, 60, 62

self-denial, 67

self-destruction, 109

self-discovery, 33, 62, 242n25

self-image, 64, 67–68

Semela, Sam, 135

separation anxiety, 188

Serpent Players, ix, 79, 243n6

sexual energy, 70–71, 104, 108, 229, 235

sexual imagery, 16, 51, 78, 233–34

Seymour, Hilary, 245n22

Shakespeare, 107; *King Lear,* 37, 110; *Pericles,* 110; *The Tempest,* 101, 110; *The Winter's Tale,* 115

Sharpeville massacre, 19, 184

Shava, Piniel Viriri, 245n22

Sheckels, Theodore F. Jr., 249n17, 251n44

Shelley, Percy Bysshe, 182, 183, 186

Shepard, Suzanne, 169, 176

Shoki (*My Life*), 203–12

Sichel, Adrienne, 204

silence as acquiescence, 2, 8

Silkworms. See *People Are Living There*

Silvester, Victor, 144, 145, 152

Simon, Barney, 44, 46, 47–48, 51, 53–54, 72, 167

Simon, John, 226, 227

Sizwe Bansi Is Dead, 68, 79–87, *83,* 245n21, 245n26; Buntu, 84–87, 178; Sizwe Bansi, 76, 84–87, 178, 197; Robert Zwelinzima, 76, 82, 87; Styles, 80–87, 153

Slabolepzy, Paul, 196, 250n37, 254n23

Smetalov (*A Place with the Pigs*), 172

Smuts, Jan (Gen.), 79, 124, 134, 144, 250n38

Solberg, Rolf, 245nn24,28,31, 254n27, 255n20

Solomon, Alisa, 250n28

South West African People's Organization. *See* SWAPO

Soweto, 184

Space Theatre, ix, 88

Spacey, Kevin, as Gideon, 190, *201*

Spivak, Gayatri, 205, 236

SS *Graigaur*, 1–2, 223–24, 227, 235, 257n45

Statements after an Arrest under the Immorality Act, 69–79, 71, 74, 243n6; Detective Sergeant, 72, 76; Errol, 70–79, 243n5, 243n6; Frieda, 70–79

Steyn, Jennifer, *233*

story-telling, 114–15, 175, 246n47

Strindberg, August, 153–54

suicide, 109

suspension of disbelief, 29

Suzman, Helen, 211

SWAPO (South West African People's Organization), 194–200 passim

swartgat, 27, 31, 147–48, 243n36

Sylwain, Duart, *137*

symbolism, xi, 20, 189, 192, 199. *See also* metaphors

teaching, 117–52, 178, 234

Technical College of Port Elizabeth, 2, 103–16, 247n13

theatre, 104, 106–107, 237; political effects, 2–3, 187

"Therapy" (Sheila Fugard), 132

time, 38–39, 44–45, 114–15, 177; lack of future, 49, 60, 111. *See also* clocks

Toller, Ernst, 172

tragedy, 9–10, 16, 101, 115, 127, 170

transgressive urges, 17, 19, 73, 75, 182

trans-real, 25–26

transvestism, 36, 76, 92–93, 173–74; racial, 22–23, 26–27, 29–30, 31

Trauerspiel, 134–35

triangle relationships, 26, 56–57, 108, 180,

241n13; in *"Master Harold,"* 135, 137, 151–52

trying for white. *See* passing as white

Tucci, Maria, 49–50, *54*

Tucker, A. Christopher, 101, 102

Valley Song, 212–23, *221*, 255n23, 256n31; Author, 218–19; Buks, 215–18, 222–23, 256n31; Caroline, 215; Veronica, 212–23, 256n28

Vandenbroucke, Russell, ix, 2, 3, 117, 151, 167, 207; *Dimetos*, 100, 101; *Statements*, 69, 70

Verdi, Giuseppe (*Rigoletto*), 216, 217, 219

vicarious experience, 31

violence, 254n21

Visser, Nick, 187

von Staden, Heinrich, 250n39, 251n42

Waddell, Rebecca, 203, 205, 206, 209, 210

Walder, Dennis, ix, xi, 17, 56, 69, 100; on *"Master Harold,"* 148, 150

Wertheim, Albert, 250n37, 254n23

Western culture, 180, 182–83

Weyers, Marius, 102, 213

Whitaker, Richard, 101

whiteness, 27–28, 31; trans-real, 25–26

Wilson, Andrew, 225

Wilson, Derek, 102

Winer, Laurie, 225

words, 78, 243n36, 253n7

writing against injustice, 211, 228

Yale Repertory Theatre, ix, xii, 142, 167

Yeats, William Butler, 116

Albert Wertheim is Professor of English and of Theatre and Drama at Indiana University. He has published widely on modern and classic British and American drama and on post-colonial writing; directed several NEH seminars on politics in the theatre and on new literatures from Africa, the West Indies, and the Pacific; and served on the editorial boards of *American Drama, Theatre Survey, South African Theatre Journal,* and *Westerly.*